AF600314

CRITICAL ALLIANCES: ECONOMICS AND FEMINISM IN ENGLISH WOMEN'S WRITING, 1880–1914

Critical Alliances: Economics and Feminism in English Women's Writing, 1880–1914

S. BROOKE CAMERON

UNIVERSITY OF TORONTO PRESS
Toronto Buffalo London

Toronto Buffalo London
utorontopress.com

ISBN 978-1-4426-3755-9

ISBN 978-1-4426-2561-7 (ePUB)
ISBN 978-1-4426-2560-0 (PDF)

Library and Archives Canada Cataloguing in Publication

Title: Critical alliances : economics and feminism in English women's writing, 1880–1914 / S. Brooke Cameron.
Names: Cameron, Brooke, 1976– author.
Description: Includes bibliographical references and index.
Identifiers: Canadiana 20190161213 | ISBN 9781442637559 (hardcover)
Subjects: LCSH: English literature – Women authors – History and criticism. | LCSH: Women in literature. | LCSH: Sex role in literature. | LCSH: Feminism and literature – English-speaking countries – History – 19th century. | LCSH: Feminism and literature – English-speaking countries – History – 20th century. | LCSH: English literature – 19th century – History and criticism. | LCSH: English literature – 20th century – History and criticism.
Classification: LCC PR119 .C36 2019 | DDC 820.9/3522 – dc23

This book has been published with the help of a grant from the Federation for the Humanities and Social Sciences, through the Awards to Scholarly Publications Program, using funds provided by the Social Sciences and Humanities Research Council of Canada.

University of Toronto Press acknowledges the financial assistance to its publishing program of the Canada Council for the Arts and the Ontario Arts Council, an agency of the Government of Ontario.

Canada Council for the Arts | Conseil des Arts du Canada

Funded by the Government of Canada | Financé par le gouvernement du Canada | Canada

Contents

Acknowledgments

Critical Alliances grows out of my ongoing work on gender and feminist collaboration. In my early research I was interested in women's use of economic models to theorize different conceptions of bodily bonds. Over the years, however, my study of feminist collaboration shifted to look at more concrete examples of women in the professions, perhaps not by accident as I navigated the academic job market. In many ways, then, *Critical Alliances* is a tribute to my own struggle to enter the profession – if not a tribute to all women still seeking gender equity in the modern labour force. It is my sincerest pleasure to offer a heartfelt thank-you to the many people who played a part in the composition of this book.

Critical Alliances would not have been possible without the support of my advisors who shaped me into the academic I am today. To that end, I thank Chris Vanden Bossche, who helped me navigate the many challenges of the job market. I am grateful for his expertise on Victorian class, from which I draw here in my own study of middle-class women's economic agency and navigation of the gendered marketplace, and which has also since inspired my recent work on working-class women and slum reform in the nineteenth century. His boundless support and generosity made me into a better scholar and, I would like to think, a better mentor of my own graduate students. I would also like to extend special thanks to Barbara Green, who often served as a second advisor to me, especially in my work on Virginia Woolf. My interest in feminist communities can be traced back to our early conversations on gender and writing. Her continued encouragement of my research on feminism and sexuality over the years has meant the world to me.

I am also indebted to my professors who set me on the path to a career in Victorian studies. Maud Ellmann and Sara Maurer made me into a better scholar and conscientious member of the academic community.

Kathy Psomiades was also a wonderful mentor to me, and her work has had a lasting influence upon my own research on fin-de-siècle aestheticism and Victorian feminist literature. Susan Harris introduced me to gendered themes in nineteenth-century Irish writings, which played a part in my chapter on George Egerton. I would also like to express my gratitude to Greg Kucich for teaching me about feminist poets in the nineteenth century and for employing me as managing editor of *Nineteenth-Century Contexts* (2005–6), where I gained invaluable first-hand knowledge about writing for the profession. I was also fortunate to work for Glenn Hendler and Bruce Burgett as project assistant for the *Keywords of American Cultural Studies*. I also owe a special thanks to Chris Keep and Richard Dellamora for first inspiring my passion for nineteenth-century women's writing.

I am grateful to have been the recipient of an Edward F. Sorin Postdoctoral Fellowship and National Endowment for the Humanities summer fellowship in 2008 and 2009, respectively, when I began planning my book project. As a participant in the NEH summer seminar "Decadent 1890s" at UCLA and the Williams Andrew Clark Memorial Library I worked with Joe Bristow, who helped me to rethink my case studies for examination. I am forever grateful to him for his enthusiastic support of my research. During the seminar I also worked with Margaret Stetz, who had already helped me with my research on Michael Field and since inspired my work on George Egerton. She is a model of critical generosity.

It is, perhaps, not surprising that in writing a book on feminist collaboration I looked repeatedly for inspiration to my own community of female scholars and friends. I would like to thank Diana Maltz for serving as an informal advisor these many years. She read countless drafts of my prospectus and job materials, and I really do not think I would be where I am today were it not for her constant help and outstanding advice. I must also express my gratitude to Kristin Mahoney for her help with my book prospectus and for her encouragement regarding the job market. Lara Karpenko was a good friend and mentor through school and, later, the job market and writing process. Lisa Hagar and Kate Kruger were both important influences on my discussion of George Egerton's writings. I also thank Cynthia Quarrie for her friendship and help with Modernist war poetry. Heather Edwards was an ally during the job market years, and my appreciation for her advice on Irish fiction and New Woman writings cannot be overstated. Thank you to Emma Peacock and Laura Ludtke for the uplifting talks on the writing process as I neared completion of the manuscript and needed that extra push.

I must also extend my gratitude toward my colleagues whose community oftentimes inspired my own thoughts on professional alliances. I thank Jason Camlot for giving me my first job with Concordia University's Department of English. I thank the members of Dawson College's English and Continuing Education Departments. And I am grateful to my many friends and colleagues in the Department of English Language and Literature here at Queen's University. A special thanks must be extended to Shelley King, John Pierce, Maggie Berg, Heather Macfarlane, and Petra Fachinger. Their friendship and enthusiasm for *Critical Alliances* often provided the fuel I needed to keep writing. I am also grateful to Ellen Hawman for helping me to proofread the final manuscript.

Research for *Critical Alliances* was completed at several libraries and with help from numerous librarians whose patience and innovative problem solving were a godsend to me at critical points in the project. I would like to thank the University of Notre Dame's Hesburg Library, U.C.L.A. Library, Concordia University Library, and Queen's University's Stauffer Library and W.D Jordan Rare Books and Special Collections. I also visited several archives and rare books libraries while completing this project, including the British Library, the Women's Library at the London School of Economics, and the William Andrews Clark Memorial Library.

I have very much enjoyed working with the University of Toronto Press on the production of *Critical Alliances*. I thank Richard Ratzlaff for first showing interest in my project, and I am grateful to editor Mark Thompson for helping me prepare the manuscript to its completion. I am tremendously grateful to associate managing editor Barbara Porter and copy editor Miriam Skey for their eagle eyes in catching those last-minute errors. And I am indebted to the three anonymous readers for the press whose thoughtful feedback helped make *Critical Alliances* into a better book.

I can't imagine having written *Critical Alliances* without the love and support of my family. My partner, Jamie, was always a willing sounding board for ideas, and as a result of our many conversations, became an unintentional expert on Victorian feminism (which is not a bad thing). I would like to thank my parents, Marie, Carl, Bob, and Barb for instilling in me a passion for education that has carried me through even the toughest of times. I must also acknowledge the important role of my fur-family in supporting this project. Sadly, three dogs (Tuk, Indiana, and Jake) and two cats (Sammy and Walter) passed over the rainbow bridge in recent years; Emma Grace the dog and Kiki cat are still with me at the time of publication. Each and every furkid logged countless hours in my office, providing invaluable emotional support through their mere presence and perfectly timed snuggle breaks.

This book is dedicated to my children, Raina and Zachary. Watching you grow is one of the greatest pleasures in my life. You are in my heart when I write about gender equity and feminist futures.

CRITICAL ALLIANCES

Introduction

Critical Alliances: Economics and Feminism in English Women's Writing, 1880–1914

Woman as woman has something radically distinct to contribute to the sum-total of human knowledge, and her activity is of importance, not merely individually, but collectively and as a class.

– Olive Schreiner, *Woman and Labor*

What were they working for in the nineteenth century – those queer dead women in their poke bonnets and shawls? The very same cause for which we are working now.

– Virginia Woolf, *Three Guineas*

With the publication of her 1911 book on *Woman and Labor*, Olive Schreiner presented readers with a precise and powerful argument for cooperative alliances between women in the fight for equal employment. Writing at the turn of the century, Schreiner looked to old forms of domestic labour – including what she characterized as the socially vital work of mothers – as well as employment in the modern or skilled professions. *Woman and Labor* would later become, as Vera Brittain claimed in the 1930s, "that 'Bible of the Woman's Movement' which sounded to the world of 1911 as instant and inspiring as a trumpet-call summoning the faithful to a vital crusade" (*A Testament of Youth*, 41). Brittain's reference to a gendered "crusade" certainly picks up on Schreiner's celebration of feminist consciousness as culminating in a mass movement or collectivity, and *Woman and Labor*, as promised by its very title, goes on to frame this coalition in almost exclusively economic terms, signalling that the gendered marketplace is key to understanding women's sexual oppression as well as their liberation. The text catalogues at length how women, by virtue of their sex, are denied the opportunity for meaningful labour and, thus, how their productive potential is wasted or otherwise devalued. By the second chapter, Schreiner therefore insists that the feminist fight for equal work intrinsically depends upon rewriting those gender roles limiting women's access to the modern workforce: "For let it be noted exactly what our position is, who today, as women, are demanding new fields of labor and a reconstruction of our relationship with life" (*Woman and Labor*, 71). By placing gender at the heart of economic reform Schreiner builds upon arguments articulated in her first novel, *The Story of an African Farm*, published almost three decades prior to *Woman and Labor.* This earlier text uses the proto New Woman character, Lyndall, to voice – albeit somewhat clumsily through didactic prose – the author's complaint against the current conventions of sex and gender: "We all enter the world little plastic beings," she tells her young friend Waldo, adding that this same world then "shapes us" according to the specific "ends it sets before us" (*The Story of an African Farm* [1883], 185). "The power to labor is with [men]," Lyndall continues, but to women the world "says – Strength shall not help you, nor knowledge, nor labor ... And so the world makes men and women" (185). Lyndall will also, like her author, call upon women to stand together so that they might fight against, and reform, this restrictive gendered economy. In 1883, this call marked a new epoch in the Victorian Women's Movement focused on gendered and economic bodies as discursive constructions and, therefore, as rewritable through acts of critical collectivity and feminist resistance.

Victorian feminists made tremendous strides, throughout the nineteenth century, in the collective fight for employment equity and women's professional advancement. This is a point that Woolf acknowledges in her 1938 discussion of modern feminism, *Three Guineas* (excerpted above). One might harbour mixed feelings toward the Victorian feminist, but as the novel-essay suggests, this gender pioneer and her "queer" friends laid the groundwork for twentieth-century conversations or "causes" concerning women and gender roles (102). The question of gendered labour, including the separate spheres ideology, played a key role in the rise of this historic Women's Movement. Victorian women were keen to rethink dominant models of gender and domesticity, in particular, restricting their work and social relevance to the unpaid private sphere. These women wanted access to the public realm of paid employment and economic status, as well as the social and sexual independence associated with many of the modern professions. As one reviewer wrote in 1888, in response to a new and independent-minded generation of Victorian women:

> The good old days, when our grandmothers worked samplers and studied their recipe books, have passed away long ago; our spinster aunts, who

> would have died rather than soil their hands with anything that savoured of "ungentility," are fast fading out; and the present generation of girlhood, with enlarged ideas as to woman's brain and woman's work, is standing on the threshold of life eager to mingle in life's warfare. ("Artistic Professions for Women" 296)[1]

Within a single century, spanning "grandmothers" to "spinster aunts," women managed to rethink the place and purpose of feminine labour as something that was no longer restricted to the domestic economy of cooking and home decor ("recipe books" and "samplers"). The reviewer is certainly anxious regarding this "new generation of girlhood" (note the patronizing tone), with their "enlarged" ideas of women's intellectual and social capabilities, and he/she clearly longs for those "good old days" when "gentility" bound women to home and family. Still, the 1888 review nonetheless admits that a cultural shift has taken place and that the women working at the end of the century are on the "threshold" of change. This new generation, he/she writes, is "eager" to embrace the challenges of modern life or "warfare," including the right to paid employment without social stigma or loss in sexual status ("ungentility").

In order to understand this history of women's work, *Critical Alliances* investigates efforts by late-Victorian feminists to rewrite dominant gender roles and, more specifically, to redefine the relationship between women and the modern workforce. The nineteenth-century Women's Movement worked hard throughout the period, and across generations, to change the definition of what it meant to be a "woman" and, by association, the form and function of "women's work." Middle-class women played an especially important role in this history because it was this demographic that was supposed to perpetuate by example the Victorian ideal of feminine domesticity. Respectable "ladies" were supposed to devote themselves to familial care-giving and maternal self-sacrifice, forms of gendered labour typically restricted to the unpaid private sphere.[2] By the later decades of the century, women's collective pursuit of an independent income challenged the separate spheres ideology underwriting such models of gender difference and feminine labour. As Schreiner argues at length in her treatise *Woman and Labor*, for example, women's "entrance ... into new fields of labor" did not necessarily undermine heterosexual plots (that "primordial physical instinct which draws sex to sex"), but it most certainly required a "readjust[ment]" in "the relations of certain men with certain women," including a new accommodation and respect for women's "increased freedom and economic independence" (249–50). A woman's independent income, in other words, required a revised understanding of sexual difference and gendered division of labour.

In the chapters that follow, *Critical Alliances* investigates representative examples of fin-de-siècle feminist authors who imagined alternative gender narratives for working women. My use of the term "feminist author" remains deliberately loose in order to capture the wide range among women writers' efforts to redefine gender roles limiting their sociosexual mobility. This study is interested in those authors who make it their business to engage with, and in some way rewrite, the social narratives that define what it means to be a "woman," including Victorian domestic ideology, and the impact of such gender roles upon women's access to the modern workforce. These gender radicals understood that "feminine labor" was itself a product of cultural institutions and market practices. Each chapter is therefore devoted to women's intervention into one of these specific facets of the modern workforce. I begin with representations of women's work in care-giving professions, from teaching to nursing, because these vocations were closely affiliated with domestic ideology, while subsequent chapters describe women's pursuit of emergent professions such as photography, journalism, and aesthetic criticism. In their representations of these gender pioneers, fin-de-siècle feminist authors were forced to rethink (if not defy) local institutions of gendered education, kinship, or the sexual economy of the gaze shaping the social meaning of women's work. Chapter 1 argues that late-Victorian women sought to legitimate their work as teachers and nurses through specialized education or skills training (what Schreiner describes as "increased mental training and wider knowledge") (*Woman and Labor*, 249), erudition which was a necessary precursor to women's successful competition in the modern workforce. The second chapter contends that feminist kinship structures allowed working women the right to a self-possessed sexual and economic contract, thus negating the need for maternal self-sacrifice in the marriage plot. Many women also fought for equal access to the modern city, as explained in chapter 3, looking for urban mobility and economic opportunity without social-sexual stigma. Still other late-Victorian women resisted the popular role of feminine muse and instead reclaimed the artistic gaze for themselves as writers and connoisseurs of art (chapter 4). The fifth chapter is a capstone chapter on feminist cultural inheritance and the "post-Victorian" dialogue between Modernist writers and their nineteenth-century foremothers. Though widely differing in their feminist strategies and points of market intervention, these feminist authors were willing to challenge dominant narratives on gendered labour, including domestic ideology, in order to produce new gender roles and economic opportunities for modern women.

Critical studies of Victorian women's work have tended to focus on the New Woman figure as the beneficiary and, thus, high point in a long-fought feminist battle for economic and sexual-social equality. For example, Krista Cowman and Louise A. Jackson's *Women and Work Culture, Britain c. 1850–1950* brings together a collection of essays that share a common interest in the independent-minded woman's rejection of high Victorian gender roles and the separate spheres ideology. Early chapters by Sandra Stanley Holton ("Religion and the Meaning of Work") and Emma Robertson ("It was Just a Real Camaraderie Thing") suggest that fin-de-siècle women enjoyed unprecedented access to the modern professions, where they attempted new negotiations of service work beyond the private sphere (Holton) and struggled to balance labour networks and heterosexual plots (Robertson). Emma Liggins's recent study, *Odd Women?: Spinsters, Lesbians and Widows in British Women's Fiction, 1850s–1930s* (2014), also traces the rise of the modern feminist from the mid-nineteenth century to the fin-de-siècle New Woman. Yet Liggins's study is most interested in figures such as the spinster or career woman who rejected the conventional heterosexual marriage in favour of sexual and economic independent plots beyond the confines of domesticity. Also in the spirit of historicist analysis, Gillian Sutherland (*In Search of the New Woman: Middle-Class Women and Work in Britain 1870–1914*) focuses on the contrast between real New Women who worked for a living and helped pave the way for subsequent female professionals and the caricature of this figure found so often in the exaggerated plots of fin-de-siècle fiction. We will only find this elusive feminist figure, Sutherland argues, by "examining the opportunities for earning money, achieving independence, available to middle-class women in Britain in the last third of the long nineteenth century" (8).

Critical Alliances, however, is not restricted to a singular focus on the literary figure of the New Woman. While some of the authors discussed in the following chapters (such as Schreiner and Levy) most certainly made important contributions to this tradition of New Woman fiction, others are better defined more loosely as feminist authors without affiliation to this specific category – indeed, Egerton adamantly rejects the label "New Woman"[3] and Michael Field (Katharine Bradley and Edith Cooper) are more properly described as aesthetes.[4] Again, this kind of loose approach to fin-de-siècle feminisms helps us to remember the many different fronts upon which women were working to rewrite gendered labour, as well as literary narratives for feminine types. Still, I share in common Liggins's and Sutherland's interest in late-Victorian women's mass movement from the domestic to the public sphere of paid employment and economic independence. Yet in surveying this history, *Critical Alliances* also shifts the focus to literary representations of feminine collaboration and argues that female cooperation played a vital role in challenging the gender spheres ideology and securing women's success in the modern workforce.

Though *Critical Alliances* is focused on representations of feminist collaboration at the turn of the century, this study will at times discuss fin-de-siècle feminists' work within the context of the long nineteenth-century Women's Movement and earlier examples of women's socio-economic struggles. This kind of historical contextualization is necessary in order to appreciate both the lasting influence of dominant gender roles and feminist inheritance (a key theme throughout this study), and it also enables us to see what sets late-Victorian feminist writers apart from their predecessors. Key to this distinction in generations is the turn to gendered cooperation underwriting women's market strategies and women's access to modern professions. By collectively inhabiting the role of "woman," the Victorian feminists presented in this study understand gender to be a social category widely applied to plural individuals. At the same time, these authors imagine how feminists might work together to change the social meaning of "feminine labour" and therein gain new access to modern economic roles and professions. These gender radicals produced alternative representations of "women" employed in various forms of labour that extend beyond, and also redefine, the feminine domestic sphere. Olive Schreiner (chapter 1) and George Egerton (chapter 3), for example, rethink how feminine caregiving can also include women's employment as teachers and nurses, while Amy Levy (chapter 2) and Michael Field (chapter 4) show us how feminine feelings, from impressions to sexual desire, are requisite to women's success as professional artists, photographers, and aesthetic connoisseurs. In reflecting upon feminist pioneers like Schreiner, Modernist writer Virginia Woolf (chapter 5) also shows readers how cultural inheritance represents an opportunity to critique gender and its impact upon modern women's social opportunities or "causes."

Literature is an obvious and powerful means by which these feminists attempt to rewrite dominant social narratives on gender and work. Despite the differences among their representations of women's cooperation, these feminist authors understand that storytelling is a socio-political act and that the narratives we circulate play a formative role in one's sense of self and world view. The fictional work is, by this account, just one of many social narratives – including religious, scientific, and legal narratives – through which identity categories are reproduced and/or negotiated. Within this larger context, literature can strive to reaffirm certain socially agreed-upon gender roles and relationships; still other literary works, like the texts analysed in this study, exploit the contradictions that inevitably arise out of ongoing conversations on contested cultural concepts such as sexual difference and gendered labour. *Critical Alliances* presents readers with representations of women's work that challenge domestic ideology and, through that challenge, open the door to alternative economic and gender plots for women. Poetry and fiction are just as important as socio-legal constructions of identity, and as argued in *Critical Alliances*, literature can also play a key role in resisting or, even, rewriting the social definition of "woman" and "feminine labour."

There are good historical reasons for limiting my study of women's collaboration to the late-Victorian period. First, the latter decades of the nineteenth century mark women's effort to move beyond restricted employment within only those professions associated either directly or ideologically with domesticity – vocations such as governessing, teaching, and nursing. Victorian middle- and upper-class women were eager to participate in the modern labour market, with its abundance of both professional and skilled positions. These feminists wanted to break free from prior gender conventions that, at the mid-century, limited women to so-called respectable work in the already over-supplied domestic fields.[5] In her *The Education and Employment of Women* (1868), for example, Josephine E. Butler claims that "the principal employments open to women are teaching, domestic service, and sewing" (5), while Jessie Boucherett's *Hints on Self-Help* (1863) warns that all of these professions are terribly overcrowded, especially teaching, because "there is no other profession open by which gentlewomen can earn their livelihood without loss of caste, and many [women] prefer poverty to a loss of social position" (23–4).[6] The second reason for my historical focus can be explained with reference to the sheer number of vocations open to women at the turn of the century. By the century's end, an increasing number of women gravitated to commercial or white-collar forms of employment, including work in offices and shops. A. Amy Bulley and Margaret Whitley's 1894 study of *Women's Work* lists several such vocations which women had penetrated to varying degrees of success – such as literature (including novel writing), journalism, teaching (from elementary to high-school), law, medicine (including pharmacy, dentistry, midwifery, and nursing), painting, music, and theatre (chapter 1, "Women's Work: Literary, Professional, and Artistic," 1–38), as well as several forms of routine clerical work, from typewriting and bookkeeping, to work in the post office, the telegraph office, and varying forms of shop work (chapter 2, "Women's Work: Clerical and Commercial," 39–65).[7] Of course, the number of female teachers continued to grow throughout the century, from 89,239 in 1871 (73.1 per cent of the total occupation), to 144,393 (74 per cent) in 1891, and 171,670 (74.5 per cent) in 1901; though comparably smaller in total results, however, the amount of women working in new commercial and white-collar professions also grew exponentially as females gradually comprised a greater percentage within each employment category.[8] For example, there were no women working in "civil service" (officers and clerks) in 1871, but by 1891 there were 8,546 (21.3 per cent) women registered in this same category, and another 14,312 (25.2 per cent) were counted in 1901; the same census also registered 1,412 (1.6 per cent) women as "commercial clerks" in 1871, and by 1891 there were 17,859 (7.2 per cent), and 55,784 (15.3 per cent in 1901. The number of women registered under "telegraph," one of the more popular employers of the New Woman, also rose steadily from 222 (7.6 per cent) in 1871, to 4,356 (29.1 per cent) in 1891, and 9,256 (40.6 per cent) in 1901. This steady growth in the number of working women was dependent upon a change in attitude toward both class and gender, as both employers and employees let go of outmoded constructs like the separate spheres ideology.[9] This same rebellion against feminine domesticity also underwrote women's access to many of the consumer pleasures promised by the modern marketplace. Many middle- and upper-class women outright rejected patriarchal institutions such as chaperonage in order to assert their equal rights to the city (made easier by modern transportation systems), where they happily enjoyed the urban market's many goods and forms of entertainment – from shopping or the theatre to newly popularized restaurants and diners.[10] Victorian women were, in other words, eager to participate in both markets of production and consumption by the fin de siècle, and in the process, helped to redefine the relationship between gender and economics.

From its very inception, the nineteenth-century Women's Movement advocated cooperation as one of the most effective means by which feminists might realize these emergent professional opportunities. This was Jessie Boucherett's point in her early appeal for some kind of recognition of mutual interests among working women ("sisterly love and mutual sympathy"):

> When we reflect how many interests in common women have, it is sad to see how little union there is among them ... Like sticks in the fable, they are easily broken one by one, instead of being bound together by the ties of sisterly love and mutual sympathy ... Every woman who has her own

> livelihood to earn, whatever her station may be, has suffered more or less either from a deficient education, or from ill-judged restriction excluding her from well-remunerated employments. Even those who are successful suffered from these causes early in their career. Truly, these mutual misfortunes, this common suffering ought to form a strong bond of union among all who work for their bread, whether they belong to the higher or lower section of society. (*Hints on Self-Help* [1863], 133–4)[11]

All women know, Boucherett argues, what it is like to labour under conditions of sexual inequality, such as poor remuneration or lack of education barring access to social and sexual advancement, and so all women have it as their best interest, she concludes, to form out of this "common suffering" a "strong bond of union" in the ongoing fight for the right to earn their own "bread." In answer to such appeals, the number of women's organizations grew exponentially throughout the second half of the century, in tandem with the rising number of women flooding into the modern workforce. There were generalist organizations in support of women's employment, such as Boucherett's own "Society for Promoting the Employment of Women," founded in 1859 with Barbara Bodichon and Adelaide Anne Procter,[12] as well as the Society for Promoting Female Welfare, established in 1866 for the placement of "women and girls of good character."[13] There was also the National Union of Women Workers, founded in 1874 by Emma Paterson and devoted to the organization of female workers, and the 1877 Working Ladies Guild, which restricted its support to middle- and upper-class women. Some organizations focused their efforts on the professional advancement of women through education, including the Women's Education Union (established in 1871), dedicated to teacher-training, and the Medical Women's Federation (established in 1877), which supported the instruction and placement of female doctors. Organizations devoted to the promotion of women in specific vocations also grew in number toward the later decades as women successfully infiltrated many of the new professions; there were organizations acting in support of women's nursing (Metropolitan and National Nursing Association [1874]), female journalists (Society of Women Journalists [1894] and the Women's Press Association [1894]), as well as women's clerical work (Civil Service Typists Association [1903]). Throughout the period, women's professional and work associations were, in the vast majority of cases, both a source of refuge as well as a powerful force for social change in the fight for sexual and employment equality.

There is no single form, or universal function, of women's economic collaboration advocated by feminist authors at the fin de siècle. Instead, the strategy of feminist intervention varies in direct relationship to the particular iteration of the gendered marketplace, just as each author's literary mode depends upon the intended site of representational intervention. *Critical Alliances* therefore considers depictions of feminine collaboration within several different literary modes, including nonfiction prose, poetry (as the translation of visual media), and multiple novel genres. Each author's contribution to representational modes is an act of resistance, a critical strategy that still reproduces, as well as questions, dominant narratives on women's gendered and economic embodiment. Schreiner's proto-New Woman novel *The Story of an African Farm* (1883) offers compelling arguments for female education while still drawing upon essentialist narratives of motherhood, for example, and Amy Levy's *The Romance of a Shop* (1888) also rewrites the typical heteronormative marriage plot novel to include professional women's mobility across gendered spheres. George Egerton's city novel *The Wheel of God* (1898) celebrates female cosmopolitanism at the expense of cross-class alliances between working women, while Michael Field's *Sight and Song* (1892) takes advantage of the gendered contradictions of aesthetic connoisseurship in order to express (or "translate") an ethical lesbian aesthetics. Finally, Virginia Woolf's post-war writings in *The Years* (1937) and *Three Guineas* (1938) do not memorialize, but nor do they outright refuse or break from (in typical Modernist fashion), her Victorian predecessors and inherited narratives of feminist coalition. Through such innovative negotiations of literary modes, the authors discussed in this study thus understand that the gendered marketplace is, itself, textual in nature and that women must therefore be able to read and also collectively rewrite the symbolic plots limiting the terms of feminine embodiment and economic agency.

1 Victorian Women's "Critical Alliances" and the Cultural Construction of Gender

By the end of the century, ambitious feminists interested in the modern workforce turned their attentions to literature and to rewriting inherited models of gender, more specifically, after notable political reforms reinforced the idea of women's rights to sexual and economic autonomy. Of course gender reformers had been, throughout the nineteenth century, focused on the legal construction of ideal femininity and its role in limiting women's access to economic agency. The 1882 Married Women's Property Act, for example, passed just one year prior to Schreiner's *The Story of an African Farm* (1883), marked one of several significant gains in such efforts to guarantee women's legal and property rights.

Under the new act, the wife (or *feme covert*) was finally, for the first time in British history, legally allowed to own and bequeath her separate property on terms similar to her single (*feme sole*) counterpart. Yet feminists such as Schreiner, writing on the heels of the 1882 Act, pushed the conversation even further to reconsider women's economic agency beyond the legal constructions of marriage. By placing equal emphasis on women's domestic and professional work, feminists after Schreiner instead took as their target for reform the very social construction of gender limiting women's self-possessed agency within, and movement beyond, the unpaid private sphere. These feminists wanted the opportunity to participate in the growing number of lucrative and, often, skilled professions established toward the latter decades of the century thanks to advances in industrial production and the modern capitalist marketplace. In her work on the late-Victorian New Woman, Sally Ledger explains how, "[a]t the turn of the century new employment opportunities were rapidly evolving with the advent of the typewriter, with the expansion of metropolitan department stores and with the professionalization of nursing and of the teaching profession" (*The New Woman*, 19).[14] Though not always self-proclaimed "New Women," the writers analysed in this book are very much invested in this late-Victorian question of gender reform and women's access to their fair share of the modern labour market – from education and nursing, to work in new journalism, or balancing professional ambitions with rights and responsibilities within the domestic sphere. "It is a satisfactory sign of the time," as one reviewer wrote in 1878, at the dawn of this fin-de-siècle Women's Movement, "that women are nowadays not ashamed to confess that they support themselves by honest toil" ("The Old and New Ideals of Women's Education" [1878], 85).[15] Turn-of-the-century feminists wanted to work, and the effort to rewrite social narratives of gender, especially domesticity, was central to their pursuit of professional opportunities within the modern workforce.

As signalled by its title, this study is interested in the tendency toward "critical" exchanges, and even debate, among those women working together to rewrite gender and labour. The idea of a nineteenth-century feminist coalition was by no means without its skeptics who debated both the movement's cohesive nature and its aspirations.[16] In his 1887 review of *The Story of an African Farm*, for example, the British clergyman Canon Malcolm MacColl finds it inconceivable that women might find purpose outside of domestic plots, and thus he criticizes Lyndall's pursuit of "independence" as "self-centered" and unrepresentative of the will of women in general. A feminist movement only makes sense, in MacColl's estimation, insofar as the collective takes as its goal ("help[s] forward") the reformation and elevation or "righteousness" of heterosexual love between men and women ("An Agnostic Novel" [1887], 362). Still other literary works by Victorian authors represent female relationships as often limited by feelings of antagonism and sexual rivalry, not cooperation or mutual identification. Examples of this kind of sororal competition include relationships between Maggie Tulliver and her cousin Lucy Deane in *The Mill on the Floss* (1860), or Nora and Magdalen Vanstone in Wilkie Collins's *No Name* (1862), as well as the sexual rivalry between Rosamond Vincy and Dorothea Brooke in George Eliot's *Middlemarch* (1872), or Jane Eyre and Blanche Ingram in Charlotte Brontë's *Jane Eyre* (1847). But to talk about women's economic collaboration is not to deny the power of sexual competition among women operating within, and defined by, heterosexual domestic plots. Rather, I am interested in how the feminist alliance often assumes the form of a strategic coalition when late-Victorian and Modernist women look beyond the domestic sphere in search of different gender plots and economic opportunities. When it comes to representations of economics and women at the end of the century, the tendency is clearly toward strategic cooperation born out of critical resistance. The concept of "critical resistance" means women working against dominant and/or inherited models of gender, including those put forth by preceding feminists.

Because feminist inheritance is one of its central themes, *Critical Alliances* often reads fin-de-siècle women's writings as responding to, or rethinking, efforts by earlier Victorian gender reformers. This contextualized approach underwrites the project's larger effort to develop an understanding of "inheritance" as a form of dialogic exchange, whereby late-Victorian feminists critique both outmoded gender roles as well as earlier examples of feminism. Inheritance thus represents a unique form of feminine connection (or collaboration) across generations that is attuned to difference and disagreements between women. Though critical in nature, these conversations among women nonetheless represent a bond in the ongoing struggle for gender reform. Indeed, Woolf did not always identify with the women discussed in her writings on gender and culture, but she did express a certain "respect" for pioneers like Schreiner and other Victorian feminists in their "bonnets and shawls" who worked hard to rethink (to "queer") restrictive gender binaries (*Three Guineas*, 102). In an earlier review of *The Letters of Olive Schreiner* (1925), Woolf even admits that Schreiner's feminist vision is not perfect, nor is its earnest admiration for self-sacrifice – especially at the expense of aesthetic quality – shared by the Modernist writer: "It is impossible," Woolf writes, "not to feel for [Schreiner] something of the pity and respect which all martyrs inspire in us, and not least those martyrs who are not required to sacrifice their lives to a cause, but sacrifice, perhaps more disastrously, humor and sweetness and sense of proportion" (103). Despite these flaws in both argument and style, Woolf claims that Schreiner's work presents readers with notable "compensations": "the cause itself – the emancipations of women – was of the highest importance, and it would be frivolous to dismiss [Schreiner] as a mere crank, a piece of wreckage used and then thrown aside as the cause triumphed onwards" (103). Feminist writings by both Schreiner and Woolf (including the latter's response to the former) represent the very complicated and often qualified approach to female cooperation embraced by women writing on gender and social reform at the turn of the century. Far from cohesive bonds of sameness, the feminist alliances examined in this study instead model the social instability of "woman" as a gendered category that can be rewritten or expanded to include women who want careers beyond the home and domestic plots, therein practising a discursive approach to gendered labour that participates in strategies of feminine cooperation across place (within contemporary movements) and time (the cultural inheritance of gender roles). As is implicit in Woolf's measured appreciation for Schreiner's important but imperfect contribution, such feminist alliances are also capable of ongoing and self-reflective deconstruction of the very categories of gender around which women mobilize.[17]

In foregrounding the discursive construction of gender, *Critical Alliances* contributes to conversations among feminist historians and literary scholars on the cultural terms (or social construction) of women's work in the nineteenth century.[18] *Critical Alliances* thus argues that fin-de-siècle feminists, through their collaborative acts of resistance, recognized these socio-discursive forces limiting women's economic roles and professional mobility in the nineteenth century.[19] The mass movement of women into the modern workforce at the end of the nineteenth century cannot, according to this methodology, be explained solely with reference to economic pull factors, such as a market demand for cheap female labour, or push factors, such as the decline in marriageable husbands; rather, social ideologies of gender and cultural assumptions of what constituted "respectable" work for "ladies" played a far larger role in shaping women's attitude toward employment throughout the period.[20] The middle-class emphasis upon feminine domesticity, in particular, is essential to this history. Dominant Victorian conceptions of "genteel femininity" worked to deter women from entering the workforce decades earlier, when the demand was in fact there, but then nineteenth-century gender reformers and feminist authors helped to rewrite the social meaning of "femininity" such that middle- and upper-class women were eventually able to enter the workforce without any sexual stigma or loss in social status. This later history is also why feminist historian Ellen Jordan looks to the Women's Movement, specifically, as a key sociological factor in the historic change in women's economic roles and employment throughout the nineteenth century: "The considerable expansion [of feminine occupations] after mid-century cannot," she avers, "be explained without reference to the arguments and activities of the Women's Movement which opened the eyes of employers to the benefits and viability of employing young women, and convinced young women that it was in their interest to train for an occupation and practice it before marriage" (*The Women's Movement*, 14).[21] *Critical Alliances* looks at how fin-de-siècle feminists found in literary representations of feminist collaboration an opportunity to rewrite Victorian femininity and, with it, women's relationship to the gendered marketplace and the proliferation of middle-class professions at the turn of the century.

Not all Victorians, however, were firm believers in the cultural construction and, thus, malleability of gender roles. Indeed, the late-Victorian Women's Movement, with its critique of feminine domesticity, sparked a sharp backlash among those critics worried about heteronormative divisions of social spaces and labour. These nineteenth-century critics believe in the gendered spheres as a biological correlative of innate sexual difference. A woman's place was in the home, they argued, and for feminists to pursue lives and careers beyond maternal domesticity was a violation of natural order. In 1874, as the Women's Movement gained increasing momentum, psychiatrist Henry Maudsley warned that the growing number of women clamouring for work outside of the home would inevitably culminate in widespread sexual degeneration. In his estimation, these women not only went against nature, thus endangering their own biological systems, but they also therefore threatened the reproductive health of the nation.

> It will have to be considered whether women can scorn delights, and live laborious days of intellectual exercise and production, without injury to their functions as the conceivers, mothers and nurses of children. For it would be an ill thing, if it should so happen, that we got the advantages of a quantity of female intellectual work at the price of a puny, enfeebled, and sickly race. ("Sex in Mind and in Education," 471–2)

This same essentialist argument would again be levelled against the new generation of feminists and gender radicals in the 1880s and 1890s.

In his "Plain Words on the Woman Question" (1889), for example, Grant Allen worried that educating women "like men – giving alike training for totally unlike functions" – threatened women's supposedly natural predisposition toward maternal labour. "The result is that many women became unsexed in the process, and many others acquired a distaste, an unnatural distaste," Allen stresses, "for the maternal functions which nature intended them to perform" (19). Charles G. Harper, writing in 1894, similarly warns that "nature, which never contemplated the production of a learned or muscular woman, will be revenged upon her offspring" in the form of "a puny, enfeebled and sickly race" (*Revolted Woman*, 27).[22] The idea that gender roles were socially malleable and not, in fact, tied to anatomy was a deeply disturbing – if not threatening – prospect to these male conservatives who had, up until the later decades of the century, enjoyed a relative monopoly over the public sphere and its paid professions. Feminist writers and gender radicals working at the fin de siècle sought to upend this heternormative (and exclusionary) balance of power. They also, in the process, sought to undo the popular assumption that women were defined strictly in terms of their (re)productive labour.

Scholarship on the intersection between gender and economics in nineteenth-century women's writing has largely focused around what critics frame as separate and competing models of production and consumption, a dichotomy that is often exacerbated with reference to the 1870s Marginal Revolution. It is worth briefly outlining this historical paradigm shift in economic thought in order to better understand the two sides of this scholarly debate.[23] Most economists since Adam Smith have understood that the modern marketplace plays a primary role in shaping individuals' relationships to each other or structures of exchange. Smith was, for example, among the first political economists to describe in thorough detail the way in which modern structures of production often define individuals as bodies of labour that are differentiated according to specialized and complementary tasks, sometimes even at disastrous cost to higher mental functions (think of the "pin factory" example in Book One of *Wealth of Nations*). However, massive growth of the commodity marketplace in the later decades of the nineteenth century required a new or "neoclassical" theory of economics focused on consumption. Led by William Stanley Jevons, Léon Walras, and Karl Menger, the Marginal Revolution in economic thought refocused attention onto bodies of desire (consumer pleasures) as the driving forces of market exchange and value (demand).[24] Lawrence Birken (*Consuming Desire* [1998]) claims that many late Victorians, both male and female, drew upon this emergent field of consumer economics in order to celebrate the gendered body as a site of idiosyncratic and pleasurable exchange.[25] Alternatively, Regenia Gagnier (*Insatiability of Human Wants*) argues that the late-Victorian writers' investment in economic theories is divided along gendered lines. While Victorian men might have celebrated a new "neoclassical" model of sexual desire, their female counterparts looked back to political economy's logic of divided labour in order to advocate for women's economic and reproductive rights as part of a larger and progressive social good.[26] Gagnier's work also looks at how many feminist writers, despite their nostalgia for the labouring body of political economy, often positioned themselves as withholding (restraint) or working toward (delayed gratification) some future pleasure not yet available to women within the current gendered marketplace.[27] This context might also, then, help us to understand the problematic turn to pronatalism modelled by so many late-Victorian feminists. "When [Sarah] Grand, [Olive] Schreiner, and other New Women rejected sex for pleasure in favour of pronatalism," Gagnier asks, "were they choosing biological sex as a higher destiny, or a Kantian freedom in perfect service to the state?" or were they, she continues, "choosing a kind of Kantian autonomy in the face of apparent heteronomy, the being buffed about by desire, of male Aesthetes and consumer society?" (*The Insatiability of Human Wants*, 175). These Victorian women, Gagnier suggests, saw the reclamation of their bodily labour as an essential precondition to the kind of individual choice so important to neoclassical economics, be that choice in service of individual pleasure or some higher service to the state. In other words, then, feminist reformers did not see pleasure and production as mutually exclusive, but instead saw gender as an important factor influencing the economic modes women might adopt and the specific reformist ends to which they might strive. Of course, not all fin-de-siècle feminist writers were preoccupied with maternal rights, but in order to rewrite women's relationship to the marketplace, these women would have to address gender constructs, including domestic (re)production, as limiting their access to employment and/or consumer choices.

The feminist authors discussed in the following chapters are particularly interested in women's ability to work together and, through such cooperation, to rewrite gender roles that determine women's access to emergent forms of skilled labour and new modes of professional mobility at the end of the nineteenth century. Here my work is very much in conversation with recent scholarship on women's complex contributions to the Victorian marketplace. Relevant texts include Deanna Kreisel's *Economic Woman*, Krista Lysack's *Come Buy, Come Buy*, Lise Shapiro Sanders's *Consuming Fantasies*, and Jill Rappoport's *Giving Women*.

Both Kreisel and Rappoport focus on Victorian women's investments in nineteenth-century theories of labour and productive relationships of exchange. *Economic Woman* looks at how Victorian authors, such as Thomas Hardy and George Eliot, "generously larded their narratives with metaphors and concepts drawn from contemporary political economy and philosophy" (14). Kreisel is particularly interested in how these metaphors are often gendered and, specifically, how representations of feminine embodiment are tied to economic anxiety, including Victorian fears around surplus desire and the circulation of wealth. Economic language and models drawn from political economy thus present Victorian authors with an opportunity to explore alternative social narratives of gendered embodiment. Rappoport is also interested in the subversive potential of political economy for Victorian women looking to rewrite gender roles. The sub-category of gift exchange, with its interest in sacrifice and the destruction of wealth, often circumvents traditional structures of production and divided labour underwriting gender difference and the subjection of women. Rappoport demonstrates how, through acts of charitable giving (as a kind of sacrifice), Victorian women instead produced "volatile and profitable economic negotiations of power and created diverse forms of community" (*Giving Women*, 5).

Shifting the conversation from production to consumption, Lysack and Sanders suggest that many Victorian feminists embraced emergent neoclassical models of economic agency in their pursuit of liberatory desire. Both critics focus on the economics of pleasure, not labour, in writing alternative gender roles and market opportunities for modern women. Lise Shapiro Sanders looks specifically at the shopgirl as a key figure in this late-Victorian shift to the consumer marketplace, as seen in the explosion of urban professions open to women at the turn of the century, as well as women's new and complex relationships with pleasure and economic desire. The Victorian shopgirl was often in a liminal position, as both object and agent of consumption, given that "her vocation required that she mediate the desires of consumers on the other side of the counter" (Sanders, *Consuming Fantasies*, 1). Indeed, many of her customers often treated her as an object of their pleasurable gaze, while at the same time demanded the fantasy of a model who partook in the pleasurable consumption of goods and leisure products (1). Sanders explains how literature of the period participates in this same complex treatment of the shopgirl, "replicatin[ing] this slippage between subject and representation" (2). In this slippage, the urban woman found for herself an opportunity to explode conventional gender norms, including the sexual economy of the gaze and gendered spheres (both assuming private feminine passivity). Like Sanders, Lysack challenges those histories which cast Victorian women as passive objects within a sexual economy of pleasurable consumption. Instead she argues that nineteenth-century female shoppers, and their acts of pleasurable consumption, often exceeded the "norms of self-regulating femininity" prescribed to women at the turn of the century (*Come Buy, Come Buy*, 6). Drawing on Michel de Certeau's theory of resistance, *Come Buy, Come Buy* explains how Victorian women saw in modern forms of shopping a means to "fashion the world around them rather than regulate themselves according to it" (8). *Come Buy, Come Buy* "examines the ways in which literary and popular writing represented the woman shopper as going to market on her own, not as an object of exchange but as a subject, and the expansive forms of identity that became possible when she took her desire with her" (12).

Taken together, these studies complicate the dichotomous model implicit in the Birken-Gagnier debate. There is, in other words, no single model for women's economic embodiment, just as there is no single or homogenous gendered marketplace. However, critics have yet to offer an extensive study of the important role that female bonds play in Victorian women's effort to navigate varying sites of market intervention (a market that cannot be reduced to a binary model of production/consumption). Intervening in this critical conversation, *Critical Alliances* therefore surveys women's participation in varying economic coalitions – from kinship, to professional bonds, or the intellectual labour union – in an attempt to rewrite gender and, with it, women's access to the modern economies of work and pleasure.

For those nineteenth-century women writers who did focus on bodily rights, political economy's emphasis upon labour presented them with a way to describe their own feminist fight against exploitative structures of gender difference and domestic ideology, as well as a way to imagine the cumulative power of (re)productive connections between women spanning generations. Writings by Schreiner framed motherhood as "the mightiest and noblest of human work" given to women (*The Story of an African Farm*, 189), while self-fashioned New Woman author Sarah Grand advanced pronatalist claims in support of sexual education as a solution to intergenerational conflict between mothers and daughters (*Heavenly Twins* [1893] and *The Beth Book* [1897]).[28] However, other fin-de-siècle women recognized and critiqued the rhetorical hold such reproductivist arguments tended to exercise upon feminist writings, and instead suggested that this essentialist logic (linking women with biology) was counterproductive in its service to patriarchal structures of family and work. Mona Caird (*The Daughters of Danaus* [1894]) is, perhaps, the most famous figure to advance such a claim, and in her 1893 "A Defence of the So-Called 'Wild Woman,'" rejects the assumption (by Eliza Lynn Linton) that women must look to motherhood as their only and true calling (thus denying women's right to participate in economic or political economies): "Have we not gone far enough along this path of destruction," Caird asks, "or must women still make motherhood their chief task, accepting the old sentiment of subservience to man, until they drive yet further into the system the cruel diseases that have punished the insanities of the past" ("A Defence of the So-Called 'Wild Woman,'" 297). As Richardson persuasively argues, Caird's rhetorical question effectively "turns biological determinism on its head" (*Love and Eugenics in the Late Nineteenth Century*, 205) by describing how the social "system" of compulsory motherhood, and not sexual reproduction itself, is responsible for the transmission of "diseases" from "victims of ill-usage [mothers]" to "children from generation to generation" (Caird, "A Defence of the So-Called 'Wild Women,'" 297).[29]

At the same time as nineteenth-century feminists were debating the relationship between labour and gender equality, still other Victorian women and sexual reformers were investing in the idea of pleasurable – including proto lesbian – female exchanges. Helena Whitbread's 1988 publication of Anne Lister's secret diaries (spanning 1806–40, her death) shows us that nineteenth-century women had their own and very complicated investments in female-female erotics.[30] At the opposite end of the century, poets and lovers Katharine Bradley and Edith Cooper ("Michael Field") also found pleasure in the beauty of feminine desire, and would often channel – or "translate" – this sexual inspiration into poetic works of aesthetic expression.[31] In her study of Victorian women's "intimate" friendships, Martha Vicinus (*Intimate Friends*) looks at how the mother-daughter trope was frequently cited as a "formative love experience" for those women who found happiness in sexual relationships with other adult women (113). In the concluding pages of her autobiography, for example, Frances Power Cobbe alludes to her partner Mary Lloyd in maternal terms: "God has given me two priceless benedictions in life; – my youth a perfect Mother; in my later years, a perfect Friend" (*Life as Told By Herself* [1904], 710).[32] Cobbe's romantic declaration depends upon a clever mix of both erotic and maternal structures, indicating that some Victorian women did not see the need to discriminate between pleasured or (re)productive economies when thinking about female-female bonds.

While working to acknowledge the variations among (re)productivist and pleasurable bonds between women, nineteenth-century feminist authors and reformers also found themselves necessarily rethinking the political form and function of these feminist alliances. The Women's Movement throughout the nineteenth century was largely preoccupied with the fight for equal sexual and economic rights, or a rights-based feminism associated with the rise of modern individualism. This form of "liberal feminism" can be traced back to early pioneers such as Mary Wollstonecraft, who fought for women's equal education, through mid-century reformers like Caroline Norton, who fought against marital coverture (successes include the 1857 Divorce Act and, later, the 1882 Married Women's Property Act), to Millicent Garrett Fawcett, who served as president of the National Union of Women's Suffrage Society (from 1897 to 1919). Yet, as Ledger argues in her study of *The New Woman*, many liberal reformers felt increasingly compelled to address economic issues and women's employment rights as more and more working women joined their ranks.[33] Some of these later gender reformers left liberal feminism behind altogether, choosing instead to ally themselves with the newly formed Labour Party or, alternatively, socialist organizations that focused specifically on working conditions and labourers' rights. Positioning herself as an advocate for labour, Eleanor Marx (Karl Marx's daughter) justified her rejection of liberal feminism – and individualists such as Millicent Garrett Fawcett – as motivated by a larger sense of social responsibility to working women: "If every demand raised by these women [the 'equal rights' feminists] were granted today, we working women would still be just where we were before," she explains, adding that "[w]omen-workers would still work infamously long hours, for infamously low wages, under infamously unhealthful conditions" (quoted in Ledger, *The New Woman*, 38). Other gender reformers who turned to socialism in order to critique structures of economic exploitation include Olive Schreiner (one of the founding members of the Women's League in the Marxist-inspired Social Democratic Federation), Beatrice Webb (member of the Fabian Society and co-author, with husband Sidney Webb, of *The History of Trade Unionism* [1894] and *Industrial Democracy* [1897]), and also Margaret Harkness (whose slum novels combine socialism and feminism; see *Out of Work* [1888], *A City Girl* [1887], and *In Darkest London* [1889]).[34] In her analysis of this history, Ann Ardis argues that many fin-de-siècle social reformers had a hard time seeing the connection between socialism and the so-called Woman Question, and would, therefore, default to either one of two ways of incorporating some analysis of gender into their theories of social reform: they would either exclude "individualist" subjects like the private family from their larger collective pursuits, or they would reframe gender as a mere symptom of larger economic structures of capitalist exploitation and economic inequality (*New Women, New Novels*, 17). Isabella Ford's work *Women and Socialism* (1907), for example, falls into this latter category insofar as it claims that both feminism and the labour movement "arise from the common evil of economic dependence, or rather economic slavery" (3). Disagreements between Victorian thinkers aside, the wide range in forms among feminine bonds suggests that, throughout the nineteenth century, feminists were themselves aware of, and actively debated, the complex relationship between gender and economics, and that their models of gendered cooperation deliberately varied according to their sexual and economic priorities.

With its focus on the wide range among feminist collaborations, *Critical Alliances* contributes to a growing and, often, opposing body of scholarship on Victorian representations of female partnerships. In many ways this recent resurgence in scholarship on female alliances can be read as a response to earlier works, such as Helena Michie's *Sororophobia*, critiquing second-wave feminism as erasing difference or conflict among women.[35] Michie's study focuses particularly on representations of sisterly bonds, from the nineteenth and twentieth centuries, because the sororal trope has enjoyed such a long and lasting influence in feminist writings about women's collaborative resistance against patriarchal structures. According to Michie's critique, the sisterly bond is in fact "competitive, problematic, and theatrical," and through this attention to division and differences between women, *Sororophobia* claims to acknowledge this complexity and to add a "dimension of dignity and choice to friendships between and among women" (21). Still more recent scholars, however, resist the idea that women's strategic coalitions were ever about sameness or lack of choice (no agency), and are, instead, attentive to material circumstances as well as difference. On this point, studies by both Martha Vicinus (*Intimate Friends*) and Sharon Marcus (*Between Women*) push us to reconsider how the female-female bond challenges our own modern and, often, reductive, heterosexist gender binaries.[36] Vicinus, for example, insists that we must think of Victorian representations of female-female desire as an "embodied history" attentive to shifting meanings of sexuality and gender within different cultural contexts (xxii). *Intimate Friends* is particularly interested in the varying ways that women's intimate bonds are an expression of self-conscious resistance (agency), claiming for themselves terms such as "wife" or "marriage."[37] Conversely, Marcus argues that our modern tendency to think in terms of same-sex desire encourages us to misread the many different forms of intimacy between women as categorized within "a subset of lesbianism and as a subdivision of gender norms" (29). Rather, *Between Women* surveys a wide range among different forms of women's friendships, female-female love, and even marriage between women that refuse easy assumptions of sameness or categorization within a single rubric of desire. Heeding the example of both Vicinus and Marcus, *Critical Alliances* reframes the variation among female alliances as the product of women's different interventions in the gendered marketplace (including cultural capital, aesthetic consumption, or urban cosmopolitanism).[38] Specifically, the authors discussed here demonstrate how feminists' different market interventions culminate in an equally diverse and strategic range in female partnerships.

By focusing on the variability and instability of gender as a social category, late-Victorian feminist reformers anticipated some of the ongoing debates among contemporary gender scholars on the power of feminist collaboration to rewrite structures of sexual difference and domestic ideology. Much of this contemporary criticism is divided over the question of agency or the degree to which the woman-identified-woman can possibly transcend heterosexual plots. One side of this critical conversation associates feminine bonds with a liberatory expression of lesbian desire, independent of men or masculine economies of heteronormativity.[39] In this "continuum model," the female-bonded woman takes as her object of self-definition a primary identification with other women – no matter where this identification falls on the lesbian continuum – and therein rejects misogynistic models of gender difference (including the feminine as "Other").[40] Still other critics propose an alternative "tension model" that separates gender from sexuality and allows us to recognize those moments where bonds between women might still work in cooperation with – even if redefining – heterosexual structures of exchange.[41] Female friendships might, in this second model, teach women to prioritize others (their girlfriends) above themselves and thus to become the ideal self-sacrificing "Angel of the House."[42] Marcus's queer methodology in *Between Women* presents readers with a more recent attempt to reconcile both sides of this critical debate. Marcus acknowledges the primary role that female bonds frequently played in Victorian women's lives, including "the marriage between women" (1), but also rejects the idea that feminine intimacy was always opposed to or exceeded heterosexual institutions (per the lesbian continuum). This latter assumption, Marcus continues, can cause us to forget how "many nineteenth-century women in what some Victorians called 'female marriages' were not seen as challenging the conventions of kinship," but instead "saw themselves, and their friends, neighbors, and colleagues saw them, as a variation on the married couple" (12).

The authors discussed in this study also experiment with a wide range in forms of feminine intimacy, including everything from the lesbian marriage (Michael Field) to affective alliances (Olive Schreiner and George Egerton) and female-centred kinship (Amy Levy and Virginia Woolf). Yet these Victorian and Modernist gender reformers do not subscribe to the image of female-female bonds as somehow transcendent or liberatory (the continuum model); instead, collaborative alliances allow these gender reformers to rewrite – and therein still reproduce – structures of heterosexual difference and what it means to be a "woman" (the tension model). Through their critique of domestic ideology, for example, these feminist texts present collaborative bonds as an integral part of women's lives and, more important, women's efforts to redefine the terms and sexual limits of the gendered marketplace. Contemporary scholarship on nineteenth-century representations of bonds between women must therefore acknowledge, if not reconcile, the continuum and tension models in order to account for the wide variety of forms and aspirations these bonds may assume.

Critical Alliances argues that late-Victorian and Modernist authors generated new and inventive models of gender and economics that do not neatly fit into stable or mutually exclusive categories such as (re)productive vs. pleasured bodies. Instead, the wide range among representations of women's bodily bonds at the turn of the century – including the lesbian marriage, intimate friendships, sororal kinship, or labour coalitions – represent expressions of resistance that, in their aspirations to feminine agency or autonomy (the continuum model), must still negotiate structures of gender difference and sexual pleasure (the tension model). The reciprocal relationship between gender roles and the modern marketplace is vital to understanding the subsequent variation among representations of feminine bonds. *Critical Alliances* looks at how, through strategic forms of feminine cooperation, feminist authors attempted to rewrite Victorian femininity and, as a result, redefined women's access to modern forms of economic consumption and professional mobility. This reading of "strategic" alliance is, of course, informed by post-structuralist models, as popularized by Judith Butler (*Gender Trouble*), that refuse the idea of feminist critique as working outside of, or transcending, dominant constructions of power.[43] Thinking in terms of discursive resistance, Butler instead asks "[w]hat possibilities of gender configurations exist among the various emergent and occasionally convergent matrices of cultural intelligibility that govern gendered life" (*Gender Trouble*, 31). *Critical Alliances* claims that women's turn to varying forms of economic cooperation represents an attempt to rewrite the cultural terms of both gendered as well as economic embodiment. For the feminist writers discussed in this study, those "matrices of cultural intelligibility" include the mutual relationship between structures of gender (domestic ideology, compulsory maternity, patriarchal kinship) and economics (paid employment, consumerism, and participation in the modern marketplace) in shaping Victorian women's lives and relationships. Literature plays a vital role in these negotiations insofar as it is a means through which to explore, and also exploit, the contradictions within the existing ideological narratives that define women's relationship to economic modes – or as Catherine Gallagher explains, "[l]iterary forms often disrupt the tidy formulations and reveal the inherent paradoxes of their ostensible ideologies" (*The Industrial Reformation of English Fiction*, xiii).[44] Possible contradictions in the history covered by this study include the tension between women's role as domestic caregivers and the increasing professionalization of childhood education throughout the nineteenth century, or the unequal application of modern contractual rights (as applied to both structures of marriage and property) to Victorian husbands and wives. Possible points of intervention (exploiting contradiction) include women's collaborative reclamation of feminized work, such as nursing, or the appropriation of the masculine gaze by the lesbian aesthete in order to translate into poetry (and therein celebrate) female-female desire. In each case, the literary representation of feminist alliances plays a vital role in the discursive reconstruction of "women" and their relationship to the gendered marketplace at the turn of the century.

2 Outline of My Argument

Critical Alliances resists the assumption that a single gender model or economic theory can explain fin-de-siècle representations of women's partnerships. In its analysis, *Critical Alliances* instead employs a synthetic method that selects theories relevant to each writer's particular intervention in, and contribution to, representations of women's gender and economic roles. Nor is *Critical Alliances* intended as an exhaustive study of the various forms and representations of women's collaborations. There is, in other words, no single model or "grand narrative" of feminist cooperation at the fin de siècle; rather, representations of women's alliances vary in direct accordance with the specific site, and intended outcome, of strategic intervention into the gendered marketplace. Schreiner's work on feminist coalitions, for example, reads as a response to nineteenth-century restrictions on women's education, while Levy's work on sisterly bonds is framed by a close analysis of Victorian women's rights to sexual contract. Egerton's professional women must negotiate the gendered cityscape (particularly the objectifying gaze of the male *flâneur*), while Field's lesbian erotics respond to the masculine gaze of aesthetic consumption. The final chapter on Woolf is intended as a concluding discussion of post-Victorian inheritance and the transition to Modernist feminisms.

Just as the authors selected are meant to highlight the range among representations of fin-de-siècle feminist bonds, so too are the following chapters discussing their feminist writings meant to highlight the many different and growing number of professions open to women at the end of the nineteenth century. I include Schreiner because her work marks the beginning of the New Woman tradition and, at the same time, the redefinition of hitherto domestic work into respectable vocations open to women. *The Story of an African Farm* and *Woman and Labor* invite readers to consider the redefinition of women's care-giving work (from governessing to nursing) across the century, to the point where women enjoy newfound access to knowledge and careers beyond domestic plots as independent teachers and even medical professionals. Conversely, Levy's fiction impresses upon readers women's exciting social and sexual freedoms within commercial spaces and business establishments. *The Romance of a Shop* imagines how women's employment as shopgirls might underwrite feminine mobility between private and public spaces, as well as facilitate women's access to a new urban economy of visual consumption and economic autonomy. Egerton's writings extend this idea of women's urban mobility to consider several emergent white-collar and modern vocations open to independent-minded women in the city at the fin de siècle. *The Wheel of God* looks at urban women's secretarial work and feminist contributions to popular journalism, and is also interested in how women's public mobility redefines care-giving work (such as nursing) into a respectable career option for women. The chapter on Michael Field traces women's struggle for recognition as artistic connoisseurs and aesthetic critics. Though this chapter offers a slightly different discussion of gendered economy by shifting attention to consumption, it continues earlier discussion of women's writings as generating new representations of feminine agency and the (literary) marketplace. The lyric poetry of *Sight and Song* records the authors' powerful insistence on their right to look at and record their pleasurable consumption (translation of) the beautiful work of art. Finally, Virginia Woolf's modernist writings offer a powerful defence of women's work as professional writers and the producers of the very narratives or social plots that define modern gender and women's economic roles. Intended as a conclusion, this chapter highlights the modernist's dialogic conversation with her fin-de-siècle sisters as they look back at, and resist, dominant Victorian domestic plots in order to write new gender and economic opportunities for the modern woman. Throughout these different chapters, *Critical Alliances* emphasizes that the range among different representations of women's market intervention is meant to complement the study's overarching theme of the variation among forms of feminine collaboration, for again, the form of feminist resistance varies in direct accordance with professional ambitions, and by the century's end the number of professions open to women had multiplied almost exponentially.

Because domestic ideology had such a powerful influence upon the gendered marketplace, I begin my book with a discussion of Victorian women's work as skilled care-givers, such as teachers and nurses. Victorian feminists recognized that many of the careers associated with the modern marketplace required a level of education typically denied women destined for the unpaid private sphere. These feminists understood that they needed first to rewrite Victorian gender roles and, in particular, to redefine the limits of domestic ideology prohibiting their access to higher or skilled training. The first chapter, "Educating New Women for Feminist Futures," argues that late-Victorian authors like Schreiner presented readers with innovative representations of women's care-giving that extend well beyond the private sphere and, thus, which require educational support. While the feminist campaign for educational reform can be traced back as far as the sixteenth century, the nineteenth century marks a watershed of new initiatives, such as the 1858 Royal Commission Report on a national system of girl's secondary instruction, as well as the foundation of several institutions devoted to women's higher learning – including Bedford College in 1849, Girton College in 1869, Newnham College in 1871, Somerville College in 1879, St Hugh's College in 1886, and St Hilda's College in 1893.[45] These institutions were inspired by, and also sparked further public debate on the form and social value, of women's work as mothers and teachers of the nation. Detractors such as Grant Allen (*The Woman Who Did* [1895]) worried that gender-neutral edification would corrupt women's (re)productive social purpose, while proponent Eliza Lynn Linton ("The Higher Education of Women" [1886]) countered that women's equal but separate education would in fact benefit the larger nation.[46] Still other feminist radicals, such as Mona Caird ("Marriage" [1888]) and Ella Hepworth Dixon ("Why Women Are Ceasing to Marry" [1899]), outright rejected the compulsory marriage plot as an unsustainable social fiction limiting women's intellectual development and, thus, wider cultural contribution. An early advocate of women's skilled labour, Schreiner (*The Story of an African Farm* and *Woman and Labor*) is a key figure to understanding this feminist history and the role of women's intellectual collaboration in negotiating the increasingly permeable boundary between the domestic and public spheres. In her proto-New Woman novel *The Story of an African Farm,* for example, Schreiner rejects traditional models of feminine instruction as servicing the conventional heterosexual marriage plot. With reference to *Pierre Bourdieu*'s theory of cultural capital ("The Forms of Capital"), this chapter claims that Schreiner's writings redefine the currency and structure (transmission) of the gendered marketplace. Education grants women access to the modern economy, and for Schreiner, this edification also transforms private reproductive bonds between mothers and daughters into a larger form of cultural labour. Writing well into the twentieth century (in *Woman and Labor*), Schreiner presents readers with a model of (re)productivist cooperation that re-imagines women's relationships to both biological as well as social care-giving.

Women's (re)productive bonds are also the main subject of the second chapter, "Sisterly Kinship and the Modern Sexual Contract." This chapter argues that feminist kinship and, specifically, women's self-possessed bodily bonds underwrote women's fluid movement between the private home and the public sphere of paid employment. When Henry Sumner Maine published his legal treatise *Ancient Law* in 1861, he singled out the Victorian period as a time of possibility, hovering on the brink of an historic shift from status to contract. In this touchstone text, Maine explains how this history depends upon a woman's right to sexual contract as a self-possessed agent of exchange.[47] As with the revolution in education, Victorian attitudes toward marriage reform were mixed, with some aligning ideas of sexual contract with a new era of gender "topsyturvydom" and the end of old world stability (status) under the patriarch (Eliza Lynn Linton, "The Judicial Shock to Marriage" [1891]). Other radical feminists argued that marital inequality had more to do with cultural constructions of gender and the family than liberal property rights (Caird, "Marriage" [1888]). Chapter 2 focuses on this second group of feminist thinkers and, in particular, their literary representations of sisterly bonds as rewriting the marriage plot novel to include women's sexual and economic contractual agency. Published on the heels of the Marriage Act of 1882, Amy Levy's *The Romance of a Shop* (1888) emphasizes how sisterly bonds play a formative role in women's equal pursuit of marriage and work. The novel's four protagonists, the Lorimer sisters, participate in an alternative structure of kinship – or sororal alliance – that substitutes old structures of "patriarchal" traffic in female bodies with a new economy in which women act as self-possessed agents; this female-centric economy therein liberates sexual desire from reproduction (including private patrilineal bloodlines), enabling women to participate in sexual-economic exchange for and by oneself. In this way, Levy's writings culminate in a model of gender indifference typically associated with Modernist and Postmodernist feminisms.

The majority of modern careers for which late-Victorian women competed were located in growing, global cities, and so in order to find work, many of these women were compelled to challenge outmoded gender roles (including domestic ideology) limiting women to the unpaid private sphere. Chapter 3, "Cosmopolitan Communities of Female Professionals," argues that affective alliances played a vital role in supporting women's cosmopolitan mobility. Pushing against old Victorian institutions such as chaperonage and the separate gendered spheres, these modern women struggled to redefine, and therein legitimate, their unique relationship to new "pink-collar" careers in the city. For many women at the turn of the century, access to the urban marketplace depended critically upon the classed and gendered definition of feminine labour. George Egerton's *The Wheel of God* (1898) reminds readers how early feminized professions such as nursing granted ladies limited access to public spaces (thanks to Florence Nightingale's pioneering efforts). The novel's more radical feminist characters also signal how, by the end of the century, many of the skilled professions were opening their doors to (and taking advantage of) the growing number of independent-minded middle-class women. Similar works by Dorothy Richardson (*The Long Day* [1905]) and Ella Hepworth Dixon (*The Story of a Modern Woman* [1894]) look at how vocations such as typewriting and journalism facilitated women's dual investment in modern forms of work and creative expression. In staking their claim to urban spaces, the female characters in these novels rewrite the sexual politics of the city. Whereas the male *flâneur* is a creature of leisured visual detachment, these professional women are instead embedded within and must, therefore, like Charles Baudelaire's "ragpicker" ("The Rag-Picker's Wine" [1857]), negotiate the material conditions of the city in terms of both class and gender. It is also here, on the margins of the gendered marketplace, where many working women discovered a cosmopolitical community of support. In Egerton's *The Wheel of God*, popular journalism itself facilitates creative expression and, thus, "political" connections among professional women (per Walter Benjamin's definition in "The Work of Art in the Age of Mechanical Reproduction" [1936]).

In order to be taken seriously as producers of cultural content, feminist writers also had to counteract the popular Victorian trope of woman as artistic muse, including the celebration of beauty's body as a passive object for men's visual pleasure and aesthetic inspiration.

The fourth chapter argues that nineteenth-century women's writings on artistic connoisseurship, including travel writing and cultural tourism, played a key role in redefining the aesthetic economy of gender and, therein, legitimating the female artist. This chapter also shifts the discussion slightly to consider women's intervention into consumer economics and, specifically, the right to act as authorities on the artistic gaze. "Women's Artistic Connoisseurship and the Pleasures of a Lesbian Aesthetic" explains how fin-de-siècle women's writings about, or poetic translations of, artworks reconfigure the gendered economy of the aesthetic gaze to create new spaces for autonomous and self-possessed feminine pleasure.[48] Building upon a long tradition of women's travel writing, late-Victorian writers such as Alice Meynell and Vernon Lee (Violet Paget) use aesthetic criticism as a way to "collect" and therein validate women's artistic experiences. Taking their cue from these contemporary feminist aesthetes, Michael Field (Katharine Bradley and Edith Cooper) celebrate erotic bonds between women as a means to navigate the gendered economy of pleasure and to assert women's contribution to the pleasures of artistic collecting. Through lyric "translations" of famous paintings, Field's *Sight and Song* (1892) draws attention to, and therein interrogates, the artist's dual investment in sexual erotics (including the masculine gaze) and possessive consumption of the beautiful feminine body. The chapter compares *Sight and Song*'s highly sexualized ekphrastic poetry with other representative texts on late-Victorian artistic collection (or art tourism) – including works by Field's friend and renowned art critic Bernard Berenson – to demonstrate Field's radical approach to the gendered gaze and visual consumption. Field's erotic translations resist dominant modes of appropriative desire and commodification; instead, the poets show us how women might, through their mutual enjoyment of feminine art, experience a new kind of aesthetic pleasure for, and to be shared among, a community of women. It is also through the medium of non-possessive lesbian erotics that Field's aesthetic translations offer readers a glimpse of an artistic subjectivity that is both engaged with, but also critical of, the gendered marketplace.

"Virginia Woolf's Post-Victorian Feminism" is a capstone chapter on female-centered kinship as an act of feminist resistance across generations. In discussing her Victorian foremothers (and Olive Schreiner, specifically), Woolf disavows the idea of women's shared sacrifice as culminating in a linear inheritance of feminism. Woolf's post-war writings, *The Years* (1937) and *Three Guineas* (1938), instead present readers with a model of women's strategic alliances through dialogic resistance at both the local and historical levels.[49] Woolf had initially planned to combine both texts into a single experimental novel-essay on women's lives. Though Woolf eventually separated the texts, both still share a common interest in women's social and economic relationships following the traumatic events of the First World War.[50] Woolf's novel *The Years* focuses on war as rupturing women's kinship (the familial plot spans the late-Victorian and Modernist periods), while her essay collection *Three Guineas* rethinks women's inheritance (per daughters, specifically) as a form of cooperative resistance. As suggested by her 1925 review of Schreiner, Woolf admits a certain respect for nineteenth-century feminists, and argues that women in the early twentieth century were still, in fact, continuing a similar fight for equal gender and economic rights beyond the domestic sphere. However, like many of her Modernist contemporaries, Woolf also refuses to memorialize Victorian narratives of self-sacrifice as heroic and as necessarily contributing to a uniform narrative. Yet neither do her post-war writings claim a definitive break from preceding feminisms and their fight against patriarchal structures delimiting women's economic mobility. In coping with the trauma of war, *The Years* and *Three Guineas* instead reframe feminist kinship and, specifically, the bonds among Victorian and Modernist women as strategic alliances formed in dialogic resistance to inherited plots that bar women's access to the gendered marketplace. Women's economic cooperation is then, in this account, implicitly self-conscious of its own temporality and, thus, conducive to a politics of difference across alternative social axes. Both novel and prose works by Woolf imagine how women's gender coalitions might work as post-Victorian (not Modernist) resistance to masculine structures of sexual and economic (re)production.

If women's economic collaborations can cross generations, then *Critical Alliances* is part of an ongoing dialogue (or "dialogic resistance" per Woolf) on women's relationship to gender roles and the impact of feminism more broadly upon the changing gendered workforce. At the heart of so much of this conversation is the question of gender roles – including domestic ideology and the gendered spheres – limiting women's upward mobility in both work and social status. Fin-de-siècle feminist authors were preoccupied with middle- and upper-class women's access to equal employment, and yet their varying critique of bourgeoisie domestic ideology carried through to post-Victorian analyses of the gendered marketplace and made possible a legacy of women's work that influenced Modernist and, even, second-wave feminists in the twentieth century on women's consciousness-raising and further deconstructing the socioeconomic (and classed) constructions of gender and women's work. What these representations of fin-de-siècle women's alliances show us is that both categories of "women" and "labour" are historically specific cultural constructions and that gendered cooperation can change the definition and, thus, composition of the gendered marketplace. It is clear that, for the feminist authors analysed here, women's relationship to the marketplace was not immutable; these turn-of-the-century feminists instead looked at gendered and economic identities as unstable points of contestation, and through varying forms of economic coalition, as well as ongoing dialogic resistance, these feminist authors reproduced new roles or narratives of gendered exchange. Indeed, the idea of a critical conversation across generations of women writers further amplifies the idea of a gendered coalition that is both strategic and also the source of ongoing debate (deconstructing the category of "woman"). Several of the feminist authors covered in this study struggle to realize some kind of ideal or utopian economic future for women, and yet the persistent variation among their different forms of female partnership defies any sense of such a singular – let alone progressive – historical narrative. The ongoing variation among female alliances instead serves as a powerful reminder that, just as the categories of gender and labour remain under constant cultural contestation, so too does the literary inheritance of feminist bonds inspire ongoing dialogue or "critical alliances."

1 Educating New Women for Feminist Futures

[W]e demand that high and complex culture and training which shall fit us for instructing the race which we bring into the world.

– Olive Schreiner, *Woman and Labor*

"There is nothing helps in this world," said the child [Lyndall] slowly, "but to be very wise, and to know everything – to be clever ... I must learn."

– *The Story of an African Farm*

On 10 September 1886, Olive Schreiner wrote to her close friend Karl Pearson, telling him "I have scribbled down some such plan of a Woman's Book as has been in my mind for many years" (Rive, *Olive Schreiner Letters*, 103). The book in question was *Woman and Labor*, published in 1911, and even though it took Schreiner the better part of two decades to complete this text, its feminist principles were always on her mind and motivated much of her writing. As implied by its title, this "Bible of the Woman's Movement" (to quote Vera Brittain)[1] discusses at great length the relationship between gender and labour, focusing extensively on how outmoded constructs of sexual difference often limit the form and function of women's work. Throughout her six chapters (three on "Parasitism," as well as chapters "Women and War," "Sex Differences," and "Certain Objectives"), Schreiner also identifies how education might restrict, as well as rewrite, women's access to modern forms of labour. Schreiner argues that boys are, from an early age, promised an advanced education befitting of the modern workforce, while their sisters are stuck with only the most rudimentary training and instead spend most of their time learning and working within the domestic sphere. "Till at nine or ten, the son in certain countries often leaves his home forever for the public school, to pass on to the college and university," Schreiner writes, "while the daughter, in the hands of trained instructors and dependents, owes in the majority of cases hardly more of her education or formation to maternal toil" (*Woman and Labor*, 51). Schreiner could see that the modern workforce was changing as a consequence of industrial capitalism, and she could also see how girls were being denied the same economic opportunities as boys because of the negative effect that gender roles had upon female education and skilled employment. As an answer to this problem, *Woman and Labor* places gender at the very centre of larger philosophical questions such as social (re)production and modern economics – for as Schreiner tells her friend Pearson in the aforementioned letter, "we want to raise the question of sex to its true place as one of the deep, reaching problems of the Universe" (103).

Schreiner's "woman's book" was really an extension of many of the same questions about gender and labour raised by her earlier novel, *The Story of an African Farm* (1883), whose proto-feminist heroine Lyndall would later become a role model for self-proclaimed "New Women" and sexual radicals around the world.[2] Through this unconventional heroine, Schreiner first debated controversial topics such as domestic ideology and its influence upon women's socio-sexual independence. In an early conversation with her cousin Em, for example, a young Lyndall confesses that it is her ambition to "learn" – "to know everything" and "be clever" (57). This quotation, excerpted above, not only sets the stage for Lyndall's feminist plotline, but it also draws a clear link between education and women's opportunities for social and economic advancement in a world that is still largely dominated by patriarchal structures of authority. Her cousin Em will ultimately inherit her father's farm, for example, but young Lyndall "[has] nothing" and must either find a husband to support her or "go to school" in order to make her own way in an increasingly skilled economy (57). Lyndall does eventually attend a boarding school, where she quickly discovers that the gendered education typical of such an institution is meant to make female students into dependent wives and mothers and that this curriculum does very little for the ambitious woman who longs to find her own way in the modern workforce: "I have discovered that of all cursed places under the sun, where the hungriest soul can hardly pick up a few grains of knowledge, a girls boarding-school is the worst," she tells her friend Waldo, adding that the ironically named "finishing schools" in effect "finish everything but imbecility and weakness, and that they cultivate" (182). Lyndall's brave, though ultimately tragic, rejection of compulsory domesticity inspired a new wave of late-Victorian gender reformers dedicated to the very same interrogation of women's education and labour. Through this proto-feminist heroine Schreiner first articulated the claim that some form of advanced training – be it skilled or intellectual training – is requisite to women's equal access to the modern professions. With the later publication of *Woman and Labor*, Schreiner would continue to argue that the form and value of feminine labour had changed under industrial capitalism and that current institutions of gendered education were thus in need of immediate reform so that women might keep pace with, and become satisfied contributors to, the fin-de-siècle workforce.

Critical Alliances begins with a chapter on Olive Schreiner because, as mentioned in the introduction, her work on women and labour helped usher in a new era of feminist writings and so-called New Woman fiction at the fin de siècle. Like Schreiner, these late-Victorian feminists were preoccupied with middle-class women's professional mobility and work beyond the private sphere. Schreiner devoted much of her life and writings to the question of women's work, and was, more specifically, concerned with women's equal access to skilled professions in light of a changing economy. In her own life, as well as her writings, Schreiner wrestled with the spectre of female domesticity that limited women's access to the modern professions. She was inheritor to a long tradition of feminist writing working in resistance to domestic ideology, but she was also part of a new, fin-de-siècle feminist movement interested in the changing gendered marketplace and the role of fiction in imagining the modern female professional. As a late-Victorian writer, she was acutely aware of the proliferation in modern careers and women's growing access – thanks to writings such as her own – to these more lucrative economic opportunities. Her writings thus marked the beginning of a new era of so-called New Woman literature, which as described by Ann Ardis and Sally Ledger, pioneers in the study of this genre, forced a discussion among late Victorians on women's sexual and economic independence by leaving open-ended women's narratives that push against or even transcend the domestic plot.[3] Schreiner's later writings, especially her treatise *Woman and Labor*, helped to define the feminist's defiant claim to modern forms of work and social equality that informs so much of fin-de-siècle women's writing on economics and gender.

In her own life, Schreiner was actively invested in sexual and economic reform. She joined the Men and Women's Club, an organization led primarily by Karl Pearson and dedicated to the interrogation of dominant cultural norms and inequalities.[4] As a member of the Club, Schreiner found an opportunity to debate the merits of socialism and the intersections between economics and gender.[5] She also formed close friendships with Havelock Ellis and Edward Carpenter, both of whom were active members of the utopian-socialist Fellowship of the New Life. These friendships would last the better part of four decades and provided Schreiner with a vital forum for discussing the intersection between sex and economics.[6] In a letter to Carpenter, composed 11 April 1887, for example, Schreiner expressed her reservations toward Karl Pearson's *Socialism and Sex* (1887), admitting that she agreed with the argument "except with regard to the state supporting childbearing women, etc." (Rive, *Olive Schreiner Letters*, 125).[7] Nor did Schreiner wholly embrace Carpenter's model of sexual reform.[8] In *Marriage: A Retrospect; A Forecast* (1894), Carpenter explains how economic capital stifles any real love between individuals, and instead wonders how increased sexual liberty, including extramarital intimacies, might successfully counter the "egoism à deux" typical of the bourgeois marriage (93). In her letter to Carpenter, dated 8 October 1894, Schreiner describes the pamphlet as "splendid," but insists that "you don't perhaps dwell QUITE enough on the monetary independence of women as the first condition necessary to the putting of things on the right footing: but you do mention it" (quoted in Rive, 241).[9]

While Schreiner's response to the marriage question might have framed "monetary independence" as the "first condition" to sexual equality, her expanded writings on gender reform more broadly recognized the value of an equal education as a precondition of the modern labour market and, thus, the very means to women's economic self-determination. She was, after all, writing at a time when women were pushing for increased access to higher schooling and, at the same time, the definition of feminine work – with an emphasis on care-giving – was expanding to include various professions or paid employment beyond the traditional domestic sphere.[10] Schreiner herself was trained to work as a governess, a vocation considered appropriate for her middle-class standing, but like so many ambitious young ladies in the late nineteenth century, she longed to work in one of the prestigious modern professions, such as medicine. This was not an impossible dream given that, by 1874, Elizabeth Garrett Anderson and Sophia Jex-Blake had founded the London School of Medicine for Women.[11] Jex-Blake would go on to develop the Edinburgh School for Women in 1886, while Anderson established the New Hospital for Women in 1890.[12] Still, modern historians Joan N. Burstyn (*Victorian Education and the Ideal of Womanhood*) and Carol Dyhouse ("Social Darwinistic Ideas and the Development of Women's Education in England 1880–1920") are both quick to caution against an overly optimistic view of such changes to women's curriculum as implicitly progressive.[13] Indeed, Victorian women's increased access to higher education and advanced forms of skilled training were gradually won, and even by the latter decades, elementary and secondary curricula for young ladies continued to stress domestic skills and to exclude supposedly masculine subjects such as math or science.[14] Yet, this outmoded education system was under increased pressure to catch up with a gendered workforce that was changing, and from the 1880s on, it opened its doors to middle- and upper-class women interested in employment beyond the private sphere. Even those jobs defined as "feminine" – from teaching to nursing – required some form of advanced training hitherto unavailable to girls bound by the traditional domestic plot.

Taking as its focus Schreiner's extended writings on women and labour, this chapter intervenes in scholarly debates on the history of Victorian women's education and its role in female employment. There are several, and sometimes conflicting, explanations as to what sparked nineteenth-century efforts to reform women's education. These explanations can be organized into roughly four critical camps. The first camp interprets the growing support for women's education as the consequence of a much wider push for democratic reforms and the rise of a liberal or rights-based feminism from the 1840s on.[15] Other critics cite economic push factors, such as the rise of industrial capitalism, which required women's skilled retraining for a modern labour market. Critics in the third camp argue that the call for women's education reform was a response to the rising number of respectable young ladies forced to earn their own living because of their parents' poor finances and/or the decline in marriageable husbands.[16] Finally, the Victorian Women's Movement, which grew in momentum and number of supporters throughout the nineteenth century, is another and often-cited causal factor in the fight for women's equal education.[17] Feminists invested in the idea of sexual and social equality recognized that advanced learning, or some form of skills training, was a necessary precursor to women's economic mobility. While this chapter considers all four historical frames, the last school of criticism on feminist collaboration is particularly relevant to the late-Victorian gendered marketplace and Schreiner's contribution to the debates on women's education and labour. This chapter argues that Schreiner's extended writings on Victorian gender and economics foreground the primary importance of education in feminists' efforts to revalue women's work, including efforts to challenge the restrictive role of domestic ideology in limiting women's skills training. Through Schreiner we can see how the gendered terms of education helped reproduce social constructions of sexual difference and, therein, the subsequent limitations imposed upon so-called feminine labour.

Yet it is her focus on women's collaborative bonds in the fight for education and skilled labour that sets Schreiner's writings apart from her feminist predecessors', as well as many of her contemporaries', work on gender and economic equality. Indeed, Schreiner's representation of a kind of intellectual union among women radically reconfigures the gendered terms of female kinship, especially the supposed biological imperative that women work as mothers within the domestic sphere. Schreiner was, after all, writing in response to a long tradition of Victorian feminism, particularly women's fight for equal education and careers beyond those forms of work tightly associated with feminine domesticity (such as governessing, teaching, or nursing). Writing in response to this tradition, Schreiner stresses the importance of female cooperation as a way to rethink biological determinism. Schreiner imagines how women might work together to produce new forms of feminist inheritance that exchange biology for other socially meaningful forms of labour. She envisions this cooperation working not just in terms of inheritance, or as dialogical response to and benefiting from women's previous struggles, but Schreiner also recognizes the importance of feminist cooperation and its ability to rewrite inherited gender roles and, with them, women's access to knowledge and skills training. Schreiner thus reimagines feminist kinship in very social terms whereby women might form bonds of alliance that stress the transmission of knowledge and cultural capital in the ongoing pursuit of modern, skilled professions.

To understand Schreiner's unique take on gender and economics, one must read her touchstone texts, *The Story of an African Farm* and *Woman and Labor*, as intervening in late-Victorian theories of female education and/as resistance against domestic ideology. Both works are a response to, and critique of, period-specific theories of women's work and women's role within the transition to a new economy of industrial capitalism. This chapter looks at how Schreiner's literary representations of the feminist collective, with its transmission of cultural capital between women, played an integral role in changing the cultural meaning of "feminine" labour. *The Story of an African Farm* represents Schreiner's earliest effort to pioneer a unique theory of gender reform that is focused on education and the transmission of knowledge between generations of feminists. Schreiner returned to this ideal of women's intellectual inheritance in her treatise, *Woman and Labor*, and added references to social evolution (per Herbert Spencer) in an attempt to rationalize the feminist cooperative as working in support of some larger vision of socio-sexual progress (ie., a natural extension of domestic care-giving). Schreiner does not, in other words, simply promote a feminine trades-unionism wherein women reclaim their lost rights to outmoded or undervalued forms of domestic care-giving; rather, Schreiner's writings on feminist collaboration redefine the very form and function of women's labour and, thereby, suggest how women might, through education, become meaningful contributors to a modern economy that values intellectual and skilled (re)production. Her feminist vision of education and employment equity lives on in the writings by New Women after her, feminists who worked hard to rewrite domestic ideology as inclusive to middle-class women's professional mobility.

1 Women's Education and Rewriting Gender

Schreiner was, in her own life, all too aware of the social and sexual economies limiting women's access to education. For the majority of her youth she was home-schooled by her mother Rebecca,[18] and it was only after her brother Theophilus ("Theo") took a job as headmaster in Craddock that Schreiner (who went with him) enjoyed some formal schooling. However, when Theo later moved for work in the diamond fields, Schreiner was unable to follow and instead took her first position as governess. It was also during these first years of independent work that Schreiner discovered first-hand the reciprocal relationship between gendered education and professional opportunity. Despite her early work as a governess, Schreiner's passion was always medicine, and in 1880 she set sail from South Africa for England in the hopes of completing her formal training and earning an MD. By 1876 there were no official legal barriers prohibiting women from studying medicine, but there still persisted several informal and prohibitive social barriers to women's success in this career path.[19] Women first had to find admission to a medical college with facilities for clinical training (in 1877, only London's Royal Free Hospital offered beds for female students), and even though the 1882 Royal Commission on Medical Education permitted women to register as doctors, the British Medical Association stood by its 1878 decision not to admit women among the ranks of practising medical professionals. Yet perhaps the biggest challenge was the preliminary exam for admission to medical school, which required students to have a working knowledge of Latin, algebra, geometry, physics, and chemistry. Of course, such an exam was easy for male students from elite backgrounds with access to a classical education. For female students like Schreiner, however, with only an informal education from their mothers or poorly trained governesses, the exam would prove an insurmountable barrier to the medical profession. Schreiner spent the summer of 1881 trying to teach herself Latin and algebra, but as biographers Ruth First and Ann Scott conclude, "there is no record of her ever having sat, let alone passed, the preliminary examination" (*Olive Schreiner*, 114). Instead Schreiner redirected her attention to nursing, applying for work at the Women's Hospital in Endell Street. Nursing was a more accessible profession for women, and most hospitals required that applicants for nursing positions have only some form of experience with domestic service. Hospitals of the period were largely intended for the poor (those with more means usually employed a private nurse within the home), and thus gave many middle- and upper-class working nurses their first encounter with the overwhelming suffering and despair of poverty. Schreiner was quickly dissatisfied with nursing as some sort of professional compromise, and eventually, as well as begrudgingly, abandoned her pursuit of a career in medicine.

Schreiner's situation was not that unusual for the period. Many late-Victorian women were confronted with, and pushed back against, a system of gendered education that was increasingly out of touch with their social and economic ambitions. In their work on nineteenth-century women's education and employment, critics Joan N. Burstyn (*Victorian Education and the Ideal of Womanhood*) and Philippa Levine (*Victorian Feminism*) describe how mid-century advances in technologies and the rise of industrial production radically redefined both the form and function of feminine labour, especially along class lines. Much of the current conversation on Victorian women's education was set by 1980s and 1990s feminist critics interested in recovering women's literary histories. Yet it is worth returning to this body of scholarship, not to revise but to enhance; like these critics, I stress the important role of feminism in economic history and, in particular, the role of equal education in underwriting women's access to the modern workforce. "By the end of the nineteenth-century," Burstyn writes, "the factory and the sweatshop had displaced the home as the primary unit of production, while the school was displacing the family as the guardian of morality and culture" (134). The ideology of gendered spheres was gradually stripped away as many working-class women flocked to the factories or took in piecemeal contracts (home industry) to support their families, while at the same time middle-class ladies found their domestic service supplanted by paid housekeepers and educated governesses or public school rooms. A decline in eligible bachelors also placed increasing pressure on many middle-class women's aspiration to marriage as a form of economic security, and instead forced these young ladies to search for their own independent income.[20] As a result, it became increasingly normal, if not necessary, for young girls to pursue an education as a means to some form of financial stability.[21] Yet this education was still, for the better part of the Victorian era, both gendered and classed. Indeed, despite its increasing irrelevance, the "separate-spheres" ideology continued to dominate both private and publicly funded institutions for women's education and skills training.[22]

Schreiner's own short-lived career as governess reminds us of the limited – though gradually expanding – number of skilled professions open to educated women by the end of the nineteenth century. This history of the Victorian governesses is an important context for this chapter because it illustrates the overwhelming influence of domestic ideology in limiting the type of vocations available to women throughout the period. Of course, women's work as teachers in both domestic and public settings figures in much of the literature throughout the period, particularly in the so-called Governess Novel. This unique genre began to take shape in the 1830s and 1840s and focused almost exclusively on tropes such as sudden impoverishment and class conflict between the governess and her employer – examples include Mary Martha Sherwood's *Caroline Mordaunt, or, The Governess* (1835), Julia Buckley's *Emily, the Governess* (1836), Marguerite Blessington's *The Governess* (1839), and Miss Ross's *The Governess; or, Politics in Private Life* (1843).[23] Other mid-century examples, such as Dinah Mulock Craik's *Bread upon the Waters: A Governess's Life* (1852) and Anna Maria Hall's *Stories of the Governess* (1852), assumed a more "dogmatic" approach in support of the marginalized heroine as social debate around the "governess question" intensified.[24] Again, late-Victorian feminists found themselves pushing back against such assumptions of women's work as tied to the home and care-giving in order to access the many modern vocations available at the end of the century.

As Mary Poovey convincingly argues in *Uneven Developments*, Victorians' fascination with the governess figure has much to do with the change in, and tension between, women's economic and domestic roles throughout the nineteenth century: "the governesses' 'plight' articulated the contradiction between the moral role women had been assigned in capitalist society and the economic position into which they were being driven in increasing numbers" (162). Jane Austen's early nineteenth-century novel *Emma* (1815), for example, illustrates how, within a single generation, the governess changed in definition from a domestic figure, with close ties to the family, into a professional woman forced to contend with the public pressure of economic employment and self-sufficiency. Emma's former governess, Mrs Weston (née Taylor) is seamlessly integrated into the Highbury community through marriage, yet the younger Jane Fairfax is forced by the threat of downward social mobility to seriously contemplate what she terms as the "sale – not quite of human flesh – but of intellect" (*Emma* [1815], 242). Emma's idealization of Mrs Weston as more of a sister than employee serves as both a narrative device, setting in motion the subsequent marriage plot (the remaining "sibling" must now find a husband), and it also signals Emma's understanding that her sororal friend circulates within a system of feminine patronage, not the workforce. Governessing was one of the few ways in which financially vulnerable women could secure social support without compromising their status as proper "ladies." The plight of Jane Fairfax, by contrast, highlights the tenuous position of young ladies trying to secure work in an increasingly competitive profession. The dwindling number of positions, outpaced by the rising number of applicants, threw into question the possibility of respectable women's seamless transition from governessing to conjugal plots, and it also compounded the professionalization of the governess by realigning her with the public job market and remunerated work.[25] Indeed, Jane has a hard time securing a reliable patron (her time at the Campbells's has run out, and her aunt and grandmother Bates are too poor to keep her), and the only volunteer, Mrs Elton, is quick to market Jane in explicitly economic terms to her friend, Mrs Smallridge.[26] Later establishments such as the Governesses' Benevolent Institution, founded in 1841, would provide some moderate relief for the growing number of women in need of economic aid and placement. Still, the prospects grew increasingly dire throughout the period for the majority of young Victorian ladies hoping for placement and preservation of social status in the competitive field of governessing.

Work as a governess was not the only option available to gentlewomen in need, and in fact, many ladies looked to teaching as an alternative and equally respectable means of financial self-support. This profession was considered suitable for ladies because it complemented – and explicitly promoted – domestic ideology. As Leonore Davidoff and Catherine Hall explain, teaching "was seen as an extension of childrearing" (*Family Fortunes*, 29), and Ellen Jordan includes education among other Victorian occupations coded as "women's work" (including work as a governess and dressmaking) because it was considered "useful to a married woman," often "carried on in a more or less domestic setting," and because women were often denied a living wage (*The Women's Movement*, 61). Published almost thirty years after *Emma* (1815), Charlotte Brontë's *Jane Eyre* (1847) effectively registers this expansion in educational training open to Victorian women. Brontë's novel is also confirmation of the close relationship between the governess and the school teacher, both of whom were considered "respectable" working women by virtue of their shared investment in female domesticity. While a student at Lowood, for example, Jane becomes proficient in those subjects meant to service a young woman's pursuit of domestic plots, including French language skills, or painting watercolour landscapes, and playing the piano (158). This education ensures her future employment as governess to Adele, to whom Jane then transfers the aforementioned skills and thus transforms her student into a cultured lady eligible for an advantageous marriage. With this curriculum in mind, Sandra M. Gilbert famously argues that Jane is not unlike Grace Poole insofar as both women, "acting as agents for men, may be the keepers of other women," adding that "both keepers and prisoners are bound by the same chains" ("Plain Jane's Progress," 484).[27] The "chains," in the case of Jane and Adele, refer to a feminine curriculum binding women to domestic plots.

This construction of the governess as a figure working on the margins of, but also reproducing, traditional gendered power structures continues to inform later Victorian examples of the novel genre – including *Margaret Stourton, or a Year of Governess Life* (1863, published anonymously), Henry Courtney Selous's *The Young Governess: A Tale for Girls* (1871), and Irene Clifton's *The Little Governess* (1900).[28] Though it is not a traditional governess novel per se, Henry James's *The Turn of the Screw* (1898) responds directly to Brontë's *Jane Eyre* when his heroine alludes to the earlier novel as a frame through which to interpret the cross-class romances between her predecessor Miss Jessel and the valet Peter Quint, as well as herself and her rich employer.[29] Late-Victorian women working in the home schoolroom could continue to earn a respectable income, thanks in large part to the many upgrades in education and improved certification options. Real-life governess May Prinhorn, for example, records in her unpublished memoirs, "Some Account of the Life of Mary Blanche Pinhorn" (1926), a salary that effectively increased fourfold over the course of her employment during 1888–99.[30] Still the fact remains that by the end of the century work as a governess faded in popularity, both in terms of literary representation (including the so-called Governess Novel) and in terms of real-life employment as women instead flocked to the many new and exciting vocations made possible by the expanding modern marketplace. "Yet the fact remains that from 1900 less and less was heard about the Victorian governess in periodicals, novels and domestic literature of the day," writes Kathryn Hughes, in her touchstone study *The Victorian Governess*; "By the turn of the century [the governess] had been joined in the employment place by teachers, nurses, clerks and bookkeepers, all of whom expected to work until they married" (203). This turn from traditionally feminine vocations in home education to emergent white-collar work had much to do with the continued socio-sexual stigma attached to the governess figure.

While some readers were certainly sympathetic toward the marginalized governess, many other Victorians felt increasingly anxious about this feminine figure's liminal position between the home and workforce, feelings of discomfort that were exacerbated by debates over women's education. Some recognized the governess's in-home education as an attractive means by which to safeguard the economic status of genteel daughters through the transmission of domestic knowledge. For this group the governess served as a public symbol of her employer's middle-class prosperity,[31] and at the same time the governess figure worked in support of a gender economy that limited the gentlewoman's social mobility to the marriage market.[32] Newly solvent middle-class families also jumped at the opportunity to have an in-home educator who could share with their daughters the knowledge and skills hitherto reserved for women of the aristocracy. Yet there were still some Victorians who took issue with the exploitation of these women working to disseminate domestic plots. In an editorial titled "Hints on the Modern Governess System" (1844), *Fraser's Magazine* points to the already glutted profession as justification for reforming the content and purpose of women's education: "[l]et women labour in other fields, and thus diminish the superabundant stock of teachers," the author writes, adding that "[t]here are many women as capable of discharging the office of clerk and book-keeper as men" (575). In her *Hints on Self Help: Book for Young Women* (1863), Jessie Boucherett explains that "no profession is more overcrowded than that of the teacher" because "there is no other profession open by which gentlewomen can earn their livelihood without loss of caste" (23–4). The implicit call to expand the definition of "appropriate" employment for women would prove all the more pressing as the number of female teachers continued to grow through the second half of the nineteenth century, particularly in those marketable disciplines such as music or the arts.[33] What many Victorian women wanted, then, was not only the right to train in different disciplines, but also the right to use this education in pursuit of various professional ends, from teaching or work as a governess to new and more ambitious forms of white-collar and skilled employment.

Interested in expanding women's economics options, some reformers fought to overhaul the education system more broadly, creating new schools and curriculum intended to prepare women for the modern marketplace. Inspired by feminist arguments originating in the enlightenment period, reformist groups such as the bluestockings began pushing for a new curriculum that supported women's independent and critical thought – associated texts include Charlotte M. Yonge's *Womankind* (1877), Mary Wollstonecraft's *A Vindication of the Rights of Woman* (1792), Hannah More's *Strictures on the Modern System of Female Education* (1799), and Maria Grey and Emily Shirreff's *Thoughts on Self Culture Addressed to Women* (1850).[34] These reformers proposed a new education for girls which was markedly different from boys' training in classics and religion; instead, feminist reformers advocated for women's training in contemporary subjects such as history, science, as well as European literature and culture. As Shirreff argues, in 1858, women are more than capable of moral and intellectual reason, both of which are necessary to productive citizenship: "The *intellectual capacity for being just,* must be cultivated no less than the love of moral justice," she explains, "and that can be done only by strengthening the reasoning power, to counterbalance the natural predominance of feeling; and by forming habits of accuracy and discrimination in all matters of opinion" (*Intellectual Education and Its Influence on the Character and Happiness of Women* [1858], 116–17).[35] Despite growing support among many Victorians, changes to girls' curriculum advanced slowly throughout the second half of the century. J.A. Banks's work on the *Year Books* records the establishment of sixty-nine schools for boys and seventy-eight schools for girls in the years between 1840 and 1890; however, the vast majority of the girls' schools (sixty-nine, in fact) were established after 1870, while half (or thirty-five) of the boys' schools were opened before this date (Banks, *Prosperity and Parenthood,* 228–30).[36] Regardless of the reason, the push to reform female education took on a new form in the latter half of the century, and these changes were of immense importance to women's social and economic mobility. Founded in 1848, in a small house next to the Governess's Benevolent Institution, Queen's College intended to provide all female applicants, including those destined for teaching, with a rational education. The college was so successful that it also inspired several similar institutions devoted to the intellectual training of women – such as Bedford College (founded in 1849 as "The Ladies College, Bedford Square"), Cheltenham Ladies College (founded in 1854), and North London Collegiate School (founded in 1850).[37] These institutions also provided graduates with teaching opportunities outside of the already glutted profession of governessing. Bedford College and Queen's College were later asked by education reformer Emily Davis to prepare female students working toward

Cambridge University's examinations. Both colleges declined, and so in 1869 Davis, along with Barbara Bodichon and Lady Stanley of Alderley, founded Girton College which taught female students according to Cambridge's curriculum and exams.

For some late Victorians the changes to women's education raised serious questions about the gendered spheres and, in particular, women's work as mothers and caregivers to the nation. These critics tended to rely upon eugenic models that defined women in terms of biological difference, and argued that sexual "specialization" was necessary to the heterosexual reproduction of the social body. Through his early appropriation of Charles Darwin's evolutionary theory, for example, Hebert Spencer convinced many detractors that women were by nature distinct from men and that the maternal drive (women's "reproductive power") would most certainly suffer if women over-extended themselves through academic study (*Principles of Biology 2* [1867], 486).[38] Spencer even claimed to have personally observed higher rates of infertility among mothers with an advanced education, and worried that those "flat-chested girls who survive their highest-pressure education" would be too "incompetent to [raise children]" (*Principles of Biology 2*, 486).[39] Using a similar brand of Social Darwinism, George J. Romanes argued that men and women are physiologically distinct and "complementary to one another," and that to "try artificially [through education] to make of woman an unnatural copy of man" can only result in a "sorry and disappointed creature who is neither the one thing [female] nor the other [male]" ("Mental Differences Between Men and Women" [1887], 29).[40] As support for his analysis, Romanes deferred to the gender expertise of famous women writers such as Millicent Garrett Fawcett and Eliza Lynn Linton. In the former he claimed to find an ally on the subject of women's separate and domestic education: "No one of those who care most for the woman's movement cares one jot to prove or to maintain that men's brains and women's brains are exactly alike or exactly equal," and as the Fawcett quote continues, "[a]ll we ask is that the social and legal status of women should be such as to foster, not to suppress, any gift for art, literature, learning, or goodness with which women may be endowed" (Fawcett quoted in Romanes, "Mental Differences Between Men and Women," 30). But Linton's writings were especially helpful insofar as they differentiated between, what Romanes describes as, "mental development" and "intellectual specialisation" (29); the point was not to deny women education (or development), but to ensure that such cultivation preserved sexual difference (that it did not "athwart" biological "specialization") and, with it, the reproductive health of the "social organism" (29). Linton is, of course, best known for her sustained critique of the educated New Woman or so-called Wild Woman, a critique that employed rhetoric of essentialist difference and maternal duty in order to discount women's social contributions in everything from work and education ("The Wild Women: as Social Insurgents" [1891]) to politics ("The Wild Women: as Politicians" [1891]). This next section will look at how Schreiner's writings on women's education responds to, and revises, these political debates on the changing meaning of motherhood and women's (re)productive contributions to the social body.

2 Women's (Economic) Collectivity

Mid-way through *The Story of an African Farm* (1883), Schreiner's protagonist and feminist mouthpiece, Lyndall, offers a powerful critique of Victorian gender roles as limiting women's access to education. In a conversation with Waldo, the farm hand's young son, Lyndall recalls how her intellectual potential was wasted on a domestic education at a ladies' boarding school that trained her in menial domestic tasks, such as making "cushions, and hideous flowers that roses laugh at, and a footstool in six weeks that a machine would have made better in five minutes" (183). Though her work is inefficient (a machine could do it better, Lyndall insists), the skills she has acquired through her boarding-school lessons are not entirely unmarketable, for the woman trained in decorative arts is destined to attract a husband. Lyndall explains this gendered difference in social plots to Waldo.

> To you it says – *Work*; and to us it says – *Seem*! To you it says – As you approximate to man's highest ideal of God, as your arm is strong and your knowledge great, and the power to Labor is with you, so shall you gain all that human heart desires. To us it says – Strength shall not help you, nor knowledge, nor Labor. You shall gain what men gain, but by other means. And so the world makes men and women. (185)

Through such didactic moments, Schreiner's novel thus takes aim at the typical gendered education reinforcing women's economic dependence upon men. Men are meant to pursue both physical and intellectual labour, modes of production that are performed within the paid public sphere and thus socially valued or associated with economic status; conversely, women must look to the domestic sphere and, therein, trade upon their good looks and acquired charm in exchange for men's financial support. In other words, the current sexual economy does not value women's intellectual work, nor does it fairly remunerate feminine forms of domestic labour. Like the pillows they make, these unskilled women are essentially decorative and their economic status is purely vicarious.

By framing women's education as a matter of sexual and economic independence, Lyndall became what Ledger describes as a "prototype of the New Woman," a figure that was officially "'christened' eleven years after the publication of *The Story of an African Farm*" (*The New Woman*, 81).[41] The novel's appeal for women's intellectual training did in fact set the tone for a new type of fin-de-siècle feminism that sought to redefine women's social roles as extending well beyond the private sphere.[42] However, unlike many of her more radical inheritors, Schreiner did not entirely abandon the principles of domestic ideology in her call to reform women's education.[43] Instead, her novel valorizes women's work as mothers and nurturers of the social body, while it also tries to imagine how education might serve a key role in redefining this social labour. Motherhood is, as Lyndall insists, "the one great and noble work left to [women]"; "*we* bear the world, and *we* make it," and for this reason, she continues, women "must have knowledge of men and things in many states, a wide catholicity of sympathy, the strength that springs from knowledge, and the magnanimity which springs from strength" (189, emphasis in original).

Schreiner's emphasis on the larger or socio-political work of mothers seems, at first glance, to reproduce a Social Darwinist model of women as necessarily beholden to (re)productive functions. In fact, such accusations of gender essentialism have dominated much of the criticism on Schreiner over the past decades. The critics associated with this discussion can be divided into two camps. On one side are scholars such as Cherry Clayton (*Olive Schreiner*), Liz Stanley (*Imperialism, Labour and the New Woman*), and Carolyn Burdett (*Olive Schreiner and the Progress of Feminism*) who insist that Schreiner's emphasis on domestic labour is part of her larger interrogation of the gendered terms of modern capitalism.[44] All three critics explain how this dominant gender economy excludes women from intellectual (and thus socially valued) forms of modern labour. On the other side of the debate are scholars such as Rita Felski (*The Gender of Modernity*) and Angelique Richardson (*Love and Eugenics in the Late Nineteenth Century*) who interpret Schreiner's theory of gender as part of a larger eugenic project.[45] As Felski concludes, Schreiner champions the "laboring, healthy, and virile body" while demonizing the "insidious threat of passivity, femininity, and disease" (157). Though Schreiner does not explicitly state this eugenic agenda, she is nonetheless condemned by virtue of her social affiliations. After all, she was a good friend of Karl Pearson, who was himself an avid supporter of

Francis Galton's eugenics,[46] and she was also an enthusiastic fan of Herbert Spencer, particularly his writings on political economy. In fact, Schreiner was not only reading Spencer while she composed *The Story of an African Farm* (1883), but she also worked into the narrative several references to Spencer's sociology.[47] With this context in mind, critics such as Ledger and Richardson position Schreiner as part of a general movement at the fin de siècle uniting the New Woman's demands with eugenics in order to imagine a productive progress.[48]

Given his influence upon Schreiner's thought, it is worth spending a brief moment on Spencer's theory of labour. For Spencer, society's gradual turn to specialized labour parallels the biological organism's natural evolution towards increasing complexity. In other words, early or "less-evolved" organisms/societies are marked by simple structure, with cells/individuals performing multiple tasks, while more advanced or "evolved" organisms/societies are complex in their structure, in which cells/individuals perform highly specialized but interdependent tasks. Consider, for example, his use of naturalistic language in the following passage from *Social Statistics* (1851):

> as surely as a blacksmith's arm grows large, and the skin of a laborer's hand thick; as surely as the eye tends to become long-sighted in the sailor, and short-sighted in the student; as surely as a clerk acquires rapidity in writing and calculation; as surely as the musician learns to detect an error of a semitone amidst what seems to others a very babel of sounds; as surely as a passion grows by indulgence and diminishes when restrained; as surely as a disregarded conscience becomes inert, and one that is obeyed active; as surely as there is any meaning in such terms as habit, custom, practice; – so surely must the human faculties be moulded into complete fitness for the social state; so surely must evil and immorality disappear; so surely must man become perfect. (32)[49]

In Spencer's theory of social organization, the subdivision of labour is driven by an underlying impulse to improved "efficacy," or what political economists refer to as "efficiency." It is this assumed tendency to complex subdivision that therein guarantees Spencer's absolute faith in labour as "so surely" (or naturally) progressing toward physiological specialization – the blacksmith's arm grows "large" while the musician's ear becomes refined. Perhaps Spencer's biggest leap of faith, however, is evidenced by his emphasis on evolution as progressive; he believes that complexity is not only a higher form of social organization but also that the composite parts, or individuals, will eventually achieve a perfection (human faculties "moulded into complete fitness for the social state"). At the same time, his biological analogy (the social body as organism) therein "naturalizes" this supposedly inevitable push to industrialized capitalism, with its emphasis on divided and specialized labour as the more evolved – and thus ideal – form of organization.

Writing in the later decades of the century, Schreiner worked hard to reconcile her dual interests in gender reform and Spencer's political economy, as well as emergent forms of popular socialism. She was for many years an important member of the Fellowship of the New Life (FNL), a utopian organization critical of economic and sexual inequalities. But when the offshoot Fabian Society formed on 4 January 1884, Schreiner was among many of the FNL members who felt conflicted regarding the latter's stronger breed of Marxism. In a 29 March 1885 letter to friend and fellow reformer Havelock Ellis, Schreiner explains her reservations as a question of "individual freedom."

> Ah, freedom, freedom, freedom, that is the first great want of humanity. That is why I sympathise so much more with the Herbert Spencer school than with the Socialists, so called. If I thought Socialism would bring the subjection of the individual to the whole I would fight to the death. But human nature will assert itself under Socialism as elsewhere. Better to die of cold or hunger or thirst than to be robbed of your freedom of action, of your feeling that you are an absolutely free and independent unit. (Rive, *Olive Schreiner Letters*, 63)

Schreiner's critical response to "the Socialists" draws implicitly upon Spencer's theory of the reciprocal relationship between the individual and the social body. She is particularly bothered by the fact that the Fabian Society privileges the latter (the social body) and ignores the necessity of the former (individualism) – or as she explains to Ellis, it is in the individual's "human nature" to want "freedom," and socialism cannot curb this "great want."[50] She rails at the thought of being robbed of one's freedom, but then she also confesses her own willingness to "fight to death" for that which might "bring the subjection of the individual to the whole." And in the same letter to Ellis, Schreiner also imagines how money, or "£200 of my own," is vital to "perfect freedom and independence!" (63). Yet as Schreiner knew from personal experience, an independent income was becoming increasingly inaccessible to those without an advanced education or training for work in the modern professions. Women would need to work together in support of, or to "subject" themselves to, the collective pursuit of an equal education and, with it, women's economic opportunity.

Schreiner's effort to reframe women's education within Spencerian terms of economic individualism anticipated the kinds of rhetorical moves made by many conservative-minded feminists at the fin de siècle. Unwilling to heed essentialist constructions of gender roles, late-Victorian reformers and so-called New Women worked hard to refute eugenicists' fear-mongering claims regarding the negative socio-sexual consequences of women's education; these gender reformers instead argued that women's intellectual development was of invaluable benefit to relations between the sexes and that feminine edification thereby represented a positive force within hetero-reproductive plots. In order to make this latter claim, however, these fin-de-siècle feminists often drew upon, but also refurbished, the very same Social Darwinist models employed by their eugenicist detractors.[51] Sarah Grand certainly subscribes to the idea of the educated woman as catalyst for positive socio-sexual evolution in her 1894 essay "The New Aspect of the Woman Question" (in which the "New Woman" is named publicly for the first time).[52] Grand argues that education ensures better relations between the sexes by doing away with women's limited roles as either subservient to, or manipulative of, men (the "cow-woman" or "scum-woman," respectively [271]). Like so many of her feminist contemporaries, Grand sees in education a way for women to "articulate" (271) their social discontent and, therefore, to transform themselves into self-sustaining adults, not "apath[etic]" and ignorant "children" (271).[53] Grand's "New Woman" (271) of the future is instead "stronger and wiser" (272) and, thus, requires a "better" partner in man (272). In her own life and writings, Grand was more than willing to demand more of men, and often directly challenged male authority on issues such as sexual knowledge and the scientific bias against the intellectual New Woman.[54] She was, for example, expelled from the Royal Naval School, which she attended between 1868–9, after expressing controversial views on religion and for working in support of Josephine Butler's campaign against the Contagious Diseases Acts. Her later marriage to Army Surgeon David Chambers McFall (21 years her senior) gave Grand increased access to scientific discourses, and she quickly became one of the best-informed feminist novelists on medical matters affecting women.[55] Some of Grand's best-known novels, including *The Heavenly Twins* (1893) and *The Beth Book* (1897), offer compelling arguments for women's sex education as a preventative against domestic problems, including spousal abuse and the spread of sexually transmitted infections.

Not all New Woman writers, however, were as eager to employ evolutionary theories in their defence of women's social and sexual advancement. In her now infamous essay "Marriage" (1888), Mona Caird argues that sexual inequality is the product of cultural constructions of gender, not nature. Victorian gender roles, she explains, teach women "to regard [marriage] as their destiny," despite the statistical reality that many "cannot marry" and are therefore "thrown on the world to earn their own living" (78).[56] Caird therefore concludes that the feminist pursuit of sexual equality must first address those gender roles and corresponding institutions limiting women's socio-economic mobility. Changes to education would, for example, help women to secure economic independence and, as a result, "rescue" marriage from its "mercenary" connotations by instead creating cultural conditions conducive to "free" partnership between consenting equals (79).[57] Yet even Caird's feminism cannot help but invoke larger pseudo-scientific forces – or what Katharina Rowold describes as an "energy economy" (*The Educated Woman*, 61) – when defending the virtues of women's social equality.[58] This line of argument is best seen in Caird's work *The Morality of Marriage* (1897), in which she chastises "men of science" for invoking the "danger of race degeneration" in order to bid women "keep solely to their maternal functions" (136). Within the very same paragraph, however, Caird claims that compulsory motherhood is a drain on women's nervous systems and that it therefore threatens the overall health of the "race" more generally: "One-half of the race [mothers], in short, is to be rescued at the expense of the other ... Women, who already are crippled in body and mind by excessive performance of the duties of maternity, are to plunge yet further in the same disastrous direction" (136). In other words, the current domestic plot is a drain on women. Caird's extended writings also suggest how this negative energy economy might be reversed by the positive effects of education, an optimistic vision that looks forward to egalitarian heterosexuality: "We see a limitless field of possibility opening before us," Caird concludes, "and we look forward steadily, hoping and working for the day when men and women shall be comrades and fellow-workers as well as lovers and husbands and wives" (79).[59] There is, in this account, only a positive relationship between education and marriage, and for Caird, intellectual equality effectively underwrites women's social and sexual progress (79).

A unique figure within this history, Grant Allen is worth mentioning because his writings on sexual reform single out Schreiner by name as an example of the misguided New Woman writer who overlooks the link between sex and social evolution. Yet Allen is not easily grouped among male eugenicists, either, because he did not invoke the traditional marriage plot as part of his larger reproductivist argument.

Instead, like many later feminists, he drew upon Spencer's theory of Social Darwinism in order to protest against dominant domestic narratives imposed upon women. Allen was especially upset by the concept of marital monogamy, which he defined as unnatural and thus harmful to the social body. He instead espoused a kind of free love as better for both sexual partners and society more generally: "What we need," he explains, "is not more compulsion, more restriction, more artificial unions, more arbitrary interference, but more freedom, more latitude, more readjustment, more ease in following out the divine impulse of the moment" ("The Girl of the Future" [1890], 55). Yet it is this same emphasis upon free love or unrestricted sexual selection that leads him to take a very negative view of women's advanced education. The same essay, "The Girl of the Future," for example, argues that "Newnham has slain its thousands, and Girton its tens of thousands" (56). Allen singles out New Woman writers Mona Caird and Olive Schreiner for characterizing the Woman Problem "as a problem of Sex rather than as a problem of Paternity and Maternity" (49), or for emphasizing gender equality in all matters (including education) and therein forgetting about women's reproductive duty to the social body (what he terms the "the Child Problem" [49]). Allen instead promotes a revised program of intellectual training that encourages female students to recognize their higher calling as mothers and nurturers of the next generation.[60] Women must, he insists, "be taught to understand their own body, and the light cast upon it by the analogy of other bodies," as well as "the society of which they are members, and the origin and development of its structure and functions" ("The Girl of the Future," 57).[61] Once taught to see herself as mother to the human race, that woman will, he wagers, "take the noblest and purest man she can get, and become by him the parent of sound and beautiful offspring" (62–3). Implicit in Allen's argument all along is the fear that improperly or overly educated women will abstain from sexual reproduction, or worse yet that they will pick an inferior mate. His Girton-educated heroine Herminia Barton, in *The Woman Who Did* (1895), commits this latter mistake. While Herminia is described as intelligent and attractive (an ideal candidate for sexual reproduction), her lover Alan Merrick is both dull and much older (his prolonged bachelorhood is a symptom of his sexual shortcomings); their selfish daughter Dolores (Dolly) is the degenerate offspring of this unsuitable union.[62] Ultimately, then, Allen's eugenic theory of motherhood revises Spencer's model to include educational intervention as necessary to "healthy" or "reproductive" bonds between the female individual and the larger social body: "if things in the future turn out as I believe they will among the most cultivated families, then a tiny beginning will have been made towards the slow evolution of a new social order" (63).

Schreiner's interpretation of the relationship between women's education and social (re)production was not entirely different from Allen's, despite the latter's claim otherwise. Still, her writings on the sociosexual benefits of erudition are always careful to distinguish between women's socially constructed gender roles and their physiological biology.[63] It was this early effort to distinguish between gender and sex that also precipitated Schreiner's break from Karl Pearson, pioneer of modern sexual eugenics. As a fellow member of the Men and Women's Club, Pearson presented himself as sympathetic to the Woman Question, and yet his writings on gender were, in fact, often limited by his views on reproductive biology. In his 1888 essay "The Woman's Question," delivered as the inaugural lecture for the Men and Women's Club, Pearson is careful to qualify his support for women's education only in situations where such intellectual training does not detract from higher "child-bearing" duties: "The higher education of women may connote a general intellectual progress for the community, or, on the other hand, a physical degradation of the race, owing to prolonged study having ill effects on woman's child-bearing efficiency" (371).[64] Preoccupied with racial fitness and social progress, Pearson defaults to a model of sexual reform that privileges collective (or eugenic) interests over and above individual (or feminist's) rights.[65] Within the same essay, "The Woman's Question," he insists that even "those who are the most earnest supporters of woman's independence ought to be the first to recognise that her duty to society is paramount ... before they appeal to the market-place with all the rhetorical flourish of 'justice' and of 'right'" (371). For Schreiner, however, intellectual cultivation did not conflict with, but instead enhanced, women's work as childbearers and caregivers; as she explains in a letter (7 August 1866) to Pearson, "[a]s far as my experience goes it is an invariable rule that in proportion as a woman has a strong active, intellect, well wȯrked, she desires to have children, & if she has them devotes herself to them, & if she has none thinks with longing almost passionate of the joy of training & caring for them" (Rive, *Olive Schreiner Letters*, 100, emphasis in original).[66] Schreiner eventually left the Club in 1886, an act which many historians assume to be the result of her "unrequited love for Pearson, and Pearson's horror at her sexual advances" (Lucy Bland, *Banishing the Beast*, 44),[67] but as Bland points out, this departure probably had more to do with conflicting ideologies and the question of women's intellectual equality, more specifically (21). For Schreiner, women's intellectual development is not consequent to, or limited by, natural biology;

rather, her feminist writings look at how education is dependent upon cultural norms and might, when enhanced, allow recipients to see into, and revise, these same social structures.

3 From Mothers to Cultural Capital

In its defence of women's education, *The Story of an African Farm* focuses on cultural knowledge and its vital role in shaping women's relationship to work in gendered spheres. The transmission of knowledge is, for Schreiner, at the very heart of the way that women think of themselves and their role within the larger social body. One of the more obvious ways that the novel stages this sociological argument is through its representation of reading (or self-education through books) as a transformative experience that alters one's sense of self and subsequent communal affiliation. While Lyndall is the novel's obvious mouthpiece, many critics also focus on Waldo as a complementary character who is almost a biographical stand-in for Schreiner's dual interrogation of education and economic systems.[68] Waldo's earlier years at the farm are marked by an acute sense of social isolation, especially after his closest friend, Lyndall, leaves for school and the ranch is taken over by 'Tant Sannie's tyrannical lover, Bonaparte Blenkins. It is only after he stumbles across a copy of J.S. Mill's *Principles of Political Economy* (1848) that Waldo happily realizes that "he was not alone, not alone" in this quest for knowledge (*The Story of an African Farm*, 115).[69] This search for an alternative intellectual community is then replayed by the novel's feminist heroine, Lyndall, during her unhappy stay at the girls' "finishing" school (182). Lyndall dreams of becoming a professional actress, but these hopes are crushed by a gendered education that limits women's labour to the domestic sphere. Desperate for some form of larger cultural connection, she saves the money earned from her decorative projects (making cushions and flowers) in order to buy books and newspapers through which to explore her own intellectual aspirations. "[A]t night I sat up" and read, Lyndall explains, and "epitomised what I read; and I found time to write some plays, and to find out how hard it is to make your thoughts look anything but imbecile fools, when you paint them on ink and paper" (183). Writing is hard work, and the skill required of this labour cannot be denied, but in books Lyndall finds the means to acquire ideas and training otherwise denied her by a domestic education.

Lyndall understands that the book – and the knowledge it contains – opens a door to an alternative community with new forms of social exchange based on ideas and (self) edification. Books, in other words, represent what Pierre Bourdieu would describe as a "form of capital."[70] Capital can, according to Bourdieu, be broken down into three interdependent categories – social, cultural, and economic – and is essential to determining an individual's position within a hierarchy of power. Social capital refers to the power and privilege inherent in "social obligations," or what we now describe as "connections" ("The Forms of Capital," 243); while economic capital refers to material wealth, or that "which is immediately and directly convertible into money and may be institutionalized in the form of property rights" (243); and finally, cultural capital includes different forms of knowledge or ideas that one needs in order to navigate social life. Schreiner's work on gender anticipates what Bourdieu would describe as the transmutable quality of cultural capital as a means to both economic and social mobility – for as Bourdieu points out, cultural capital is "convertible" (243) and can be used to gain access to, or validate one's place within, otherwise exclusive networks of power and privilege (249). Her writings explore women's access to cultural capital in its many different forms, including embodied (state of mind) or objectified (books or material instruments) and, later, cultural capital in its "institutionalized form" (educational qualifications or certification). Under the strictures of domestic ideology, however, women are consistently denied access to institutionalized capital, and thus, like Lyndall, must make do with other forms of accessible or objectified knowledge as a means to social and economic mobility.[71] Schreiner is particularly interested in how cultural capital might redefine women's access to modern forms of production, a hypothesis that therein cements her alliance with other fin-de-siècle constructivist feminists. *The Story of an African Farm*, for example, does not portray woman's educational preparation as the logical consequence of innate biological forces; rather, Lyndall's powerful protest highlights the way that gender ideology reproduces feminine labour which is bound by the domestic sphere. Schreiner's later work, *Woman and Labor*, elaborates at great length on how women's constricted education woefully under-prepares them for a modern industrial economy.

This is not to say, however, that Schreiner's emphasis on the cultural conditions of gendered labour prevents her from using Social Darwinist logic in defence of women's intellectual and economic rights. By focusing on women's cultural knowledge, Schreiner deconstructs eugenic arguments against modern female education, but then, in the same breath, imagines how a revised program of women's intellectual training might thereby enhance social (re)production. This is why her treatise *Woman and Labor* takes to task Pearson's claims that erudition will somehow undermine woman's natural calling as "Divine child-bearer! Potential mother of the race" (210).[72] With a sarcastic tone, Schreiner notes how this same "lofty theorist" (209) is not in the least bit concerned about "the haggard, work-worn woman and mother [...] who destroys health and youth in the sweater's den" (211–12). Indeed, Pearson seems to celebrate "the woman, who, on hands and knees, at tenpence a day, scrubs the floors of the public buildings, or private dwellings," because "that somewhat quadrupedal posture is for him truly feminine, and does not interfere with his ideal of the mother and child-bearer" (212). Eugenic-inflected language (the "quadrupedal's" physical degeneration) is used to emphasize Schreiner's point that the excessive demands of domestic labour not only demean but also dehumanize women. Using Pearson's own logic against him, Schreiner thus explains how traditional domestic ideology is out of sync with a modern industrial economy and that the latter requires a new program of intellectual training so that women might continue to play a meaningful role within the larger system of social (re)production. Schreiner even goes so far as to imagine how women's work within new and skilled professions might underwrite advanced sexual selection: "The female doctor or lawyer earning a thousand a year will always," Schreiner insists, "and to-day certainly does, find more suitors than had she remained a governess or cook, laboring as hard, earning thirty pounds" (242). Her confidence in this social projection has much to do with the idea of both intellectual and economic contributions to the family. Unlike the underpaid cook or governesses, the female doctor or lawyer is more marketable – both sexually and economically – because their specialized training demands fair remuneration. And Schreiner insists that, when looking for a mate, "the human male has a strong tendency to value the female who can contribute to the family expenditure" (242).

Motivating Schreiner's feminism, then, is the sustained appeal for the revaluation of the form and function of women's role within social (re)production, a proposal that means rethinking Victorian domestic ideology limiting women's access to knowledge and skilled labour. Through a brief but important reference to famed pedagogue Friedrich Froebel, Schreiner signals her unwillingness to restrict women's social roles by virtue of, what she describes as a "correlation of appearance" between motherhood and education (*Woman and Labor*, 170). Froebel believed that early childhood education (or what would later become known as "kindergarten") should be placed in the hands of women educators, whom he believed enjoyed a natural bond with young students by virtue of the maternal instinct.[73] This representation of teaching as another form of "social mothering" struck a chord with Victorian education reformers, such as Mary Carpenter (1807–77) and Anna Brownell Jameson (1794–1860), and Froebel continued to find support with female educationists throughout the century and beyond – some of his influential advocates include Helen Keller, Elizabeth Peabody, Phoebe Hearst, Jane Stanford, Frances Folsom Cleveland, and Elizabeth Harrison. Unlike Froebel (and many of his followers), however, Schreiner resists the idea of an inherent link between sexual physiology and women's work as teachers. Schreiner instead references the education reformer as support for her claim that no individual, regardless of sex, should be prohibited from doing what he/she does best or is "most fitted": "That one male Froebel should be prohibited or hampered in his labor as an educator of infancy, on the ground that infantile instruction was the field of the female," is not only unjust, she argues, but also "makes an unnecessary deficit in the general social assets" (*Woman and Labor*, 170). For women to be social assets, not "deficits," they must have access to adequate instruction befitting modern industrial society. Elsewhere in *The Story of an African Farm*, Lyndall concisely outlines the relationship between women's mental development and modern forms of labour. In the same aforementioned conversation with Waldo, this outspoken heroine describes how women's domestic education is a dehumanizing process that, emptied of any real intellectual rigour (her brain is "diluted and squeezed out of [her]" [182]), trains women to produce decorative goods that "a machine would have made better in five minutes" (183). The implication that domesticated women are no better than mindless automatons would have certainly shocked readers for its irreverent rejection of the idealized "Angel of the House," but this rhetorical gesture would have also appealed to those anxious about the role of the machine in the transition to modern capitalism. Throughout her extended writings Schreiner argues that mechanization has fundamentally altered the socio-economic landscape, rendering obsolete older forms of physical production – including women's domestic labour.[74] The traditional Angel of the House is effectively isolated from, and ignorant of, the modern world, and so the modern "child is of necessity removed from the hands of the mother, and placed in those of the specialized instructor" (*Woman and Labor*, 50). Modern women need education in order to rear the next generation of modern workers.

Yet, as Schreiner stressed throughout her writings, not all women could or should be mothers, and so all women must have access to an education that is best suited to their specific strengths and social potential. It is also on this point of women's social potential beyond the domestic sphere that class politics enters into, and plays an exclusionary role within, Schreiner's writings. *Woman and Labor* explicitly rejects the assumption that all women should devote themselves to "the bearing and suckling of children" (62), and describes the concept of compulsory motherhood as both "antiquated" (63) and factually unnecessary within modern society – it is, instead, Schreiner insists, a holdover from so-called savage societies (*Woman and Labor*, 62). In Schreiner's estimation, only middle- and upper-class women have social resources requisite to transcending the brute functions of reproductive biology. First, a decline in infant mortality rates means that population replacement is not as pressing a problem for this group: "the number of children reared to adult years among the more intelligent classes probably equals or exceeds those of the lowest, owing to the high rate of infant mortality where births are excessive" (63, n1). Second, Schreiner's reference to "the more intelligent classes" also betrays an underlying assumption about the middle- and upper-classes' ability to contribute to modern industrial society. The working-classes, "owing to lack of intellectual power or delicate manual training, have now no form of labor to offer society which it stands really in need of" (38). Schreiner's feminism is, therefore, a movement by and for "ladies" of privilege. Her treatise, in *Woman and Labor* certainly undermines the eugenic logic of compulsory motherhood, but it also reverses the class dynamics of domestic ideology: now working-class women are limited to biological reproduction, while middle-class women are the ones who can and must transcend the machinery of their own physical bodies in order to be meaningful contributors within a modern industrial society.[75]

It is also at this point, in her critique of compulsory motherhood, that Schreiner outlines a new theory of feminist kinship as mediated by the cultural transmission of knowledge – or "cultural capital." In both fiction and prose, Schreiner imagines how education is necessary to women's participation in skilled labour, but she is also interested in how this pursuit of knowledge might bring with it an added opportunity for women to restructure their relationship with each other and the social body. Put simply, she imagines a "Woman's Movement" in which contributors' "efforts are not, and cannot be, of immediate advantage to themselves, but that they almost of necessity and immediately lead to loss and renunciation, which gives to this movement its very peculiar tone" (*Woman and Labor*, 126). Cultural knowledge is, within this feminist vision, both embodied and convertible into a new form of social capital that is shared among, and serves as support for, women's ongoing intellectual and economic advancement (including their access to "a new form of labor" [126]). At the same time, Schreiner is confident in the transformative power of this cultural capital to mediate bonds between women and therein produce an entirely new social economy. This is also why she compares the "Woman's Movement" to previous "religious developments" (125), and envisions a feminist devotee who "bends over her books with the passion and fervor with which an early Christian may have bent over the pages of his Scriptures" (127). Only, Schreiner's feminist envisions a new world (a new gendered economy) made in woman's image, not God's – just as she "fits herself by each increase of knowledge," so too will her inheritors after her (128).

In looking to these future generations, Schreiner's *Woman and Labor* assumes the form of a utopian vision. Her feminist is part of a shared "consciousness of great impersonal ends, to be brought, even if slowly and imperceptibly, a little nearer by her action, which gives to many a woman strength for renunciation" (128). This visionary tone is there from the very start of *Woman and Labor*, in which the first chapter, "Parasitism I," outlines a forward-looking feminism: "We do not ask that our ancient spinning-wheels be again resuscitated and placed in our hands," nor does Schreiner "demand that society shall immediately so reconstruct itself that every woman may again be a child-bearer (deep and over-mastering as lies the hunger for motherhood in every virile woman's heart!); neither do we demand that the children whom we bear shall again be put exclusively into our hands to train" (64–5). Schreiner understands that these forms of feminine labour are out of step with the modern economy, and so she instead "demand[s] that … in this new world we also shall have our share of honored and socially useful human toil, our full half of the labor of the Children of Woman" (65). The repeated use of the plural possessive pronoun, coupled with the reference to "socially-useful" (re)production, implies a new form of inheritance mediated by the transmission of cultural consciousness, not biological kinship. Looking forward to future generations (to the "Children of Woman"), Schreiner's feminist collective works hard to transform cultural consciousness (convertible "cultural capital") into other forms of material or institutional knowledge (education and skilled training) and thereby secure economic opportunities and capital hitherto denied women within the current gendered economy. "We demand nothing more than this, and we will take nothing less," the first chapter projects, "This is our 'WOMAN'S RIGHT!'" (65).

Conclusion: New Women on the Horizon

Olive Schreiner's writings on gender and economics had a powerful and lasting influence upon the Women's Movement and the feminist fight for employment equity at the turn of the century. Her *Woman and*

Labor was, as mentioned from the outset of *Critical Alliances*, hailed by gender activists such as Vera Brittain as the "Bible of the Woman's Movement."[76] Being a nurse herself, who served in the First World War's Voluntary Aid Department, Brittain was particularly inspired by Schreiner's impassioned and repeated directive to women to "take all labor for our province!" (172, 173, 202). "I can still tingle with excitement," Brittain writes, "of the passage which reinforced me, brought up as were nearly all middle-class girls of that period to believe myself predestined to a perpetual, distasteful but inescapable tutelage, in my determination to go to college and at least prepare for a type of life more independent than that of a Buxton young lady" (41). In Schreiner's *Woman and Labor* (1911), Brittain clearly found the call to arms that validated her pursuit of some kind of larger or "independent" life beyond domestic "tutelage" typically prescribed to all proper young "ladies." Her entry in *A Testament of Youth* (1933) goes on to quote at length Schreiner's long list of modern professions to which educated women must stake their claim.

> From the judge's seat to the legislator's chair; from the statesman's closet to the merchant's office; from the chemist's laboratory to the astronomer's tower, there is no post or form of toil for which it is not our intention to attempt to fit ourselves; and there is no closed door we do not intend to force open; and there is no fruit in the garden of knowledge, it is not our determination to eat. (*Woman and Labor*, 172; quoted in Brittain, 41)

One can easily imagine how, after reading the above and confident passage on women's professional ambitions, the young Brittain would have "visualised in rapt childish ecstasy a world in which women would no longer be the second-rate, unimportant creatures that they were now considered, but the equal and respected companions of men" (41). This "vision" of gender equality was first articulated almost three decades earlier, in *The Story of an African Farm*. A 1911 review of *Woman and Labor,* for example, complains of the "distance" in subject matter between Schreiner's earlier novel and her later "treatise on women's rights," but then goes on to explain how the breadth in material effectively replicates the author's argument regarding women's ongoing fight for equal employment, from the days in which "we bore the race" and "laboured free together" to the modern skilled economy in which women's "traditional labours ... have shrunk away forever" ("Woman and Labour," in *Good Health* [1911], 915). The review is confirmation of the ongoing battle by feminists, after Schreiner, for access to "new fields of labor from which women are barred" (915). Schreiner's call for women's education and employment reform was first articulated in 1883 by her radical heroine Lyndall, and in 1911, when a young Brittain picked up *Woman and Labor*, the author was still working hard to realize this feminist vision.

That there is a continuation between Schreiner's *The Story of an African Farm* (1883) and her later treatise *Woman and Labor* makes sense insofar as Lyndall's sad ending leaves open, rather than answers, questions about the feminist figure and her cultural legacy for later generations of women. Towards the novel's end, Gregory Rose eventually finds Lyndall abandoned by her lover and dying from illness after her child is stillborn. It is important to note that he does not use this opportunity to reassert his romantic intentions, but instead takes on the role (and even clothing) of feminine nurse so that he might lovingly tend to the broken and dying woman. In his review of Schreiner's novel, Andrew Lang claims that Lyndall's narrative "would astonish a reader of penny fiction" (363); he takes particular issue with the aforementioned scene in which "a young man dresses like a young woman," and claims that one "scarcely understands" why "[t]his incredulous heroine has a love affair, has even a baby, [but then] refuses to marry its father" ("Theological Romances" [1888], 363).[77] Lang was not the only reader to wonder at the feminist meaning of Lyndall's tragic demise in *The Story of an African Farm*. H. Rider Haggard claims that the novel must be the "result of inward personal suffering on the part of the writer" ("About Fiction" [1887], 363), while Edward Aveling argues that Lyndall's "pathetic" attempt at sexual independence simply proves the need for "the great socialist revolution that is rapidly approaching" ("A Notable Book" [1883] quoted in First and Scott, *Olive Schreiner*, 124).[78] Still another critic, writing for *The Englishwoman's Review* (1883), contends that the key to Lyndall's frustrated life can be found in those conversations with Waldo on gendered education: "We have been more especially attracted, however, by some remarks on the narrow education of women," the anonymous reviewer writes, adding that such didactic moments in the novel "tend to show that the Colony has quite as necessary lessons to learn as the mother country" (quoted in First and Scott, *Olive Schreiner*, 123). This last reviewer's attempt to align Schreiner's novel with Victorian conversations on gender reform proves prescient, for later critics well know that Lyndall's unfinished quest inspired many New Woman writers and feminist reformers to continue the fight for sexual and economic equality.

This feminist legacy is especially evident in the subsequent generation of New Woman novelists who, like Schreiner, employ an open-ended narrative structure in order to cultivate readers' investment in ongoing gender reform. Some examples of the New Woman's unresolved or unhappy endings include Mary Erle in *The Story of a Modern Woman* (1894), a professional journalist who is disappointed in the traditional lover and romance plot, or Hadria Fullerton in *The Daughters of Danaus* (1894), whose career as a professional composer is thwarted by family obligation. Schreiner's narrative influence can also be found in Amy Levy's *The Romance of a Shop* (1888), the subject of the next chapter on feminist kinship and women's open-ended struggle to balance work and family at the fin de siècle. For contemporary critics Ann Ardis (*New Women, New Novels*) and Sally Ledger (*The New Woman*), these unresolved narratives take their cue from Lyndall's valiant struggle against the traditional marriage plot. Ledger sees in Lyndall's tragic demise a rather cynical message about the feminist's narrative alternatives to domesticity in the early 1880s: "And yet despite the energy of her protests, by the close of the novel, Lyndall is dead," Ledger writes, for "in 1883, the New Woman could not survive the hostile climate into which she was perhaps prematurely born" (*The New Woman*, 81). Ardis is, by contrast, much more optimistic about the literary inheritance of this early gender radical and her narrative protest. "Lyndall dies, yet the resolution of her life's narrative cannot cancel out the power of her disruptive speech," Ardis explains, adding that Lyndall's voice instead lives on beyond the text to inspire a generation of feminist writers after her in the fight for sexual and economic equality: "To put it another way," Ardis continues, "[Lyndall] speaks "beyond the ending," even if she cannot write or live beyond it" (*New Women, New Novels*, 68). This radical rebellion against narrative closure, or what Ardis describes as "traditional narrative strategies of containment," is part and parcel of the text's larger vision of women's right to "self-definition" – Lyndall "asserts an agency that is not enclosed or controlled by narrative omniscience" (68). As with her fictional and real-life successors, Lyndall is instead necessarily part of, and inspires, a feminist inheritance dedicated to the collective fight for women's education and economic equality.

In her final call to arms, Schreiner's feminist thus impresses upon readers the wider or political dimensions of women's cultural knowledge as possibly mediating an alternative gendered economy. This chapter has argued that, through such bonds of cultural inheritance, Schreiner's feminism seeks to redefine what it means to be a woman and, therein, the kind of work or social roles open to later generations of women. However, as is so often the case with such strategic feminism, this vision of a "New Woman" on the horizon of modern economics is not necessarily open to all. While her call for female collaboration might seem inclusive in its open-endedness, Schreiner's final vision of a feminist labour movement was in fact, by definition, hostile toward those women deemed "unproductive" threats to the progressive effort. There was, in other words, no room in this Women's Movement for what Ardis describes as the "polyphony" of voices speaking back to "monologic discourse" (68). Instead, Schreiner's model of feminist collectively reinforces what Ann Heilmann describes as "Western points of view," in which the progress of the nation rests with the reformation of white middle-class women. "Black characters are relegated to the sidelines and treated with little or no sympathy" Heilmann writes (*New Woman Strategies*, 139), and as discussed previously, working-class women are also excluded from Schreiner's progressive vision by virtue of their association with physical labour. Schreiner was instead preoccupied with intellectual and skilled production, and thus fixed on middle and upper-class women of privilege and their role vis-à-vis so-called modern production. As Rowold explains, "[m]iddle-class women's education and professional work in Schreiner's argument was important to counteract race-deterioration and continuing evolutionary advancement in conditions of 'modern civilisation'" (*The Educated Woman*, 63). This is why Schreiner spends nearly three out of six chapters in *Woman and Labor* railing against what she labels as the "parasitical woman" who is dependent upon her husband for the vicarious consumption of goods and status, and who makes no meaningful social contribution through labour or ideas. In this model, the woman who trades sex for financial support ensures that both the "old forms of domestic labor" and the "new" expressions of socially meaningful labour "inevitabl[y]" "slip" from womankind's grasp (*Woman and Labor*, 115). As a solution to this social problem, Schreiner imagines how the feminist coalition might work to secure alternative education and economic options for women and therein save the social body from this perceived threat of social "degeneration." "The female labor movement of our day is, in its ultimate *essence*," she insists, "an endeavor on the part of a section of the race to save itself from inactivity and degeneration, and this, even at the immediate cost of most heavy loss in material comfort and ease to the individuals composing it" (123–4; emphasis mine). Despite this claim to an "essential" purpose among feminists, Schreiner's extended writings on women's education repeatedly stress the ideological (and thereby malleable) construction of gender and economic roles for women. The irony is, of course, that her constructivist arguments prioritize white and middle-class women, a selective approach to gender that ultimately reproduces ideological structures of racial and classed privilege.[79]

My next chapter will continue this discussion of middle-class constructions of gender, focusing specifically on the role of (re)productive feminisms in revising domestic ideology. As one of Schreiner's New Woman inheritors, Amy Levy worked hard to imagine middle-class women's role within the modern workforce. By the time Levy published *The Romance of a Shop* in 1888, Victorian ladies were already flocking to the city in search of employment within the many skilled and white-collar vocations. Yet Schreiner herself also witnessed this continued expansion of career opportunities for later generations of women. Her own nieces, for example, enjoyed both the medical training and employment denied to Schreiner two decades earlier. In a 1911 letter to Andre Murray, Schreiner brags of her youngest niece Ursula who is "doing very well with her ~~legal~~ ^medical^ studies at Cambridge" (ll. 15–16), and the same letter also mentions her other niece, Lyndall Schreiner, who "is studying law … [and who] passed her first LLB exam last Xmas, & will take her final next year" (ll. 11–13).[80] But in reference to Lyndall, Schreiner is quick to add that "[t]hen we will have to fight a big fight to get the parliament to pass a law allowing women Barristers to practice" (ll. 13–14). It was always clear to Schreiner that the "fight" for women's equality was ongoing and would involve continued contributions for several generations beyond her own immediate descendants. For Levy, however, writing five years after Schreiner, the feminist's (re)productive inheritance would also require a return to domestic plots and the fight for women's sexual self-possession underwriting modern contract. In Levy's writing we thus find a new opportunity to think of pleasurable exchanges by and for women that are part of, not antithetical (or "parasitical") to, the feminist cause.

2 Sisterly Kinship and the Modern Sexual Contract

We want a home and an occupation ... a real, living occupation.
– Gertrude, in Amy Levy's *The Romance of a Shop*

there is sometimes a bond existing between sisters, the most endearing, the most pure and disinterested of any description of affection which this world affords.
– Sarah Stickney Ellis, *Women of England*

Published in 1888, Amy Levy's *The Romance of a Shop* follows in the footsteps of Schreiner's attempt to write new narrative possibilities for women beyond traditional expectations of marriage and motherhood. Like her predecessor, Levy herself saw in higher education an opportunity for women's social advancement. She was, in fact, one of the "thousands" of modern feminists whom Allen claimed was "slain" by Newnham College ("Girl of the Future" [1890], 56). Levy was the second Jewish woman to gain admittance to the prestigious college in 1879, but left after two years (in 1881) without completing her tripos examinations.[1] Allen specifically names the feminist author in his nightmare vision of "a few hundred pallid little Amy Levys sacrificed" in the interests of women's "higher cultivation" (56), a characterization meant to stress the supposed correlation between women's education and socio-sexual degeneration.[2] Yet Levy's *The Romance of a Shop* directly challenges such pronatalist arguments by showing how women's pursuit of a skilled profession does not undermine domestic plots. While the novel does not focus at length on the link between higher education and gendered economics, regarding Schreiner's contribution to the New Woman movement, it does contain progressive representations of women's self-directed training as professional photographers.

Schreiner's feminist influence can instead be seen in *The Romance of a Shop*'s challenge to dominant gender roles and the domestic plot, specifically, limiting women's access to the world of business. In Levy's hands, the domestic sphere is redefined as a space of sisterly kinship underwriting women's professional aspirations. This is Levy's point when, in an early conversation with cousin Constance "Conny" Devonshire, protagonist Gertrude Lorimer offers an impassioned defence of women's dual pursuits of "a home" as well as "a real, living occupation" (epigraph above). That she uses the plural form "we" is telling, for Gertrude speaks not only of herself but also of her sisters – Fanny, Phyllis, and Lucy – and their plan to establish a successful photography business at 20B Upper Baker Street, in the heart of urban London. With this representation of sisters' professional collaboration, Levy's novel stages a critical intervention into dominant Victorian models of feminine domesticity, models described in many of the period's conduct manuals for women. Writing on and for *Women of England* (1843), for example, Sarah Stickney Ellis invokes the sororal bond as the perfect formulation of women's shared impulse to familial service over and above self-interest. Levy's *The Romance of a Shop*, however, imagines women working together and toward a goal that extends beyond the private sphere, and in doing so the novel therein poses innovative questions about the form and function of sisterly bonds and their relationship to the gendered spheres. Gertrude's early articulation of both familial and professional commitments begs the question whether or not women can in fact enjoy fluid movement between home and work, while also implicitly asking whether sibling bonds are meant to support or subvert the dominant domestic plot that would limit women's roles within the private sphere.

In trying to imagine a place for women's paid work in support of the home, Levy's novel taps into nineteenth-century conversations on marriage and the modern sexual contract, conversations that became all the more urgent after the 1882 Marriage Act. As Ann Ardis explains, in *New Women, New Novels*, several feminist authors had already begun, in the latter decades of the century, to refuse the cultural assumption of marriage as a form of narrative closure whereby women were safely ensconced within the private sphere to work as unpaid and selfless caregivers for both husband and children.[3] Still other Victorian women who did embrace the domestic plot continued to push for legal and economic reforms to the institution of marriage, demanding that wives be granted property rights equal to their husbands. When it was finally passed into law in 1882, the Married Women's Property Act was hailed by many as a watershed moment for feminists' efforts to attain self-possessive agency within the structures of sexual exchange. While the Act was certainly flawed in many ways, it nonetheless represented a significant attempt to redefine the familial bond in terms that mirror modern constructions of sexual and economic contract.[4] Under the new 1882 law, the "married woman [was] capable of entering into and rendering herself liable in respect of and to the extent of her separate property on any contract, and of suing and being sued, either in contract or in tort, or otherwise, in all respects as if she were *feme sole*." For many late Victorians, however, the Act's repeated turn to "contract" in place of marital "coverture" signalled a growing cultural investment in sexual choice and mutual exchange, a construction of desire which was especially troubling when applied to women. During the 1880 parliamentary debates of the bill, for example, Sir Henry James (Attorney General) worried that new legislation "would effect a *great revolution* in the matters not merely within but outside the household of every married man," particularly in terms of women's economic and political representation (quoted in Mary Lyndon Shanley, *Feminism, Marriage, and the Law in Victorian England*, 129; emphasis mine). Writing almost a decade later, in reference to *Regina v. Jackson* (in which a husband sued his wife for the "restitution for conjugal rights"),[5] professional author and popular anti-feminist Eliza Lynn Linton lashed out against recent legal reconstructions of the "voluntary union" as threatening "the destruction of the family by the virtual abolition of marriage" ("The Judicial Shock to Marriage" [1891], 692).[6] Though responding to notably different political cases, both critics nonetheless blamed the 1882 Act for marital discord and, therein, insisted that contract (sexual and/or economic) was antithetical to women's natural loyalty to, and restricted social movement within, the domestic sphere.

While Linton and James seem confident in their dichotomous models (familial loyalty versus sexual contract), modern critics remain divided as to the precise role that contract might play in the constitution of the modern family. Much of this debate hinges on the causal relationship between economics and kinship. For critics such as Margaret R. Hunt (*The Middling Sort*), the marriage contract formed alongside the emergent capitalist culture of individualism and liberal self-interest.[7] Other critics such as Alan Macfarlane and Ruth Perry focus on varying economic influences and correlating factors in the history of kinship or family systems. In *Marriage and Love in England 1300–1840* (1986), Macfarlane credits patrilineal kinship and the linear descent of property through males as inspiration for a new culture of private individualism and contract. Conversely, Perry's *Novel Relations* interprets the gradual disaggregation of the family, shifting from bilateral consanguineal bonds to private conjugal bonds, as the product of an emergent culture of industrial production and capital accumulation. Focusing on the eighteenth and early nineteenth centuries, Perry's study explains how "the weakening of consanguineal ties, the dispersion of communities, and the growing power of individualism – manifest in a range of legal, economic, and cultural signs – repositioned women with respect to their families of origin, leaving them more dependent than ever on the goodwill of their husbands" (195).[8] In *Incest and the English Novel, 1684–1814,* Ellen Pollak makes a similar point when describing how capitalism both "renders the kinship structures archaic" and also "preserves [these structures] in a residual way in the ideology of the biological family which posits the nuclear family with its oedipal structure as a natural rather than culturally created phenomenon" (13).[9] According to Pollak, these supposedly innate drives of biological family thus mask, rather than truly supplant, kinship and social structures such as the gendered descent of property.[10] This is also why modern twentieth-century feminists writing on psychoanalysis and the family find themselves returning to older social structures of affiliation, such as kinship, to explain the relationship between gender and economics (including capitalism) per concepts such as mutual exchange and modern contract.

This chapter will look at how fin-de-siècle author Amy Levy sees in social structures of kinship an opportunity to rethink women's gendered work, particularly with respect to women's right to sexual and economic contract. Unlike her late-Victorian contemporaries, such as James or Linton, Levy does not view kinship and contract as opposing social structures; rather, her novel *The Romance of a Shop* imagines how familial bonds between sisters can support an alternative gendered economy in which women enjoy the right to contract and, with it, fluid movement between domestic and professional plots. *The Romance of a Shop* is, in other words, an example of what critics such as Kathy Alexis Psomiades and Elsie Michie describe as the Victorian novel's active role in rewriting sexual and economic systems.[11] Psomiades's "The Marriage Plot in Theory" considers how the nineteenth-century marriage-plot novel actively reproduces heterosexual difference (53),[12] while Michie's *The Vulgar Question of Money* focuses more closely on the Victorian heiress as disrupting patrilineal exogamy (the heiress must instead circulate within an endogamous economy) (425).[13] Levy's novel, by contrast, is interested in how the female-centred kinship system might underwrite both women's professional and romantic ambitions – the ability to "have it all," so to speak: a family and an occupation.

The Romance of a Shop marks an innovative contribution to late-Victorian representations of feminist collaboration by virtue of its emphasis on female-centred kinship as mediating women's access to the modern marketplace. Other chapters in *Critical Alliances* focus on feminisms that celebrate educational and labour unions, professional cooperation, or mutual erotics, while this chapter looks specifically at the family and women's literary investment in sisterly bonds. This interest in familial bonds is not new among Victorian feminists looking to rewrite gender difference and women's social mobility. Indeed, this chapter reads Levy's novel as inheritor to earlier conversations among Victorian women writers, from Emily Brontë (*Wuthering Heights* [1847]) to George Eliot (*The Mill on the Floss* [1860]), on the powerful hold of sibling bonds (the consanguineal family) limiting women's relationship to socio-sexual independence. Yet Levy's turn to sisterly kinship is new and marks the fin-de-siècle transition from patriarchal status to sexual/economic contract. With its innovative representation of the sisterly bond, *The Romance of a Shop* reimagines the familial private sphere as a space of feminist support for women's domestic as well as professional plots. To make this point, this chapter compares Levy's novel with other late-Victorian representations of the shopgirl torn between romance and work, including notable examples from male writers such as George Gissing (*The Odd Women* [1893]) and Henry James (*The Princess Casamassima* [1886]) to works by women writers such as Ella Hepworth Dixon (*The Story of a Modern Woman* [1894]) and Katherine Mansfield ("The Tiredness of Rosabel" [1908]). In these later works, the female shop assistant's economic aspirations are figured as marginal to heterosexual plots, and eventually the shopgirl must even choose between her profession and romance, as if women's conjugal obligations preclude careers. *The Romance of a Shop* instead suggests that women can have both the career and marriage plot, so long as kinship bonds are rewritten to privilege women's self-possessed or female-centred sexual/economic exchange. Sisterly kinship is, in other words, central to women's fluid movement between the domestic sphere and the public sphere of employment and business.

The Romance of a Shop presents readers with a definitive argument on sisterly kinship as vital to the historic transition from status to the modern contract. It is worth noting that this chapter does not attempt an exhaustive comparison of Victorian anthropological models of the family; rather, analysis is limited to contextual Victorian texts and conversations insofar as they are relevant to understanding the innovative work of Levy's representation of sisterly kinship. For example, the Lorimer sisters' running conflict with their elder Aunt Caroline Pratt dramatizes competing nineteenth-century theories on women's duty to the family and the strategic differences between linear and lateral sororal bonds. In making this point, section one of this chapter references Henry Sumner Maine's *Ancient Law* (1861) and the Deceased Wife's Sister Controversy (1835–1907) as evidence of Victorians' wide-ranging views on women's relative role within the family. Section two reads Levy's novel in relationship to Victorian theorists such as Friedrich Engels (*The Origin of the Family, Private Property, and the State* [1884]) on the link between economic and conjugal structures of exchange. Unlike many other texts from the period, *The Romance of a Shop* does not see women's sexual choice as separate from, or a threat to, familial allegiances; instead, Levy's novel reverses the Marxist formula to emphasize kinship bonds as the primary force shaping the gendered economy which thereby limits women's access to the modern workforce. The third and final part of the chapter focuses specifically on the relationship between sisterly bonds and sexual/economic contract. This section theorizes the relationship between the sisterly bond and women's self-possessed desire. As Levy's novel suggests, real contract recognizes women's right to bodily self-possession and the associated principle of independent pleasure (or consumption). *The Romance of a Shop* thus closes with an alternative marriage plot built upon, and reinforcing, woman's right to own and freely exchange her (re)productive labour and desire.

1 Old and New Women

Amy Levy's *The Romance of a Shop* opens with a picture of the Lorimer family in transition: the four adult sisters – Gertrude, Lucy, Phyllis, and Fanny – have lost their father and, with him, their immediate means of financial support. Though the women are in deep mourning, they are also extremely enthusiastic about the possibility of embracing a new life of feminine self-subsistence. The four sisters decide together that they will move from suburban Campden Hill to the West End of London and set up a photography studio, and as part of this new life, the women will also attempt to redefine Victorian gender roles.

> "Gertrude and I," went on Lucy, "would do the work, and you Fanny, if you would, should be our housekeeper."
>
> "And I," cried Phyllis, her great eyes shining, "I would walk up and down outside, like that man in High Street, who tells me every day what a beautiful picture I should make." (55)

With this early scene, Levy signals to the reader that this is a novel about family and, specifically, a narrative interested in cooperative bonds between sisters. Together the sisters devise a new structure of family which will grant them both mutual support and also access to the urban world of work and pleasure.[14] Lucy and Gertrude will fulfil the role typically assigned to the middle-class man who works and thus financially supports the household, while Fanny (the oldest sister) will play the role of Victorian wife and tend to the house, an assignment which makes sense given that she is "behind the ages ... belonging by rights to the period when young ladies played the harp, wore ringlets, and went into hysterics" (56). Phyllis, the youngest sister, will not work at all; rather, she plans to play the part of consumer and enjoy the sights and pleasures the city has to offer.[15]

Yet the sisters' plan of a female-centred household is persistently challenged by their rather cantankerous Aunt Caroline Pratt. Though "she really meant well by her nieces," as the narrator tells us, Aunt Caroline nonetheless enters the plot as a source of conflict (64). As maternal aunt, she bears a certain amount of responsibility toward the sisters: "You are my dead sister's children, and I have done my duties toward you, or I would wash my hands of you all from this hour" (66). With this threat, Aunt Caroline not only disavows the sisters' commitment to each other, but she also rejects their authority to define their own familial and economic destiny. She is instead intent on dividing up the Lorimer women among relatives; she proposes that Fanny and Phyllis go with the Sebastian Lorimers (64), while she and her husband Septimus will care for Gertrude and Lucy, only – "Either as permanency, or until you have found suitable occupations" (65). Rather than take in all four of her nieces, Aunt Caroline instead betrays a very limited sense of sisterly responsibility across generations. On the one hand, her plan for Fanny makes sense insofar as the latter is Mr Lorimer's daughter by an earlier marriage and, thus, not related to the Pratts through maternal blood. On the other hand, however, the aunt's decision to group Fanny with Phyllis, who is her sister's daughter, clearly signals that her plan of placement has very little to do with sororal loyalty. In fact, her irreverence for sibling allegiance is made manifest in her dual attempt to divide up the sisters and take only those "better able to look after themselves" (64). Aunt Caroline wants only those nieces who promise minimal effort and who might more easily transition into occupations she deems as "suitable" (65). Her rather quick disregard for sisterly obligation serves as a powerful reminder of how, throughout the nineteenth century, the lateral familial bond faced increasing pressures, especially following the historic shift to linear conjugal plots.

Aunt Caroline's coercive approach is instead indication of how, for many Victorian women, the turn to domestic plots was the product of social and economic compulsion, not personal or romantic attachments. Aunt Caroline firmly believes that the best "occupation" for women is marriage, and she does not hesitate to voice this opinion to her nieces: "it is a pity that none of you has married," she laments, just before she dives into her extensive plans to relocate all four sisters among appropriate households (64). In an effort to remind her nieces of this preferred conjugal plot, she characterizes the Lorimers' scheme as "dangerous and unwomanly" and warns against their potential "loss of caste" or "damage to prospects," dual threats which draw attention to the social and economic pressures compelling women to marry (72). She worries that the sisters will not only unsex themselves, and thus risk their status within the family, but she is also concerned that this unsexing will then damage the women's marriage prospects and culminate in their further fall in class ("caste"). This leap in logic – jumping from gender roles to social exile – is motivated by Victorian anxieties toward the independent woman. As Claudia Nelson explains, single and unmarried young women "could not readily live alone without appearing alarmingly independent," but "sisters could set up household and enjoy their freedom" (*Family Ties in Victorian England*, 101).[16] In other words, then, the sororal family was only an acceptable alternative to marriage insofar as it was subordinate to, or a back-up plan in the absence of, the conjugal ideal.[17] For Aunt Caroline, however, sibling responsibility is supplanted by the economically advantageous conjugal plot. She is eager to see the sisters married off as soon as possible, and laments that they are not more like the "well-disciplined" and "well-dowered daughters of the house of Pratt being in the habit of 'going off' in due order and season" (64–5).[18] This is also why, when Aunt Caroline hears that the sisters will move to the city rather than pursue lucrative marriage proposals, she responds with horror and calls the sisters "willful, foolish girls" (65). The sisters' plan lacks what she calls "common sense" (65), as if to say that women's pursuit of a home life and career independent of marriage is so radical that it completely defies social comprehension. In an attempt to force her nieces to adhere to gender propriety, Aunt Caroline invokes the threat of masculine authority: "But your uncle shall talk to you; perhaps you will listen to *him*; though there's no saying" (65–6). This conflict between aunt and nieces is never resolved and, instead, the persistent tension between both – as stand-in for the clash between consanguineal and conjugal plots – serves as a powerful reminder that Victorians themselves were actively engaged in contemporary debates on gendered plots and kinship systems.

In labelling women like Fanny as "behind the ages," Levy's opening chapter also suggests that Victorians thought of the change in family structures as part of a larger and progressive social narrative. Even Aunt Caroline's emphasis on conjugal bonds fits within this historic schema. The idea of a progressive shift to mutual bonds between individuals also informs Henry Sumner Maine's construction of kinship and history in *Ancient Law* (1861), a text which was hailed by many Victorians as an instant "classic" on modern contract law (J.H. Morgan, introduction [1917], vii).[19] *Ancient Law* reads like an origin story, tracing the formation of modern society from its so-called primitive state to its modern formation – or, rather, its modern aspirations. In his fifth chapter, "Law in Primitive Society," Maine explains how the familial bond plays a central role in this historic evolution.

> [S]ociety in primitive times was not what it is assumed to be at present, a collection of *individuals*. In fact, and in the view of the men who composed it, it was *an aggregation of families*. The contrast may be most forcibly expressed by saying that the *unit* of an ancient society was the Family, of a modern society the Individual. (*Ancient Law* [1861], 74; emphasis in original)

So-called primitive society, or the world of "status," is marked by the subordination of individuals to the aggregate family.[20] The distribution of power and property is determined by blood or the "consanguineal bond" among siblings and descendants.[21] Indeed, there is no such thing as the individual in this world of status: "Men are," Maine explains, "regarded and treated, not as individuals, but always as members of a particular group" (*Ancient Law*, 108). The transmission of goods and power within the family is safeguarded by a kind of corporate figurehead, comparable to a "Public officer" within a "Corporation" (108). Even this familial head does not stand out as an individual with exceptional powers or a distinct identity; rather, the patriarch – because this position of authority is inherited through male bloodlines – is no more than a "trustee" who guards the interests and property of the family, his "children and kindred" (108). Eventually, with social evolution, the blood bond (the consanguineal family) is displaced by private bonds or "contracts" between individuals. "We may," as Maine concludes his chapter, "say that the movement of the progressive societies has hitherto been a movement *from Status to Contract*" (100; emphasis in original).[22]

Despite Victorians' increasing investment in the conjugal contract as structuring familial descent, still so much literature of the period nonetheless remains fixated on lateral consanguineal bonds as vital to siblings' social and sexual development. Some of the more infamous examples of bonded siblings include William and Dorothy Wordsworth (she is mirror to his "former heart" and "former Pleasure")[23] or Percy Bysshe and Elizabeth Shelley (whom Percy described as his spiritual "twin" [quoted in Teddi Chichester Bonca, *Shelley's Mirrors of Love*, 47]).[24] Throughout the nineteenth century, the sister is often positioned as the passive complement to men's self-definition and creative agency.[25] Her supporting role in the family plot is largely the product of Victorian assumptions regarding women's passive constitution. As Sarah Stickney Ellis explains in *Women of England*, females "are, in fact, from their own constitution, and from the station they occupy in the world, strictly speaking, relative creatures" (57).[26] One thinks of Catherine Earnshaw, in *Wuthering Heights* (1847), who cannot even imagine a life independent of her adoptive brother Heathcliff: "He's always, always in my mind," Catherine insists, "not as a pleasure, any more than I am always a pleasure to myself, but as my own being" (103).[27] George Eliot's *The Mill on the Floss* (1860) also frames the sister, Maggie, as relative mirror in her brother Tom's heterosexual marriage plot.[28] In the early chapters of the novel, Maggie and Tom are "still very much like young animals" who "ate together and rubbed each other's cheeks and brows and noses together, while they ate, with a humiliating resemblance to two friendly ponies" (*The Mill on the Floss*, 82). As an adult, however, Maggie continually tries, but tragically fails, to find the same emotional intimacy that defined her childhood bond with Tom.[29] The awkward sexual tension between brother and sister, as represented in novels by Eliot and Brontë, is also a reminder of how the Victorian shift to conjugal bonds placed increased pressure on, if not outright erased, the lateral bond between siblings. After all, as both Maggie and Catherine advance into adulthood, they are compelled to give up the intimate brother-sister bond for marriage plots and can only return to this primal sibling intimacy through death (Heathcliff is eventually buried beside Catherine per his final wish to "have her in my arms again" [272], while Maggie and Tom drown together in "close embrace" [517]).

The Victorian gravitation toward conjugal plots placed particular pressure upon sisters due to their already insecure economic position within the family. For women, especially, the compulsion to marriage as substitute for the sibling bond is largely a result of the changing financial constructions of the family and the associated descent of property. Under the old consanguineal structure, fathers and brothers readily assumed financial and legal responsibility for wives and sisters – even after the latter took husbands with fortunes of their own. This sense of familial responsibility was born of a deep valuation for women, in which sisters and daughters were viewed as equal partners and "co-decision" makers in the preservation of the familial corporation (Ruth Perry, *Novel Relations*, 128).[30] But the historic transition to the conjugal family brought with it, what Ruth Perry describes as, "increasingly asymmetrical legal arrangements in inheritance and succession" (111). The modern conjugal kinship system erected an invisible, or "gendered," barrier between brothers and sisters, leaving women's subsequent social and financial situation entirely dependent upon "the economic circumstances of the persons they married" (111). The shift from lateral cooperation to linear competition also changed the long-term affective structure of sibling bonds.[31] As Valerie Sanders explains, in *Brother-Sister Culture in Nineteenth-Century Literature*, the cross-sex sibling relationship became "the very cornerstone of middle-class family life," training youth for their own eventual private and linear families (12).[32] Boys and girls learned to think of themselves as sexually differentiated individuals destined for – and, in the case of females, as defined through – the heterosexual marriage plot. The linear structure of the conjugal plot also ensured that the lateral sibling bond would be supplanted by cross-sex bonds between husbands and wives or father and daughters.[33]

The role of women's bonds in this ongoing tension between consanguineal and conjugal plots is best illustrated by the debates surrounding the 1835 Marriage Act, a piece of legislation which prohibited marriage between a widower and his sister-in-law on the grounds that the two were effectively defined as siblings under English common law.[34] Efforts to repeal the Act began in 1842 with the unsuccessful "Marriage to a Deceased Wife's Sister Bill," and continued into the Edwardian period, when the Act was finally repealed in 1907. Implicit in the original 1835 prohibition was the valorization of sisterly bonds as morally superior to, and thus necessarily more socially important than, the cross-sex conjugal bond. Writing in defence of the original 1835 Act, A.J. Beresford-Hope paints a picture of this "moral" bond as both selfless and sexless – or selfless because sexless – and untainted by the jealous rivalries which he assumes are implicit in conjugal plots.

> So long as the wife's sister continues the unmarried guardian of her nephews and nieces, they will be to her the nearest and dearest, and only objects of love and care, but as soon as she marries their father she incurs the risk of having children of her own, who will be much nearer to her than her former charge ... A good aunt may often be changed into, if not a bad, at least a less devoted step-mother; a step-mother perhaps, on account of the very relationship previously existing, more jealously alive to trifles than a stranger would have been. (*The Report of Her Majesty's Commission on the Laws of Marriage* [1850] 75)[35]

In Beresford-Hope's estimation, the sister will instinctually look upon and care for her nieces and nephews as her own flesh, but once she is transformed into a step-mother, all feelings of sororal responsibility are supplanted by self-interest and jealousy.[36] His defence of the lateral sibling bond relies heavily upon the assumption of women's "relative status" within the family (per Sarah Stickney Ellis, *Women of England*, 57), a supposition that continued to inform debates on the Act throughout the century. Half a century later, for example, Beresford-Hope's treatise on the "The Lords and the Deceased Wife's Sister Bill" (1883) argues that the sexualized "sister" represents a competitive threat to the "sacred" family (762), while in the same year Dr Charles Cameron's 1883 speech to the Marriage Law Reform Association asserts that responsible aunts are "so imbued with love for their dead sister and her offspring" that they are more than "willing to defy the sneers of a scandal-loving and calumnious world, and risk their reputation on the shrine of a sacred duty" (*Marriage with a Deceased Wife's Sister* [1883], 15). In other words, defenders of the Act believed that sisters were bound by, and defined through, a higher calling to familial service, a gendered role that superseded any individuating characteristics or desires.

Despite its vehement supporters, the 1835 Marriage Act was also the source of much criticism throughout the century, with many cultural and political opponents targeting the underlying legal assumption of sexual desire as self-interested. In novels such as *The Hand of Ethelberta* (1876) and *Tess of the D'Urbervilles* (1891), late-Victorian author Thomas Hardy challenged the dichotomous construction of sisters as either selfless or selfish, and instead proposed a third version of female bonds that allowed for sexual cooperation. Proponents of the 1835 Marriage Act would have been scandalized by the former novel's titillating chapter in which Ethelberta convinces her lover Christopher Julian to open his heart to her younger sister Picotee: "Placing her arm round Picotee's waist, who had never lifted her eyes from the carpet, [Ethelberta] drew the slight girl forward, and whispered quickly to him [Christopher Julian] – 'kiss her, too. She is my sister, and I am yours … Care for us both equally!'" (273). This theory of triangulated sisterly desire is something to which Hardy again returns in *Tess of the D'Urbervilles* (1891). Faced with her impending arrest and execution, Tess asks that Angel take as a substitute lover her younger sister Liza Lu, who is an improved version of herself: "[Liza] has all the best of me without the bad of me," Tess insists, "and if she were to become yours it would almost seem as if death had not divided us" (381).[37] When Angel balks at the prospect of an illegal union, Tess is quick to counter "[t]hat's nothing" and "[p]eople marry their sisters-in-law continually around

Marlott" (381). Tess is able to reject the 1835 prohibition as "nothing" because she and her sexualized sister in no way threaten the primacy of the patriarchal family. Yet criticism of the 1835 Marriage Act was not limited to fiction. There was also, for example, William Holman Hunt who openly defied the law by marrying Edith Waugh (in 1873), the sister of his deceased wife, Fanny. While Hunt's marriage was the source of much controversy, it was also supported by many Victorians, including Dinah Mulock Craik whose novel *Hannah* (1872) offered a compelling defence of marriage between a widower and his deceased wife's sister. As with Hardy's novels, the sisters in Craik's story are not presented as self-interested sexual competitors; rather, the eponymous heroine feels both love for her husband, Bernard Rivers, as well as a strong sense of familial love toward her sister's child.

Like her contemporaries, Levy suggests that the sexualized sister is not an inherently competitive subject whose desire undermines the sororal bond. Yet her novel also presents a new twist on this theme by stressing the variation among sisters, and imagining how these differentiated women might work in support of the family unit. In *The Romance of a Shop* sisterly bonds are not shorthand for women's relative gendered sameness; rather, the Lorimer sisters are written as notably distinct in both their productive and pleasured activities, variations in gendered attributes which are then confirmed through their different contributions to the shared household. Fanny is the oldest, but she is also one of those outmoded Victorian "ladies" who cannot quite understand her more "modern young" sisters – she is, the narrator explains, "a round, sentimental peg in the square, scientific hole of the latter half of the nineteenth century" (56). It thus falls to the second-oldest, Gertrude, to save the sisters from destitution by "propose[ing]" the very "progressive" notion that they start their own business and, therein, break from "the dull little ways by which women, ladies, are generally reduced to earning their living" (54, 55). This isn't to say that Gertrude is the most modern of the sisters; that role belongs to Phyllis, who both explicitly identifies, and takes the most pleasure in, the sisters' defiance of even the most entrenched gender conventions. When Lucy and Frank walk together through the London streets, for example, Phyllis turns to Gertrude and proclaims, "all this is delightfully unchaperoned, isn't it?" (96). Though Gertrude herself enjoys unescorted movement through the city, she cannot go as far as Phyllis and openly admit this break with social/sexual customs. Instead, Gertrude thinks that "[t]he question of propriety" is "best left to itself" (something "she hated … to discuss"), and so it is little wonder that she feels a certain discomfort at her younger sister's open disavowal of sexual customs: "her own unconventional sense of the fitness was a little shocked at seeing her sister [Lucy] walk out of the house with an unknown young man [Frank], both of them being bound for the studio of the latter" (97). Still, Gertrude's "shock" does not necessarily translate into a "conventional" response, such as repression or disapproval; her concern is instead largely borne of her acute sense of sisterly solidarity and, with it, responsible concern.

Other characters in the novel recognize the differences among the sisters, without assuming that these variations in some way undermine the tie of sororal loyalty. Even Fred and Conny debate the strengths and virtues of their cousins in a way that underscores how each of the Lorimers has a distinct role to play in the unconventional sororal family. Fred describes Gertrude as "the cleverest" and Phyllis as "the prettiest," but when he insists that "Lucy is far and away the nicest of the Lorimer girls," his sister Conny quickly and "crossly" responds that "Gerty is worth ten of her [Lucy]" (91). While Conny's defence might be somewhat biased (she and Gertrude are close friends), it also nonetheless signals a new valuation for feminine intellect (to be "clever") that runs throughout the novel and supersedes any impulse to petty jealousies. This is not to say that there are not moments where the sisters are placed in potentially competitive situations. For example, Lord Watergate makes an immediate "impression" upon Gertrude (87), but when she later hears him declare that "[Phyllis] is very beautiful," the older sister is "suddenly" overcome by a "vision" of the widower's dead wife ("her golden hair, and haggard beauty") (115). Gertrude's "vision" of the deceased wife raises the "specter" (or another vision of sorts) of sexual competition as outlined in the debates surrounding the 1835 Act. However, the Lorimer sisters are not related to the departed, and more important, Gertrude's sexual desire (her attraction to Lord Watergate) in no way compromises her feelings of responsibility toward her younger sister and the sororal bond more generally. There is no jealousy between sisters, only the urge to support and protect one another. In the same scene, she critically evaluates the growing romance between Sidney Darrell and Phyllis, and when she later catches Lord Watergate smiling at her sister's "nonsense," Gertrude promptly whisks away Phyllis from further risk and condescension (116).

While the sisters' sexual desires (or conjugal plots) are a central theme throughout *The Romance of a Shop*, it is also important to note that the Lorimers do not outright reject older systems of kinship, particularly the consanguineal bonds of blood. As demonstrated by their initial brainstorming session, the Lorimer sisters maintain a continued investment in what Maine refers to as the "corporate" family; the sisters' loyalties lie with one another and, for this reason, they vow to "keep together" (*The Romance of a Shop*, 54). Yet their determination to include Fanny, who is in fact their half-sister (52), also signals a radical attempt to rewrite the terms of lineage implicit within the consanguineal bond. By including their half-sister, the Lorimers appropriate what Maine refers to as the "the power of the father" (Patria Potestas) in order to decide their own lateral bonds of alliance. In his history, Maine explains how this form of "agnation" (adoption) is possible because the corporate family is both biological and, sometimes, constructed.[38] The power of agnation, Maine continues, rests solely with the patriarchal head: "Where the Potestas begins, Kinship begins; and therefore adoptive relatives are among the kindred. Where the Potestas ends, Kinship ends; so that a son emancipated by his father loses all rights of Agnation" (88).[39] In other words, men are the ones who typically enjoy the exclusive authority to name or benefit from adoption, while women's role within the corporate family is instead defined in terms of "natural" contributions (descent through biological reproduction). As Ruth Perry explains, in *Novel Relations*, "Agnatio," or "kinship created through the male," "was a function of being subject to *patria potestas* or the father's power," and "[w]omen could only create cognito, or natural kinship, 'devoid of the privileges attached to legal kinship'" (109). By naming Fanny as equal participant, the Lorimer sisters effectively reject this ancient model of the male corporation and, specifically, the law of the father (Patria Potestas); the sisters instead replace patriarchal power with their own lateral structure, governed by the siblings themselves, and thereby signal their intention to "unanimously" write their own feminist futures, "never mention[ing] that [they] have seen better days" (*The Romance of a Shop*, 67).

2 Sisterly Solidarity

Once in the city, the Lorimer sisters decide to renovate their newly rented shop and, through their collective labour, create a gendered space that will then support their pursuit of economic and sexual rights beyond the domestic sphere. One of the rights the sisters quickly claim is their ability to act as agents in sexual plots. In the same early scene, for example, the sisters take a brief break from their hard work so that they might enjoy "the spectacle of that gorgeous youth [Fred] hammering away in his shirt sleeves on a pair of steps" (78). Not passive, the sisters are instead assertive agents of desire who take pleasure in the masculine object of their gaze. Words like "gorgeous" and "immaculate" tell us that the Lorimers are not disappointed consumers. Through the remainder of the novel, the sisters will assert their claim to pleasurable consumption as reward for, and supported by, their collaborative work. Yet, the sisters also discover quite early that their pursuit of urban pleasures will not go unchallenged by those characters steeped in traditional Victorian gender roles – characters who tend not to acknowledge, let alone fairly remunerate, professional women. The novel makes this latter point about gendered pay in reference to the "Lorimers' customers, [who] seemed to think the sex of the photographers as a ground for greater cheapness in the photographs" (82).[40] When Conny asks Gertrude why the sisters don't want to work as assistants rather than entrepreneurs, Gertrude quickly explains that the latter "[is] life and the other death" (68). Their goal is, from the very start, economic independence through sisterly cooperation, and anything short of this objective smacks of failure or even "death." While such a statement might seem hyperbolic, it makes sense when we remember that the sisters' collaborative venture guarantees them a form of feminine autonomy hitherto denied under the old patriarchal family.[41] By focusing on the radical gendered possibilities of sisterly bonds, *The Romance of a Shop* imagines how women might reclaim their productive and pleasured bodies, and better yet, how this self-possession then enables women to look back at, and demand the equal right to contractual exchange with, men.

Levy was not, of course, the only late-Victorian writer to propose a theory of the female-centred domestic sphere as sustained by, and sustaining, women's paid labour. Her friend and political activist Clementina Black, compelled by social circumstance to work outside of the home, also counted herself among a new generation of women interested in rethinking the separate gendered spheres.[42] It makes sense to compare the two authors given that the Lorimers were modelled after the Black sisters (Clementina, Grace, and Emma), who briefly shared a flat on Fitzroy Street in London (1879) as part of their socio-political activism.[43] In her essay "The Organization of Working Women" (1889), Black explains how so many of these new female workers want to live off of the proceeds of their own earnings rather than depend upon "the wages of others" by performing their own domestic labour that, though "useful and valuable, [is] not measured by a market price" (258). The right to an independent income was essential to middle-class women's social and sexual empowerment, but in order to obtain this economic agency, many aspiring female professionals found that they also needed to redefine the conventions of gender limiting their economic mobility. To make this point, Black contrasts earlier feminist Harriett Martineau, who insisted that life in the urban boarding house "would not be respectable" (quoted in Black, 259), with the "[h]undreds of women" who are "living precisely in that manner at the present day and enjoying the respect of their neighbors" (259). Still, the primary obstacle faced by this latter group of urban women was the fair remuneration for their equal work: "the lingering tradition that women do not, or should not, work for money, still causes their work to be treated with less regard, and by this very circumstance helps to prevent it, in too many cases, from rising to an equal standard of efficiency with that of men" (259). Black's loyalties lay primarily with working-class women's labour; she was an active member of the Women's Trade Union League, for example, and she helped to found the Women's Trade Association in 1889, and spent her later years working and writing for the Anti-Sweating League and the Women's Industrial Council, both of which supported the 1909 Trades Board Act per the minimum wage. Some of her notable works on working-class women's labour rights include *Sweated Industry and the Minimum Wage* (1907) and *Makers of Our Clothes* (1909, with Adele Meyer).

Though they were friends and fellow gender radicals, Levy did not share Black's commitment to socialism as a tool for gender reform, a point which is obfuscated by many critics who are preoccupied with biographical interpretations of Levy's writings on women and economics.[44] Deborah Nord, for example, is eager to assume that Levy shared her friends' radical politics, describing the author as part of "an amorphous community" (which included radicals such as Beatrice Webb and Margaret Harkness) who "understood their own marginality [...] as a condition of their sex but also as a product of their socialist politics, of their aspirations to enter male-dominated areas of work, or of their religion or class" (*Walking the Victorian Streets*, 183–4). For Emma Francis, however, Nord's reading is part of a long tradition of scholarship that misrepresents Levy's political activities – some of the earliest offenders include Edward Wagenkecht, who misidentified Levy as secretary for the Beaumont Trust charity organization, and Warwick James Price, who "produce[d] a fantasy of Levy as bona fide working class" (Francis, "Why Wasn't Levy More of a Socialist?", 48). Yet as critic Linda Hunt Beckman points out, Levy's name is "conspicuously lacking" in minutes taken during her friends' socialist gatherings (*Amy Levy*, 83), and in an 1886 letter to Violet Paget (a.k.a. "Vernon Lee"), Levy herself expresses discomfort with the Black sisters' Fitzroy-flat plan to do their own housework and "attend Socialist and Anarchist meetings" (letter dated November 1886, quoted in Beckman, 255). Two years later, *The Romance of a Shop*'s representation of the sororal economy at 20B Upper Baker Street suggests that Levy eventually warmed to the idea of women's collaborative work, but the text still avoids any mention of working-class women or cross-class cooperation. Levy's novel instead focuses on middle-class women and their professional advancement through work as photographers and shop owners.

The real feminist innovation of *The Romance of a Shop* lies in its representation of women as self-sufficient and capable economic agents, even capitalizing on the newness of women's professional work as a means to both sexual and social ends. While the Lorimer sisters must fight for fair remuneration, they also discover that their work is in strong demand among those who are "curious and fond of novelty" and who therein subscribe to the more progressive "theories about women's work" (135). The sisters, however, use this market opportunity to push for further recognition in the form of equal social mobility and economic contract with men. In an early scene Gertrude refuses an interview with *The Waterloo Place Gazette,* which would transform the Lorimers' enterprise into a marketable story for readers' titillation; she instead insists upon the sisters' professional standings as "photographers, not mountebanks!" (90), a claim which draws attention to the women's dual status as both subjects and producers of spectacle. For critic Elizabeth F. Evans it is precisely this emphasis upon women's professional authority which marks the novel as "unusual" for its time. Other contemporary representations of the shopgirl – from Monica Madden in George Gissing's *The Odd Women* (1893) to Millicent Henning in Henry James' *The Princess Casamassima* (1886) – limit women's economic role to work as paid assistants, but Levy's "women in business" often explicitly distance themselves from, and insist upon, their authority over "commodities on display" ("We Are Photographers, Not Mountebanks!", 26).

Yet Levy's ambitious and empowered approach to the shopgirl figure can perhaps best be seen in comparing her novel with contemporary works by female writers. Other turn-of-the-century women writers who referenced this figure in their fiction include Ella Hepworth Dixon, in *The Story of a Modern Woman* (1894), and Katherine Mansfield, in "The Tiredness of Rosabel" (1908). Like their male contemporaries, Gissing and James, these other feminist writers tend to downplay women's sexual agency in their work as shop assistants. Published shortly after Levy's novel, *The Story of a Modern Woman* contains the tragic subplot of #27, a shopgirl who is seduced and abandoned by Dr Dunlop Strange and who later dies from illness after a failed suicide attempt.[45] The story of this "wretched creature" who was once "a respectable girl – a shop assistant" (164) highlights for readers the sexual danger that often accompanied women's work in commodity culture and the easy slide from an agent of sales to an object of masculine consumption.

Mansfield's short story, "The Tiredness of Rosabel," takes as its primary focus this easy slippage between the shopgirl and the objects she promotes for sale. Rosabel is an assistant in a hat shop and is often asked by prospective customers to model the wares. This labour is the source of both frustration and fantasy, as customers are rude but also a source for Rosabel's romantic projections. These dual impulses collide one day when a young, attractive couple asks Rosamond to model for them a fancy hat with feathers and a velvet rose. The girl looks at the hat on Rosabel and excitedly decides that it is "adorable" and "suits [Rosabel], beautifully" (2), while the young man is much more aggressive in his objectification of the shopgirl and, as soon as his companion is out of earshot, asks if Rosabel has "ever been painted," adding that she's "got such a damned pretty little figure" (3). Yet it is the young girl's consumer gaze that most upsets Rosabel (she is "seized" by a "feeling of anger" and "longed to throw the [hat] in the girl's face" [3]), while the man's sexual advances instead inspire a prolonged fantasy in which Rosabel and the girl switch places as agents of consumerism and pampered enjoyment of riches.[46] "The Tiredness of Rosabel" gestures toward the sexual risks often faced by shopgirls, but at the same time the story highlights the working woman's aspirations to some form of economic agency and authority within commodity culture – the kind of agency promised by Levy's sisters in their collaborative ownership of a photography business.

At the same time as Levy was writing – and as a consequence of such innovative representations – many real-life Victorian women were, in fact, making tremendous strides in the world of business, and by the end of the century it was becoming increasingly acceptable for women to work as shop proprietors or assistants.[47] Women's increased access to these commercial spaces is directly tied to the industrial revolution and standardized production of goods, both of which redefined the knowledge and skill-sets required of those working in the sales industry. Expertise in the preparation and presentation of goods was rendered redundant, and the new sales economy instead gave way to a polarized labour market comprised of both highly trained and unskilled workers. The former group was usually populated by men with specialized knowledge in management or accounting, while women often made up the majority of the latter group of shop assistants and customer-service workers.[48] Even prior to such deskilling, however, many middle-class women in the early nineteenth century participated in retail work and even owned shops (especially clothing businesses or rural shops), and trade consistently represented "the largest single occupation" by which these women could "[earn] their livelihood in their own right as well as assisting their male relatives" (Davidoff and Hall, *Family Fortunes*, 301). Yet a new labour economy and, with it, an increased need for customer-service employees presented late-Victorian women with a unique opportunity to legitimate their role within the retail industry. In her history *The Women's Movement and Women's Employment in Nineteenth Century Britain*, Ellen Jordan explains how, by as early as the 1870s, shop employers favoured middle-class women for service positions that implicitly required social grooming in manners and personal presentation (37).[49] The middle- and upper-class customers frequenting such establishments also helped to establish retail as "suitable" employment for middle-class women (on a par with teaching and domestic service), and the rising popularity of the sales industry also gave, what Jordan refers to as, "a hint of where future opportunities were to lie" for independent-minded women (37).

Just as middle-class women were seeing some success in the world of retail, so too were they playing a leading role in the professionalization of photography at the end of the nineteenth century. Indeed, many Victorian women were already steeped in traditional art forms such as painting and music, fields coded as feminine and genteel, and thus did not require a new form of skills training or erudition; instead, the challenge for these women lay in their efforts to penetrate that "borderland" of career artists – or in making that transition from unpaid amateur to a remunerated professional.[50] Gains in some of the older and thus more established artistic fields were slow but steady. An 1841 census counts 264 women (7.3 per cent of the category) who identify as professional musicians, but that number jumps to 1,618 in 1861 (17.1 per cent); a similar survey in 1851 counts women as comprising "5 percent" of professional "painters, sculptors and engravers," but then this number steadily increases to "8.3 per cent in 1861, 9.2 per cent in 1871, 24.7 per cent in 1891, 26.5 per cent in 1901, and 26 per cent in 1911" (Jordan, *The Women's Movement*, 114). It is, however, in the category of "paid and professional photographers" where women made some of the fastest and largest gains – although often women worked as both tinters and printers of photographs, rather than producers.[51] An 1861 census counts 168 women (6.6 per cent of category) working as professional photographers, but that number jumps dramatically to 1,301 women (19.6 per cent) in 1881.[52] The rapid rise of women working in this field has much to do with the newness of the photographic technology, which made it very difficult for men to maintain a monopoly over the market. While women were often excluded from traditional art academies, photographic studios frequently advertised for female students or apprentices,[53] and early practitioners such as Lady Clementina Hawarden (1822–65) and Julia Margaret Cameron

(1815–79) made some of the most visible and lasting contributions to the field while it was still in its infancy. Cameron's experiments with copy and painterly collage forced photographers to rethink the relationship between "authentic" art and science, while Lady Hawarden's images of domestic women looking outward through windows, and/or inward through mirrors, implicitly questioned the gendered ideology of separate spheres.[54] With their contributions to both process and content, both female artists helped to pave the way for Amy Levy's later meditations on the female photographer who moves between the private and public spaces in search of professional legitimacy.

Levy's professional women are unique, however, because they rely upon sisterly kinship as underwriting their access to both sexual and professional equality. Even when compared with other New Woman representations of shopgirls in the city, such as Dixon's *Story of a Modern Woman* or Mansfield's "The Tiredness of Rosabel," *The Romance of a Shop* stands out by virtue of its emphasis upon this female-centred family structure as requisite to women's successful navigation of the modern marketplace. Mansfield's short story instead suggests that the store model, as the object of visual pleasure, is reduced to a competitive relationship with other women in positions of economic power greater than her own; at the end of the work day, Rosabel reflects upon the many "awful" (2) female customers who objectify her and, at the same time, she dreams of trading places with the attractive girl and enjoying her life of leisure consumption. *The Story of a Modern Woman*, likewise, paints a very bleak picture of the shopgirl as existing purely for men's disposable pleasure. Yet Dixon's novel is not as cynical in its representation of feminine bonds; rather the plot's primary focus on the friendship between Mary Erle and Alison Ives suggests a certain commitment to female solidarity. Both women will eventually forgo romantic plots with men (Alison rejects Dr Dunlop Strange and Mary breaks ties with Vincent Hemming) rather than participate in the sexual betrayal of another woman (Alison honours the memory of #27 while Mary refuses to betray Vincent's wife). "If we [women] were only united we could lead the world," Alison insists, adding that "all we modern women are going to help each other, not to hinder" (164). Still the closing chapters of *The Story of a Modern Woman*, with Mary left all alone to her career as a popular society journalist, would seem to imply that sexual and family plots are antithetical in the fin-de-siècle woman's professional aspirations. Levy's novel, by contrast, brings together familial and female bonds through her emphasis on sisterly kinship, and through this combination, suggests that women might rewrite the relationship between gender (or domesticity) and the marketplace.

In *The Romance of a Shop*, it is the sisters' collaborative bond that guarantees their financial support and mobility between the gendered spheres. This is a novel about female-centred kinship specifically, not friendly or social alliances more broadly, and it is this feminist kinship system that provides the necessary support for women as they navigate the work/family divide barring professional mobility. Even when Aunt Caroline tries to remind the Lorimers of "how [they] stand" (64) economically, the sisters will not be bullied. Shy Fanny even throws herself into the fray in defence of her sisters: "we are poor, and we are not ashamed that any one should know it. It is nothing to be ashamed of" (64). Still, Gertrude's momentary internalization of her Aunt Caroline's views suggests just how hard it is to transcend traditional plots of feminine domesticity: for one brief moment, after she dropped "her bomb," Gertrude saw "herself and her sisters as they were reflected in the mind of Mrs. Septimus Pratt: naughty children, idle dreamers" (65). However, Gertrude is able to resist her Aunt Caroline by turning to her sisters for support, and together they "make some good resolutions" as they carry forward with their plan (66). These latter resolutions represent the substitution of one familial kinship system for another: the conjugal patriarchy is supplanted by the consanguineal sisterly bond. Once they are collectively established in the city, the sisters also enjoy newfound freedom to form social attachments and exchange with like-minded individuals: "The calling which they pursued brought them into contact with all sorts of men, among them, people in many ways more congenial to them than the mass of their former acquaintance; intercourse with the latter have come about in most cases through 'juxtaposition' rather than 'affinity'" (135). Sisterly bonds thereby underwrite women's efforts to move beyond the restrictive confines of tradition ("juxtaposition") and, instead, to enjoy new socio-sexual choices ("affinity").

The Romance of a Shop's emphasis upon sisterly kinship also paves the way for a new marriage plot that does not preclude women's sexual and economic agency. In this way, too, Levy's novel stands alone as one of the rare examples of a late-Victorian narrative showing women who continue to work even after they marry. Even later representations of sisterly bonds and shopgirls, as found in *The Odd Women* (1893), do not revise the marriage plot to this extent. In Gissing's hands, romantic seduction is pictured as a divisive wedge that comes between both women's solidarity and professional ambition. Once she is married to Edmund Widdowson, for example, Monica Madden gives up her apprenticeship with Rhoda Nunn and Mary Barfoot, and a later romance between Rhoda and Everard Barfoot (Mary's cousin) forces the bluestocking to choose between marriage and work, as if the two are mutually exclusive.[55] While Gissing is unable to reconcile romance and women's economic aspirations, still other novelists such as H. Rider Haggard looked at how women's right to contract necessarily culminates in a new marriage plot. Published the same year as Levy's novel, Haggard's *Mr. Meeson's Will* (1888) focuses on the savvy legal maneuverings of Augusta Smithers, a young writer who lets herself be tattooed in order to secure her lover's inheritance. Augusta's bodily sacrifice is a powerful representation of women's possessive individualism (women's ownership of both body and legal testimony), and her eventual marriage to Eustace Meeson is both reward for her gift and also provides her with the financial security to continue writing and publishing independently.[56] As with Levy's novel, then, Haggard's closing representation of the working woman reminds readers of the modern marriage contract as described in Maine's *Ancient Law* (1861), a text that Haggard certainly would have known given his early training as a lawyer (passing the bar in 1884). But unlike Haggard, Levy reframes women's right to modern contract as grounded in kinship, not sacrifice, and places sisterly bonds at the very forefront of women's economic and sexual agency. Marriage need not undermine women's economic or sisterly collaborations; rather, *The Romance of a Shop* shows us how sisterly collaboration underwrites women's agency within sexual and economic plots.

3 Sisterly Bonds and the Modern Marriage Plot

In *The Romance of a Shop*, Levy imagines how sisterly collaboration underwrites women's access to the modern city as a space of both work and embodied pleasure.[57] In one of the most cited passages from the novel, Gertrude travels to the British Museum by an Atlas omnibus; sitting "boldly" atop her public carriage, she enters into the public sphere of urban work and mobility, as well as visual consumption.

> for Gertrude, the humours of the town had always possessed a curious fascination. She contemplated the familiar London pageant with an interest that had something of passion in it; and, for her part, was never inclined to quarrel with the fate which had transported her from the comparative tameness of Campden Hill to regions where the pulses of the great city would be felt distinctly as they beat and throbbed. (80)

It is worth noting that Gertrude travels to the British Museum in pursuit of a "course of photographic reading" (79) that will, in turn, help the sisters build their shop and reputations as professional photographers. As such, Gertrude is not only taking in the sights of the city, but she is also entering into the public sphere of paid work per the Lorimer sisters' aspirations to economic independence. Yet it is also in this critical scene of urban mobility (quite literally) that the novel signals its dual interest in the relationship between women's collaborative work and embodied desire, the latter of which is experienced as visual consumption rife with sexual connotations.[58] Shifting quickly from a state of "fascination" to "contemplation," Gertrude practises what many late Victorians hailed as a modern urban consciousness. In "The Metropolis and Mental Life" (1903), for example, Georg Simmel explains how the city, with its "rapid crowding of changing images," stimulates the "higher layers of the psyche" ("his head instead of his heart") and therein paves the way for a reflective or psychological response (410).[59] In *The Romance of a Shop*, however, Levy imagines how this urban consciousness might underwrite women's pursuit of self-possessed pleasure, both visual and sexual. Gertrude transforms visual sensation into insight ("interest") and then reflects upon past events leading up to this moment in time (from "tame" Camden Hill to "the pulses of the great city"). As she makes her way through the busy streets, her visual enjoyment of the "London pageant" approaches "passion," and it is clear that she derives both mental and physiological energy from the city. Regarding the latter, it is as if her and the city's "pulse" "beat and throbbed" together as one, an image which is both sexual and life-affirming.

Though relatively brief, the omnibus scene introduces lasting questions about the sisters' access to an alternative plot that recognizes women's inalienable desires and thus their right to mutual sexual exchange. While collaborative work will afford the sisters a certain degree of access to the city (beyond the private sphere), the Lorimers' quest for such sexual recognition will be challenged by men like Sidney Darrell, whose disregard for feminine agency threatens to undermine both the sisters' bond and their innovative domestic narrative. Upon their first introduction, "Gertrude found herself rather cowed by the man and his indifferent politeness, through which she seemed to detect the lurking contempt; and as his glance of cold irony fell upon her from time to time, from beneath the heavy lids, she found herself beginning to take part not only against herself but also against the type of woman to which she belonged" (108). Darrell presents as the quintessential *flâneur*-figure, whose gaze maintains a certain distance between himself and his chosen object. His "cold" and privileged affect reminds one that the original French *flâneur* figure was related to the English dandy, a character of both boredom and leisure.[60] Gertrude immediately recognizes how Darrell assumes a position of "indifferen[t]" masculine authority and that his half-open eyes (as if unconscious) confirm this dismissive or disrespectful "view" of women. Thanks to the support of sororal bonds, however, Gertrude refuses to be "cowed" into submission (108). As she later explains to her sisters, he is "the sort of man; – if a woman were talking to him of – of the motions of the heavenly bodies, he would be thinking all the time of the shape of her ankles" (110). Gertrude knows that Darrell dislikes her "type" because she thwarts his expectation of what a woman should be, and through collaborative conversation, she and her sisters reclaim feminine subjectivity by reversing the gendered power dynamic; together, the Lorimers transform Darrell into an object to be scrutinized and exchanged among women who are equal and empowered sexual subjects.

Despite this momentary victory, Sidney Darrell continues to play a prominent role as misogynist villain throughout the remainder of the novel, and his continued presence therein demonstrates the ongoing need for sororal bonds as underwriting the sisters' sexual and social agency. He resurfaces later in the narrative as Phyllis's fatal love interest. Phyllis knows that her sisters will disapprove of the match because Darrell is already married (Gertrude does indeed object), and so she secretly absconds with her lover and thereby severs the ties of sororal loyalty. When Gertrude realizes the situation, she races over to Darrell's flat to reclaim her sister and to defeat the masculine threat once and for all. What ensues is a symbolic and compelling battle of the gendered gazes.

> His face was livid with passion; his prominent eyes, for once wide open, glared at her in rage and hatred.
>
> Gertrude met his glance with eyes that glowed with a passion yet fiercer than his own.
>
> Elements, long smoldering, had blazed forth at last. Face to face they stood; face to face, while the silent battle raged between them.
>
> Then with a curious elation, a mighty throb of what was almost joy, Gertrude knew that she, not he, the man of whom she had once been afraid, was the stronger of the two. For one brief moment some fiercer instinct in her heart rejoiced.
>
> ... a moment and Darrell had dropped his eyes. (172)

This time it is Darrell who is forced to look at and engage Gertrude with his eyes "wide open"; he must meet her "face to face" in this "fierce" test of wills. Empowered by her love for her sister, Gertrude stands up to this man "of whom she was once afraid" and whose masculine gaze formerly made her "cow" in self-loathing. And this time she emerges victorious. She forces Darrell to "drop his eyes" in submission to *her* feminine authority, and then she takes Phyllis away. As readers know, however, Gertrude is still too late: Phyllis dies. Why exactly she dies is the cause of much debate among critics. Elizabeth F. Evans ("We Are Photographers, Not Mountebanks!"), for example, argues that Phyllis is punished for being a "fallen" woman, while Deborah Nord (*Walking the Victorian Streets*) adds that Phyllis's death reaffirms the rigid gender barriers limiting women's access to the city.[61] While the gendered spheres (and masculine desire, specifically) are most certainly a factor in Phyllis's downfall, it is still more important to understand her death as symbolic of women's fate outside of sisterly kinship. In lying to and running away from her sisters, Phyllis abandons the consanguineal bond in favour of the conventional heterosexual plot. As we know from Darrell's previous encounters with Gertrude, this plot transforms women into sexualized objects befitting masculine expectations and enjoyment. As such, Phyllis effectively chooses a romantic narrative that kills off, rather than recognizes, her feminine subjectivity.

In stressing the primacy of kinship bonds, Levy's novel also offers a very different theory of the relationship between women and economics as compared with those put forth by contemporary Marxist feminists after Friedrich Engels. In his touchstone text *The Origin of the Family, Private Property and the State* (1884), Engels paved the way for gender and economic theorists to come together in their joint critique of capitalism and its devastating impact upon women's relationship with property and the family. Drawing heavily on Lewis Henry Morgan's anthropological history *Ancient Society* (1877), Engels charts the history of human civilization, from savagery and barbarism, as dependent upon the gradual formation of private property and accumulative capital (*The Origin of the Family, Private Property and the State*, 57). For Engels, this latter stage of so-called economic "civilization" also corresponds with the rise of the conjugal family and the subsequent "world *historic defeat* of the *female* sex" (87).[62] Citing Marx, Engels explains women's sexual subordination as analogous to the capitalist's exploitation of labour: "The modern family contains in germ not only slavery (servitus), but also serfdom, since from the beginning it is related to agricultural services. It contains in miniature all the contradictions which later extend throughout society and its state" (Marx quoted in Engels, 88). This history thus frames economics as the primary force both shaping familial bonds and therein driving women's subsequent subordination to masculine capital. Contrary to Engels, however, Levy imagines how the family – or kinship structures, more specifically – might revise women's economic opportunities and even socio-economic mobility. Her innovative take on the Victorian family points to what Gayle Rubin later describes as the social formation of kinship and its influence upon sexual/economic exchange. Rubin's 1975 essay "The Traffic in Women" is now infamous for its challenge to classical Marxism as "fail[ing] … to fully express or conceptualize sex oppression" (107). This "failure," Rubin continues, is due largely to Marxists' inability to think of sex as a social structure shaping economics.[63] It is this ancient history of kinship, not capitalism, that determines individuals' relationships to bloodlines and private property, and for this reason Rubin insists that we "look for the ultimate locus of women's oppression within the traffic in women, rather than within the traffic of merchandise" (118). One must, in other words, look to kinship systems in order to understand women's socio-economic oppression, as well as women's rights to self-possessed exchange and the modern contract.

In its affirmative representation of sisterly cooperation, Levy's *The Romance of a Shop* thus reverses the model of economic determinism made popular by many Marxist feminists. Whereas the latter focus on capitalism as the source of sexual oppression, Levy instead looks to the social structure of kinship as shaping gender roles and, through these roles, women's access to socio-economic opportunities within and beyond the domestic sphere. Her emphasis on the sororal economy, both in terms of gender and economics, enables Levy to imagine an alternative domestic plot that does not preclude women's careers after marriage. After all, *The Romance of a Shop* concludes with the remaining three sisters happily married, a conjugal plot that for many critics limits the feminist potential of Levy's narrative. Deborah Parsons, for example, complains that "Levy backs down from the implied female radicalism by concluding the girls' stories with the conventional endings of marriage or fall and death" (*Streetwalking the Metropolis*, 93). Victorian reviewers were equally conflicted in their responses to the novel's conclusion: the *Jewish Chronicle* writes, "[f]or the Lorimer girls work meant a very novel and interesting life, the finding of new friends, and for each the unfolding of a love story" ("The Romance of a Shop" [1888], 196), while *The Academy*'s George Saintsbury is much more critical in his complaint that "Miss Levy really must not fold her heroine to her lover's breast at the end 'like a tired child'" ("New Novels" [1888], 198). Yet these critics fail to appreciate how the novel's unfailing investment in sisterly kinship culminates in a very different or feminist romance plot. Even Fanny, the most traditional of sisters, must first procure her sisters' support before marrying her lover: though Fanny "would have dearly liked a 'white wedding' and secretly hoped that the sisters would suggest what she dared not," the sisters are themselves more "practical" in their approach and send Fanny "soberly to the altar in a dark green travelling dress, which was becoming if not festive" (158). It is her sisters, and not her husband, who set the tone for Fanny's married life.

Far from a retreat (per Parsons's analysis), Levy's novel instead offers a radical revision to the marriage plot that preserves both the lateral consanguineal bond between sisters and, with it, the support necessary to women's continued sexual and economic autonomy, even after they become wives and mothers.[64] In contemplating her newborn son, for example, Gertrude wonders if he "will prove to have inherited his father's scientific tastes, or the literary tendencies of his mother" (193). Within the patriarchal family, the child is defined through his linear relationship to the father, or the male bloodline. But in reclaiming her son as possible heir to her talents, Gertrude instead positions herself as part of a matrilineal kinship system in which women's reproductive labour is by and for themselves. In this inalienable feminine bond, children are defined through the mother and her sisters. That Gertrude's child is male is important insofar as it signals how matrilineal descent is not governed by heteronormative sexual difference (i.e., precluding lineage from mothers to sons).[65]After all, heterosexual difference only matters in patriarchal structures of kinship where tracing descent involves a division between sexual reproductive labour (mother) and the object choice (father).[66] By contrast, the matrilineal kinship system privileges female bloodlines and thereby defines children through their mother (reproduction) – not the father (object choice) – and does not discriminate between daughters and sons (both are heirs to their mother). The female-centred family, refigured here as women's bonds through children, instead allows for a new sexual economy that is "gender indifferent," or not limited by the sex of partner.[67] Rather, a woman enjoys absolute freedom of sexual choice and the object of her affection matters only insofar as he/she/it/etc. contributes to, or detracts from, her pleasure.[68] Looking toward a matriarchal future, then, Levy's *The Romance of a Shop* promises a new romantic narrative wherein the self-possessed woman is free to exchange with whomever (or whatever) brings her pleasure. Lucy, for example, asserts this right to sexual choice when defending her impending marriage to Frank Jermyn in terms of love. Upon learning of the engagement, Aunt Caroline promptly asks if the sisters "have found out who Mr. Jermyn *is*?" in which her reference to "who one is" serves as code for socio-economic class and those other financial forces that compel women to marry for support as opposed to desire. Yet Lucy is insistent in her rebuttal, "We never wanted to know," using the plural pronoun ("we") as shorthand for both the sororal bond and/as women's right to self-determination (156).

While sisterly kinship acts as a protective barrier against sexual objectification or appropriation, the new contractual marriage plot still depends upon the partner's respect for, and exchange with, the self-possessed female subject. Such an exchange can be seen in Gertrude's relationship with Lord Watergate. Toward the end of the novel, the newlyweds unhappily find themselves at a dinner party with Sydney Darrell, against whom Gertrude still holds a grudge regarding Phyllis's death. Upon spotting her old nemesis, Gertrude "turn[s] pale" and "los[es] the thread of her discourse, and her appetite," while Darrell, by contrast, simply continues "on eating his dinner and looking into his neighbor's eyes, in apparent unconsciousness of, or unconcern at, the Watergates' proximity" (194). The Dandy-figure is still, as much as ever, oblivious to the feelings of women in his company, and so a desperate Gertrude must look to her husband for mutual understanding: "looking up into his face, into the lucid depths of his eyes, [Gertrude] felt all that was mean and petty and bitter in life fade away into nothingness" (192). George Saintsbury objects to the image of Gertrude as a "tired child" ("New Novels" [1888], 192), but his reading forgets that our heroine is, by this point, exhausted by the death of her sister Phyllis and, also, overwhelmed by her own feelings of desire for Lord Watergate – feelings she has spent the better part of the novel trying to suppress. Consequently, Lord Watergate's embrace is quite literally an example of male support for the female-identified woman. Readers will also note how Lord Watergate, in looking at Gertrude's "weary, haggard face," acknowledges, rather than disavows, "the pathetic look in her eyes as they yearned towards him in entreaty, in reliance, – in love" (192). This exchange is yet another example of his willing participation in the modern sexual contract: he looks into her eyes and recognizes both her "weary" sadness for her sister, as well as her "yearning" desire for him. It is significant, moreover, that Gertrude gives into her desire only *after* she is certain of both his respect for her and for her sororal loyalty – she has not forgotten that her sister's death was precipitated by a man who disavowed women's bonds and, with them, feminine subjectivity.

In rewriting the marriage plot as a story of mutual contract, Levy makes possible a new and open ending in which wives and mothers might continue to pursue their professional careers beyond the domestic sphere. Just as sexual contract is defined by the mutual recognition of women's right to self-possessed exchange of (re)production and pleasure, so too then must its narrative form (or the new marriage plot) avow women's right to continued work and economic agency. In her epilogue to *The Romance of a Shop*, Levy paints a picture of this modern conjugal plot, with a twist: after informing the readers that Gertrude and Lucy are also happily married, the narrator quickly shifts to a discussion of the photography studio, which "is let to an enterprising young photographer," and then adds that the flat above remains vacant (194). This closing image privileges the space of work alongside the domestic sphere – a work/home balancing act that the sisters themselves continue to practise even after they are married. Lucy continues her employment as professional photographer, having even "succumbed to the modern practice of specializing, and only the other day carried off a medal for photographs of young children from an industrial exhibition" (193), while Gertrude is now a writer, which was always her preferred profession (54). The sisters' continued work thus contravenes what Ann Ardis describes as the "traditional" romance plot in which the chosen bride is returned to the domestic sphere to live out her destiny as wife and mother. In their continued appeal to sisterly bonds, the Lorimer sisters are instead more akin to a new generation of feminist writers and activists who, as Ardis also explains, supported each other's "'monstrous' ambitions to be something – anything – besides wives and mothers" (*New Women, New Novels*, 134).[69] Levy's novel is still surprisingly distinct, even within this historical context, because of its bold representation of sisterly bonds in support of wives' continued professional ambitions. Even Aunt Caroline, that unrelenting advocate of the old patriarchal order, cannot help but admire the Lorimers' accomplishments, and "speaks with the greatest respect of her niece, Lady Watergate, though she has been heard to comment unfavourably on the shabbiness of the furniture in Sussex Place" (193–4). This latter point regarding conspicuous consumption is a firm reminder of Aunt Caroline's material aspirations (the kind of values which lead to mercenary marriages), but even she is forced to admit within polite circles this new breed of professional woman (both "lady" and writer). Times are changing by the novel's end, and even this begrudging recognition from the "Old Guard" implies new hope for alternative narratives in which married women enjoy fluid movement between the domestic and public spheres.

Despite its happy and hopeful picture of the Lorimer sisters' marriage plots, however, Levy's *The Romance of a Shop* nonetheless retains a certain ambivalence as the narrative draws to a close. Returning to the now-empty flat at 20B Upper Baker Street, the novel's "epilogue" resists closure by leaving the fate of the flat open-ended: "When last I passed the house they were to let unfurnished, with great fly-blown bills in blank casements" (194).[70] By also omitting the shopkeeper's gender, this last scene hints at a possible feminist future where, with the advent of the modern contract, gender difference is irrelevant and no longer limits women's movement between home and work. Still, the more cynical reader might insist that this omission is a sign of Levy's hesitation or, worse yet, pessimism regarding the self-empowered working woman's future. Indeed, our fears would almost seem to come to fruition with Darrell's return, earlier in this same epilogue. However, the man who stands out most in that dinner scene is Gertrude's supportive husband, whose "reassuring glances" set the stage for future men to advocate on behalf of their wives and sisterly bonds. So if there is a note of uncertainty in this last chapter of *The Romance of a Shop*, then it must be attributed to the men who continue to populate domestic spaces and plots. Readers are left to wonder whether these men will choose – or contract with – the empowered New Woman. The closing image of the unlet flat leaves this question open-ended, as if contingent upon those domestic arrangements in which supportive partners (and readers) recognize women's right to contract in and beyond the domestic sphere.

Conclusion: Sisters in the City

In titling her novel "The Romance of a Shop," Amy Levy cleverly signals to readers that the urban marketplace and the shop, in particular, play an integral role in rewriting the terms of domestic romance and women's access to the modern (sexual/economic) contract. The gendered gaze and visual consumption, specifically, figure largely throughout the novel as one way to imagine this self-possessed New Woman and her bold claim to the urban marketplace, with its many opportunities as well as pleasures. During her second omnibus ride, for example, Gertrude spots Frank who then waves his sombrero "in exaggerated salute" (99). Given his unwavering support of the Lorimer sisters throughout their time in the city, Fred's excessive greeting implies both a moment of humour but also, and more important, an undeniable gesture of mutual recognition – if not respect ("salute"). He is, in other words, among a new generation of liberal-minded men who welcome the New Woman's presence in the modern city and her demand for equal economic and visual exchange. Yet this visual encounter with the progressive "new man" is quickly overshadowed by Aunt Caroline, whose "frozen stare of nonrecognition" (99) immediately reminds Gertrude of the "old" patrilineal economy which denies – or, rather, refuses to acknowledge – women's right to urban agency. Thanks to her aunt's surprise appearance, Gertrude is reminded that she cannot ignore the social structures of kinship, especially those sororal ties that bind her to other women; she must, therefore, return to the collaborative space of women's work as necessary support for her continued effort to assert her role as an equal subject in modern economies of gendered exchange, including her later interactions with Lord Watergate or Sidney Darrell, men who either engage the sisters in a mutual gaze (even salute, as Frank does), or who look at and reinforce the idea of women as objects circulated among men.

Levy's novel, with its powerful representation of the female-centred family, poses interesting possibilities for a feminist model of inheritance that is open-ended in its vision of gendered plot. I have in this chapter argued extensively for the important role that sisterly kinship played in rewriting fin-de-siècle women's relationship to the modern economic and sexual marketplace. In *The Romance of a Shop*, this sororal bond underwrites the sisters' fluid movement between gendered spaces and, ultimately, their ability to reimagine a marriage plot that does not preclude women's professional aspirations. Indeed, the sisterly bond facilitates women's reclamation of their (re)productive and pleasurable bodies, and better yet, their self-possession then enables women to look back at and demand mutual exchange between men *and* women. Still, to say that *The Romance of a Shop*'s rather ambivalent ending throws into question any linear vision of feminist inheritance after the revised domestic plot would not be unwarranted. The shopkeeper's gender is withheld and the unlet flat remains an open-ended question, as if waiting for modern women's unlimited access to the city and work, as well as alternative domesticities. However, this unresolved ending also looks outward toward larger and ongoing efforts by feminist writers to disrupt social and sexual narratives for women. *The Romance of a Shop* thereby leaves open the gendered possibilities of women in work and love, as if to say that professional women's stories will depend upon collaboration with generations of feminists who continue to challenge the old narratives (the Aunt Caroline Pratts and Sydney Darrells) restricting women to domestic spaces/plots. Yet feminist writers' contribution to this conversation and the stories generated through dialogical collaboration across generations will vary depending upon the specific site of market intervention, thus resisting any form of cumulative or "progressive" descent from woman to woman. The next chapter, on George Egerton (Mary Chavelita Dunn Bright), signals this diversity in feminist strategies of cooperation by shifting attention to modern women who are not afraid to traverse domestic and even national boundaries in search of professional mobility within the urban marketplace.

With its bold representation of women's visual pleasure, *The Romance of a Shop* raises questions about the possibility of a female *flâneur* (or *flâneuse*) and, more specifically, about women's contribution to new and distinctly feminine forms of urban (visual) consumption. The *flâneur* was, by the end of the century, the quintessential urban wanderer whose gaze was firmly associated with both visual pleasure and authority. In tracing the origins of this figure, critics often cite nineteenth-century Parisian poet Charles Baudelaire's essay "The Painter of Modern Life" (1863).[71] This is not to say that Baudelaire was the first to discuss idle urban spectatorship, or "*flânerie*." In *Streetwalking the Metropolis*, for example, Deborah Parsons argues that the figure can be traced back to an 1806 French pamphlet "detailing a day in the life of a *flâneur*, M. Bonhomme" (17). But it was Baudelaire's essay "The Painter of Modern Life" (1863) that cemented the *flâneur*'s recognition among international audiences, including English authors and readers. His essay helped popularize the figure's definition as an urban man who aimlessly wanders the city streets in search of visual stimulation. Yet the *flâneur*'s relationship to urban space is complex, caught somewhere between intimacy and distance, as a consequence of mounting anxieties toward the homogenizing crowd. In Baudelaire's hands, this unease gives way to a mode of visual consumption that draws stimulation from the urban mass, but that also, and simultaneously, polices the distance between his privileged position as subject and the object of his gaze.[72] The crowd is described as "his element, as the air is that of birds and water of fishes," and "[h]is passion and his profession are to become one flesh with the crowd" ("The Painter of Modern Life," 9).[73] Still, his communion with the crowd is limited by a persistent desire "to see the world, to be at the centre of the world, and yet to remain hidden from the world" (9). He is, as Baudelaire continues, "a prince who everywhere rejoices in his incognito" (9). This history is important for it also explains why so many feminist critics, such as Janet Wolff (*Feminine Sentences*) and Griselda Pollock ("Modernity and the Spaces of Femininity"), deny the possibly of feminine *flânerie*, for as they explain, only men enjoy the privilege of leisurely and objective – or objectifying – urban consumption.[74]

The Romance of a Shop is markedly distinct from such contemporary accounts of modern *flânerie* as a form of distanced consumption as power.[75] Instead, Levy's novel suggests how women must practise different modes of urban mobility and pleasurable consumption that are situated in the material conditions of gender and economics. Even the fact that Gertrude chooses to travel by omnibus would immediately distinguish her from the male wanderer. As Ana Perejo Vadillo explains, the *flâneur* exerts authority through aimless walking, but transit "passengers are not in control of their journeys" and thus have no authority over urban space or the crowd (*Women Poets and Urban Aestheticism*, 25). Though transit provides a temporary form of urban mobility, the sisters' lasting transformation of gendered economies depends upon their position within an alternative and female-centred kinship system. This is also why the vast majority of the sisters' visual exchanges takes place within domestic interiors, as if to remind readers of the familial systems underwriting sexual/economic exchange. While men like Darrell might refuse the opportunity for mutual exchange with such self-possessed women, still other 'new men' of the future – including Lord Watergate and Frank Jermyn – are eager to participate in modern marriage plots that respect women's right to contract.

The novel's closing picture of self-possessed working women is very much in the spirit of fin-de-siècle feminist fiction and New Woman novels which, after Schreiner, worked hard to envision for ambitious young women a new path to professional opportunities. In Levy's hands, the modern New Woman's labour is her own and she need not, therefore, sacrifice body and blood (or family) for restrictive domestic plots. *The Romance of a Shop* instead proposes a new model of "womanhood" for subsequent generations of feminist readers and activists working together, in a common "sisterhood," for both family and careers. Almost ten years later, Egerton would seem to answer Levy's call for an empowered woman whose participation in the modern workforce affords her easy movement between the private and public spheres. But whereas Levy's heroines look to sororal kinship as support for their urban mobility, Egerton's ambitious women instead embrace professional alliances as a means to access the cityscape and, through which, to write new gendered and economic roles. The next chapter will look at how Egerton's 1898 publication of *The Wheel of God* presents readers with a new cosmopolitan woman whose feminist consciousness underwrites fluid movement between domestic spaces/plots and modern careers as typists, nurses, professional writers and journalists.

3 Cosmopolitan Communities of Female Professionals

Life [in NYC] seemed less concrete, less inside the houses and warehouses; it was everywhere, pounding like a gigantic steam-hammer, full speed, in the air, in the streets – insistent, noisy, attention-compelling.

– George Egerton, *The Wheel of God*

The way her silky garments undulate
It seems she's dancing as she walks along
Like serpents that the sacred charmers make
to move in rhythms of their waving wands

– Charles Baudelaire, "The Way Her Silky Garments" in *The Flowers of Evil*

On 1 August 1897, "George Egerton" wrote to her editor Grant Richards promising imminent submission of her new novel, *The Wheel of God*. In the letter, she described the novel as a "study of a woman's life, [showing the] development of her character through outward circumstances, the elimination of [the] baser part of her dual nature" (quoted in Margaret D. Stetz, "'George Egerton,'" 114). "George Egerton" is, of course, the pen-name for Mary Chavelita Dunne Bright, best known for her popular collection of short stories, *Keynotes*, published five years earlier in 1893.[1] With the publication of *The Wheel of God* in 1898, the author made good on her promise to Richards and delivered an extended "life study" of a modern woman named Mary Desmond (later, Mary Marriott) who struggles to define herself (her "character") in the midst of changing social institutions of gender and women's work.[2] So-called life novels were already, by the century's end, an established means through which to treat modern-day issues, such as the marriage question or women's employment equity, through a focused study of a single character's social development – contemporary examples combining both themes include Ella Hepworth Dixon's *The Story of a Modern Woman* (1894) as well as Grant Allen's *The Woman Who Did* (1895) and *The Type-Writer Girl* (1897).[3] While *The Wheel of God* did not necessarily revise the form or content associated with this novel genre, it nonetheless capitalized on its popularity in order to place women's struggle with "outward circumstances," including the gendered marketplace, front and centre in the cultural imagination. Egerton's narrative focuses on the female protagonist's effort to navigate the modern cityscape and, therein, to capitalize on the many opportunities for work in the proliferating professions open to women at the turn of the century.

This chapter will look at how the modern woman's urban mobility is mediated by the interdependent relationship between work and gender. *Critical Alliances* has, up until this point, focused on late-Victorian women's collaborative efforts to rewrite domestic plots. George Egerton's feminist fiction shows us that fin-de-siècle women also asserted a collective claim upon the gendered city and the economic opportunities promised by the urban marketplace. In *The Romance of a Shop*, the Lorimer sisters find support in each other or feminist kinship while moving between private and public spaces. Following in Levy's footsteps, Egerton places the public cityscape at the very heart of late-Victorian feminists' efforts to rewrite dominant narratives of gendered labour and women's work, specifically. In boldly staking her claim to the urban workforce, *The Wheel of God*'s heroine, Mary Desmond, shows fin-de-siècle readers how the female professional must also defy dominant gender roles and gendered modes of exchange, including the *flâneur*-figure's sexualized gaze limiting women's access to public spaces and associated economic opportunities. In the poem "The Way Her Silky Garments" (1857), excerpted above, Baudelaire describes the *flâneur*'s expectation that the urban woman serve as an object for his visual consumption, no matter whether this consumption be an act of desire or repulsion; while her garments are, for example, a source of sexual fascination, there is still a seeming "serpentine" danger in her assertive expression of feminine desire as she moves through this shared urban space and tempts his gaze. Still, this male observer understands the seductive power of feminine artifice and can therefore enjoy, without being overpowered by, the urban woman's "polished eyes … made of charming stones" (l. 9).[4] The *flâneur*'s gaze is, in other words, a means to sexual objectification that contains, without admitting equal respect for, women's efforts to participate in modern modes of urban (visual) exchange. This poem and its representation of cross-sex interaction thus begs the question, can women enjoy a form of public agency equal to that of her male *flâneur* counterpart, and if so, how might her employment in the modern workforce facilitate this shift in the gendering of cityscape?

The possibility of the *flâneuse*, as a gendered complement to the male wanderer, has motivated much debate among recent scholars. As Janet Wolff explains in her essay "The Invisible Flâneuse," "[t]here is no question of inventing the *flâneuse*; the essential point is that such a character was rendered impossible by the sexual divisions of the nineteenth century" (45).[5] The female figures who do appear in Baudelaire's writings on the cityscape include the prostitute, the widow, the old lady, the lesbian, the murder victim, and the passing unknown woman – all sexualized objects by and for masculine consumption (41). "[W]hat is missing in this literature," Wolff argues, is an account of how these women might have played an active part in shaping the modern urban experience, including first-hand or fictional narratives by feminists, or "a poem written by 'la femme passante' about her encounter with Baudelaire, perhaps" (47). Still other critics, such as Deborah Nord (*Walking the Victorian Streets*) and Judith Walkowitz (*City of Dreadful Delight*), explain how, even for those women who did venture into the public sphere, Victorian domestic ideology undercut any possibility of female *flânerie*. For Nord this means that "the *flâneuse* remains a thing of the imagination" and that "the gaslight must be enjoyed by women in private" (201–2), while Walkowitz explains how narratives of sexual danger oftentimes circulated as a means to control the increasing onslaught of women's "disorderly sexual conduct in the city," including "fashion and self display" and "non-familial attachments" (6). The present chapter takes up Wolff's challenge by reading *The Wheel of God* (1898) as interested in the idea of an urban woman whose sexual and economic demands might rival (and therein threaten) her male contemporaries. It is worth noting that Egerton herself did not consciously identify with the label "New Woman" and was even horrified, as Margaret Stetz notes, to discover that she was being compared to feminist authors such as Olive Schreiner or Sarah Grand ("'George Egerton,'" 67).[6] Yet, with its underlying critique of domestic ideology limiting women's social mobility, *The Wheel of God* in many ways builds upon the literary techniques and popular successes of earlier New Woman novels – including works by feminist authors such as Schreiner and Amy Levy, pioneers of the novel genre.[7] Still, this chapter will not force the connection between Egerton and those earlier self-proclaimed feminists by relying on the category of New Woman as a shorthand for *The Wheel of God*'s innovations in gender and economics; instead, this chapter will focus on the novel's investment in the very specific figure of the urban woman who migrates to the modern city in search of professional opportunity and socio-sexual independence. The urban marketplace, with its promise of new employment options, proved an essential factor in this independent-minded heroine's search for alternative (or nondomestic) narratives.

To reject the traditional heterosexual marriage plot is not, however, to deny the important role that love might play in the urban woman's "life story." Rather, like other feminist writers before her (especially Levy), Egerton imagines how affective bonds between women might enable its participants to move beyond, and therein rewrite, domestic plots and spaces. The novel's first book, "The Seed in the Sheath," quickly establishes that Mary's story will be driven by her overwhelming need for emotional connection; in the "Awakening" chapter, for example, Mary is not only in tune with nature's rhythms of seasonal change, but she also feels herself drawn to some kind of "great cry for love, love, love, that is as the voice of the wind, calling over the waste of the world's waters" (64).[8] However, the final two books, "The Blossom in the Bud" and "The Ripening of Fruit," are wholly preoccupied with women's migration to, and struggle to adapt within, the global metropolis. This plot trajectory thereby reminds us of what Kate Krueger and Tina O'Toole describe as the central role of the urban city in Egerton's feminist fiction. In *British Women Writers and the Short Story, 1850–1930*, Krueger explains how Egerton's unconventional heroines must participate in a process of "deterritorialization" that challenges or breaks down the gendered and economic borders limiting women's access to public spaces (105).[9] O'Toole's *The Irish New Woman* shifts the conversation to global migration and Egerton's interest in the urban encounter as mediating "fluid" or transnational subjectivities (130).[10] Both critics help us to see how Egerton's cosmopolitan woman is not a detached or transcendent figure of global mobility; rather, Mary is situated within, and often works against, the local and material conditions that make up the city and its economic relationships or opportunities.[11] Building upon the critical conversation, this chapter stresses the importance of feminine bonds, as an expression of situated gender, in mediating women's access to the modern marketplace. This gendered marketplace will push our unconventional heroine to find emotional and economic support within a community of fellow working women, as opposed to a sense of self defined through cross-sex bonds or the heterosexual marriage plot.

It is also this emphasis on cooperation among professional women that marks *The Wheel of God* as a new and innovative fin-de-siècle feminist text. Sections one and two of this chapter will therefore position

Egerton as part of a new branch or late-Victorian movement of women writers interested in female-female bonds as underwriting women's economic mobility, including access to the global city. Egerton is, in other words, different from earlier generations of feminist writers, as well as many contemporaries even, by virtue of her celebration of cosmopolitan communities of professional working women. My use of the term "cosmopolitan" to describe Egerton's feminist fiction is influenced by Deborah Parsons's study *Streetwalking the Metropolis* on women and urban mobility. Parsons explains the "cosmopolitan" as a modern extension of the Victorian *flâneur*-figure, the city wanderer who enjoys a kind of power or authority of detachment and panoramic viewpoint of the city (14). What sets the cosmopolitan apart from the *flâneur*, however, is simply the scale of mobility from a single city to, now, a "host of cities" – a new form of global mobility or wandering that transcends national boundaries (14). Yet my analysis here is also influenced by Parsons's careful qualification of the gendered terms of this kind of global mobility. Women writers did not enjoy the same kind of access to detached urban authority as their male counterparts, but instead wrote about and experienced the city in very concrete or material terms. In Parsons's account, therefore, the writings by modernist women writers "emphasize the tangible and walkable metropolis rather than the conceptual and, by definition, unlocatable cosmopolis, a factor that perhaps offers some explanation for the uneasy position of women writers in canonical accounts of the 'cosmopolitan' nature of modernism" (*Streetwalking the Metropolis*, 14).[12] This chapter will use Parsons's theory of the cosmopolitan woman and her concrete interaction with the cityscape to understand women's participation in the fin-de-siècle urban marketplace (anticipating feminist innovations in the modernist period upon which *Streetwalking the Metropolis* is largely focused).

The first part of this chapter will draw upon established theories of urban *flânerie* by Baudelaire and Benjamin in order to understand how the cosmopolitan woman's urban experience is different from men's by virtue of the fact that her mobility is always mediated by gender difference. The second part of the chapter will look at how this situated relationship to the cityscape then plays a direct role in limiting the kinds of employment or professional opportunities open to women at the turn of the century. Parts two and three argue that this career-minded woman must therefore look to feminist alliances or, specifically, a cosmopolitan community of women (traversing national and even temporal boundaries) in order to negotiate the modern gendered marketplace. In thinking about Egerton's unique contribution to fin-de-siècle conversations on women's economic communities, section three of the chapter will also compare *The Wheel of God* with other late-Victorian representations of women's global mobility, including representations by Irish women writers interested in – and often writing against – female migration to the New World. Egerton's fiction certainly stands out against such works (even those by her compatriots) by virtue of its positive representation of emigration and women's access to a global city. However, *The Wheel of God* does not suggest that transatlantic relocation alone is enough for women's successful infiltration of modern careers; rather, the novel's heroine must look to other like-minded professional women as support for women's fluid movement from domestic roles to the urban marketplace with its many modern career opportunities. Like Levy before her, then, Egerton sees in feminist cooperation a way to rewrite inherited domestic plots to include new narratives on women's socio-economic and, even, cosmopolitan mobility.

In *The Wheel of God*, Egerton imagines how collaboration among middle-class professional women produces new sexual and economic opportunities and, with them, new feminist narratives. Although it begins as a global romance, the life novel quickly transitions into a story about gender consciousness and feminist cooperation.[13] In pursuit of this reading, the structure of this chapter will also, therefore, mirror the narrative of character "development through outward circumstances" (per Egerton's 1897 letter to Richards) – circumstances that include the urban conditions of gender and labour. Over the course of her life story, Mary learns to recognize the restrictive power of gender difference, as embodied by the male *flâneur*. Like Gertrude Lorimer in Levy's *The Romance of a Shop*, Mary must stare down these male *flâneur*-figures who bar her access to city space and its economic opportunities. Whereas Levy's characters find support in sisterly kinship, Egerton's unconventional heroine boldly traverses gender spheres to forge cosmopolitan bonds with other female professionals. Mary becomes, what later critics such as Walter Benjamin ("The Paris of the Second Empire in Baudelaire" [1938]) and Deborah Parsons (*Streetwalking the Metropolis*) might describe as, the female "rag-picker" working through, and rewriting, the material conditions of the cityscape limiting women's economic mobility. It is also here within the situated space of material or market encounters that Mary learns to appreciate the political potential of women's labour. She discovers that certain pink-collar professions, like typewriting, undermine her aspirations to feminist community, but thanks to her close friendship with professional writers, Mary eventually realizes a new feminist consciousness that is grounded in – and works on behalf of – political bonds between women.

1 The Modern Cosmopolitan Woman

George Egerton's novel *The Wheel of God* opens with the story of migration as a dual solution to the problems of urban poverty and women's limited professional mobility. In an early scene, the novel's young protagonist Mary Desmond is sent into the streets of Dublin to beg for financial assistance from family and friends, only to discover the Irish city is a space of "squalor and sordid poverty" exacerbated by economic divestment (12).[14] Walking "as in a dream of her own," the protagonist offers an impressionistic "history" of the city that implicitly frames the "neglected" children and "yelping curs" as the unhappy products of an economy in decline, leftover ruins not unlike the "houses and courts where the Huguenots had lived" or the now vermin-filled mansions that remind her of "long-vanished tenants" (13). Through this formative encounter with the Meath Street poor and abandoned, Mary discovers that she must look elsewhere – or westward, to the American metropolis – for an economic future, and so in a later chapter and at the ripe age of seventeen she sets sail for New York City and therein "pass[es] from girlhood to womanhood" (64).[15] Book one closes with a picture of Mary "trembling" with excitement as she looks forward to what she thinks will be the beginning of her own fairy-tale adventure, complete with "castles in the fire, luring dragons, and a knight in virgin armour, pricking along the road of life to strains of romantic music" (63). Mary's romantic aspirations are not unusual, for as Christine Stansell explains, the American city represented newfound freedom from both the "confines of the village and the drudgery of the cottier's plot," as well as a chance to "[marry] better than one could ever hope to in Ireland" (*City of Women*, 84). As evidence Stansell cites an 1850 letter in which a young woman from County Cork tells her father that "this [America] is a good place and a good country" for the female migrant: "The Lord had not it destined for me to get married to Some Loammun or another at home that after a few months he and I may be an Incumberance upon you or perhaps in the poor house" (Diarmaid O Muirithe, *A Seat behind the Coachman*, 138, 140). In *The Wheel of God*, however, the narrator's editorial insertion forewarns readers that the subsequent life journey will not, in fact, be an "answer" to the "great cry for love ... calling over the waste of the world's waters" (64). The story that follows instead focuses on the single woman as she struggles to find work and happiness in the modern American metropolis.

It is worth mentioning at this point that there are significant areas of overlap between Egerton's own biography and some of the key events in her "life novel." Born in 1859 in Melbourne, Australia to an

Irish father, Captain John J. Dunne, and Welsh mother, Isabel George, Egerton quickly learned to think of herself in cosmopolitan terms. It was not long before her father's financial troubles forced the family to move among New Zealand, Chile, and finally Ireland, where Egerton spent the majority of her youth. In all of her fiction, Egerton drew upon these formative experiences as material for her literary representations of woman's "character" (1 August 1897 letter to Grant Richards) at the turn of the century. Like Mary Desmond, Egerton spent her young adulthood travelling between London and New York in search of employment (after her mother's death in 1875),[16] and she was also very unlucky in love. In 1887 she left New York for Norway with her lover Henry Higginson (who was already married), but after he passed away in 1889, Egerton returned to England and, in 1891, married George Egerton Clairmonte (a source of inspiration for her pen-name).[17] After her husband's numerous infidelities, Egerton eventually left Clairmonte, and the two were officially divorced in 1895. *The Wheel of God* replays the author's own global travels to Ireland, New York, and England, for example, and while elements of Higginson can be glimpsed in the loveless D'Arcy, Clairmonte is clearly the inspiration for the unfaithful spendthrift, Cecil Marriott.[18] One theme emerges through both fictional and biographical narrative arcs: women must travel far and wide, traversing national and gendered borders, in search of professional and emotional fulfilment.

Irish immigration has always been recognized as one of the critical forces contributing to New York City's transformation into a world-class metropolis by the end of the nineteenth century.[19] This history of relocation can be attributed to catastrophic events such as the Great Famine of 1845–52, during which as many as 1.5 million Irish left for the United States,[20] or the later Land Wars 1870s–90s, which saw another wave of Irish newcomers fleeing civil unrest and the poverty of the "long depression." An 1875 census counts 199,084 foreign-born Irish among the city's 1,041,886 total population (*Census of the State of New York for 1875* [1875], 37), and these high numbers hold strong to 1880, in which another census lists 198,595 Irish-born immigrants living in Manhattan and 78,814 in Brooklyn (Ronald Bayor and Timothy J. Meagher, *The New York Irish*, 289).[21] These migrants came in search of the "American Dream," or the myth of opportunity and wealth as immortalized in texts such as Horatio Alger's *Ragged Dick* (1867). In his short story "Home Sickness" (1903), George Moore reflects upon the American City's role in the Irish imagination as a place of escape from both poverty and the contemplative life.[22] Suffering from an acute case of blood poisoning, the story's protagonist James Bryden leaves his Bowery home (where he has lived for the past thirteen years) and returns to Ireland in search of rest and recovered health. During his convalescence in his native Irish village, Bryden is confronted by many individuals who recycle the same myths of the west which no doubt motivated his own travels more than a decade ago. Despite Bryden's claim that the New World "isn't all you think it" (159), the Irish "peasants" still envy him and "regret ... that they had not gone to America when they were young" (161).

The American city held out particular promise to Irish women as a place of new social and sexual freedom. New York City was, as Stansell records, "full of single young women" who, by 1860, outnumbered their male counterparts five to four (*City of Women*, 83).[23] By the century's end (1900), one out of every five women (married or single) received a wage income, and 34 per cent of New York City's labour force comprised female workers (women also made up 18 per cent of the national workforce).[24] A New York City census from 1875, just prior to Mary's arrival,[25] shows that immigrants account for almost a quarter of the single working population: 24 per cent of single women and 22 per cent of single men.[26] Single men and women alike were drawn to New York City in search of new employment opportunities which accompanied the economic expansion in the latter decades of the Gilded Age. As Ronald Bayor and Timothy J. Meagher note in *The New York Irish*, "[t]he expansion of certain industries in the city, especially textiles and light manufacturing, allowed thousands of male Irish Americans to move into the lower rungs of management and middle-class respectability" (312). Women migrants also sought economic advancement by responding to the increased demand for teachers and nurses, as well as new and growing professions such as shopgirls and clerical work. Regarding the last category, *The Census of the State of New York for 1875* counts 982 males to 71 female "clerks and copyists" (secretaries and typists), but these numbers do not include in this category the even greater numbers of clerks and copyists who worked in stores (48,861 males; 2,042 females), banks (2,581 males; 18 females), express companies (118 males; 1 female), or telegraph offices (35 males; 2 females) (440). As America's capitalist economy continued to grow, so too did the number of middle-management and white-collar professions, providing female migrants such as Mary with the increased possibility of economic mobility and socio-sexual independence.

Eager to take advantage of these proliferating career options, ambitious young women were forced to reject outmoded or Old World gender roles limiting proper Victorian ladies' social mobility to domestic plots and spaces. When her law-student neighbour invites her on a day-trip to New Jersey, for example, Mary "hesitate[s]," for "the old home ideas of propriety, the chaperon idea, cropped up," but then "she wisely put them aside and consented" (*The Wheel of God*, 128). The narrator's approval of Mary's "wise" decision to put aside such prohibitive concerns implies a marked difference between American and European attitudes toward female chaperonage. The assumption that American culture is more permissive or progressive regarding women's public mobility is something that expatriate author Henry James wrote about extensively in his own late-nineteenth-century fiction. In *The Portrait of a Lady* (1881), Isabel Archer is surprised to find that her cousin Ralph Touchett disapproves of her and Henrietta Stackpole's plans to travel through London without an escort: "Do you mean it's improper?" Isabel asks, adding that "[Henrietta] has travelled over the whole American continent and can at least find her way about this minute island" (136). James's eponymous heroine Daisy Miller also discovers, at great personal cost, that her European friends are scandalized by her very American assumption of physical and sexual agency: "Flirting is a purely American custom; it doesn't exist here," Winterbourne explains to the eponymous heroine, "So when you show yourself in public with Mr. Giovanelli, and without your mother – " "Gracious!" (*Daisy Miller* [1879], 86).

Egerton's protagonist, Mary, will not go unchallenged in her effort to access urban spaces. Early into her stay in New York City, Mary takes to the streets in search of some form of mental relief from her exhausting work as a typist, but then she quickly discovers that the commercial districts such as Broadway are filled with men who "stared so" (*The Wheel of God*, 87). Her later migration to London, akin to a reverse migration back to the Old World, suggests an effort to return to, and directly challenge, traditional gender roles. Early into this return, Mary finds herself missing the "colour" and "polyglot atmosphere" of New York City (146) and concludes that "one felt more at home in America" (147). However, her nostalgic reverie is abruptly disturbed by the revelation of a passing man whose gaze serves as a stark reminder that sexual objectification is a constant risk faced by women within any city: Mary "felt his eyes run over her," and "[a]n overpowering, violent sense of irritation seized her" (147). Full of indignation, Mary looks back and both visually as well as metaphorically refuses the man's unwelcomed advances: "Why should he come and stare at her?" she thinks to herself before "[s]he turned and looked at him" (147). Her time spent in the American metropolis has clearly taught Mary a thing or two about women's ongoing need to refuse those traditional gender roles barring women's equal access to the cityscape.

Through such references to the masculine gaze, Egerton's novel invokes a much longer and complicated body of writing on the *flâneur* figure and the socio-sexual power dynamics underwriting urban mobility. This literary tradition is often traced back to Baudelaire's 1863 essay, "The Painter of Modern Life," which famously defined this urban figure as a "passionate spectator" and "a prince who everywhere rejoices in his incognito" (9). Baudelaire's emphasis upon seeing without being seen (his "incognito" Prince) transforms urban experience – both cosmopolitanism and *flânerie* – into an expression of gendered and economic authority. Judith Walkowitz (*City of Dreadful Delight*) describes this as the "powerful streak of voyeurism" that both Victorian cosmopolitanism and urban *flânerie* share in common, and that makes both a distinctly bourgeoisie masculine mode of experience (16).[27] Yet the turn to detached authority can also be understood as the *flâneur*'s defence mechanism against the overwhelming and homogenizing pressures of the urban mass. In "The Paris of the Second Empire in Baudelaire" (1938), for example, Benjamin draws a distinction between the pedestrian, who "wedge[s] himself into the crowd," and Baudelaire's *flâneur*, "who demand[s] elbow room and [is] unwilling to forgo the life of a gentleman of leisure" (30).[28] Benjamin's account of the urban traveller's need for visual distance effectively echoes fin-de-siècle sociologist Georg Simmel's discussion in "The Metropolis and Mental Life" (1903), on how the mental faculties (as opposed to the heart) serve as a barrier "protecting" the observer "against the threatening currents and discrepancies of his external environment" (*The Sociology of Georg Simmel* [1950], 410). Egerton's novel, by contrast, describes a career woman who strives for distance, only to fall back upon and therein tacitly admit her situatedness. In one powerful scene, in the New York City section, Mary attempts a walk "down Broadway" only to find that the street is "thronged with men" who make it "difficult" for her to negotiate this urban space (*The Wheel of God*, 139). Though she disregards Old World propriety without any subsequent regret, Mary's access to the modern city is not, in other words, without its gendered obstacles. She cannot make her way through the city street without feeling that her sexual autonomy and, with it, her status as a respectable lady are somehow under threat by those who "stare" at her and turn her into an object for masculine visual pleasure. She is, instead, forced to negotiate a masculine gaze that challenges her right to urban subjectivity and thereby denies her equal participation in visual exchange.

Though she is sexually situated and suspect, the urban woman can still look to class difference as protection against the homogenizing masses. In Dorothy Richardson's *The Long Day* (1905), for example, the unnamed narrator-heroine makes her way through Greenwich Village at midnight in search of a Working Girl's Home, only to be confronted by an older vagrant woman who warns her that "it's late for a lady to be out, with the streets full of drunks and lazy longshoremen; and I know you *be* a lady" (145). The elder woman's allusion to fallenness should serve as a deterrent, but the narrator instead seizes the (socio-economic) high ground by escorting this "strange chaperon" to shelter for a "good meal and a hot cup of coffee" (148) and then gives a "twenty-five-cent piece" to the "poor creature" upon leaving (149). In Egerton's *The Wheel of God*, the working woman's chosen route through the city serves as a similar allusion to prevailing social narratives on the intersections between gender and class status. Though readers are given only the slightest clue as to the location of Mary's place of employment (somewhere along Canal Street, close to Broadway), the novel is very specific with regard to her flat, which "was in Seventh Avenue, between block twelve and thirteen – it was like living in a slum" (87). Even more important, however, is the detail given regarding her commute home: she "used to avoid Broadway going home," and would instead "go along Bleeker Street and Lower Fifth Avenue until she reached Thirteenth Street" (87).[29] Mary's chosen route cuts through Washington Square Park and thereby takes her past some of the richest neighbourhoods in the city.[30] The prestige associated with Washington Square in the nineteenth century is well-catalogued in works by Henry James (*Washington Square* [1880]) and Edith Wharton (*The Age of Innocence* [1920]),[31] while its outlying areas were much more mixed in terms of class and culture (hence Mary's ability to live in Greenwich Village).[32] By the latter decades of the century, the park also saw an influx of Bohemian residents and genteel poverty.[33] It is this latter group to whom Mary is particularly drawn during her urban commute. During a stopover in the park one humid July afternoon, for example, Mary is struck by how the "'coloured ladies' on the stoops, or lolling in the doorways, or gossiping from the windows had muslin 'waists' or print matinees, whilst her beige gown stuck to her shoulders" (125). For critics such as Tina O'Toole (*The Irish New Woman*), Egerton's cosmopolitan woman would seem to transcend racial difference insofar as Mary "identifies more with the African Americans … than with the English people she encounters" within the city (145).[34] Yet any such progressive reading is undone by the fact that Mary's subsequent reflection emphasizes economic difference, as opposed to empathetic identification that transcends material conditions such as class (to recall Parsons' theory of women's situated cosmopolitanism). It is the next line – "No season is favourable to genteel poverty" (*The Wheel of God*, 125) – that betrays Mary's socio-economic ambitions. With her beige dress sticking to her, Mary is clearly the implied "genteel" individual; yet she cannot help but compare herself to, and admire, the African American women who do a much better job of making the most out of a difficult situation, both in terms of work and fashion. Far from a utopian or multicultural bond, Mary's implicit comparison is instead a reminder of the physical (her rumpled dress) and social (class ambiguity) discomfort imposed upon the working woman. Her chosen route through Washington Square and her subsequent study of the African American women populating its doorsteps are telling examples of an underlying desire for a class status which ensures her distance from any homogenizing or integrated crowd.

Whether travelling by foot or public transit, Egerton's heroine is still forced to contend with her fellow city subjects, and it is this persistent situatedness that then inspires her search for an alternative or distinctly "feminine" mode of urban mobility. The same passage from the New York City section notes that Mary's work is right by an elevated train (86), which by the 1880s would have a run from Broadway West, to Third Street, and up Sixth Avenue, all the way past her apartment and up to 59th Street.[35] Travel by train would seem to position Mary above the surrounding cityscape and its inhabitants, giving her the kind of spatial distance typically associated with urban *flânerie*.[36] Yet *The Wheel of God* only recounts Mary's New York City commute by foot, and even in the later London chapters, when she does travel by omnibus, Mary cannot escape the urban crowd as it "presse[s] forward," forcing her to "[shrink] back" as if in protection (153). She tries, in one of the early London scenes, to rise above the traffic by "[going] on the top of the bus, although the conductor had looked surprised," but even there she cannot transcend the urban traffic that, like a "great heart," "sen[ds] a shock right through all London" and makes her feel both "curious" and "dizzy" at the same time (152). By the century's end, omnibuses were forced to maintain low fees in order to compete with newer forms of mass transit (including trams and the underground train), making it the favoured mode of transportation for working- and lower-middle-class commuters.[37] As London's population neared five million by the 1880s,[38] public transportation contributed to the city's increasing congestion, and it also promised a quick means of escape to the city's surrounding suburbs for those elite travellers who could afford the higher train fare.[39] Mary's short trip by omnibus from Goodge Street ("running into Tottenham Court Road" [151]) up to and along Gower Street thus serves as an acute reminder that the suburban escape was beyond the reach of most working commuters. By comparing London with New

York City, *The Wheel of God* also implicitly celebrates the latter as representative of a certain mobility that seems to be lacking in the Old World. Mary herself "define[s] the difference" as a question of women's employment opportunities: "She felt that she would not dare mount one of the stairs here and boldly ask for work, as she had done in New York, relying on her need and her personality to awaken an interest, even though only momentary" (146).

To effectively navigate these gendered city spaces, and to take advantage of the economic mobility promised by the urban marketplace, Mary will have to look to affective bonds between professional women for social and sexual support. This positive revaluation of the cosmopolitan woman's situated relationships, and their role in mediating feminine mobility within the cityscape, is best illustrated by Mary's early and formative friendship with fellow typist "Sep" (Septima). The two women first bond following a chance encounter amid a "compact mass" of people outside of Macy's on Sixth Avenue one Christmas Day (92),[40] and as they both make their way through the "impossible" crowd Mary gradually sheds her "overpowering sense of loneliness" (92). She instead looks into Sep's "brilliant" eyes (like "stars in her odd little soft face") and feels "something vibrant, glad, emanat[ing] from [Sep] to Mary and thaw[ing] the gathering ice in her [Mary]" (92). This immediate connection with the fellow female wanderer teaches Mary to feel at home in her urban environment, and more important, this female friendship provides her with the necessary support to guide (like a "star") her movements through even those most foreboding or "compact masses." Yet the power of this affective bond between working women is something that Mary will have to relearn upon her return to London. From the outset, Mary feels exhausted by the English city and, in particular, threatened by the prospect of cross-class contact: "It seemed years since she used to long to mix with crowds," and she no longer "find[s] exhilaration in the sight of multitudes," nor "feel[s] her pulses throb to the beat of all the myriad feet" (155). Mary's negative response has everything to do with her "forced" immersion within the city crowd: "the sordid squalor forced itself upon one; the great, aching pity one had for each unit was only another cause of pain, for the people in bulk repelled one" (155). Constant exposure to urban suffering and poverty, in particular, overtaxes Mary's bodily sympathy, and thereby exacerbates her yearning for individual difference and/or distance. She will, in later chapters, embrace affective alliances among professional women as a means to transcend this classless mob and, in the process, to realize her aspirations to urban cosmopolitanism.

2 Women's Working Lives in the City

After moving from New York City to London, Mary Desmond takes up residence in a women's boarding house, where she is quite physically confronted with the lives and bodies of other working women who are struggling to survive in the busy metropolis. An early scene recounts how the protagonist looks to "Aston House" for some form of "escape" or "solitude" from the city (154, 155). Yet Mary will find no reprieve. Instead, "the smell of overcrowded women, struck her as she opened the door of the sitting-room, made her feel faint, flushed her face" (155). Mary's corporeal response is appropriate given that these fellow boarders, as bodies of desire ("all wants" and needs [158]), serve as visceral reminders of the city as a place of overcrowded and often competing economic pursuits, as well as disappointments and even physical enervation. Mary is certainly bothered by many aspects of the modern metropolis, a point which is particularly evidenced by her defensive response to the homogenizing crowd, and life in the boarding house teaches her that these urban forces can often spill over into the private sphere. Indeed, Mary is frequently kept awake by her fellow boarders who come and go at irregular hours and who sometimes bring their noisy work home with them. These working women make continual demands upon Mary, who is then emotionally and physically exhausted by their personal stories of suffering: "life in this great hive pressed in upon her; lives within lives, scandals, whispers of tragedies, and quiet heroism" (184). Through this forced contact, Mary is early confronted with the realization that her effort to negotiate the cityscape will require a new understanding of her own relationship to other working women, including women who have different class or economic experiences.

Among scholars working on gender in the nineteenth-century, the boarding house is widely recognized as a catalyst for middle-class women's urban opportunity and economic mobility. Martha Vicinus's *Independent Women* traces how, in response to the growing numbers of working women, several fin-de-siècle feminist organizations "vigorously advocated the establishment of 'suitable house accommodation at reasonable rents to ladies of small incomes, where, while retaining their entire independence, they may live with greater comfort and economy than in lodging houses of the ordinary type'" (*Englishwoman's Review* [15 March 1889], quoted in Vicinus, 295). Yet this careful distinction between "ordinary" and so-called suitable housing also betrays an ongoing need to protect the genteel woman from her working-class contemporary, a social divide which is reproduced by many of the British and American novels of the period. In *The Tunnel* (1919), for example, British novelist Dorothy Richardson is careful to qualify that her heroine Miriam Henderson lives only briefly in a "decayed Gentlewoman's" hostel (256, 258), while the American novelist Dorothy Richardson (no relation to the aforementioned author) begins her fictional autobiography *The Long Day* (1905) by recounting her early introduction to the "Young Women's Christian Association" during a search for both "*respectable* and cheap boarding-houses" (6, emphasis mine). This same unnamed narrator will later be forced to accept living conditions similar to Mary Desmond's London hostel, in which working women's sleeping cubicles afford little privacy or physical autonomy.

Many nineteenth-century working women looked to ladies' organizations and labour collectives in an effort to preserve their genteel status. Egerton's reference to real-life organizations such as the Society for Promoting the Employment of Women (SPEW), from whom Mary seeks repeated assistance (145, 188), serves as a stark reminder that even Victorian philanthropist organizations were not without their class biases. SPEW was established in 1859 by Barbara Bodichon, Adelaide Anne Procter, and Jessie Boucherett as an organization devoted to the retraining and placement of middle-and upper-class ladies in need of employment.[41] The mid-century push for gender equity in education and training had made it increasingly difficult for such women to procure respectable work as a governess or teacher. Reflecting upon this history, Newnham College lecturer Sarah Harlant (1884) explains how "the usual opening for impecunious gentlewomen, that of teaching, had been taken up by others with higher qualification for the work, who are without the impulse of poverty" (quoted in A. James Hammerton, "Feminism and Female Emigration, 1861–1886," 54). SPEW thus attempted to broaden women's employment options by legitimating various new professions within the expanding commercial and white-collar sectors (such as office and secretarial work). Yet their emphasis upon gendered respectability nonetheless created a classed hierarchy among working women and their different fields of employment – some of the positions which caused concern included semi-menial and mechanical work in telegraph offices, printing, lithography, or typewriting.[42]

By focusing on the urban working woman, novels such as *The Wheel of God* and *The Long Day* offer an almost sociological account of the limited number of so-called respectable professions open to ladies, and chart the classed hierarchies that often structured this female labour at the fin de siècle. After losing her position as a teacher, for example,

Richardson's protagonist is forced to consider less prestigious or less "respectable" forms of work; the "unskilled, friendless, [and] almost penniless girl of eighteen" (5) tries a range of jobs, including everything from work as a match-box maker and seamstress to a shopgirl and laundry shaker. She quickly discovers that each occupation is poorly remunerated, paying anywhere between $2.50 and $4.00 a week. It is not until she takes up skilled work as a stenographer-typist that the narrator finally makes the jump to middle-class "prosperity" and earns between twenty and twenty-five dollars a week (268). The middle-class woman's fascination with marketable skills, such as typewriting, as means to economic mobility is a theme that dominated several feminist novels of the period.[43] In Grant Allen's *The Typewriter Girl* (1897), for example, the unnamed female protagonist quickly secures work in a publishing firm, and it is not long before she is offering her employer editorial advice and, even, by the novel's close, writing her own fictional biography. *The Wheel of God* instead reads as a counterpoint to such an uplifting narrative trajectory, showing readers that typewriting did not in fact guarantee favourable pay or socioe-conomic status for women workers. In her early days as a typist in a New York business firm, Mary Desmond works alongside "all sorts and kinds" of women – "girls of sixteen, women of thirty; shabby, well-dressed, 'stylish,' dowdy, pretty, [and] homely" (81). While Mary may be better dressed than these girls, any such signs of individual distinction are quickly obliterated by the crushing pace of secretarial work in the modern city: Mary "scarcely" has time to be "miserable" or even "think of her position" because she is "too bewildered by the feverish air of this monstrous international sifting sieve" (77). The reason Richardson's protagonist can make the jump in social status while Egerton's cannot has to do with training: the former acquires additional training in composition and grammar through self-study and night school, while Mary "persevere[s] doggedly" to master her work on the spot (77). Thanks to her special skills, Richardson's heroine makes the fantastical leap from stenographer to author-journalist, while Mary's work allows little opportunity for personal expression, let alone professional advancement.

As if the alienating effects of typewriting were not problem enough, the typist's close affiliation with the trades also placed at risk her social status as a respectable Victorian lady. Mary herself witnesses SPEW turn away several female applicants with "trade" knowledge – such as "typewriting (then beginning), bookkeeping, [and] a bodice hand" – because their skills deem them less needy than their genteel counterparts (189). *The Wheel of God* is, in this way, more accurate than other late-Victorian novels insofar as it questions the assumption of women's work in the feminine vocations, such as typewriting, as means to socio-economic mobility. Indeed, the increasing over-supply of women typists by the end of the century had the dual negative effects of gendering the profession as feminine and, thus, encouraging poor wages.[44] Angel Kwolek-Folland cites an 1890 United States census which counts women as making up to 64 per cent of the category "stenographers and typists" (30), with these numbers rising to 77 per cent in 1900 and 83 per cent in 1910 (*Engendering Business*, 30).[45] These female typists were often paid between 25 to 50 per cent less than their male counterparts, and this disparity in wages helped drive the demand for cheaper female labour and made women's economic independence quite impossible.[46]

In addition to being underpaid and undervalued, work as a female typist effectively erased any markers of individuality or (class) difference. Much of this devaluation was due to the typewriter itself as a machine of mass reproduction.[47] The very form of typewriting – using standardized font to create texts – makes Mary's individual contribution (and personal style) completely indistinguishable from that of another copyist's. Walter Benjamin describes this as the loss of artistic "aura." His essay "The Work of Art in the Age of Mechanical Reproduction" (1936) explains how, in pre-industrial cultures, the work of art was recognized as an individual's artistic expression, and consumption of this rarified creation affirmed its "cultic value." In the age of mechanical industry, however, new technologies of mass reproduction made art readily available to the majority, and the bulk replication and distribution of the copy thereby undermined the work's "aura" as both original and rare. As an instrument of this kind of mechanical reproduction, Mary's typewriting likewise erases her "aura," making her individual insights not only invisible but also completely unnecessary.[48] Very early into her position, Mary realizes that her special talents, including "style" or "languages," are of "no use" in a work environment that prioritizes "typewriting" as women's most important marketable skill (77). For critics such as Victoria Olwell, this erasure of the individual thus culminated in the "double meaning" of the term "typewriter" as reference to "both the machine for typewriting and the person – usually and iconically the woman – who operated it for a living" ("Typewriters and the Vote," 55). Egerton's novel is clearly aware of this "iconic" understanding of women's typewriting, as indicated by the events surrounding Sep's suicide at the end of Book Two. Upon learning of Sep's death, fellow typists take a brief moment to mourn, but then the "pendulum [swings] back" and the office quickly "regain[s] its cheerfulness" (136). Sep is not missed because she was, effectively, no more than a mere machine. Yet Sep "had been her [Mary's] only intimate" (140), and so the suicide has a devastating effect upon Mary's work and life in the city. Lost without her friend, Mary decides to leave New York for London. She also knows that there will be "no difficulty" in leaving her position because, like Sep, she will be efficiently replaced by another "typewriter": "Her place could be filled up on Monday morning," Mary thinks to herself, for "one writing machine was as good as another" (140).

While Egerton's heroine is most certainly selective in her professional and personal alliances, she nonetheless recognizes the power of working-women's cooperatives as underwriting the cosmopolitan woman's access to the city and, with it, economic and gendered opportunities. In fact, by the time *The Wheel of God* (1898) appeared in print, there was already in both England and the United States a growing labour movement promoting women's collective rights to fair wages and mobility across a range of professions. Early pioneers such as Emma Paterson, for example, founded the Women's Trade Union League (in 1874; originally called the Women's Protective and Provident League), dedicated to the protection of female employees from wage depression, exploitative competition, unregulated working hours, and other forms of gender discrimination in the workplace.[49] Inspired by Tina O'Toole's work in *The Irish New Woman*, some critics might be tempted to position Egerton's novel within this history of feminists working to break down or "deterritorializ[e]" economic difference (144).[50] In her use of this latter term, O'Toole invokes feminist Rosi Braidotti's related writings on the "nomadic subject" as an alternative mode of economic embodiment that is both affective and affirmative, rather than alienated and alienating (O'Toole, 146). In place of "difference-minded" and "schizoid" logic of capitalism, the nomadic encounter instead represents a positive and mutually affirming relationship that facilitates ethical inclusion (or recognition) and also, in Braidotti's terms, encourages us to rethink the subject as always in the process of becoming: "To disengage the process of subject formation from negativity to attach it to affirmative otherness means that reciprocity is redefined not as mutual recognition but rather as mutual definition or specification" (Braidotti, *Nomadic Theory* [2011], 287). It is also this affirmative response which then marks the nomadic subject as distinct from exiled or migrant subjects. Using Braidotti's terms, O'Toole describes what she sees as Egerton's innovative representation of urban emigration "as a way of being in the world rather than a journey between two fixed points" (*The Irish New Woman*, 130). Mary is, according to this reading, comfortable inhabiting liminal social spaces, and her affective bond with fellow city dwellers effectively undoes cultural differences, including class divisions.[51]

This next section complicates such an optimistic account of Mary's urban travels and, instead, argues that *The Wheel of God* (1898) presents readers with a version of the fin-de-siècle feminist whose cosmopolitan mobility is made possible by, and therein reproduces, the material conditions of class difference.[52] Reflecting upon her fellow boarders at Ashton House, for example, the best Mary can offer in terms of an affective, cross-class alliance is the weak admission that "[l]ife wasn't so bad" and that the "women were nice when you got to know them" (187). It is important to note that Mary draws this conclusion only once she is "upstairs," and after she gazes upon a "bright, fiery-blue star" that "blink[s]" at her "like an encouraging eye" (187). In other words, Mary can only appreciate her working-class roommates after establishing some kind of physical and mental (reflective) distance. This is, therefore, a far cry from the nomadic subject who welcomes contact with a range of urban subjects and who positively inhabits those in-between socio-economic spaces; rather, Mary clearly still aspires to some form of female *flânerie* that preserves the difference between herself and the homogenizing mob. It is this kind of detachment, as a protective barrier around the individual, that she misses most about New York City. While in the United States Mary had her own private room in "Uncle Hiram and Aunty Sadie's" boarding house (87), and she also enjoyed frequent visits to the building's rooftop where she revelled in the act of looking from above (108–9), but in London Mary is unable to attain this same separation and must therefore submit to being affected by the city, both physically and psychologically. This next section will consider in more detail how Mary's aspiration to spatial and social distance is facilitated by carefully negotiated alliances with other middle-class women like herself, women who pursue professional mobility while still adhering to (even if rewriting) the conventions of class difference.

3 Women's Professional Cooperation

The third and final book, "The Ripening of the Fruit," in Egerton's three-part *The Wheel of God*, opens with an impressionistic picture of summer life in Buckinghamshire, England, just outside of London. This is the bourgeois world of "tennis" and "champagne-cups," where "people from town" who are "fagged at the end of the season" seek refuge or "escape," and where resident "country people" are thus afforded "glimpses of town and fashion" (219). Readers eventually learn, after several descriptive paragraphs on "white flannels" and "silk parasols" (219), that Mary is among the elite crowd, thanks in large part to her late-husband's fortune (227). While the first two books ("The Seed in the Sheath" and "The Blossom in the Blood") chronicle Mary's struggle to find her place in the modern urban workforce, from Dublin to New York City and then London, this third volume instead transports readers to the relatively sequestered (if not stagnant) world of married life in suburban England. Margaret Stetz is right in her claim that "The Ripening of the Fruit" is part of the author's sustained critique of marriage ("'George Egerton,'" 128–30), and yet it is also important to note that Egerton wages this argument in service of a larger vision regarding women's socio-economic mobility. In this final book Mary is forced to contend with domestic ideology and, specifically, the bourgeoisie marriage plot underwriting social distinctions between the middle-class professional woman and her working-class sister. Mary's failed marriages – first to D'Arcy and then, in Book Three, to a dissolute gambler and womanizer named Cecil Marriott – serve as powerful reminders that heterosexual romance often undercuts women's aspirations to economic and sexual equality. The relationship with Cecil, for example, proves a problem of unequal investment, and the union fails because Mary's husband cannot match her emotional and financial contribution: "It was a sign of the breach between them that she was beginning to think of her money as separate from his" (292). Feelings of "irritation" eventually give way to "repulsion" and then "hate," and it is not long before the disappointed wife longs for her former existence as "independent Mary Desmond" (292). A trip to town is, moreover, an opportunity for "relief" (263) and recollection of how "she was happier in the old days," in New York, when all she had to think of was herself and to "earn her supper" (285). The longing expressed in this moment is not for a specific place but for a form of possessive individualism that Mary best associates with the cosmopolitan cityscape.

In qualifying her desire as tied to the city, Egerton's novel also presents readers with a representation of the migrant subject that differs markedly from those offered by many of her Irish contemporaries, including other fin-de-siècle female authors. There were Irish women writers in the late-Victorian and Modernist periods whose work celebrated global migration as offering new social and gender opportunities for independent-minded women. For example, Florence Dixie (*Gloriana, Or the Revolution of 1900* [1890]) looked to her American sisters as potential allies in debates on the "Woman Question,"[53] while later author Maeve Brennan's short fiction ("The Bride" [1953], "The View from the Kitchen" [1953], "The Anachronism" [1954], and "The Servants' Dance" [1954]) focuses on female migrants' work as domestic servants and the sometimes subversive potential of the "outsider inside" structures of middle-class domesticity.[54] However, most of the fiction produced around the time Egerton was writing, including works by her female compatriots, actively discourages female migration and instead interprets such cosmopolitan aspirations as a form of self-interested disregard for community and tradition, including the heterosexual domestic plot.[55] Early Edwardian fiction by Irish writers Katharine Tynan, Mary Butler, and Rosa Mulholland instead stress women's emotional and bodily loyalty to nation and culture. Their narratives celebrate Ireland's rural countryside and its people and propagate images of the global city as a place of moral corruption and sexual downfall. Butler's semi-autobiographical *The Ring of Day* (1906) refers to the Irish peasantry as "the chosen people" (260) caught up in the nationalist struggle and rightful inheritors of the late nineteenth-century land wars. While the middle-class and clergy must take care of this noble population, the novel argues that the greater responsibility lies with women, especially rural women, who must stay and, through work as wives and mothers, ensure the preservation of Ireland's cultural heritage (66).[56] In Tynan's *The French Wife* (1904), middle-class protagonist Alison Barnard embraces the idea of women's responsibility to Irish culture and devotes herself to the remaining inhabitants of her native Ballycushla, teaching home industry and library classes to the peasantry. She also becomes involved in national politics and volunteers her time to the anti-immigration candidate Sir Gerard Molyneux's campaign for a seat in parliament.[57] Mulholland's *Father Tim* (1910) contains the familiar anti-immigration interpretation of the city as a place of moral danger (a naïve rural peasant girl is taken advantage of, and eventually dies as a result of, sexual corruption);[58] and Mulholland's later work, *Norah of Waterford* (1915), has the priest Father Columba explicitly discourage women (Norah) from immigrating by stressing national responsibility over personal ambition: "You are better where you are, child [...] an Irish girl like you is better half starved at home than earning good wages in New York. Emigration might do if you had a farmer husband – one like Joe Aherne – [...] Such a pair, with a little money to start with, might well take land and prosper" (154).[59] In all of these novels, women are told that they belong in Ireland, and there is throughout each narrative a distinct tone of nostalgia for, and desire to get back to, an idealized home (both family and nation). Egerton's cosmopolitan woman is not entirely unlike these nationalist representations insofar as Mary does express a certain longing for her former home; yet that lost "home" is distinctly urban in nature, and her desire is absolutely tied to the global city's promise of sexual freedom and mobility beyond the confines of nationalist and domestic plots.

In balancing women's nostalgia with feelings of desire or even passion, Egerton's representation of the urban woman as migrant also stands in distinction to many contemporary male writers' conception of the global traveller as a kind of "exile."[60] This difference can be explained through close analysis of gendered differences in the city's promises of both escape (the exiled subject) and socio-economic opportunities (the migrant subject). Joyce's "Eveline" (1904) imagines how emigration represents for women the fantasy of sexual liberation: his eponymous heroine longs for "escape" ("She must escape!"), and wonders how relocation to the New World with her lover Frank will "save her" and "give her life, perhaps love, too" (47).[61] Yet Eveline is, in the end, unable to leave behind domestic duty to her native land and family, and so concludes the story with feelings of regret and longing. With this frustrated ending, Joyce's story stresses feelings of separation and nostalgia typical to what Braidotti classifies as the "exiled subject," a subtype within the larger genre of migrant literature. "Exile literature," Braidotti explains, "is marked by a sense of loss or separation from the home country, which, often for political reasons, is a lost horizon" (*Nomadic Subjects*, 59). Insofar as she longs for her lost life in New York City, Egerton's heroine would also seem a variation of the exiled subject, but it is also in her definition of the city as a space of gendered mobility that Mary sets herself apart from the latter type and instead signals her forward-looking aspirations to new horizons. Mary is, in other words, what Braidotti would call a "migrant subject" who inhabits an "in-between state whereby the narrative of the origin has the effect of destabilizing the present" (59). Her ability to recall the past in order to rupture the present and motivate the future is also a key feature that distinguishes Mary from the defeated women who populate Henry James's *Daisy Miller* and *Portrait of Lady*. In James's fiction the American heroine travels to England and Europe only to be disappointed in her expectations of sexual and social freedoms.[62] Unlike these "innocents abroad," Mary does not lose sight of her former freedoms and instead conjures up a mental image of the American city in order to gain new insight into her present domestic disappointments.[63] In true migrant fashion, she exists in a "suspended" or "often impossible present" that is consistently challenged by both her nostalgia as well as her "blocked horizons" (to use Braidotti's terms in *Nomadic Subjects*, 59). The metropolis is always with Mary, not as a specific destination but as a psychological opportunity both to remember and to strive toward new economic horizons.

The final book in *The Wheel of God* suggests how women's migrant relationship to domestic plots – caught in between both "home" countries and familial bonds – effectively mediates, as well as limits the cosmopolitan woman's situated mobility within the modern cityscape. Ladies well-versed in Victorian gender conventions knew that they needed to define themselves in relationship to the private sphere in order to legitimate their work and/or social mobility as appropriately "feminine." Mary's work in support of Cecil's medical clinic, for example, allows her fluid access to professional work without compromising her status as a proper Victorian lady and guardian of the hearth, while Richardson's unnamed heroine in *The Long Day* (1905) finally achieves economic independence only to find herself envying her friend Minnie Plimpton whose marriage is a reminder of "the only real way a woman can, after all, be successful" (266). In both novels, domesticity not only serves as a buffer against the urban crowd, but it is also a way for upper-class women to preserve their gendered status as respectable or "successful" ladies.[64] Egerton's novel also references feminine domesticity and, specifically, the self-sacrificing mother figure through Mary's modest claims that she only wants to "give herself" to her patients, and that "[loving] is the only thing I can do well" (343). Such efforts to legitimize women's work in nursing as a kind of professionalized domesticity can be traced back to Florence Nightingale, who is hailed by most scholars as a key pioneer of the vocation.[65] In her touchstone work, *Uneven Developments*, Mary Poovey explains how Nightingale's own narrative often "underwrote" and "capitalized upon the contradiction inherent in the domestic ideal in order to make even more contradictory claims for women than contemporary feminists did" (166).[66] Like these nurses before her, Mary imagines how her appropriately "feminine" care-giving might also facilitate public contact and, even, cosmopolitan exchange. She proudly recalls her many visitors from diverse locations, including Mexico, Japan, Copenhagen, Luxemburg, and Christiania: "they come and see me when they return from their tours, and I hear a great many extraordinary tales from the women" (342). It is also through her work as a nurse that Mary meets and befriends professional writers Miss Ingleton and "John Morton," women who also move freely between the gendered private and public spheres.

Both Miss Ingleton and Morton serve as powerful reminders of the growing number of late-Victorian women who found economic mobility through work in modern vocations, such as journalism or professional writing – Morton is a published author and Ingleton is a journalist for women's magazines. In her history of Victorian women's work, Ellen Jordan notes how women made consistent socio-economic gains through work as "authors, editors, and journalists": by the end of the century, in 1901, as many as 1,249 women (or 11.3 per cent of the total category) count themselves as working within this field of paid writing (*The Women's Movement*, 79). In *The Wheel of God*, Miss Ingleton's repeated reference to "ladies" (she sub-edits a "ladies' paper" on "sport for ladies") hints at how many of these new authors were still limited by the classed gender ideology aligning women with the domestic sphere (310).[67] Of course Victorian women began to stake their claim to journalism as early as mid-century, when feminists Bessie Rayner Parkes and Barbara Smith Bodichon first launched the *English Woman's Journal* in 1858 (and *The Englishwoman's Review* in 1866) and Isabella Beeton (with her husband Samuel) began the *English Woman's Domestic Magazine* in 1856 – these women had different and, even, opposing ideas about the role that social reporting might play in gender reform. Egerton's representation of the professional also suggests how many of these independent women were quite innovative in their attempts to redefine the public/private divide as permeable in their pursuit of so-called "respectable work."[68] Miss Ingleton self-identifies as a "woman" (not "lady") and happily traverses urban space without a chaperone – in fact, she travels by mass transit or "crowded" public trains (310). At the same time, however, she longs for an alternative domestic sphere that can accommodate her professional aspirations – this support is not possible in the "ladies' homes," which she quickly abandons because she has "no freedom" and nothing in common with the other boarders (she was always "shocking" them with her intellect and smoking) (310). In Mary, John Morton sees a woman with the opposite problem: alienation that is brought on by domestic seclusion. Morton's invitation to a "lecture" at the "Lady Sappers' Club" is an opportunity for Mary to exchange these lonely "cobwebs" for the excitement of women's urban mobility and intellectual exchange (346).

The Wheel of God is, however, more than a comment on the middle-class woman's careful reconfiguration of the gendered spheres (building upon the work of their feminist foremothers in nursing and journalism). Rather, the novel is also a timely glimpse into how late-Victorian women's urban mobility – including movement between public and private spheres – depends critically upon new forms of professional alliances: female-female bonds underwriting women's access to the modern marketplace. It is also at this point that Egerton's novel develops the distinction between working- and middle-class occupations as a question of autonomous expression. Unlike her working-class counterpart, the professional retains her autonomy by working through – not for – the means of production.[69] In this way the novel aligns feminist journalism with what cultural critics such as Walter Benjamin might later describe as the "political" potential inherent in mass culture ("The Work of Art in the Age of Mechanical Reproduction" [1936]). Whereas the traditional work of art is defined by an irreproducible aura, modern journalism is instead defined by, and works through, mass reproduction in order to reach a greater audience.[70] In her journalist friends, Mary thus finds feminist figures who harness new modes of mass culture in order to facilitate "political" connections and conversations among like-minded women. Miss Ingleton's own popular journalism blends together the respectable ("Ladies") and the sensational (feminist topics and sports) to reach a wider female readership.[71] Both Miss Ingleton and Morton also actively promote writing by, or about, other feminists and women reformers. When Morton shares with her friends an article on German socialists, Mary experiences first-hand the socio-political power of this popular journalism; reading through the essay, she is "astonished" to discover her old friend the "bow-maker" among the activists, and this revelation "quite stirr[s] [her] out of the apathy that had been stealing over her in the last years" (345). Mary shakes off those cobwebs of depression and instead connects with other women across time and space. This emotional response to the newspaper article thus represents a new kind of affective community (a female-centred "home") that is made possible by, and is mediated through, women's professional work.

It is also in this turn to political bonds that Egerton's novel returns full circle to the question of female *flânerie* in order to posit a very different or feminist mode by which women might move between private (autonomous) and public (shared) spaces. Together, Miss Ingleton and John Morton help Mary to become what later cultural critic Benjamin might describe as a modern "rag-picker," a counterpoint to the detached *flâneur*.[72] The "rag-picker" is one of the many figures who populate Baudelaire's modern city, but because of economic status, this urban wanderer must limit his movement to marginal spaces scavenging amid the dejected and rejected. In "The Rag-Picker's Wine" this scavenger figure first appears under the red glare of a street light "Au coeur d'un vieux faubourg" (1.2):

> One sees a rag-picker go by, shaking his head,
> Stumbling, bumping against the walls like a poet,
> And, with no thought of the stool-pigeons, his subjects,
> He pours out his whole heart in grandiose projects. ll. 5–8

In his analysis of the poem, Benjamin seizes upon the simile (comme un) comparing the rag-picker's urban wanderings with the creative process of recreating or rewriting stories of the city's future ("The Paris of the Second Empire in Baudelaire" [1938], 48). Though Benjamin's rag-picker is male, recent critics such as Parsons *(Streetwalking the Metropolis)* imagine how this situated figure can also serve as a useful or "alternative metaphor" for the urban woman – more so than Baudelaire's prostitute ("Women and Prostitutes") or the woman of fashion ("In Praise of Cosmetics") ("The Painter of Modern Life" [1863]);[73] like the rag-picker, the urban woman is a situated figure who must negotiate the cityscape's power structures and, often, work within its marginal spaces (6).[74]At the same time, this marginal subject can help us to understand Egerton's narrative on political bonds among professional women: by virtue of her gender, Mary is forced to navigate a city of men who "stare" (87) and who thus limit her urban mobility, but by the third book of *The Wheel of God*, Mary has also learned to envision herself as positioned within, and empowered by, a community of middle-class writers and artists. Morton's later invitation to a feminist lecture presents Mary with yet another opportunity to be part of this mediated urban experience: "You would find things changed now," Morton warns, "I remember when all the way from St. Paul's to Charing Cross, there was no choice between the coffee-room of an hotel, a few too expensive confectioners,' or Lockhart's" (346). Morton's quick history precludes the assumption of women's experience of the cityscape as either idiosyncratic or detached; she instead encourages Mary to think of the city as shared through, and thus mediated by, other women's histories.

In *The Wheel of God*, the *flâneuse* is recast as a cosmopolitan rag-picker whose political bond with other urban women helps to reclaim or "salvage" her place within a larger feminist narrative. Yet it is also important not to lose sight of the class dynamics that distinguish this narrative subject from the other working-class women who populate the city. As always, the difference depends upon the subject's relationship with the private sphere as a space of both physical and social distance, but in its final turn to feminist politics, Egerton's novel is also compelled to rethink the conventional domestic plot and women's restricted role within this gendered sphere. The fact that her husband Cecil Marriott must die for Mary to experience even a shred of personal and professional happiness is a reflection of Egerton's rather cynical view of the traditional domestic plot; rather, her novel rejects the heterosexual romance and instead embraces feminine collectivity as alternative source of private and professional support, as well as hope. The novel thus closes with an image of newly liberated Mary stepping off a train from London and into a collective feminist history. As Mary surveys the rural scene, she knows that the "other women" (Ingleton and Morton) are "awaiting her coming" in one of the domestic cottages in the valley below (362). One can safely assume that this is, however, a distinctly middle-class feminist utopia. The high cost of commuting would have precluded the participation of those from lower social orders to participate in suburban communities and communal culture.[75] Mary's trip from town to Herefordshire (by way of a "little station of Chalfont Road" [361]) was, in other words, well beyond the reach of most working-class and poor labouring women.

The fact that Mary travels by train immediately signals that she does not play the part of the detached urban *flâneur*;[76] her cosmopolitan mobility is instead shared with other travellers – including those on the train and, more important, those working women who await her return to their collective feminist home. This latter haven of feminist consciousness motivates Mary's subsequent mental rag-picking as she pieces together her place within an even larger history. Moving from the public to the private sphere, Mary recalls "[f]orgotten scenes" from her own "questioning childhood, ardent girlhood, [and] womanhood with its disillusions" (362). Her mental recollection ("realisation of herself" [363]) transcends the individual, as the possessive pronoun is quickly dropped and "self" becomes a mere part within a larger or metaphysical "inheritance of self" (364). In returning to her friends and their shared feminist community, Mary thus reimagines herself as part of a figurative landscape that is "filled with myriads of women" who look back at her and remind her that they are "all units, even as she, chained to the solitary cell of their mysterious woman's nature" (363). While the biblical allusion to the "valley of shadows" (364) may seem hyperbolic, readers are meant to recognize the larger political implications (per Benjamin's theory of art and modern labour) implicit in this gender consciousness: Mary has finally found her place in "the whole scheme" (306). As she makes her way toward her friends, Mary also gives herself over to this community of women and their shared struggle: "her heart seemed to grow hot within her, and to burn out the last atom of self; and she hastened down the slope with eager steps to where the women were calling in the gloom" (364). The urban woman is finally transformed into the rag-picker/poet who collects marginal or forgotten stories and pieces them together into (and rewrites) a new feminist history for the future.

Conclusion: Professional Women and Open Endings

I have, throughout this chapter, attempted to show how *The Wheel of God* portrays women's changing relationship to the urban landscape and its gendered marketplace at the fin de siècle as a question of collaboration among professional women. Egerton's novel, with its cast of independent-minded female characters, implicitly compares the growing number of new vocations open to women and their associated potential for economic mobility or "migrant" struggle. Mary is unhappy as an overworked typist and first finds relief from traditional gender roles in her work as a nurse, a field of employment that was already gendered as "feminine" given its association with care-giving. It is through her contact with female journalists, however, that she is finally able to find some sense of happiness and home within a larger and, sometimes overwhelming, urban marketplace. The novel is, in this way, absolutely accurate in suggesting that late-Victorian women's contribution to certain professions was more radical, as well as rewarding, than their contribution to other or more established gendered vocations. Between 1871 and 1911 the number of female nurses (and midwives) continued to grow, with women consistently making up the vast majority of this category: in 1871 there were 30,632 women working as nurses (100 per cent of the field), while in 1891 there were 53,057 (98.9 per cent) and in 1911 there were 83,662 women in the occupation (98.5 per cent). It is even more interesting to note the number of young women, between the ages of 15 and 25, who gravitated toward the profession: in 1871, these younger workers made up 2.4 per cent of the total population of female nurses, and in 1891 those ratios rose to 9.4 per cent and again to 11.7 per cent in 1911. Yet it is in emergent fields such as journalism where independent-minded women fought hardest for entry into the professional borderlands. There was a notable rise in women working as professional "authors, editors, or journalists" between 1881 to 1911, the dates corresponding with the rise of popular or so-called yellow journalism, but it is also clear from these numbers that women had a somewhat harder time with representation in this employment category.[77] There were 660 women working as professional writers (11.4 per cent of the category) in 1891, and those numbers rose dramatically to 1,249 (11.3 per cent) in 1901, and 1,756 (12.7 per cent) in 1911. The proportion of 15- and 24-year olds within this category of female writers remained fairly steady, from 10.8 per cent in 1891, to 11.9 per cent in 1901, and 8.6 per cent in 1911. Though the number of female journalists might seem comparatively low, especially when measured against pink-collar vocations like nursing, it is important to note that women did make significant headway in representation, even despite the best efforts of their male competitors to maintain their gendered monopoly of the profession.[78]

As suggested by *The Wheel of God*, many of the new vocations associated with the modern cityscape promised women unprecedented opportunities for economic and social mobility to move beyond traditional domestic – and even national – plots. Mary's search for work takes her on a transatlantic journey from Ireland to New York City and then London, during which she quickly learns that some jobs, such as typewriting, can be suffocating and alienating, while other professions, such as nursing and journalism, offer opportunities to form affective bonds with other women who work in, and move through, city spaces. Egerton's novel is, in this way, representative of a generation of female professionals who recognized, and who took full advantage of, the inherent link between women's economic mobility and urban cosmopolitanism. There were, of course, real-life pioneers such as Florence Nightingale and Mary Seacole who understood that women's nursing, as a form of paid care-giving, would legitimatize their (international) movement into the public sphere of paid work and national service – both women were later recognized as unofficial war heroes for their medical contributions during the Crimean War (1853–6). Still other ambitious women, at the end of the century, seized upon the bourgeoning field of popular journalism at the fin de siècle as means to move beyond the domestic sphere and to access new urban spaces and exchanges with other urban subjects.[79] By the century's end, hundreds of women gravitated toward the profession, with many of these writers pushing back against, and even rewriting, dominant social narratives about class and gender limiting their access to urban subjects and spaces.[80] There was the American writer Elizabeth Banks whose reportorial *Campaigns of Curiosity* (1890s) on the working conditions of London's female domestic labourers raised questions about class and national differences in a way that played into, and reinforced, Victorian conventions of gendered propriety (Banks's status as a "Lady" was doubly threatened by her Americanness as well as her cross-class "slumming").[81] Still other female journalists outright rejected the conventions of feminine domesticity in order to cross over into, and expose the horrors of, working-class life and labour in London's East End – examples include Annie Besant's political publications on the Match Girls ("White Slavery in London" [1888] published in *The Link*), Clementina Black and Adele Meyer's work *The Makers of Our Clothes* (1909) (portions published by *The Women's Industrial News*), and Margaret Harkness's investigative series *Tempted London* (originally published by *British Weekly*, 1887–8) and *Toilers in London* (*British Weekly*, 1889).[82] In Egerton's hands, however, the urban woman's contribution to the modern workforce both enables, and is supported by, affective bonds among other like-minded middle-class professionals. The most radical thing about her protagonist is her outright rejection of domestic plots as limiting the independent-minded woman – and yet the class barriers between working women remain firmly intact by the novel's open ending.

Egerton's *The Wheel of God* does not offer much in the way of a conclusion, but instead leaves readers with several unanswered questions. The first set of questions are stated explicitly as Mary mulls over the words of John Morton, the novel's talking-head feminist: "Was the fault in herself or in the time; or was the truth to be found in the words of 'John Morton'? – 'The men we women of to-day need, or who need us, are not of our time – it lies in the mothers to rear them for the women who follow us'" (363). The "or" in this interior monologue does not simply indicate a contradiction but, rather, Mary's effort to link one problem with another, specifically women's gendered situation with men's. In keeping with the rag-picker mentality, a state of mind that is situated and also capable of abstraction or (re)collection, Mary traces the problem of gender inequality from women to men across time and place. At the same time, she imagines how women might play a leading role in rewriting their own, as well as men's, gendered situations. The latter (men's situation) then points toward the next question regarding the outcome of this ongoing feminist struggle. Despite Egerton's reticence toward the label "New Woman," *The Wheel of God* nonetheless subscribes to what Ann Ardis (*New Women, New Novels*) and Sally Ledger (*The New Woman*) outline as the feminist's investment in narrative rupture – leaving their stories open-ended because their heroines exceed conventional plotlines. Like so many of her contemporaries, Egerton thus disrupts the domestic plot by exchanging heterosexual romance for bonds between women. With its final interior monologue, *The Wheel of God* also wonders aloud if this feminine alliance might realize an alternative "offspring," so to speak. The private self is, in this moment, supplanted by a larger connection with fellow women whom Mary hears "calling" to her in the "gloom" and "shadows." Implicit in this call are the final two questions: will women find their way out of the darkness, and will they (per Morton's invocation) bring with them, or "rear," a new "man-child" worthy of the professional woman's romance plot?

If market sales are an indication of success, then Egerton's feminists have a long way to go in their struggle for an alternative narrative.

Egerton knew that the literary marketplace could play a critical role in the dissemination of a feminist argument (or feminist "type"), and she capitalized on the popularity of late-Victorian feminist themes to pursue her own representations of women's urban mobility and emancipated sexuality. But by the time she composed *The Wheel of God*, Egerton found herself writing in response to yet another and much more conservative audience invested in normative heterosexuality as a response to the 1895 trial of Oscar Wilde (for committing acts of so-called gross indecency). Worse yet, Egerton suddenly needed a new editor willing to entertain what was, given the change in cultural attitudes, a potentially radical critique of the conventional domestic plotlines.[83] Her old publisher, the Bodley Head, had made its mark by flaunting moral conventions and literary censors, but the scandal surrounding the Wilde Trials frightened editor John Lane so severely that he watered down much of the press's subsequent output and cut ties with many decadent artists, including prominent figures such as Aubrey Beardsley (who was tainted by association with Wilde).[84] By 1897, the year Egerton began writing *The Wheel of God*, the Bodley Head had already ceased publication of its innovative side ventures, *The Yellow Book* and Keynotes Series.[85] Sceptical of what she termed the press's "milk and water" censorious approach to fiction (quoted in Stetz, "'George Egerton,'" 113), Egerton instead asked Grant Richards to publish her life novel in its full integrity. Richards honoured the author's request, and the novel was published without significant alteration the following year in 1898. Though *The Wheel of God* received favourable reviews among critics, the commercial sales were extremely poor.[86] In her biographical study of "'George Egerton,'" Margaret Stetz records how, "within a year, interest in [*The Wheel of God*] had dropped so badly that only thirty copies were sold between January and June of 1899," and that Richards even had to ask Egerton for "the return of 61/14 of the royalties she had been advanced" ("'George Egerton,'" 133).

We must wonder if the novel's commercial failure was a product of a heteronormative backlash among readers who were, after the Wilde Trials, anxious about experimental narratives that resisted domestic closure. This history also reminds us of Egerton's very literal investment in the reciprocal relationship between literary representations of working women and the real-life professional writer's socio-economic advancement. After *The Wheel of God*'s market disappointment, Egerton would continue to struggle for the remainder of her writing career. As Stetz explains, the once-infamous "'George Egerton' was, in a sense, driven out of the fiction lists by the public's changing tastes and by publishers' changing demands" ("'George Egerton,'" 145). Neither

Egerton's later turn to translation (of Knut Hamsun's *Hunger* [1899]) nor her work in drama was enough to revive the public's interest in the once-popular writer.[87] As Ruth Knechtel writes, Egerton "passed most of her final 40 years outside the literary world," and even now, "decades after her association with New Womanhood, she is remembered predominantly for her early contributions" ("George Egerton," n.p). It would almost seem, then, that the novel's closing image of a feminine commune could stand as a symbol for the author's own ongoing struggle to find a home for herself and her feminist message within the popular literary marketplace.

The next two chapters, on Michael Field and Virginia Woolf, encourage further meditation upon this notion of a collaborative literary history by and for women. Though, neither author is in direct conversation with Egerton – Field's *Sight and Song* (1892) pre-dates Egerton's popular works, while Woolf's fiction is part of a larger Modernist effort to rethink, or break with, Victorian culture and inheritance – these writers still share Egerton's aspirations to affective connection and artistic collaboration among women. Like the other authors discussed in *Critical Alliances*, both Woolf and Field also encourage readers to contemplate the social and sexual opportunities made possible when feminists produce new and empowering representations of professional women working beyond, and defiance of, inherited domestic plots.

4 Women's Artistic Connoisseurship and the Pleasures of a Lesbian Aesthetic

They [Michael Field] have poetic feeling and imagination in abundance, and yet they have preferred to work with the studious and interpretative side of the mind and write a guide-book to the picture galleries of Europe, instead of giving us a book full of the emotions and fancies which must be crowding in upon their minds perpetually.

– W.B. Yeats's "Review of *Sight and Song*" in *Michael Field, The Poet*

Art cannot be separated from life, and still less from thought.

– notes sent to K.B. and E.C., 25 January 1892, in W.B. Yeats, *Michael Field, The Poet*

In what is clearly a very negative review of *Sight and Song* (1892), W.B. Yeats insists the true poet captures through verse the unmediated world of feeling and emotion. In an obvious allusion to the Romantic-era mythology of a "spontaneous overflow of feeling," his definition of the literary form leaves little room for mental contemplation of impressions or careful and reflective expression of aesthetic experience. Indeed, the idea of an interpretive process is entirely absent from Yeats's model of poetic composition, as the music of imagination takes on a life force of its own and moves through the poet to find expression on the page. *Sight and Song* therefore disappoints insofar as its ekphrastic translations of famous paintings into verse form tend to draw attention to, rather than transcend, the poet's own subjective position as observer and aesthetic mediator, for as Yeats explains elsewhere in his review, "the two ladies who hide themselves behind the pen-name Michael Field have set to work to observe and interpret a number of pictures, instead of singing out of their own hearts and setting to music their own souls" (361).

The "two ladies" were, of course, lovers and collaborators Katharine Bradley and Edith Cooper, aunt and niece duo (respectively) who were friends with famed fin-de-siècle artists such as Charles Ricketts and Charles Shannon, as well as American art historian Bernard Berenson. The poems contained within *Sight and Song* are the impressionistic results of the poets' two-year tour of continental art galleries, focusing particularly on paintings by Italian Grand Masters. In the preface to the collection, Field promises "to translate into verse what the lines and colours of certain chosen pictures sing in themselves" (v), but as Yeats argues in his review, the poems themselves in fact fail to realize this aesthetic objective and instead read more like "a guide-book to the picture galleries of Europe." Field's experiment in ekphrastic translations seems, in his account, little more than an example of touristic collection best suited to travel writing, and not the stuff of true poetry.

With these negative remarks about Field's verse-form "guide book," Yeats implicitly dismisses an entire history of women's writings on art. As discussed in the last chapter, fin-de-siècle feminists were particularly keen to take advantage of the expanding field of professional writing and journalism, and many found in these new mediums an opportunity to reshape dominant cultural conversations on women's role in art, as well as obvious prospects for professional mobility and social status. Meaghan Clarke's excellent study *Critical Voices: Women and Art Criticism in Britain, 1880–1905*, for example, looks at how female writers such as Alice Meynell, Florence Fenwick Miller, and Elizabeth Robins Pennell were vital contributors to periodical criticism on art, and through their published works, helped shape nineteenth-century debates on the nude (Meynell), Impressionism (Meynell and Pennell), as well as feminism and women's art (Fenwick Miller).[1] Still more recently, Hilary Fraser's *Women Writing Art History in the Nineteenth Century* positions *Sight and Song* within a much longer tradition of women's travel writing on arts and culture, a history in which women often relied upon their subjective or, even, "feminine" impressions as a mode of apprehending the cultural artwork. That Field's collection of ekphrastic poetry reminds one of a tradition of art tourism makes sense given that the poets themselves were heavily influenced by contemporary critic and friend Bernard Berenson's writings on aesthetic collection and connoisseurship. In his 1892 letter to Bradley and Cooper (excerpted above) Berenson insists that the work of art "cannot be separated from life" or "thought," and his subsequent call for a cerebral response to the aesthetic work is then complemented by a theory of self-withholding (the very opposite of Yeats's unmediated "emotions and fancies"). In Field's hands this critical turn to larger questions of "life" also permits a strategic analysis of gender and the sexual economy of visual consumption. Through reflexive (or what Yeats describes as "studious") translations, the poems in *Sight and Song* thus raise questions about women's contribution to art criticism as both subjects and objects of the aesthetic gaze.

This chapter is, quite clearly, working with a different definition of economy than that outlined in previous chapters. Whereas earlier discussion has focused on women's participation in the labour force, including structures of production, this chapter instead looks at women's relationship to structures of consumption and, in particular, the relationship between visual consumption (or collection) and artistic connoisseurship at the fin de siècle. Nineteenth-century connoisseurship was, as today, meant as a designation of authority or expertise in the area of art and cultural knowledge. In the late-Victorian period, this expertise took on certain professional dimensions thanks to the proliferation of affordable print technologies and, by association, journalism and aesthetic writings dedicated to the dissemination of cultural knowledge or art collection. As Meaghan Clarke and Francesco Ventrella argue in their introduction to "Women's Expertise and the Culture of Connoisseurship," the 2017 special issue of *Visual Resources*, the field of professional writing on art was still new by the end of the century, and as a result many female writers were able to participate in, and even reshape, the form and function of this critical tradition. This chapter will show how late-Victorian women's writings participated in emergent debates about opposing methodologies of empirical self-withholding versus subjective impressionism as a means to artistic apprehension (visual consumption). This is not to say, however, that these women were immediately accepted or recognized authorities in conversations on late-Victorian connoisseurship.[2] Rather, the critical tendency to privilege empirical methods of art study (or a "masculine temperament") often worked to exclude women who were used to working in subjective or impressionistic modes. As members of some of the most elite communities dedicated to fin-de-siècle aestheticism, Bradley and Cooper acutely understood, and were personally engaged with, these conversations on the gendered dynamics barring women's access to artistic authority. *Sight and Song* is a record of the poets' attempt to reclaim feminine feeling as the source of artistic insight and, therein, to imagine a tradition wherein women might act as cultural authorities rather than passive muses of masculine consumption.

As a collection of verse translations, *Sight and Song* does not obviously fit with this feminine tradition of prose criticism on art, and yet the ekphrastic poems nonetheless serve as illustrative examples of an aesthetic theory of collection by self-consciously attending to the tension between subjective impressions and the objective work itself.[3] Despite prefatory promises of "objective" translations, the actual poems themselves offer what I will show to be highly embodied and even erotic expressions of aesthetic experience and visual consumption. It is perhaps for this reason that the preface ends with the following admission: "When such effort has been made, honestly and with persistence, even then the inevitable force of individuality must still have play and a temperament mould the purified impression" (vi). The poetic translator makes an "effort" to be objective, and yet the force of "individuality" is still an inevitable component in the aesthetic experience or "impression." This persistent subjectivity has much to do with the relationship between form and aesthetic experience: ekphrasis cannot entirely wrest the paintings free from their visual form, and as a result, the translations must record the subjective mode of apprehension or, in other words, aesthetic connoisseurship. Moreover, Field's translations present aesthetic connoisseurship in gendered terms, showing us how the observer-as-translator's gaze is oftentimes coded as masculine desire for, or pleasurable consumption of, a feminine object.[4]

There has been already important criticism on fin-de-siècle aestheticism and economics,[5] and in tracing this history, one can also see how women's foray into art criticism was complicated by the popular assumption of women as objects – rather than subjects – of aesthetic consumption.[6] For feminist writers such as Field, then, the aesthetic project involves a complex mode of cultural critique that engages with – rather than transcends (per Yeats's insistence) – the material forces of gender and cultural production.[7] The female aesthete must, in other words, resist what critic Jonathan L. Freedman describes as the tendency "to reproduce directly in the sphere of aesthetic appreciation the purely sensory engagement with a world of commodities that Marxist critics – particularly those influenced by the 'Frankfurt school' – have argued defines experience in a mature, consumption-oriented capitalist economy" (*Professions of Taste*, xix–xx).[8] For women writing at the turn of the century, gender would play a central role in their effort to lay claim to aesthetic connoisseurship and, with it, the right to pleasurable consumption of artistic works. These aspiring aesthetes could not, in other words, separate literary expression from their socially situated position as women, constrained by – and therein compelled to negotiate – the material forces of gender. Many of these female writers instead engaged directly with the sexual economy of the aesthetic gaze in a manner that foregrounds what Cherry Clayton describes as the "non-coincidence between a woman's politics and her art" (*Beyond the Frame*, 178). The sexual politics of such writing can be glimpsed in the female aesthete's careful navigation of the gendered gaze, a power dynamic which often precludes women's access to visual and artistic authority. Many of these female aesthetes wrote from the position of beautiful object or "muse" in order to resist the masculine gaze and thereby expose the socio-economic principles underwriting, and working through, the structures of visual pleasure. As Kathy Alexis Psomiades explains in *Beauty's Body: Femininity and Representation in British Aestheticism* (1997), the beautiful female is herself a site of contested meaning, embodying both "inaccessible psychological depth" and a "tangible material surface" (3). Beauty's body thus plays a critical role within the aesthetic tradition as an iconic representation of an irresolvable tension between pleasing surfaces (art) and underlying economic structures (including commodity culture).

Interested in artistic agency, Field participates in a fin-de-siècle move among feminist writers who look back and challenge the masculine gaze limiting women to the role of passive and thereby silent object. Rather, *Sight and Song* is part of a bold tradition of feminist writing at the end of the century interested in claiming women's right to connoisseurship. Indeed, Field's emphasis on a female-centred aesthetics fits within a tradition of late-Victorian mirror poems wherein women reclaim beauty's body as an active source of feminine inspiration and artistic agency. Examples within this tradition include Caroline Lindsay's "My Own Face" (1889), May Probyn's "The Model" (1883), and Mary E. Coleridge's "The Other Side of a Mirror" (1896). At the same time, however, Field's playful deconstruction of the boundaries between subjective and objective apprehension (sight verses song, respectively) also taps into concurrent debates on the gendered gaze and women's ability to practise appropriate aesthetic methods. Other late-Victorian female art critics such as Vernon Lee and Alice Meynell wrestled with these gendered terms of connoisseurship and, in particular, with an emergent masculine mode of self-disciplined withholding as requisite to critical legitimacy. Yet Field's poetry represents a distinct contribution to both feminist traditions (mirror poems and aesthetic criticism) by virtue of the poets' enthusiastic celebration of collaboration. Beyond the sheer numbers of women writing about art at the turn of the century, Field's *Sight and Song* shows how it is important for women to write together and, through this partnership, to explore the generative relationship between artist and muse in order to create a feminist or female-centred aesthetics.

This chapter reads Michael Field's *Sight and Song* as a touchstone work on late-Victorian women's effort to reclaim the pleasures of an aesthetic gaze for their own and mutual exchange. Unlike the other authors discussed in *Critical Alliances*, Field places art and aesthetic theory, specifically, at the very centre of feminist efforts to redefine the gendered marketplace. The poets' collaborative translations give back to women the power to define what it means to be feminine and the role of gender in artistic production and consumption. Field's ekphrastic poetry deconstructs the masculine gaze in order to produce an alternative, or "feminist," model of aesthetic connoisseurship that preserves the autonomy of the feminized work of art. The first section of this chapter will look at those feminist art critics who came before Bradley and Cooper, focusing specifically on women writers who blended together artistic tourism and travel writing. Building upon this feminist tradition, Field's *Sight and Song* presents women's writing as an act of reclaiming the artistic power of femininity, as both the muse and medium for impressionistic inspiration. The second section of this chapter will, by contrast, look at Field's male influences, including Berenson's writing on art criticism and a wider masculine tradition of aesthetic connoisseurship. The final section then charts Field's move from theory to practice, with particular attention to the poetic translations as expressions of collaborative and, therein, mutually pleasurable feminist aesthetics. Field's poetic translations rewrite the gendered economy of the gaze to emphasize the autonomous feminine figure who looks back and refuses to play the part of passive object to masculine possessive consumption.[9]

As a collection of lyric poetry, *Sight and Song* also presents a unique contribution to fin-de-siècle women's strategies of economic collaboration. Previous chapters have focused on works of fiction, with open-ended narratives that invite readers' active investments in the relationships and outcomes of feminist communities. Field's lyric poems instead encourage us to give ourselves over to a form of aesthetic pleasure without gratification, thereby invoking the economics of consumption or a mode of consumerism that is always in the moment (non-narrative) and persistently unsatiated. This innovative mode of aesthetic consumption is grounded in the poets' commitment to the productive power of feminist bonds between women. The poets' bold experiment in ekphrastic translation presents a new form of aesthetic collection that is non-possessive in its aim and, therefore, that takes pleasure in a shared or "lesbian" bond between the visual consumer and autonomous feminine muse. I add, however, that it would not be possible to appreciate the innovations of Field's feminist gaze without due attention to the embodied, visual dynamics of the translator's aesthetic experience. *Sight and Song*'s repeated return to the poet's position as subject of the gaze raises larger questions about the socio-economic context of literary marketplace and women's artistic authority and production of art, especially feminist art by and for women. The often personal expression of desire in these intimate lyric poems allows the dual authors to experiment with a new form of connoisseurship that celebrates and therein foregrounds women's mutual pleasure, or what I will call "lesbian erotics."

1 Women and Art Criticism

In an undated diary entry from 1890 Katharine Bradley recounts a conversation with legendary aesthete Oscar Wilde in which the two discussed Walter Pater's theory of aesthetics (quoted in Marion Thain and Ana Parejo Vadillo, *Michael Field, the Poet*, 241).[10] Both professed that Pater played an influential role in their own theories of artistic appreciation, though Bradley is quick to add that she cannot quite "forgive" the renowned theorist for his definition of "the scholarly conscience as male" (241). Bradley's further explanation indicates that, while Pater's claim may in fact be a "just" characterization of the gendered difference structuring current attitudes toward the critical "conscience," it is, also, therefore the cause of her own "suffering" and intellectual struggle (she finds it "hard to bear") (241). Wilde's response to Bradley further probes the relationship between gender and aesthetic writing by placing the onus upon women themselves as inherently different in their approach to artistic reflection: "he has a theory," the diary entry continues, that "it is often genius that spoils a work of art – a work of art that should be so intensely self-conscious," and that, "[o]wing to their imperfect education the ~~only~~ only [*sic*] words we have had from women are works of genius" (241). Women's so-called genius, in other words, runs counter to the Paterian call for rigorous self-scrutiny and "discrimination" among "one's own impression" as the only means "[t]o see the object as in itself it really is" (Walter Pater, *The Renaissance* [1873], xix).[11] Less than two years after this conversation with Wilde, Bradley and Cooper published *Sight and Song*, a collection of poetic translations of famous paintings in which they boldly claim their right to theorize art and, in the process, rewrite the gendered economy of the aesthetic gaze.

While critics are in agreement that Michael Field's *Sight and Song* represents an important contribution to the literary tradition of ekphrastic poetry, these scholars are still divided on the precise nature of the poets' intervention by virtue of the gendered nature of women's writing about art and aesthetic theory. Julia Saville ("The Poetic Imagining of Michael Field") argues that the poets wanted to "engage shoulder to shoulder with leading male intellectuals of an avant-garde, fin-de-siècle aesthetic culture" (178), and that *Sight and Song* thereby aspires to a form of "authorial self-effacement that belongs to a specifically male Victorian aesthetic genealogy" (179). Hilary Fraser (*Women Writing Art History in the Nineteenth Century*), by contrast, repositions Michael Field as inheritor to longer history of nineteenth-century women's writings; her chapter on *Sight and Song* presents a historicist analysis of women's travel guides and translations, focusing on "both their literal rendition of foreign language art texts into English, and their figurative translation of the experience of viewing art into other literary and performative media, such as ekphrastic poetry and exhibition" (63). This chapter will combine both critics' points in an effort to appreciate the gendered economy at play in *Sight and Song*. This section will position Michael Field's aesthetic poems within a larger tradition of nineteenth-century women's impressionistic writings on art and visual culture, and then the next two sections will consider how the persistent subjectivity present within their ekphrastic translations authorizes a uniquely feminine point of view and, important, a cooperative aesthetics by which the poets speak back to and refuse the masculine gaze.

Many early nineteenth-century women saw the growing industry of travel writing and guidebooks as a means to artistic expression. Landmark changes in global politics – from the British defeat of Napoleon to technological advances in international travel by steamship or rail – opened up Europe to a new wave of upper-class travellers eager to access the continent's treasure trove of cultural sites and galleries.[12] At the same time, British galleries and museums opened their doors to the general public making it easier for women to access renowned artworks and cultural artifacts.[13] Many women interested in art criticism were quick to take advantage of the "looser" and "informal" structure of "the essay, the journal, sketches and letters" in order to record their aesthetic experiences (Fraser, 64).[14] Maria Graham (1785–1842), Mariana Starke (1761/2–1838), Elizabeth Eastlake (née Rigby) (1809–93), and Anna Brownell Jameson (1794–1860) all saw in the prose form of travel writings an opportunity to record their very personal – and, even, feminine – impressions of the cultural landscape.[15] Maria Graham's many works contain vivid descriptions of both natural and cultural landscapes, as well as popular touristic attractions, encountered during her trips to India, Chile, and Brazil (*Journal of a Residence in India* [1812], *Journal of a Residence in Chile* [1824], and *Journal of a Voyage to Brazil* [1824]).[16] Mariana Starke also made a name for herself as a travel writer and is still, to this day, best known for her guides to France and Italy, including the best-selling *Information and Directions for Travellers on the*

Continent (1824), combining practical information and the author's own personal and poetic reflections upon cultural monuments and works of art.[17] Still, it took some time before female critics recognized themselves as part of an established tradition. Both Graham and Starke were, for example, overlooked by Elizabeth Eastlake's 1845 article "Lady Travellers" for the *Quarterly Review*.[18] Eastlake was the first woman to write for the *Quarterly Review*,[19] and she would later weigh in on some of the biggest aesthetic questions of her day, such as the merits of the new photographic arts (her 1857 essay "Photography" for the *Quarterly Review*) and the popularization of German and Italian artists (in *Five Great Painters* [1883], on Leonardo Da Vinci, Michelangelo, Titian, Raphael, and Dürer). Conversely, art critic and guidebook writer Anna Brownell Jameson celebrated women's influence on European art, and her earliest publications (*Diary of an Ennuyée* [1826] and *Visits and Sketches At Home and Abroad* [1834]) include references to many works by female artists encountered during her travels to European galleries.[20] Jameson also helped secure the reputation of women's art criticism among male counterparts,[21] and art historian Bernard Berenson later ranked Jameson among intellectual giants such as John Ruskin (though Ruskin himself famously argued that her knowledge of art was no better than that of his father's uneducated serving girl).[22]

These early pioneers of women's writing on art and culture eventually helped open the door to late-Victorian women's experimentation with aesthetic writings in different forms, including poetry and non-fiction prose. A. Mary F. Robinson's poetry, for example, often draws upon impressionistic techniques modelled by earlier women's travel writings on art and culture. Briefly educated at University College London, Robinson spent most of her formative years in Italy, and as a result, many of her poems express a deeply personal connection to the latter country's cultural landscape and its artworks. "Venetian Nocturne" (1886) paints a picture of Venice as a place of strange and even treacherous beauty but does so by abstaining from any kind of concrete representational description in favour of subjective thoughts and feelings. A brief glimpse of "towers and domes in moonlight brightness" (11) is quickly exchanged for morbid anxiety: "Ah! Could this be death?" (12). And her sonnet sequence "Etruscan Tombs" (1887) records the poet's encounter with ancient Italian funerary art, adding to this meditation her own personal expression of anxiety about death. As Fabienne Moine notes, in "Italian Rewritings by Nineteenth-Century Women Poets," the poet-traveller's references to artistic artefacts often stand in as "metaphors" for Robinson's own feelings (208). This impressionistic approach to the artistic work can be seen right away in the first sonnet, especially the final couplet's appeal for some kind of immortality through art ("last") after passing ("past"): "But, O my love, my life is such an urn/That tender memories mould with constant touch,/[...] A sacred urn, filled with the sacred past,/That shall recall you while the clay shall last" (ll. 9–14).[23] The second and third sonnets are equally interested in the artistic preservation of the dearly departed, imagining how the cinerary urns "keep the dead alive and as they were" (21) or how a "carven slab recalls [a dead king's] name and deeds" (41). Throughout such descriptive moments, however, the seemingly concrete artefacts are transformed into "symbols" or "emblems" of the mourner's "discontent" (20), including the poet's subjective meditations on the artistic record of her own life and death. "When I am dead may none for me/Invoke so drear an immortality!" (27–8), writes Robinson, and the final sonnet closes with an image of the ancient tombs "sewn with slender discs of graven gold" (52) that immortalize the dead in "patient sleep in altered lands" (55). Robinson's poetry, with its personal mediations on art and culture, was admired by many fin-de-siècle aesthetes, including notable feminist writers such as Michael Field and Vernon Lee (Violet Paget).[24]

Writing at the end of the century, author Vernon Lee also benefited from women's earlier travel writing on art history and culture, and as inheritor to this feminine tradition, Lee experimented with similar prose techniques (especially the turn to subjective impressions) in an attempt to remake fin-de-siècle aesthetic criticism in terms hospitable to women. Lee's two-volume study of Renaissance art, *Euphorion: Being Studies of the Antique and the Medieval in the Renaissance* (1884), is written in a fragmentary form that privileges the personal and subjective encounter with art.[25] Indeed, her work was best known for its bold defence of fin-de-siècle impressionism as both an aesthetic movement and critical practice.[26] Early into volume 1 of her study, Lee defends the "new-fangled" impressionism against charges of "charlatanry" by explaining how the subjective mode is not only more "realistic" in form but, also, the only true means by which one can come closest to apprehending the aesthetic object in question.

> The art which deals with impressions, which tries to seize the real relative values of colours and tints at a given moment, is what you call new-fangled: its doctrines and works are still subject to the reproach of charlatanry. Yet it is the only truly realistic art, and it only, by giving you a thing as it appears at a given moment, gives it you as it really ever is; all the rest is the result of cunning abstraction, and representing the scene as it is always, represents it (by striking an average) as it never is at all. (*Euphorion*, 10)

By focusing on the work of art, or the "thing as it appears at a given moment," Lee also favours the personal moment of partial and idiosyncratic apprehension.[27] "We see only very little at a time," she writes, "and that little is not what it appeared to the men of the past; but we see at least, if not the same things, yet in the same manner in which they saw, as we see from the standpoints of personal interest and in the light of personal temper" (12). To say that Lee's stated methodology resembles that outlined in *The Renaissance* (1873) would not be incorrect, for *Euphorion* (1884) was in fact dedicated "To Walter Pater, in appreciation of that which, in expounding the beautiful things of the past, he has added to the beautiful things of the present." Little surprise then that Lee's emphasis upon subjective meditations (6) might also echo the Victorian sage's attempt to know the work of art through careful reflection and questions that probe the viewer's personal and affective response – "What is this song or picture, this engaging personality presented in life or in a book, to me?" Pater famously asks, "What effect does it really produce on me?" (preface [1873], xxix).[28]

Self-positioned as part of an aesthetic tradition, by drawing from Pater and celebrated female writers before her, Lee nonetheless faced steep resistance from critics eager to guard the field of art criticism against women's innovations and claims to expertise. Some reviewers saw her as an "apt pupil" of Pater's "personal" and "subjective" criticism ("Studies of the Renaissance" in *Atlantic Monthly* [1885], 132), but then complained that her prose was deficient in "style" (136) or "polish" (Marguerite Blessington, "Books of the Week" in *Times*, 13 December 1895, 13). An otherwise favourable review by the *Australasian* (4 October 1884) objected to Lee's "long-linked and rather trailing sentences," adding that, "while full of power and suggestion," her prose is "sometimes wanting in clearness and definition" ("Euphorion," 632). Others were more intolerant in their condemnation of *Euphorion* as inferior to John Addington Symonds's work on the Renaissance (*Saturday Review*, 6 September 1884, 17–18) or of Lee herself as "devoid of aesthetic sense" (*Nation*, 22 January 1885, 76–7).[29] In each of these cases, Lee was, as Christa Zorn argues, "measured against more established writers" and male critics, specifically (*Vernon Lee*, 13). Even Pater himself could not help but qualify his praise for Lee's work – its "poetic charm" and "justly expression, sustained and firm" – with reference to gendered differences in writing and a backhanded compliment that "women's style so seldom is [firm]" (4 June 1884).[30] Still others were concerned with what they saw as Lee's incapacity for objective or impartial evaluation of her subject matter, an aesthetic sensibility which was becoming increasingly central to the professionalization of art criticism in the latter decades of the century.[31] In his review for the *Academy* (19 July 1884), for example, E. Purcell accuses Lee of "losing her grasp on reality by stretching out into associations and accidental remembrances" ("Review of *The Beautiful*," 37–8), while the aforementioned review for the *Atlantic Monthly* characterizes Lee's study as "intensely feminine" by virtue of its "quick intuition" and "rococo" affections ("Studies of the Renaissance" [1885], 136). Yet Lee's commitment to a personal and poetic method is ingenious, for it not only aligns her with the already long tradition of women's innovative contributions to art, but it also implicitly endorses the impressionistic mode by which women might stake their claim to the pleasures of visual consumption.[32]

Following in Lee's footsteps, fin-de-siècle writer Alice Meynell saw in art criticism a new opportunity to assert her right to the aesthetic gaze, and her published writings on French Impressionism look closely at cultural representations of women as muse. Meynell's 1892 article "Pictures of the Hill Collection" (*The Magazine of Art* [1882]), for example, looks at how Edgar Degas's studies of ballet dancers (no specific titles) fascinate with their "unidealised" representations of the "thin, undersized, bony, long-elbowed" female form at work – "not a line of natural grace in their attitudes, nor a hint of beauty in face, dress, or figure, but only the taught sprightliness of the ugly dance forced into their tired limbs" (82).[33] More than a simple means to professional advancement, art criticism gave back to female critics such as Meynell a means to visual authority and, with it, a way to imagine – and to describe for readers – a new "feminist" content. Indeed, the feminine figures that populate Degas's paintings and sketches are not pretty or palatable objects of visual pleasure; rather, many of these figures are "depressing and discouraging," or they look upon each other as agents of their own gaze and with "cool cruelty which is indefinably painful" (82). Meynell's writings, in other words, describe feminine figures that are not readily available to the pleasured gaze – figures that disturb and even resist any easy assimilation within the subject/object dynamic that dominate phallocentric modes of art study. And in her impressionistic account of the viewing experience, Meynell thus proposes a mode of cultural connoisseurship that is definitively feminine in its bold ownership of visual consumption, and at the same time, the female critic works hard to legitimate women's roles as complex subjects – not objects – of the aesthetic gaze, something that even later female poets struggled with in their meditations on art and gender.

For later Victorian poets, women's access to the aesthetic gaze required that women look back at and refuse the gendered hierarchy between the male artist and his feminine muse. Thus, a generation of fin-de-siècle feminist poets, starting in the 1880s, began writing so-called mirror poems that both consciously acknowledge this masculine tradition and, at the same time, reclaim femininity (or feminine reflection) as substance for women's own artistic expression. May Probyn's "The Model" (1883), for example, expresses the feminine muse's frustration and even anger toward the male artist who fails to appreciate his female muse's complexities and contributions to the aesthetic process. The same eponymous model imagines his paintings of her draped in "shoulder-slipping garb" (l. 21) with "great gold serpents coiled about the throat" (l. 22), trappings and props typical of works by Dante Gabriel Rossetti and others associated with the Pre-Raphaelite Brotherhood.[34] The poet's reflection upon these images (as if looking in a mirror) inspires a final, angry rejection of the masculine artist who misrepresents and thereby betrays her: "To me all's one,/His loathing or his loving" (ll. 12–13). In a similar way, Caroline Lindsay's "My Own Face" (1889) draws upon the extended trope of women's mirror reflection in order to imagine a mode of female-centred artistic expression. The fact that Lindsay writes in sonnet form suggests that she is looking back to a feminist tradition of love poems – from Elizabeth Barrett Browning (*Sonnets of the Portuguese* [1850]) to Elizabeth Siddal ("The Lust of the Eyes" [1850s]) and Christina Rossetti ("In an Artist's Studio" [1856]) – resisting the masculine gaze. In a kind of critical exchange with these earlier women writers, Lindsay alters the feminist tradition by giving us a fin-de-siècle artist who takes herself as muse for an extended conversation on women's complex interiority.[35] "Poor face of mine!" writes the poet, "Right often dost thou lend/A smile to his some smileless thoughts that be/Bound deep in heart" (ll. 5–7). Through meditation on this feminine reflection, Lindsay encourages others to rethink the poetic process as an act of both looking at and also listening to or exchange with the female muse: "Oft thy kind eyes see/My soul's great grief and bid their ears attend" (ll. 7–8). Rather than romanticize or idealize beauty's body, the poem instead closes with a powerful image of the feminine subject as human: "Yet God's own image thou – O human face!" (l. 14). In their anthology *Victorian Women Poets*, Angela Leighton and Margaret Reynolds argue that such representations of feminist self-inspiration were in fact "much more common in the work of twentieth-century writers" ("Caroline Lindsay," 476).[36] Whether a dominant literary mode or not, female-centred poetry by Lindsay and May Probyn – as well as Mary E. Coleridge and Michael Field – suggest how important it was for women writers at the fin de siècle to reclaim femininity as an active force in artistic creation and, therein, to rewrite the gendered economy of the aesthetic gaze to include the possibility of women artists.

Still other fin-de-siècle poets working within the tradition of the mirror poem saw an important opportunity to shift the conversation slightly but importantly to the question of feminine erotics and the woman poet's pleasurable response to beauty's body. Mary E. Coleridge's "The Other Side of a Mirror" (1896) offers a powerful representation of this secret world of feminine passion. Gilbert and Gubar famously proclaimed that the poem is preoccupied (consciously or not) with the female self's monstrous doppelganger (akin to Bertha Mason) reflected back to her by the mirror/prison (*The Madwoman in the Attic,* 16). Yet to focus only on monstrosity is to lose sight of the mirror as also reflecting back to the poet an alternative world of feminine desire and sexual frustration.[37] The mirror reflects back to the poet a face with open mouth ("parted lines of red" [l. 14]) but "no voice to speak her dread" (l. 18) and "lurid eyes" (l. 19) in which shine "The dying flame of life's desire" (l. 20). Sensual imagery mixes with language of anger to paint a picture of a female poet who wants to recover and celebrate, or take pleasure in, her own eroticized feminine self: "Shade of a shadow in the glass, O set the crystal surface free!" writes Coleridge in the final stanza, "Pass – as the fairer visions pass – /Nor ever more return, to be/The ghost of a distracted house,/That heard me whisper, 'I am she!'" (ll. 25–30). Coleridge's revelation of a unified self might be fleeting, but it is nonetheless powerful, for it gives feminist writers permission to take pleasure in those forbidden feelings of female passion and sexual longing.

Though interested in the concept of a female-centred poetics, Michael Field's *Sight and Song* represents still a different contribution to this fin-de-siècle feminist tradition of art writing. In dialogic conversation with fellow feminist poets, Michael Field does not strictly adhere to the mirror as a trope for reclaiming women's artistic agency; instead, Bradley and Cooper, through their use of the shared poetic personae, turn to feminist collaboration in order to play with, and deconstruct the roles between artist and muse. *Sight and Song* demonstrates that it is necessary for women not only to write in numbers (the proliferation of mirror poems at the end of the century) but that it is also advantageous for women to write together, literally, in order to redefine feminine social roles and visual agency. As I will demonstrate in the next section, Field's reclamation of women's visual agency represents a larger intervention into an emergent tradition of fin-de-siècle aesthetics, asking who gets to enjoy beauty's body and how does the feminine muse contribute to the artistic process. In taking pleasure in a female-centred aesthetics, Bradley and Cooper's collaborative poetry thus works to investigate and rewrite the meaning of femininity precluding women from artistic connoisseurship.

The gendered gaze and, specifically, a masculine tradition of aesthetics is therefore an important context for Field's feminist poetics. While *Sight and Song* is part of a feminist tradition that includes women's earlier travel writings on art and aesthetic translation, as well as fin-de-siècle mirror poems and their validation of the feminine muse, the collection is also an important response to masculine theories of visual consumption and aesthetic authority. Bradley and Cooper were keenly inspired by male peers such as John Ruskin, Walter Pater, and Bernard Berenson. The poets maintained a friendship and correspondence with Ruskin up until his death in 1900, despite their infamous disagreement on the question of religion,[38] and they were also familiar with Pater's work on aesthetic theory (the preface to *Sight and Sound* reads as a direct response to his essay "Prosper Mérimée" on authorial self-withholding).[39] However, it was Berenson who perhaps played the largest role in shaping Michael Field's method of poetic translation. The poets first met Berenson in Paris in 1890, during one of their tours of European galleries, and Bradley and Cooper later attended his lectures on the Italian Renaissance painters, delivered after his appointment to the National Gallery in 1891.[40] When Bradley and Cooper began their second tour of European galleries, as Saville notes, they "went armed with a list of paintings to see [provided by Berenson] and a recommendation to buy the recently released, revised edition of Morelli's book *Kunstkritische Studen über Italienische Malerei*" ("The Poetic Imaging of Michael Field," 183).[41] This next section will trace in greater detail Michael Field's response to these male intellectuals and, in particular, to the gendered economy of the masculine gaze implicit in their writings on aesthetics and artistic translation.

2 The Gendered Economy of Aesthetic Translation

Michael Field's *Sight and Song* opens with an explanation of the poets' ekphrastic project, their effort to translate original paintings into poetic form. Within this preface one can discern quite clearly the aspiration to an objective mode of apprehension that does not distort the work of art's original meaning or "song."

> The aim of this little volume is, as far as may be, to translate into verse what the lines and colours of certain chosen pictures sing in themselves;

> to express not so much what these pictures are to the poet, but rather what poetry they objectively incarnate. Such an attempt demands patient, continuous sight as pure as the gazer can refine it of theory, fancies, or his mere subjective enjoyment.
>
> "Il faut, par un effort d'esprit, se transporter dans les personages et non les attirer à soi." For *personages* substitute *peintures*, and this sentence from Gustave Flaubert's "Correspondance" resumes the method of art-study from which these poems arose.
>
> Not even "le grand Gustave" could ultimately illude [*sic*] himself as a formative power in his work – not after the pain of a lifetime directed to no other end. Yet the effort to see things from their own center, by suppressing the habitual centralisation of the visible in ourselves, is a process by which we eliminate our idiosyncrasies and obtain an impression clearer, less passive, more intimate.
>
> When such effort has been made, honestly and with persistence, even then the inevitable force of individuality must still have play and a temperament mould the purified impression:
>
> when our eyes have done their part,
> Thought must length it in the heart.
>
> M.F. (v–vi)

The first step in "objective" apprehension, as outlined in the preface, is "suppression": the poet-as-translator must "[suppress] the habitual centralization of the visible in ourselves" so that "we eliminate our idiosyncrasies and obtain an impression clearer, less passive, more intimate" (vi). The successful translator must, in other words, strive for a "continuous sight" that is free or "refine[d]" "of theory, fancies, or his mere subjective enjoyment" (v). By defining their project of poetic translation in objective terms, "Michael Field" therein aligns *Sight and Song* with an aesthetic tradition of self-withholding as described in fin-de-siècle writings by many male contemporaries, including writings by Walter Pater, John Ruskin, and Bernard Berenson.[42] The aesthetic connoisseur is, within this latter tradition, driven by the desire to apprehend the artistic work as it truly is, independent of subjective expectations or preconceptions.

Scholarship on *Sight and Song* has tended to read the poets as successful in their pursuit of impartial translation, a claim that implicitly reproduces a dichotomy between objectivity and subjectivity. This way of thinking about Field's project is largely inspired by Ana I. Parejo Vadillo's touchstone article "Sight and Song: Transparent Translations and a Manifesto for the Observer," which explains how Field's mode of translation allows the original work to retain its "own artistic achievement" (24).[43] The moment of objective apprehension of this autonomous work is thus diametrically opposed to, and must therefore expunge all traces of, the observer's subjectivity. As Vadillo further explains, "To be able to translate objectively that poetry, the viewer, gazer, and translator must, according to Michael Field, eliminate his/her subjectivity and his/her aesthetic positioning, for these may influence the perception of the art object" (21). Yet Field even admits, in the last lines of the preface, that "the inevitable force of individuality must still have play and a temperament mould the purified impression" (vi). For Vadillo, these forces of individuality do not mean that subjectivity has a role in translation; rather, "Field offers a two-phased aesthetic, one in which objective enjoyment is followed by a subjective *jouissance*" (24). Following the original work's objective incarnation (i.e., the successful translation of an independent object), Field can then – and only then – bask in a form of pleasure. The critical separation between objectivity and subjectivity remains intact.[44]

It is necessary, however, to further contextualize Field's aesthetic methodology as a response to a masculine tradition of poetic connoisseurship, particularly when we recognize within the poets' preface allusions to Walter Pater's theory of authorial self-withholding as outlined in "Prosper Mérimée" (1890).[45] Pater recognizes in the eponymous dramatist's correspondences an aspiration to "impersonality" as the basis for "literary art," and yet Pater does not say that Mérimée is in fact successful in this "central aim"; rather, the aspiration to objectivity functions more as a "precautionary maxim," even if "as little possible as a strict realism" (reprinted in 1895 in *Miscellaneous Studies*, 23). Pater's essay also invokes Gustave Flaubert as another "great master of French prose" who attempts an objective stance (23). "It has always been my rule to put nothing of myself into my works," writes Flaubert, but "luckily," as Pater continues, Flaubert "often failed in thus effacing himself, as he too was aware" (23–4). Heeding Pater's example, Field's preface cites Flaubert's "Correspondence" on authorial self-suppression as the necessary foundation for artistic creation: "Il faut, par un effort d'esprit, se transporter dans les personages et non les attirer à soi (One must, through mental effort, be carried inside the characters, not attract them to oneself)." But in taking Flaubert as an artistic model, Field not only substitutes "*peintures*" for "*personages*," the poets also, like Pater, read the French writer against his claim in order to produce a "method of art-study" that acknowledges the "inevitable" play between self-suppression ("the effort to see things from their own centre" [vi]), and the "inevitable force of individuality" (vi).[46] Given Pater's nuanced take on authorial self-withholding, it seems odd, therefore, that Field would cling to the language of objectivity, claiming to have composed poems that translate the songs which paintings "objectively incarnate" (vi). This language and its methodological implications have much to do with the influence of Bernard Berenson, who, like Pater, encouraged the poets' reverence for the Italian Grand Masters, but who also, and unlike the latter, believed it was possible to repress the authorial self in the study of art.

Berenson believed that aesthetic connoisseurship was indeed tied to refinement through self-withholding, a standard of judgment to which he held *Sight and Sound*. When Bradley and Cooper first met Berenson in 1890, the art historian was already moving away from what he saw as Pater's emphasis on subjective impressions toward, instead, a much more objective and cerebral method of art-study as modelled in works by Giovanni Morelli. In his work on the aesthetic method, Morelli argues that the conscientious student of art must conduct his/her own "independent and searching inspection of the actual works of their masters," rather than rely on the writings and theories of others, for it is "easy enough to aestheticize and philosophize about art without taking the slightest notice of *works* of art" (quoted in Samuels, *Bernard Berenson: The Making of a Connoisseur*, 95). Through Berenson, Field acquires a certain interest in Morelli's method and, specifically, his characterization of art study as an individualistic enterprise that does not require expert credentials or extensive research. In an 1891 letter to Berenson (cited in the introduction), Bradley and Cooper explain that "[f]or a year and half we have been striving to find the real poems contained in several pictures we love," and add that they know Berenson "will laugh, and Morelli feels uncomfortable in his grave – but the self-willed poets watch their pictures receive of them, and write" (Thain and Vadillo, *Michael Field, The Poet*, 316). Yet it is also the poets' continued interest in subjective impressions (per Pater) that caused Berenson, as a devotee to Morelli, to reject *Sight and Song*'s ekphrastic translations as overly "poetic" (diary entry dated 23 June 1892; Thain and Vadillo, 255). Berenson complained that the poets had "confused the material of poetry, which is feeling with colour & outline the materials of painting," but then during afternoon tea, he optimistically added that "someday [Bradley and Cooper] shall give the very pictures itself, drag the animal from its shell" and that then they "shall write a great poem, as Rossetti did on the Vierge au Rochers" (255). Berenson's expectations that Field take Dante Gabriel Rossetti as a model for ekphrastic translation implicitly gestures toward the gender dynamics with which women were continually forced to contend in their claims to aesthetic connoisseurship. In his translation of Da Vinci's "Virgin of the Rocks,"

Rossetti positions the virgin mother as mediator between the world of human flesh and "God's two-fold system" (1.7), as if to suggest that the poet/translator must inhabit a space of aesthetic distance or wonder.[47] It is, then, easy to imagine why Berenson, with his adherence to Morelli's method, would prefer such a self-conscious depiction of aesthetic distance over and above what he conceives of as Field's "poetic" language of impressions and sensual subjectivity.

Still, the question remains as to why Field would choose music, rather than stick with the conventional trope of sight, as a way to thematize objective translation. While touring European art galleries in 1891, Edith Cooper wrote to Berenson and briefly alluded to the central role aural apprehension would play in her and Bradley's forthcoming collection of ekphrastic translations: "Artistic form in all the arts tends towards music; artistic matter in all of them towards painting. It is pictures alone in which the technique is harmonious as a musician's score that lend themselves to poetry" (Thain and Vadillo, 316). Edith was clearly thinking of Pater's claim, in "The School of Giorgione" (*The Renaissance* [1873]), that "*All art constantly aspires toward the condition of music*,"[48] but while Pater wrote of music in inspirational terms, Bradley and Cooper instead committed to aural apprehension in order to think about form. This method of translation is only possible because the picture's technique is not unlike the "musician's score," and thus the painting lends itself to poetry or "song." At the same time, the poets' emphasis on sound over and above sight is the means by which they attempt what John Ruskin describes as a mode of "innocent" apprehension. In *Elements of Drawing* (1857) Ruskin describes the aesthetic mode of looking as the effort to recover "what may be called the *innocence of the eye*; that is to say, of a sort of childish perception of these flat stains of color, merely as such, without consciousness of what they signify, as a blind man would see them if suddenly gifted with sight" (*The Elements of Drawing*, 6 n.1). Modifying Ruskin's *visual* model, *Sight and Song* (1892) instead suggests that it is the innocent *ear*, not *eye*, which apprehends the aesthetic object. As outlined in the volume's preface, the translator strains to hear "the lines and colours" that "certain chosen pictures *sing* in themselves" (v, emphasis mine). While the translator might begin with "patient, conscious sight as pure as the gazer can refine it," in the end this sight gives way to a refined ear that apprehends aesthetic meaning through sound (v). Sight is therefore a trope for subjectivity, while sound stands in for the detached aesthetic truth. In fact, subjectivity seems better aligned with the realm of visual signs and signifiers as the stuff of substitution or equivalence, not the original work itself.

Shifting from theory to practice, Field's translator attempts to sing the object's original song by first eliminating all traces of such subjectivity. In the poem "La Gioconda," this objective distancing is facilitated by the non-narrative lyric form. Although it is the third poem in the volume, "La Gioconda" is essential to understanding Field's ekphrastic project both because of its well-known subject matter, and because late-Victorian readers would have immediately thought to compare Field's poem with Pater's discussion of the same artwork in *The Renaissance* (1873). Field's translation of Da Vinci's painting reads as follows:

LA GIOCONDA
LEONARDO DA VINCI
The Louvre

Historic, side-long, implicating eyes;
A smile of velvet's lustre on the cheek;
Calm lips the smile that leads upward; hand that lies
Glowing and soft, the patience in its rest
Of cruelty that waits and doth not seek
For prey; a dusky forehead and breast
Where twilight touches ripeness amorously:
Behind her, crystal rocks, a sea and skies
Of evanescent blue on cloud and creek;
Landscape that shines suppressive of its zest
For those vicissitudes by which men die. (8)

The poem begins as if a faithful description, and yet the feminine subject's "Historic, side-long, implicating eyes" (l. 1) immediately situate the work at a remove from the translator-as-poet, within the distant realm of history.[49] The action in this passage has already happened, and so the translator instead concentrates on the physical forms within the work. By stressing this distance between object and subject (the translator), Field instead negotiates what Marion Thain, in *"Michael Field": Poetry, Aestheticism and the Fin de Siècle,* describes as the impossible mix of spatial and temporal spaces typical of the ekphrastic poem. The painting is concerned with spatial (synchronic) organization, while the poem is typically associated with narrative or linear structures (diachronic) (Thain, 80). This emphasis on the spatial dynamic of the work can also be seen in the lyric's subsequent descriptions of the woman's cheek, lips, and hands, as well as the surrounding landscape of "crystal rocks, a sea and skies/of evanescent blue on cloud and creek" (ll.

8–9) – all of which are, in fact, a detailed list of objects (verbal phrases) lacking active verbs or predicates.[50]

Despite techniques of spatial distancing, however, "La Gioconda" cannot entirely transcend the subjective mode of aesthetic apprehension. The poem's reference to "implicating eyes," for example, suggests that the translator does not inhabit a neutral position, objectively removed from the work of art; instead, the observer's gaze is "implicated" by La Gioconda's "side-long" glance.[51] The translator-as-observer is thrust back into a relationship (of looking) with the aesthetic object in question.[52] The obvious question, then, is why the poem admits this persistent subject in the form of a self-conscious gaze. The answer depends entirely upon the mechanics of translation and the impossible tension between form and aesthetic experience. The persistence of an aesthetic subjectivity is evidence that, despite prefatory promises of objectivity, Field's ekphrastic project in *Sight and Song* inevitably turns to embodied practices, such as sight, in order to apprehend and translate the formal features of one artwork into another. The collection's aesthetic mode is therefore closer to what critic Marion Thain describes as "synaesthesia" (or a synaesthesic method), in which sensory perception is vital to mediating the complicated balance of, and movement between, painting (sight) and poetry (song) ("*Michael Field*," 70). Here, I use Thain's theory of synaesthesia to help us understand Field's persistent turn to subjectivity as part of, and validating, a feminist tradition of women's writings on art and embodied aesthetic experience.[53] Again, the poets would have been aware of such theories of sensory perception from reading Pater's "The School of Giorgione" (1873), which begins with the following discussion of translation:

> It is the mistake of much popular criticism to regard poetry, music, and painting – all the various products of art – as but translations into different languages of one and the same fixed quantity of imaginative thought, supplemented by certain technical qualities of colour, in painting; of sound, in music; of rhythmical words, in poetry. In this way, the sensuous element is art, and with it almost everything that is essentially artistic, is made a matter of indifference ... For, as art addresses not pure sense, still less the pure intellect, but the "imaginative reason" through the senses, there are differences of kind in aesthetic beauty, corresponding to the differences in kind of the gifts of sense themselves. (*The Renaissance* [1873], 83)

In what reads as an extension of Pater's theory, *Sight and Song* suggests that the visual mode of painting cannot be denied and that, by extension, Field's gaze must play a role within the ekphrastic translation of paintings into poetry (hence the conjunction in the title, "Sight *and* Song." As Pater explains in the same essay on Giorgione, we come to "imaginative reason through the senses," and "[e]ach art, therefore, having its own peculiar and untranslatable sensuous charm, has its own special mode of reaching the imagination, its own special responsibilities to its material" (*The Renaissance*, 83). The aesthetic experience is, according to Pater, defined in terms of sensory responses or "impressions" unique to the artwork's form, and it is precisely this "form" that is ultimately "untranslatable."[54] A painting's beauty or aesthetic content cannot, for example, be abstracted from the process of looking at, and, thus, visually experiencing the work's spatial organization, its lines and colours.

Taking their cue from Pater's synaesthesia, Bradley and Cooper stake their intervention into a masculine tradition of aesthetic translation – with its associated "manly" austerity and self-withholding – by instead drawing upon an impressionistic mode typical to female connoisseurs. In "A Pen-Drawing of Leda" we find another excellent example of the translator's persistent subjectivity in the poem's visual imagery and ongoing tension between spatial (synchronic) and narrative (diachronic) structures.

A PEN-DRAWING OF LEDA
SODOMA
The Grand Duke's Palace at Weimar

'Tis Leda lovely, wild and free,
Drawing her gracious swan down through the grass to see
Certain round eggs without a speck:
One hand plunged in the reeds and one dinting the downy neck,
Although his hectoring bill
Gapes toward her tresses,
She draws the fondled creature to her will.

She joys to bend in the lovely light
Her glistening body toward her love, how much more bright!
Though on her breast the sunshine lies
And spreads its affluence on the wide curves of her waist and thighs,
To her meek, smitten gaze
Where her hand presses
The swan's white neck sink heaven's concentrated rays. (81)

Through this careful reconstruction of Sodoma's visual scene, "A Pen-Drawing of Leda" attempts to negotiate the impossible mix of spatial and temporal spaces characteristic of the ekphrastic poem. However, the poem's early movement from Leda's "lovely" form, "wild and free" (l. 1), to her male suitor, Zeus, and the "round eggs without a speck" (l. 3) mimics the conventions of narrative plotting, and implicitly gestures toward the violent outcome of this encounter. At the same time, the poem's repeated references to light implicitly align the sun with Zeus's sexual pursuit, as if to show how the act of looking is an expression of power. Like the sun, Zeus "gapes toward" Leda's "lovely" form (l. 6), while rays of light "spread" and assert their "affluent" power as they engulf "the wide curves of her waist and thighs" (l. 11). Light thus links masculine desire with visual authority as it spreads across and envelopes the feminine object, subtly re-enacting the more familiar tale of Zeus's rape of Leda.

Both "La Gioconda" and "A Pen-Drawing of Leda" attract Field precisely because of the stories inherent within each visual work. The translation of "La Gioconda" also retells a story of masculine adventure and conquest as thematized by the play of light. Light first appears in the form of "twilight" "amorously" "touching" the "ripeness" that is La Gioconda's breast (ll. 7, 6), and then later it appears to "shine" from the surrounding landscape (l. 10). These same rays also illuminate the landscape's "zest" "for those vicissitudes by which men die" (ll. 10–11). This reference to a sadistic landscape echoes the earlier description of La Gioconda's hands folded in patient "rest of Cruelty that waits and doth not seek for prey" (ll. 4–6). Landscape and woman will not be conquered, but instead wait ominously for their masculine prey to come to them. This interest in the sexual dynamics of looking can be found in many of the other poetic translations within *Sight and Song*. While some of these ekphrastic works outright refuse the masculine gaze, still others try to imagine a way of looking that is non-possessive, yet still full of desire and visual pleasure. This next section will look at how Field's translations, as synaesthesic works, see in the subjective mode an opportunity to refuse the masculine gaze and, instead, offer in its place a visual connoisseurship grounded in ethical lesbian erotics.

3 Female Bonds and Aesthetic Connoisseurship

By the fin de siècle, feminist efforts to assert women's claim to artistic connoisseurship meant rethinking the role of gender in aesthetic methodology, including the gendered economy of the gaze and women's restricted role as objectified feminine muse. Field's poetry not only validates the inherent agency of beauty's body in the act of artistic creation, but the poets' erotic translations also carve out a place for a feminine mode of subjective apprehension that harkens back to earlier writings by women on the question of gender and artistic authority. Like the late-Victorian women writers discussed in this study, Field embraces new strategies of feminist collaboration – specifically, the erotic bond between artist and muse – in an attempt to produce new cultural representations of empowered women with socio-sexual autonomy. Writing in response to both male and female influences, Bradley and Cooper strategically reframe aesthetic translation in sexualized terms, and while *Sight and Song* clearly aspires to an established tradition of masculine self-withholding, the poems' persistent reference to, and pleasure in, feminine impressions raises obvious questions about the link between gender and an ethical consumption. As seen in both "La Gioconda" and "Pen-Drawing of Leda," Field's poetic translations emphasize not only the central role of the gaze, but the poems also align the act of looking with desire. This equation between looking and desire makes sense given that visual consumption is itself a sensory activity and, as such, evaluated in terms of pleasurable stimulation. Indeed, in his preface to *The Renaissance* (1873), Pater explains how it is the job of the art critic to isolate and analyse such aesthetic stimuli.

> The aesthetic critic, then, regards all the objects with which he has to do, all works of art, and the fairer forms of nature and human life, as powers or forces producing pleasurable sensations, each of a more or less peculiar or unique kind. This influence he feels, and wishes to explain, by analysing and reducing it to its elements. (xxx)

Field pushes this model of artistic experience even further to consider the gendered dynamics at play within the aesthetic gaze. The poetic translations in *Sight and Song* deliberately fold back onto, and challenge, the embodied subject who looks at and enjoys the work of art. Rather, it is through this self-reflexive representation of looking that the poets-as-translators establish a "feminist" way of looking that takes pleasure in, while still preserves, the sexual autonomy of the artistic object or muse.

Recent criticism on the sexual politics of *Sight and Song* tends to extend Vadillo's favourable interpretation of Field's translations as successful in their aspirations to objective aesthetics. Jill Ehnenn, for example, claims that Field's translations create "speaking-spaces for female characters and artist's models – spaces to be perceived by women readers and spectators" (*Women's Literary Collaboration*, 77), while Krista Lysack aligns Field's reflexive gaze with a form of visual "consumption that eschews ownership" (*Come Buy, Come Buy*, 936).[55] Still other critics, including Hilary Fraser (*Women Writing Art History in the Nineteenth*

Century) and Julia Saville ("The Poetic Imaging of Michael Field"), see in Field's aesthetic translations a very subjective, but tactical, expression of masculine desire that, when combined with the poets' masculine pseudonym, draws attention to the gendered economy of the aesthetic gaze.[56] I share with this latter group of critics an interest in the way that Field's poetic translations deliberately invoke, only to queer, the sexual economy of power implicit in the masculine gaze. In focusing on gender and economics, however, *Critical Alliances* also reads Field's queer aesthetics as part of a larger attempt to validate women's status as connoisseurs and, therein, to write new cultural narratives that respect women's artistic authority. Time and again, Field's poetic persona doubles as observer who, like Zeus in "A Pen-Drawing of Leda," must accept a passive position in response to the feminine form's powerful assertion of sexual evasion or outright rejection. This mode of aesthetic experience thus gestures toward a very specific and embodied translator who is caught in the moment of looking as visual stimulation. What I describe as a "feminist" gaze, then, is the subjective and highly self-reflective expression of desire – an expression that depends upon but, also, preserves the feminine object's autonomy.

Of course, *Sight and Song* also contains poetic translations that focus on a masculine object of the aesthetic gaze. Yet these poems, too, present readers with a feminist gaze that practices aesthetic consumption as a form of self-reflexive pleasure. In "L' Indifférent," for example, Field represents Watteau's painting of a beautiful dancing boy in terms that draw attention to the translator's increasingly frustrated desire for the elusive aesthetic object.[57] Initially, the translator attempts to get the object to respond by asking, "*Sweet herald, give thy message*!" (l. 3), but the boy chooses instead to "dance on" rather than reply to this invocation (l. 4). The poet stages repeated attempts at seduction, as figured in the italicized portions of the poem, yet the boy still refuses until finally the poet-narrator admits, "In vain we woo" (l. 14). The full poem reads:

L' INDIFFÉRENT
Watteau
The Louvre

He dances on a toe
As light as Mercury's:
Sweet herald, give thy message! No,
He dances on; the world is his,
The sunshine and his wingy hat;
His eyes are round

Beneath the brim:
To merely dance where he is found
Is fate to him
And he was born for that.

He dances in a cloak
Of vermeil and of blue:
Gay youngster, underneath the oak,
Come, laugh and love! In vain we woo;
He is a human butterfly; –
No soul, no kiss,
No glance nor joy!
Though old enough for manhood's bliss,
He is a boy,
Who dances and must die. (1–2)

The opening iambic lines promise an easy blend of form and subject; the bouncing and forward moving lyric would seem to suggest that the poet-translator is indeed privy to the "song" emanating from the work, the very same song motivating the boy's dance. However, this song is quickly ruptured by those colons, which mark the shift from a passive auditory experience to an italicized address and, with it, the translator's active participation in the poem.[58] The first address runs for less than a line and is met immediately with the word "no," which acknowledges the object's refusal (l. 3), and by the second stanza the address takes the form of enjambed lines (ll. 13–14), as if to signal the observer-as-translator's mounting desire. At the same time, the enjambed lines quickly regress into monosyllabic beats – "Come, laugh and love!" (l. 14) – that are both heavy and even desperate, in contrast with the musicality of the poem's iambic metre. Perhaps the most important contrast between the two stanzas can be found in what follows the denied appeals. In the first stanza, the poet is met with a definitive "no" and then moves on to describe the painting and its subject, focusing on the boy's eyes, hat, and dance. By the second stanza, the address is followed by the admission "in vain we woo" (l. 14), succeeded by a long series of negatives in describing the boy. We are, for example, told that the dancing boy has "no soul, no kiss/No glance nor joy!" (ll. 16–17), and the poem ends on a negative note when it pessimistically informs readers that, though the dancing boy is beautiful, he eventually "must die" (l. 20). These latter lines paint a picture of the eroticized object (the dancing boy) as the total embodiment of "no," a figure of absolute refusal to the point of complete negation. The object's refusal has, by the second half of the poem, culminated in the poet-translator's frustrated desire, not an objective account of the work or its song.

It is also this turn to a non-possessive gaze that underwrites Field's collaborative lesbian erotics. As many critics have already argued, the poem's sexualized representation of the boyish figure suggests a self-conscious meditation upon the poets' own lesbian desire. For critics such as Fraser, the adolescent is an "indeterminate" or "liminal" figure, caught between youth and manhood, and is therefore a particularly fruitful symbol for a range of dissident sexuality, including lesbian desire (*Women Writing Art History in the Nineteenth Century*, 85). Martha Vicinus also argues that the male adolescent was a popular symbol among many late-Victorian lesbians, some of whom even adopted a boyish look, "because he could represent visually their sense of difference from other women" ("The Adolescent Boy," 85). This youthful figure, she continues, "represented action without responsibility, a transvestite disguise that permitted either sexual or emotional aggression or childlike responsiveness" (85). Given this cultural context, I argue that the translator's desire for the youth can easily be rethought as a trope through which the poets express their shared lesbian desire; in fact, "L' Indifférent's" reference to an unsatisfied "we" (l. 14) does not invoke an abstract or monocular gaze, but instead, folds back on and therein mediates, specifically, Bradley and Cooper's triangulated desire for the unattainable aesthetic object.[59] For the purposes of this chapter, however, I want to focus on those translations that take the feminine figure as their primary subject, for it is in these poems that we best see Field's development of an ethical erotics that rewrites the gendered terms of aesthetic consumption to produce a non-possessive and collaborative feminine pleasure. Poems such as "La Gioconda" and "A Pen-Drawing of Leda" look back at and implicate the translator-observer, and through such moments of self-reflexivity, make possible a queer aesthetics. In Field's translations the feminine object consistently evades her masculine pursuer and thus demands a new mode of visual apprehension that is attentive to, and accepting of, mutual feminine exchange. "La Gioconda" and "A Pen-Drawing of Leda" describe a feminine muse who looks back at and implicates her observer, and both poems therein transform aesthetic consumption from an act of domination to a non-possessive mode of shared visual pleasure. For example, the final lines of "A Pen-Drawing of Leda" point to the feminine object's power over the male subject; when light bounces off Leda back to Zeus, it also illuminates the point of contact and that spot "where her hand presses" Zeus's neck (l. 13). The poem refuses to resolve this moment of conflicted contact – Zeus's desire is thwarted by the more powerful Leda who is the real agent of seduction – and the aesthetic gaze is, instead, reframed as an erotically charged and mutual exchange between observer and the feminine object of desire.

In keeping with its emphasis on a non-possessive aesthetic, Field's *Sight and Song* also suggests how the translator-as-observer must take pleasure in, but still respect, feminine autoeroticism. Field's translation of Giorgione's "Sleeping Venus," for example, is extraordinary precisely for its sexually charged description of female masturbation.[60] We can see an example of this self-pleasuring in the following passage:

> Her hand the thigh's tense surface leaves,
> Falling inward. Not even sleep
> Dare invalidate the deep,
> Universal pleasure sex
> Must unto itself annex –
> Even the stillest sleep; at peace,
> More profound with rest's increase,
> She enjoys the good
> Of delicious womanhood. (101–2; ll. 62–70)

"[D]elicious womanhood" is, of course, a clear reference to pleasure in feminine sexuality, but it is important to note that this is Venus's pleasure in her own sexuality. Her act of self-pleasure is described as "falling inward," a kind of introversion into herself, and her autoerotic desire is "annex[ed]" "unto itself," suggesting a dual and conflicting gesture of combination and yet separation through a single wholeness independent of the observer's desire. In her interpretation of the masturbatory image, Saville explains how Field resists the impulse to "figurative interpretations" and therein respects the independence of the original work and Venus herself ("The Poetic Imaging of Michael Field," 197). Fraser also sees in the poem a form of feminist ethics, adding that the poets' shared lesbian gaze "celebrates the scopophilic pleasure of women gazing upon the beauty of a woman's body in a paean to female sexuality" (*Women Writing Art History in the Nineteenth Century*, 92). I agree that the observer does find some degree of visual pleasure, only looking is here represented as empathetic identification. As in previous poems, the translator's gaze moves across surface objects in a way that tells a story of sexual desire and pleasurable stimulation. In this case, however, the gaze itself replicates the motions of masturbation; the poet-as-translator watches Venus's hand as it moves inward from her "tense" thigh to her "deep,/universal pleasure." The visual shift from "tense," to "peace," and finally to the "good/of delicious womanhood" thus offers a kind of narrative through which the translator traces and, at the same time, vicariously enjoys Venus's moment of stimulation, climax, and then denouement.

The poet-as-translator's stimulated response to the work of art also reintroduces the question of synaesthesia as holding in balance both the visual and auditory modes. Through structured "song," the translator attempts a feminist erotics that takes pleasure in the mutual autonomy of the visual object ("sight"). "The Sleeping Venus," for example, is composed of mostly four beat lines, taking some liberty here and there to make the metre fit (the third line reads best as five beats, while the stanza's thirteenth, or penultimate, line has three). It is a difficult poem to scan, especially given that Field often ignores linguistic stress in order to focus on relative stress. Yet this technique belies a deliberate effort to maintain self-discipline and, in controlling or suppressing subjective desire, to keep the object at the forefront of discussion. This sentiment is best evidenced by the poem's conclusion, which rhymes "sweet" and "feet" as if trying to contain subjective pleasure within the realm of reverence.

> In communion with the sweet
> Life that ripens at her feet:
> We can never fear that she
> From Italian field will flee,
> For she does not come from far,
> She is of the things that are;
> And she will not pass
> While the sun strikes on the grass. (105; ll. 119–26)

The object of the painting might remain fixed, unable to "flee" or "pass," and yet the translation fights the impulse to contain her as passive by restricting the sun's rays to the grass, an obvious connection with the observer's own expression of reverence at her "sweet" "feet." Of course, as with the forced metre, this struggle to control desire is itself telling of the inescapable subject that is at the heart of translation and the aesthetic experience.

As the conduit through which the painting (sight) becomes lyric (song), Bradley and Cooper are not only subjectively present in the act of translation, but their shared desires, mediated by the elusive object, culminates in an ethical lesbian erotics. It is no accident that *Sight and Song*'s final poem ends with an image of frustrated desire, for the feminist gaze refuses to replicate the masculine mode of possessive consumption. In this poem, a translation of Watteau's "L'Embarquement pour Cythera," the translator describes Venus as guiding young couples to the eponymous island. Because of the poem's length, I quote selectively.

Tis Venus' rose veiled barque
And that great company ere dark
Must to Cythera, so the lovers prevail,
Adventurously sail. (118; ll. 23–6)

As Vadillo reminds us, "the island of Cythera is the myth of the quest for love" ("*Sight and Song*: Transparent Translations," 31). The final stanza stands apart as a kind of postscript in which the translator admits that this pursuit has already passed and the lovers are now long "gone."

Now are they gone: a change is in the light,
The iridescent ranges wane,
The waters spread: ere fall of night
the red-prowed shallop will have passed from sight
and the stone of Venus by herself remain
Ironical above that wide, embrowning plain. (125; ll. 141–6)

The translator is left staring at the "stone of Venus by herself," and the statue seems almost irreproachable in her "irony."[61] This final meditation firmly places readers within that moment when Bradley and Cooper, standing in the art gallery, looked at and recorded their visual consumption of the Venus statue.[62] Their frustrated desire is written explicitly into the poem's postscript. The first line of this last stanza is broken in half by a censure, marked by a semicolon, which separates the "Now they are gone" from "a change is in the light." This break signals a shift in focus from the already absent object to the light and the idea of change. Yet this change is also elusive insofar as light gives way to "waning ranges" and "spreading waters." The lovers are indeed gone, and the poet-as-translator is left looking across an ever-widening and fading landscape. The semicolon in the third line introduces yet another break, marking the landscape as separate and the lovers now as a double absence. The second half of this third line then tells us that night is falling, thereby confirming that the light and, with it, the landscape (the ranges and waters) are lost to the observer-as-translator. This point is amplified when the next line tells us that the lovers' boat has passed from sight, rhyming this last word with night. Overall, then, this postscript is all about sight – or rather, losing sight of the desired object. These final lines relate that highly embodied moment when the poets stood in the gallery and gazed upon the stone statue of Venus, trying to conjure, only to lose, her story-song. The final couplet's masculine rhyme, linking "remain" and "plain," is somber in its lack of musical momentum, while also drawing attention to the tension between spatial and temporal experience. There is a clear difference between all that "remains" (the ironical stone Venus) and the poets' desire to again see across that "plain" and therein hear the lovers' "laughter" one last time (l. 133).

Though the original artwork's song might prove ultimately elusive, efforts to listen and to record one's impressions still prove fruitful and, indeed, underwrite Field's collaborative aesthetics. This is the point of "Treading the Press," which self-consciously represents the synaesthetic method in the thematic shift from singing to dance.

TREADING THE PRESS
Benozzo Gozzoli
The Campo Santo at Pisa

From the trellis hang the grapes
        Purple-deep;
Maidens with white, curving napes
        And coiled hair backward leap,
As they catch the fruit, mid-laughter,
Cut from every silvan rafter.

Baskets, over-filled with fruit,
        From their heads
Down into the press they shoot
        A white-clad peasant treads,
Firmly crimson circles smashing
Into must with his feet's thrashing.

Wild and rich the oozings pour
        From the press;
Leaner grows the tangled store
        Of vinage, ever less:
Wine that kindles and entrances
Thus is made by one who dances. (20–1)

Dominated by troches and loose dactyls, the poem reads almost like a chant, as if in an attempt to reenact the unnamed song that motivates the treaders' dance. Each stanza ends with a feminine rhymed couplet – "laughter" in the "rafters," and then "smashing" and "thrashing" – giving the impression of an overwhelming atmosphere of sound. Yet despite what seems like an overwhelming turn to "song," the poem is, nonetheless, a highly subjective account of the treaders' work and the visual pleasure this offers. As Ehnenn observes, "Treading the Press" places the dancing female wine pressers at the very centre of Benozzo Gozzoli's fresco, *The Drunkenness of Noah*, in order to rewrite "a Biblical story about a patriarch's wrathful curse into a charming scene about a happy community of women" (*Women's Literary Collaboration*, 80).[63] I would also argue that the poem's fascination with women's gendered cooperation is part of a larger effort to deconstruct the masculine gaze. The poem begins with an image of grapes "purple-deep" and overripe hanging from a trellis, and the next line then quickly moves to a description of a group of maidens with "white, curving napes" and "coiled hair" (ll. 2, 3, 4). Finally, in stanza 3, the grapes – transformed into "wild and rich oozings" – are poured from the press and left to ferment into wine. Such descriptive attention to appearances and shapes suggests the translator's initial expectation that the roundish maidens, like the grapes, are passive objects to be plucked or possessed. However, in foregrounding the female dancers' active role in production, the poem thus rejects the masculine mode of consumption which renders woman a passive object. Indeed, it is this idea of cooperation, and not objectification, that is the source of aesthetic pleasure. Specifically, "Treading the Press" points to the wine, the product of collective dance, as the final object of aesthetic consumption. At the same time, the translator's closing comment that wine is made "by one who dances" refuses to engender this creative process as either feminine or masculine (l. 18). While the pronoun "one" would seem to suggest a singular dancer, a solitary subject, its lack of gender specificity instead reminds us of the cooperative dance between men and women. The male peasant's thrashing dance can begin only after, and in response to, the females' dance – he needs these women to pass him the grapes for treading, just as the women need him to thrash the grapes into wine. In this final stanza, then, the poem encourages a new kind of aesthetic experience that takes pleasure in ("kindles and entrances") the productive agency of collaboration.

Conclusion: The Art of Lesbian Erotics

In the summer of 1903, while visiting Bernard Berenson at his wife Mary's family cottage in Haslemere, Bradley and Cooper helped themselves to a painting on silk that belonged to the latter's brother because, as biographer Emma Donoghue explains, in *We Are Michael Field*, the poets assumed that its owner (Logan Pearsall Smith) had abandoned the artwork. Pearsall Smith contacted the couple insisting they return the painting, but the poets' reply instead claimed a "pious obedience to that law of possession, which, inscribed in Heaven, if not on earth, decrees that objects of beauty belong to those who love them best" (quoted in Donoghue, 116). Krista Lysack's "Aesthetic Consumption and the Cultural Production of *Sight and Song*" convincingly interprets this event as an example of the poets' celebration of "nonobjectifying consumption" (938) – a mode of visual pleasure that continued to influence Bradley and Cooper's relationship with art well into their later life and writings. Gender is central to Field's attempt to rethink the socio-economic structures of consumption that typically govern one's aesthetic responses to art. In fact, the poets' redefinition of the artwork as a thing of "beauty," not legal property, can be traced back to their earlier representations of queer desire in *Sight and Song*. As in that earlier work, Field insists that beauty's body (the feminized artwork) cannot be owned; beauty can only be "loved" or celebrated, an aesthetic mode that therein disavows masculine modes of appropriation or possession.

For modern scholars still today, Victorian women's role as active participants in shaping the form and (feminist) content of aesthetic theory is still up for debate. Kate Flint claims that "it is hard to detect anything like a feminist agenda" in nineteenth-century art criticism by women (*The Victorians and the Visual Imagination*, 193), while Pamela Gerrish Nunn "emphatically" insists that Victorian women did not make a meaningful contribution to aestheticism and that the "art critic's voice as a public noise can be generalised as a male voice" – those female writers who did contribute to the field would have thus copied the form and content of their forefathers ("Critically Speaking," 109). Still other scholars, such as Meaghan Clarke, convincingly show us how women writers, despite their varying attitudes toward feminism and art discourse, "made a fundamental difference to the construction of the discipline, just as it was being professionalized and institutionalized" (*Critical Voices*, 156), while John Paul M. Kanwit adds that "feminist views are often embedded in the stories that women writers tell about art works" (*Victorian Art Criticism and the Woman Writer*, 4). If art journalism helped make possible the rise of late-Victorian realism,[64] for example, then female writers such as Vernon Lee and Alice Meynell (among the first to define "impressionism") must be acknowledged for their important contributions to the profession as well as its impact upon wider literary and cultural conversations and conventions (Kanwit, 5–6). By reframing aesthetic translation in gendered terms, *Sight and Song* also challenges any assumption of a masculine tradition and, instead, aligns itself with this much larger history of women's active contribution to art criticism and aesthetic theory. Writing together as "Michael Field," the poet-as-translators Bradley and Cooper inhabit the position of male observer only to deconstruct the gender economy of the gaze and give back to feminine writers and muses their voice within this aesthetic exchange.

At the same time, Field's effort to stake out for women a role within the modern gendered marketplace as respected connoisseurs and producers of artistic content is thoroughly collaborative in that it requires a community of women that extends beyond the authors themselves to include readers and future consumers of feminist content. As discussed in this chapter, *Sight and Song*'s emphasis on the subjective nature of ekphrastic translation invites readers to participate in the poets' collaborative redefinition of the "feminine" within aesthetics. First, this invitation encourages readers to think about the wider conversation among feminist authors on the gendered gaze and women's artistic authority. Late-Victorian "mirror poems" – including Caroline Lindsay's "My Own Face" (1889), May Probyn's "The Model" (1883), and Mary E. Coleridge's "The Other Side of a Mirror" (1896) – reclaim for women their agency in the act of artistic creation as both feminine muse and author of the aesthetic experience. At the same time, Field's claim to artistic authority – looking at and theorizing famous paintings – must be read as part of a tradition of women's artistic connoisseurship, which includes early examples such as Mariana Starke's travel guides or Anna Brownell Jameson's *Penny Magazine* (1834–45),[65] as well as later writings by Vernon Lee on aestheticism or Alice Meynell's art journalism.[66] Finally, and perhaps more significantly, the poets' subjective translations also invite reflection upon the primary role of gendered desire in, as well as women's contribution to, aesthetic theory. In both cases the feminine is rewritten as an active participant within the visual encounter and subsequent literary translation, and yet this second mode is all the more daring for its unabashed celebration of visual erotics as a mutual and ethical exchange that preserves feminine autonomy. Field's ekphrastic poems celebrate subjective desire and therein invite readers to enjoy, alongside the translator, women's active contribution to – and even authority over – the aesthetic experience, and this representation of the feminine as subject (not passive object of masculine consumption) thus consolidates a new construction of gender that works in support of women's artistic connoisseurship.

There can be little surprise, then, given their emphasis on the affective power of art, that Bradley and Cooper thought of their literary creations as real flesh-and-blood characters whose powerful influence could be still felt in their poets' own everyday life. As friend Charles

Ricketts recalls, in his short memoir of the couple,[67] "[t]he persons of [Bradley and Cooper's] dramas were like living beings of whom they would talk by the hour, whose opinions they would quote or surmise just as if they were shall we say Mary Berenson or Robert Browning" (*Michael Field*, 5). Of course, this same blurring of boundaries between the literary and the real can also be found in Field's *Sight and Song*, where the poems' representations of feminine autonomy clearly continued to influence the poets' life-long attitudes toward art as a force to be loved and cherished, but not owned or objectified as property (regarding Logan Pearsall Smith's painting). Elsewhere in his biography Ricketts writes that "To think of nothing else but art seems forced and affected to us" (5), but in Field's case this devotion was clearly part of a much larger commitment to the transformative influence that art might exercise in our everyday lives – including our attitudes toward gendered and economic consumption.

By drawing readers into a shared poetic relationship of female erotics, Field writes new social narratives by and for women interested in aesthetic authority. *Sight and Song* is, therefore, part of a fin-de-siècle movement by feminist artists to rewrite the gendered economy of the gaze and, with it, to affirm women's roles and professional mobility as critics and producers of modern artistic content. The next chapter builds upon this idea of women's bodily bonds and literary affect through an analysis of post-Victorian inheritance of feminist models in Modernist writings by Virginia Woolf. Though Woolf did not specifically address works by Michael Field, the former shared her Victorian predecessors' preoccupation with literature as shaping gendered relationships of exchange and women's access to socio-sexual autonomy. Writing in the early decades of the twentieth century, after the trauma of the First World War, Woolf challenges the idea of a definitive break between generations, and instead her writings on women and economics see in literary kinship between women an opportunity to redefine the gendered economy handed down from Victorians before her.

5 Virginia Woolf's Post-Victorian Feminism

Killing the Angel in the House was part of the occupation of a woman writer.
– Virginia Woolf, "Professions for Women"

[Olive Schreiner] remains even now, when the vigor of her books is spent, and her personal sway, evidently of the most powerful, is a memory limited to those who knew her, too uncompromising a figure to be so disposed of.
– Virginia Woolf, "Olive Schreiner"

On 21 January 1931, in a lecture addressed to the London National Society for Women's Service, Virginia Woolf delivered her now infamous explanation of how, in order to be a successful writer, she had to "kill" the Victorian Angel in the House, that icon of feminine self-sacrifice and domestic servitude. To "kill," in this context, is framed an act of "self-defence" (2), for as Woolf continues, "[h]ad I not killed her she would have killed me," and "[s]he would have plucked the heart out of my writing" (2). The lecture was eventually republished as "Professions for Women," and the ideas it expressed, especially regarding cultural inheritance of gender roles and their impact on women's economic mobility, became the seed for later texts, *The Years* (1937) and *Three Guineas* (1938). For feminist scholar Elaine Showalter, "Professions for Women" neatly articulates the author's ongoing interest in gender as a contested category that straddles both the past and present. Woolf was, on the one hand, "fighting off the spectre of Victorian respectability so ironically named the Angel of the House" by Victorians before her, and on the other hand, "struggling to find the courage to 'tell the truth about my own experience as a body'" ("Killing the Angel in the House," 339, 340). While the second struggle is ongoing, Woolf thought she had found the answer to the first in a theory of androgyny, Showalter argues, which allowed the Modernist a comfortable distance from her literary foremothers whose "circumstances as women had made them weak" (341).[1] Yet the above excerpt on "Olive Schreiner," from the 1925 review discussed at the start of this study,[2] also belies Woolf's respect for how some of her sister-writers were made all the stronger, or "uncompromising," through their "personal" writings on gender and feminism. These Victorian predecessors, as with their counter-narratives on "women," cannot "be so disposed of" and thus require a more complicated approach to periodicity and the cultural transmission of gender narratives.

Contemporary scholarship on Woolf has long been fascinated with the author's complicated relationship with her Victorian predecessors. Jane Marcus is perhaps the scholar best known for popularizing the assumption of Woolf as writing in opposition to nineteenth-century narratives on gender and the patriarchal family.[3] Marcus's essay "Storming the Toolshed," for example, takes issue with biographer Quentin Bell's claim that Woolf "belonged inescapably, to the Victorian world of Empire, Class and Privilege" (Bell, *Virginia Woolf*, vol. 2:186), and instead insists that in her writing, Woolf "was arguing for a total subversion" of such inherited institutions (Marcus, 635).[4] Marcus's later introduction for *Virginia Woolf and the Languages of Patriarchy* also claims that Woolf's writings express "passionate hatred for the Victorian patriarchal family" and propose in place of the latter a very forward-looking (in a rejection of the past) "utopian vision of social equality for women and working-class men" (5). More recent scholarship by Steve Ellis (*Virginia Woolf and the Victorians*), however, argues that Woolf's writings defy any kind of easy or definitive periodization and that the author herself instead entertains a complex and sustained negotiation with her literary forbearers. Woolf was, after all, personally connected to some of the most significant figures whose literary careers spanned the turn of the century: "Not only were Woolf's Victorian forbearers numerous and eminent, but they all knew each other in a consolidated network that effected Woolf's "hereditary position, " and that she would spend the lengthy post-Victorian portion of her life continually remaking" (Ellis, 11).[5] In "remaking" her literary kinship, Woolf would often, therefore, find herself balancing her so-called passionate hatred (to invoke Marcus) with what Ellis describes as "an attitude of admiration, which indicates, not a desire to 'return' to the past, but the recognition of an inheritance that can be serviceable to modernity in various ways" (Ellis, 4). This chapter is interested in that "serviceable" relationship between Woolf and her sister-writers in the nineteenth century. What does Woolf draw from feminist writers before her, and how does she remake literary inheritance between women into a connection that is neither nostalgic nor overly progressivist?

Rewriting bonds between sisters across Victorian and Modernist generations means rethinking literary inheritance and the transmission of dominant gender narratives, specifically, as a process of negotiation and resistance. *Critical Alliances* argues that Woolf's representation of post-Victorian kinship implicitly responds to, and also reimagines, the Victorian feminisms discussed in preceding chapters. This is, in other words, a capstone chapter in which I read Woolf's investment in the late-Victorian Women's Movement as part of an ongoing dialogic conversation on gender reform across generations. Both *Three Guineas* and *The Years* would seem to heed the fin-de-siècle feminist's call for open-ended narratives that are inclusive of women who seek work and relationships beyond domestic plots (per Schreiner and Levy). Woolf is also, like Egerton and Field, interested in women's work as professional writers and the impact of gendered economics upon feminist art (including the gendered gaze). Unlike her literary foremothers, however, Woolf's writings reject the possibility of a progressive feminism and, instead, call attention to the cultural transmission of gender as a process of negotiation and critical resistance.[6] Critic Melba Cuddy-Keane argues that Woolf's avant-garde writings promote precisely this kind of fluid or negotiable relationship between narratives and their recipient readers. Cuddy-Keane rejects the idea of a polarizing divide between generations, and in *Virginia Woolf, the Intellectual, and the Public Sphere*, instead focuses specifically on Woolf's aspirations to a kind of democratic inclusiveness in literature that carefully deconstructs the traditional divide between so-called high and popular culture: "[Woolf] promoted a dialogic rather than an authoritarian relation between writer and reader and opposed the increasing standardization or 'massification' of the reading public implicit in the process of mass production and distribution" (Cuddy-Keane, 2). This same idea of a dialogic exchange between classed writers and readers can also be applied to Woolf's work on Victorian domesticity and particularly feminist authors' attempt to rethink the narrative construction of gender as an inclusive process that also allows for readers' critical resistance.[7]

This chapter looks at how dialogic resistance is an important feature of Woolf's writings on the intersections between gender and economics in *The Years* and *Three Guineas*. In these later texts Woolf explores at length the limits imposed upon women's work and career ambitions as a consequence of dominant cultural constructions of gender and the feminine ideal, in particular. *Three Guineas* looks back to a "Victorian psychology of the sexes" (or "infantile fixation" [126]) in order to explain the gendered prohibition on women's participation in social and political exchanges beyond the domestic sphere, including contemporary conversations on war and gendered violence. The Victorian woman must "not on any account be allowed to make money," Woolf explains, because an independent income meant that she was "free" of her father and of domestic obligations more generally (*Three Guineas*, 132–3). Working against the "general acceptance of male dominance, and still more of feminine inferiority" (126), Woolf imagines how women might form a kind of "society of outsiders" whose collective resistance both draws attention to and deconstructs the gender bias implicit in these cultural narratives of domination and exclusion. In a similar gesture of cultural resistance, *The Years* has its main protagonist, Eleanor Pargiter, look back at the Victorian past and wonder aloud if "things have changed for the better" and whether "[w]e're happier" and "freer" than before (386). As someone who was bound by domestic obligations to the patriarch for the better part of her life, from 1880 to the "Present Day" chapter, Eleanor is understandably optimistic when she looks to the younger generation, like her doctor-niece Peggy. Yet the latter's sceptical response to her aunt – "What does she mean by 'happiness,' by 'freedom'"? (386) – undercuts any sense of a unilateral and progressive narrative running throughout this intergenerational feminist critique of gender and economics.

Woolf's sceptical attitude toward the Victorians and their inherited narratives of gendered labour informs much of her writing and, thus, effectively maintains her literary connection with, but also critique of, feminisms before her. I take as an example Steve Ellis's work on the "post-Victorian" (*Virginia Woolf and the Victorians*) in order to think through these "serviceable" exchanges between Modernist and Victorian feminisms.[8] While Woolf might not reference by name the preceding authors discussed in this study (excluding her review of Schreiner, excerpted above), her representations of women's dialogic critique of inherited gender roles certainly employ similar textual strategies devoted to the narrative deconstruction of "woman" as a fixed identity category. Her narrative representations of female labour, in particular, look back at and resist the same gender tropes against which her fin-de-siècle sister writers fought in their pursuit of economic opportunity. Woolf's writings thus propose an alternative, or "post-Victorian," model of feminist inheritance in which women across generations are bonded together by virtue of their shared resistance to dominant patriarchal culture. This kinship is borne of an ongoing fight against, by and large, the persistent influence of nineteenth-century domestic ideology and is, as a result, a question of textual strategy (not biology). To "kill the Victorian Angel in the house" thus means to participate in a literary tradition that works against the assumption of periodization – including the popular assumption of an historical break by Modernists. Woolf refuses the idea of an absolute or regenerative break in literary tradition, yet her feminist fiction still strives for a critical distance in its effort to redefine inherited gender narratives and, specifically, the collective category of "woman" by which she and her literary foremothers are restricted. Her writings on gender and economics thus make possible a very different and, specifically, critical relationship between Modernist feminists and their Victorian forbearers. It is possible for Modernist writers to appreciate and even draw upon the work of feminists before them, while still trying to rewrite the narrative tradition of gender (in both form and content). In *Three Guineas* and *The Years*, Woolf models this intergenerational dialogue by presenting readers with new narrative representations of "women" who break free of their inherited Victorian domestic plots. Writing against dominant models of gendered economics, Woolf's matricidal author instead maintains an ongoing – albeit critical – dialogue with her literary foremothers, and thereby works to produce an alternative "feminist" tradition of cultural inheritance by and for women.

1 Woolf and the Post-Victorian (literary kinship)

The plot of Virginia Woolf's *The Years* begins in the 1880s and, through close study of the Pargiter family across the decades, traces the change in women's gendered relationship to the family and filial loyalty, specifically. When the matriarch of the family dies, the eldest daughter of the family, Eleanor, takes over her mother's domestic duties and the day-to-day running of the home at Abercorn Terrace. She looks after her father, Colonel Abel Pargiter, and also serves as buffer between him and her younger siblings. Yet Eleanor's work comes at the high personal cost of her physical and economic autonomy. At one point, her sister Milly remarks on how Eleanor enjoys philanthropic service in the poorer neighbourhoods "more than anything," and that it is obvious that Eleanor would even "like to live there if [she] had [her] way" (31). When pressed on the subject, however, Eleanor shifts uncomfortably in her chair, thinking to herself how "she had her dreams, her plans of course; but she did not want to discuss them" (31). This act of self-silencing foreshadows the trajectory of Eleanor's life of sacrifice, compelled to spend the better part of her youth and adult years caring for, and subordinate to, her father until he passes away. Fast-forward eleven years to 1891, Eleanor is in her thirties but still bound by filial duty to her father and his home. This novel section also reveals how the domestic economy is entirely financed by the father, thereby replicating Victorian gender ideology in which wives and daughters are figured as dependent wards of the patriarch. After tallying up the monthly grocery expenses, for example, Eleanor enters her father's study in order to ask him for remuneration, which he provides after "unlock[ing] the drawer in which he kept his cheque-book" (92). It is worth noting that Eleanor tallies up the monthly bills with her mother's pen: "she had never thrown it away because it was part of other things – her mother for example" (91). Writing with this pen and taking care of her father's domestic finances, Eleanor thereby occupies the exact same position as the former matriarch. Though the daughter performs the invaluable work of feeding and maintaining the family, the domestic income nonetheless belongs exclusively to Colonel Abel Pargiter. Eleanor's work is unpaid, and because she cannot enjoy an independent income, she literarily depends upon her father's support for food and shelter. With later chapters moving into the twentieth century and "Present Day" thirties, the plot structure of *The Years* signals to readers its overarching interest in Modernism's connection to the Victorian family. By focusing more closely on the relationship between two generations of Pargiters, the narrative structure therein replicates the idea of cultural transmission, as well as critique, of nineteenth-century models of gender and kinship.

Kinship has long served as a popular trope among authors interested in thinking through questions of cultural inheritance. Of course, this idea of "kinship" as shorthand for literary tradition predates Modernist writers like Woolf. Jane Spencer's *Literary Relations: Kinship and the Canon, 1660–1830* traces this way of thinking back to the early writers in the Renaissance, many of whom drew inspiration from biblical narratives, such as Genesis, on human beings as conduits for God's divine inspiration (9).[9] Yet several centuries later, Victorian author Charles Dickens saw in kinship a way to rethink one's relationship to cultural authority and the literary canon; his fiction regularly uses the orphaned or abandoned character (*Great Expectations* [1861], *David Copperfield* [1850], or *Oliver Twist* [1838]) in order to raise larger questions about thwarted genius, a theme which many argue is a reflection of his own traumatic childhood and how poverty briefly placed in doubt the author's claim to cultural inheritance.[10] By drawing our attention to otherwise illegitimate figures and their rightful claim to genius (their "expectations"), Dickens's fiction also encourages readers to think about the inherent "fiction" of canonicity and filial bonds between authors. Later theorist Emmanuel Levinas makes a similar point in his explanation of how such representations of kinship need not be restricted to biology but can, instead, be thought of as a metaphor for loyalty and the transmission of power from one generation to the next: "Filiation and fraternity – parental relations without biological bases – are current metaphors in our everyday life," he writes, adding that "[t]he relationship of master to disciple does not reduce to filiation and fraternity, but it certainly includes them" (*Totality and Infinity*, 71).

Many women writers also saw in kinship a powerful way to thematize their exclusion from the literary canon. Writing well before Levinas, Victorian authors such as Elizabeth Barrett Browning pushed even harder on the idea of kinship as a malleable "fiction" in order to carve out a place for female writers and their inheritors within a largely phallocentric literary canon. Early into her künstlerroman *Aurora Leigh* (1856), for example, Barrett Browning's titular heroine peruses her father's library (book 1) as she struggles to realize her own creative genius (later crowning herself poet laureate in book 2); Aurora Leigh then takes for herself a male source of inspiration, William Shakespeare (in book 1), while also trying to imagine an alternative or matriarchal inheritance as she meditates upon her deceased mother's portrait (book 1). Poets Katharine Bradley and Edith Cooper ("Michael Field") paid homage to Barrett Browning as literary foremother by co-publishing some of their earliest verse dramas (*Bellerophôn* [1881]) under the pen-names "Arran and Isla Leigh" (Bradley and Cooper, respectively). Late-Victorian women writers' bold attempt to imagine their place within the literary canon is completely refigured as a matrilineal tradition between foremothers and their feminist inheritors. Through this kind of regendering, kinship is repurposed as a powerful way to think about cultural bonds between female artists.

With the transition to Modernism, however, many authors – men and women, included – positioned themselves as writing against, or breaking from, their literary forbearers.[11] It became especially common for writers to celebrate filial continuity after the First World War (1914–18), as if the bonds of inheritance could somehow heal the trauma of war and answer for the many casualties suffered during the conflict. Some critics, such as Elaine Scarry (*The Body in Pain*), see in the literature of this period a continued effort to frame the soldier's death as contributing to a larger and heroic national legacy: war finds regenerative meaning, she explains, in "the interior content of human bodies, lungs, arteries, blood, brains, the mother lode that will eventually be reconnected to the winning issue" (137). Consider for example the opening octet of Rupert Brooke's poem, "The Soldier" (1914), composed in the early years of the war.

If I should die, think only this of me:
That there's some corner of a foreign field
That is for ever England. There shall be
In that rich earth a richer dust concealed;
A dust whom England bore, shaped, made aware,
Gave, once, her flowers to love, her ways to roam;
A body of England's, breathing English air,
Washed by the rivers, blest by suns of home.

Brooke's poem presents a powerful vision of a recuperative death as the fallen soldier's blood spills in the "foreign field of battle" and therein makes "richer" (or fertilizes) the land ("dust") that is now literally and symbolically annexed by the English imagination. Contemporary critics such as Teresa Heffernan argue that the trauma of the Great War persistently challenged any hopes of positive futurity; the Modernists instead saw themselves as living within an "end of times" scenario, but without the promise of an ending that might console or alleviate the pervasive "sense of exhaustion" (*Post-Apocalyptic Culture*, 7).[12] The Modernists were, Heffernan continues, left with "the Nietzschean challenge to either cower in terror at the randomness of the future, a future without a definitive course and without an end, or to embrace this liberation as from a chain" (42). Siegfried Sassoon's and Wilfred Owen's poems exemplify this more pessimistic – or what critic Sarah Cole describes as the "disenchanted" – view of war as a "useless and degrading slaughter" of bodies ("Enchantment, Disenchantment, War, Literature," 1639). For example, with its carefully chosen images of bodily pain and destruction, Owen's "Dulce et Decorum Est" (1920) refuses to transform the fallen soldier into a site of generative hope or heroics.

If you could hear, at every jolt, the blood
Come gargling from the froth-corrupted lungs,
Obscene as cancer, bitter as the cud
Of vile, incurable sores on innocent tongues, –
My friend, you would not tell with such high zest
To children ardent for some desperate glory,
The old Lie: *Dulce et decorum est*
Pro patria mori.

Speaking directly to the reader, Owen's poem asks that the soldier's death be recognized for what it is: a brutal death made worse by modern warfare (machine guns, trench battle, and poison gas shells). The trauma of such war, the poem insists, cannot be recycled into myths of "glory" told with "zest" to children eager to sacrifice themselves for country and culture; rather, "the old lie" of war as heroic is exposed and thus cut short, making a definitive break between Owen's poetry and the generative myths perpetrated by authors before him.[13]

Stressing the link between war and death (or narrative endings), not regeneration (or cultural transmission), many Modernists therefore saw themselves as working within an entirely new epoch that was detached from, and even positioned against, the preceding literary tradition. For many critics, this attempt to stage a definitive break from the Victorians is best seen in Ezra Pound's infamous call for Modernist artists to "Make it New!" and though Kurt Heinzelman (*Make It New: The Rise of Modernism*) accurately argues that Pound did not articulate this sentiment until 1934, the point still stands that the Modernist period is often hailed – even if retrospectively – as a point of rupture in literary kinship. F.T. Marinetti models an assertive rejection of tradition in his 1909 "Futurist Manifesto": "Why should we be looking back over our shoulders, if what we desire is to smash down the mysterious doors of the Impossible?" (14). And in his 1914 essay for *Blast*, Wyndham Lewis explains Vorticism as a total rejection of continuous temporality and, instead, asserts a new Modernism that is interested only in the present: "Our vortex is not afraid of the Past: it has forgotten its existence. Our vortex regards the Future as sentimental as the Past … With our Vortex the Present is the only active thing. Life is the Past and the Future. The Present is Art" (147).[14]

Still other writers such as Virginia Woolf, however, did not position themselves as enacting a radical break from literary kinship, but instead looked to produce new or disenchanted readings of death and the violence of war. *Three Guineas* is frank in its response to the photographic documentation of brutalized bodies and the shocking carnage of war: "They are not pleasant photographs to look upon. They are photographs of dead bodies for the most part," Woolf writes, adding that "This morning's collection contains the photograph of what might be a man's body, or a woman's; it is so mutilated that it might, on the other hand, be the body of a pig" (10).[15] As with Owen's poetry, Woolf's account of war refuses to glorify the soldier's death as working in service of a larger national tradition; instead, Woolf is deliberate in her attempt to foreground the work of interpretation ("it might … be the body of a pig") so that readers must wrestle with the notion of "dead bodies" which are "not pleasant" nor romanticized.

Woolf's complicated relationship with her literary predecessors has long been the stuff of debate among critics, with much of this conversation focused on the difference between the author's approach to history and that of her Bloomsbury contemporaries. Early work by Elizabeth French Boyd, for example, positions Woolf as part of a collective "rebel[ion] against the Victorian world," but then adds that the Group still could not avoid "being the transmitters of its traditions and its [the Victorian world's] legacies" (*Bloomsbury Heritage*, 77). Still more recent work by Steve Ellis encourages us to consider (what remains "under-acknowledged") the degree to which "Woolf's attachment to aspects of the 'Victorian world'" might set her apart from other members within the Group, including her husband Leonard, who were perhaps more antagonistic in their posture (*Virginia Woolf and the Victorians*, 2–3). As support for his line of investigation, Ellis invokes Hermione Lee's biography *Virginia Woolf*, a foundational work that understands the author as both "Modern" as well as "late Victorian." "The Victorian family past filled her fiction, shaped her political analyses of society and underlay the behavior of her social group," Lee writes, and this same nineteenth-century construct was also "a powerful ingredient, of course, in her definition of her self" (55, *sic*). Lee's biography employs the term "post-Victorian," which Ellis later takes up in order to understand Woolf's complicated approach to literary inheritance. The concept of "post-" Victorian is a way to think through the author's search for some kind of conciliation with the past; there is, as signalled by the hyphenated prefix, an undeniable tension between the present (1930s) and the past (1880s), and yet the "post" present is still "backed" by, or attached to, the past "Victorian" era. The "post-Victorian" is used throughout this chapter as a way to frame Woolf's writings on gender roles and women's cultural labour. Whereas many of her Modernist contemporaries stage a radical break from literary traditions before them, an approach made all the more imperative after the trauma of the First World War, Woolf instead embraces a different model of history as an ongoing dialogue with Victorian predecessors and their continued influence on domestic narratives and women's work in the early twentieth century.

I use "post-Victorian" deliberately, then, for the term perfectly captures the critical resistance implicit in Woolf's representation of intergenerational tensions between women. Some of her earliest novels, including *Night and Day* (1919) or *The Voyage Out* (1915), focus on the familial drama between Victorian parents and their modern daughters who long for more freedom beyond the confines of gendered domesticity. *Night and Day*'s female protagonist Katharine Hilbery is bonded to her mother, who plays a vital role in both mediating her daughter's relationship to the past (collaborating on a biography of Katharine's famous father, the poet Alardyce), but also facilitates her daughter's break with patriarchal authority by approving the final match between Katharine and Ralph Denham, despite Mr Hilbery's objections. In *The Voyage Out*, by contrast, the father-figure is peripheral to the central bond between aunt and niece, Helen Ambrose and Rachel Vinrace, respectively. Helen plays a vital role in her niece's social and sexual awaking, encouraging in the latter a habit of independent thought that will later challenge her lover Hewet's traditional expectations of feminine submission (his effort to control her literary taste is a primary example of this masculine authority). Yet it is in her fifth novel *To the Lighthouse* (1927) that Woolf strategically equates the death of the matriarch with the trauma of war in order to question the popular assumption of a Modernist break from the past. In the "Time Passes" middle section, for example, the Great War is almost entirely overshadowed by the death of Mrs Ramsay, while the same ten-year period also includes the death of Prue in childbirth and Andrew in war as if the two are parallel consequences of the disrupted, but still a formative, kinship system. In other words, the death of the Victorian mother is such a catastrophic event that it is equal to the shock of war and, therein, upsets traditional modes of self-conception which are typically associated with linear or realist plots.[16]

Like Woolf, other writers of the period used the death of the matriarch as a way to signal domestic rupture and, with it, the beginning of a new filial order. E.M. Forster's *Howard's End* (1910) implicitly aligns Ruth Wilcox with old England, especially insofar as both represent an emphasis on aristocratic blood and the filial descent of status. Yet the grand dame's decision to bequeath her home – the titular "Howard's End" – to Margaret Schlegel raises questions about rightful inheritance and the transmission of English culture.[17] The Schlegel sisters represent an unconventional generation that is both cosmopolitan (mixed English and German heritage) and democratic in its affiliations among the upper, middle, and working classes (Margaret's marriage to husband Henry Wilcox, as well as Helen's illegitimate child with Leonard Bast).[18] In a not too dissimilar fashion, William Faulkner's *As I Lay Dying* (1930) treats the death of the matriarch, Addie Bundren, as an occasion for multiple perspectives that push against the conventions of literary narrative; the decentralized narrative is told by several characters, including a contribution from Addie herself (toward the conclusion), and in multiple verb tenses that ultimately defy any assumption of a linear plot.[19] Despite their different representations of linear history, these novels all suggest that the matriarch's death marks a point of rupture in, and reinvention of, kinship bonds between the past and present generations.

Woolf's writings also represent the mother's death as an opportunity to re-imagine history as a non-linear dialogue – or "post-Victorian" critique (not break) – between generations. For some critics, however, Woolf's persistent investment in kinship is nothing more than a reactionary sentimentalism. Alex Zwerdling, for example, reads the matriarch's death in *To the Lighthouse* (1927) as part of a shared nostalgic turn by the Bloomsbury Group after the War.

> Woolf worried constantly that *To The Lighthouse* would be dismissed as sentimental [...] She had after all been trained by her Bloomsbury colleagues to think of sentimentality – especially for the Victorian past – as a bacillus, likely to bring back those dangerous nineteenth-century illnesses known as reverence and filial piety. But perhaps she need not have worried, because by 1927, when *To the Lighthouse* was published, the revolutionary impulse of 1910 had largely spent itself, and more and more of the [Bloomsbury] rebels were looking back with a sense of loss to the way of life that had disappeared. In part this was the product of World War I, the horror of which heightened, retrospectively, the positive qualities of what came before. (*Virginia Woolf and the Real World*, 200–1)

Conversely, I see in Woolf's fiction a theory of kinship that is much more complicated and, thus, defies any simple "revolutionary"/"reverential" dichotomy, to use Zwerdling's terms. Rather than claim a definitive break from history after the First World War, Woolf's representation of the dead mother instead invites readers to contemplate Modernism's continued resistance against inherited systems of gender and sexual economies.[20] In *To the Lighthouse,* for example, Cam and James are forced to confront their feelings of resentment toward their tyrannical father as they sail toward the lighthouse, while Lily Briscoe watches from the shore and thinks about the past and, in particular, Mrs Ramsay's role as angel of the house. Contemplating these different authority figures, Lily and Cam each tumble to a similar revelation at the very same moment: the ability to understand one's position vis-à-vis cultural inheritance depends upon distance (resistance) and, also, varies significantly from person to person and moment to moment (non-linear). Likewise, the mother's death in *The Voyage Out* represents a rupture in the transmission of filial loyalty; yet this earlier novel also imagines how this rupture allows bonds between women to supplant the traditional logic of patriarchal authority. After her mother's death, Rachel forms a close relationship with her (sororal) aunt Rachel, who encourages in her niece forms of intellectual and emotional agency that exceed paternalistic control. That Rachel dies by the novel's end is not a negative comment on this feminine transmission, so much as it is a reflection on the difficulty of Modernist women's struggle against masculine authority.

Like these earlier works, *The Years* suggests that the death of the matriarch facilitates a rupture in structures of filial loyalty. This later novel represents a particularly fruitful opportunity to think through the Modernist's critical response to nineteenth-century gender roles, especially the restrictions such roles impose upon women's socio-economic agency. As the eldest daughter of the Pargiter clan, Eleanor is first to assume responsibility for the family after her mother passes away. Eleanor's subsequent role as domestic manager also requires that she negotiate the patriarchal structure of capital organizing the late-Victorian home. *The Years* (1937) illustrates how women's work within this private sphere often reinforces men's monopoly of economic status and power. Eleanor is the one who purchases Maggie's birthday present, for example, but her father nonetheless pays for it and is the one to give the gift to his niece. When Maggie does not immediately love her "garish" necklace, the Colonel feels "[a] pang of disappointment out of all proportion to its object" (121, 122). His disproportionate response is indication that the gift's meaning well exceeds the receiver's pleasure; rather, the necklace serves as a public display of the patriarch's ability to satisfy his family's material needs. Though Eleanor is the one who selected the necklace, its social value still transcends her domestic economy and instead serves as a vicarious display of masculine wealth and status.

The rest of this chapter will focus more closely on Modernist women's critique of this Victorian structure of kinship. In Woolf's writings, Modernist daughters desirous of socio-sexual autonomy must refuse nineteenth-century narratives on gender and the family, including the patriarchal appropriation of women's (re)productive labour, as well as theories of ideal femininity modelled by literary foremothers. To make this point, this next section will focus on the cultural work of women's writing as both a vocation and medium for gender ideology. Writing back against dominant narratives on feminine domesticity, Woolf sees in women's work as professional authors a definitive move into the public realm of paid employment and cultural conversations on gendered economics.

2 The Economy of Artistic Resistance

Woolf's essay "Professions for Women" persuasively reframes the debate on equal access to modern vocations as a question of gender roles and, specifically, domestic ideology passed down to women from previous generations. Speaking from her own experience as a writer, Woolf argues that it is necessary for the aspiring professional to "kill" off the Victorian mother – that "Angel in the House" – lest the latter's insistence upon feminine decorum and self-sacrifice suffocate any capacity for critical distance or ambition.[21] Matricide, in this account, serves as a powerful way to imagine women's rejection of inherited gender roles and, instead, to write new narratives in which women might enjoy professional mobility and economic independence. Yet it is also important to note that, in her discussion of gender and economics, Woolf does not, herself, identify as a "professional woman" (but as a "professional *writer*") because she does not work out of necessity. "But to show you how little I deserve to be called a professional woman, how little I know of the struggles and difficulties of such lives," Woolf writes, "I have to admit that instead of spending that sum upon bread and butter, rent, shoes and stockings, or butcher's bills, I went out and bought a cat – a beautiful cat, a Persian cat, which very soon involved me in bitter disputes with my neighbors" (1–2). On the one hand, this effort to distinguish between the professional woman and the professional writer reminds readers how feminist alliances (and debts) might be fractured along class lines – Woolf is, already, financially secure and, therefore, different from those women who must work for a living. On the other hand, and more relevant to the theme of this chapter, Woolf's statement reminds readers of those pressures (the "bread and butter, rent," etc.) that typically bind women to, and make them responsible for, the private domestic sphere – these women might, instead, find their identity, as well as alliances, through vocational ambitions (shades of Egerton's cosmopolitan woman). In Woolf's own experience, women's economic independence – including artistic autonomy and the right to "tell the truth about my own experiences as a body" (4) – is a key part of this post-Victorian attempt to rewrite gender roles.

While "Professions for Women" can be read as part of Woolf's ongoing critique of Victorian domestic ideology, the essay also marks a critical turning point in her attitude toward gender roles and the possibility of some form of reconciliatory middle ground. In fact, as Ellis argues, Woolf's original 1931 lecture, delivered to the London National Society for Women's Service, pursued a "much fuller attack" on Victorian writers such as Christina Rossetti and Alfred Tennyson for promoting the "Angel of the House" ideal, a model of gender difference that made "[a] real relationship between men and women" completely "unattainable" (quoted in Ellis, *Virginia Woolf and the Victorians*, 113). The lecture overturns the more moderate opinions expressed in earlier works like

A Room of One's Own (1929) that saw in the domestic a positive substitute for the "great events" narratives which had grown increasingly popular after the First World War. The turn to professions as a suitable goal for women, instead, requires a forceful critique of the ties that bind women to the home and family, including narratives on feminine decorum handed down by literary greats in the nineteenth century. Woolf was, for example, especially offended by the literary niceties that structured gendered difference, calling the typical exchange of compliments between men and women "really disgusting" (quoted in Ellis, *Virginia Woolf and the Victorians*, 113). This pointed critique is somewhat softened in her later draft of *The Pargiters* (inspired by the 1931 lecture and which would, later, become *The Years*), wherein Woolf argues that Victorian poetry contributes to "a relationship between men and women that was both false and disagreeable" (xxx–xxxi). Despite the suggestion of compromise implied by the milder tone, Woolf nonetheless maintains her original critique of Victorian domestic ideology. By shifting attention to cultural inheritance, rather than individual authors, the published version of "Professions for Women" (1931) still builds upon this critique by explaining women's limited access to economic opportunities as a problem of gender roles and the textual construction of sexual difference. At the same time, Woolf's critique of outmoded narratives on gender marks a new refusal of filial loyalty to the past, a sentiment that informs her later writings, including *The Years* and *Three Guineas*, on women's creative and economic independence.

This investment in the cultural work of writing and, specifically, the idea of artistic autonomy has a long history within the Bloomsbury Group, of which Virginia Woolf was a prominent member.[22] Many members of the Group were particularly interested in separating out art's meaning or "value" from the material conditions of consumer demand and the mass marketplace. The Hogarth Press reprinted a series of articles by *The Nation and Athenaeum* (February to May 1927) on the declining numbers of book sales, and as part of his 1932 broadcast series, E.M. Forster worried about readers' gravitation away from the printed text toward more popular or mass media such as radio and film (28 December 1932, "Not New Books" 651).[23] Renowned economist John Maynard Keynes (*The General Theory of Employment, Interest, and Money* [1936]) was also a member of the Group and, like his literary friends, was deeply committed to culture: he collected contemporary works of art and acted as chairman for the Council for the Encouragement of Music and the Arts as well as the Trustees of the Royal Opera House.[24] In his *Collected Writings* (1972), Keynes also imagined how a redistribution of general wealth might work to support the arts and other forms of cultural production, worthy investments by virtue of their "civilizing" influence upon consumers.[25] For critics after Raymond Williams, however, the Bloomsbury Group's attempts at cultural reform are little more than a snobbish act of bourgeois self-preservation. Singling out Keynes for specific mention, Williams's touchstone essay "The Bloomsbury Fraction" explains how the Group saw itself as working to secure democratic inclusion and free choice: "From Keynesian economics to its work for the League of Nations, [the Bloomsbury Group] made powerful interventions towards the creation of economic and political and social conditions within which, freed from war and depression and prejudice, individuals could be free to be and to become civilized" (244–5).[26] Despite such high ideals, the Bloomsbury Group's macro intervention, Williams continues, suggests nothing more than the elite individual's "conspicuous and privileged consumption" and is therefore hardly the stuff of radical social critique, let alone any model of democratic cultural reform (245).

To level accusations of cultural elitism at Woolf, however, would be to miss her larger discussion on the relationship between distance and critique, in which the aspiration to artistic autonomy functions as a means to creative resistance, not transcendence. Her essay "Middlebrow" (1942), for example, argues that it is the eponymous go-between class who is, in fact, responsible for the illusion between so-called high and low (or mass) cultures: "[the middlebrow] goes to the lowbrows and tells them that while he is not quite one of them, he is almost their friend," and then, "[n]ext moment he rings up the highbrows and asks them with equal geniality whether he may not come to tea" (3). Woolf imagines how the modern artist instead engages in a critical relationship with mass culture, and that this concept of "high" thereby denotes the distance underwriting free thought and creative insight. The highbrows "are the only people who do not do things," Woolf explains, and because they are freed from material pressures, "they are the only people who can see things being done" (3).[27] Woolf's extended writings on creative resistance do not focus on the marketplace alone, but rather, her earlier *The Common Reader* (1923) also looks at the role of literary tradition and its influence upon (or limit of) artistic expression. The volume's essay "Modern Fiction" explains how early novelists – such as Henry Fielding and Jane Austen – "did well" in their "practice of the art," but because they worked with "simpler tools," "their masterpieces certainly have a strange air of simplicity" (1). It is also this same interest in literary influences or conventions ("tools") that then leads Woolf to label authors like H.G. Wells, Arnold Bennett, and John Galsworthy as "materialists" who, though they have "immense skill and immense industry," write to appease readers' demands ("Modern Fiction," 3). At the same time, Woolf notes how a new generation of modern writers, including James Joyce, "attempt to come closer to life, and to preserve more sincerely and exactly what interests and moves them, even if to do so they must discard most of the conventions which are commonly observed by the novelist" ("Modern Fiction," 4). The true aim of modern literature is, the essay therefore suggests, to show something of its own positionality through innovative – and often impressionistic – resistance against literary inheritance.

Given Woolf's position as a female writer, the context most relevant to her writings on modern art thus concerns the cultural transmission of gender roles limiting women's creative expression and authority. In working against this inheritance, Woolf's writings instead propose a form of post-Victorian kinship that maintains an aspiration to critical distance while still in dialogue with her cultural predecessors. In "Professions for Women" (1931), for example, Woolf invites her listeners to see themselves as part of a collective effort by and for "women," working over generations, to restructure gender roles prohibiting equal access to the modern vocations (hence the essay's title). It is also in this touchstone essay that Woolf imagines how women's artistic freedom must be credited to previous generations of female writers whose work helped redefine – or even erase – the gendered terms of these new borderlands. Woolf herself identifies as a professional writer ("My profession is literature") and admits that, thanks to the efforts of these women before her, "when I came to write, there were very few material obstacles in my way"; "For the road was cut many years ago," she continues, "by Fanny Burney, by Aphra Behn, by Harriet Martineau, by Jane Austen, by George Eliot – many famous women, and many more unknown and forgotten, have been before me, making the path smooth and regulating my steps" (1). Woolf also describes how her earliest forays into journalism were well-received, both in terms of readership as well as pay ("one pound ten shillings and sixpence," for her first publication [3]). As discussed throughout *Critical Alliances*, the modern woman's ability to earn a living by her pen owes a certain debt to New Women, like Schreiner and Levy, or female professionals and aesthetes, like Egerton and Michael Field, whose writings on the cultural arts helped secure women's fair remuneration and status within the field. The "post" construction of cultural kinship therein perfectly captures Woolf's critical response to her feminist predecessors and their influence upon Modernist women fighting for similar socio-economic opportunities. "Professions for Women" concludes with a reference to an alternative inheritance of women's hard-won freedoms: "You have won rooms of your own in the house hitherto exclusively owned by men," and "You are earning your five hundred pounds a year," but all of these freedoms are "only a beginning," Woolf cautions (5). The Angel may be dead, but this break in kinship does not mean that generations after her are not still wrestling with her influence and trying hard to write new narratives in answer to "what is a woman?" (3). The definition of "woman" is, in other words, still under collaborative reconstruction.

What it means to be a "woman" is something that Woolf consistently invites readers to contemplate, and through this invitation to collaborative dialogue, Woolf places culture and, specifically, the narrative transmission of gender roles at the very heart of modern feminism and women's economic mobility.[28] Yet as she points out time and again, women's access to cultural expression and resistance depends critically upon their material conditions, and for this reason, in texts such as *A Room of One's Own* (1929), Woolf adamantly stresses that "a woman must have money and a room of her own if she is to write fiction" (4). Two years later, in her 1931 lecture "Professions for Women," Woolf tells her listeners among the Women's Service League that they now have those rooms: "You are able, though not without great labor and effort, to pay the rent" because "you are earning your five hundred pounds a year" ("Professions for Women" [1931], 5). This assumption of a sufficient income has much to do with the audience in question, a group of professional women who would likely accept her claim that "there is nothing to prevent a woman from being a doctor, a lawyer, a civil servant" (5). Yet Woolf is also quick to caution that, "even when the path is nominally open" to such careers, the professional woman will still find that there remain "many phantoms and obstacles … looming in her way" (5). Those "looming phantoms" are, of course, a reference to persistent cultural narratives on gender to which Modernist women themselves might subscribe. With these "obstacles" in mind, Woolf thus concludes her lecture to the Women's Service League with a question about domestic spaces as a metaphor for gender ideology: "how are you going to furnish this space," she asks, and "with whom are you going to share it, and upon what terms?" Woolf writes, adding that "these, I think are questions of the utmost importance and interest" (5). In her later texts, *The Years* and *Three Guineas*, Woolf attempts her own answer as to how women might rewrite gender roles. Both texts position themselves within a post-Victorian inheritance of feminism in order to write back against dominant cultural narratives on gender and to produce their own definition of the professional "woman."

3 Feminine Collaboration in *The Years* and *Three Guineas*

The Years introduces its protagonist Eleanor as a figure of post-Victorian resistance whose development throughout the novel marks a movement toward modern feminism. After her father passes away in the "1911" chapter, Eleanor promptly sells the old family house and embarks on her own independent adventure abroad, travelling to Spain and Greece. At fifty-five years of age Eleanor knows she is "getting old," but she is not too old to break free from the traditional definition of women as confined to the domestic sphere (198).[29] Though she was raised as a Victorian, Eleanor nonetheless refuses to carry her ancestors' outmoded domestic ideology with her into the twentieth century. This refusal is made explicit when, almost three decades later, in the "Present Day" chapter, Eleanor directly contradicts her nephew North's assertion that "everybody ought to marry" and, instead, explains how such a domestic plot "isn't for everyone," a point which she has clearly modelled in her own life (372). With her female relatives, Eleanor is positive in her interpretation of the present day as offering women new social opportunities. She regularly shares with her niece recollections of the past in order to stress "how things had changed" (326) and how such transformations are "for the better" (386).[30] Though Peggy struggles to understand Eleanor's stories, particularly her aunt's claim that she is now "happy in this world – happy with living people" (387), the younger woman cannot help but be affected by Eleanor's contagious laughter (390). In "The Novels of the 1930s and the Impact of History," Julia Briggs argues that the radical potential of *The Years* rests on the novel's ability to inspire feminist consciousness in a younger generation of characters and readers. The novel does this by using characters' dialogue as a means of "conveying to a younger generation the sense of exhilaration felt by older women like Eleanor and Kitty, women who have discovered the modern pleasures of freedom and of living their own lives" ("The Novels of the 1930s and the Impact of History," 80).[31] Yet it is important to note how this feminist consciousness also depends upon a sense of collective debt, as well as a shared battle against sexism, between generations of women. Eleanor's story helps Peggy to reconsider her own independent income as a doctor within the context of women's history: she is encouraged to see herself as one of many present-day women who are economically "freer" (to use Eleanor's words) thanks to the struggles of generations before them. Like this modern pupil, the reader also listens to Eleanor's story and interprets her example as a reminder of women's ongoing effort to redefine gender roles and what it means to be a "woman."

In both form and content, *The Years* is consistent with Woolf's extended writings on feminist dialogue as both collaborative and ongoing, a means rather than an end to gender and social reform. The reader cannot close her copy of the novel assured that an egalitarian gender economy is imminent. Indeed, one might recall characters such as North who, despite Eleanor's example of feminist resistance, is still completely enamoured of masculine authority, as is evidenced by his awe for his "established" uncle Martin (406). One must also compare North with Peggy, who is herself openly critical of her brother's superficial ambitions: "You'll marry. You'll have children. What'll you do then? Make money. Write little books to make money" (390). At issue for Peggy is a type of masculinity that sacrifices both art and meaningful relationships for power, and for this reason she advises North to devote his energy and talents to "living … living differently" (391). Read on the heels of her prior conversations with Eleanor, Peggy's recommendation to North appears part of a larger feminist critique of domestic plots in which money and status are hoarded by men. The placement of this conversation, in the novel's final chapter, is a reminder that the answer to Woolf's feminist critique is still unrealized – it is, rather, part of a post-Victorian resistance against traditional gender roles.

Published one year after *The Years*, Woolf's three-part prose work *Three Guineas* looks at how the female pressure group might function as a catalyst in this ongoing effort to produce alternative social narratives for women. The need for this push-back by women, Woolf explains, has much to do with the already divisive nature of the gendered spheres: on the one side men jealously guard their monopoly of material capital, while on the other side women fight for equal access to the professions and an independent income. This "fight" alone "wear[s] down [a woman's] strength and exhaust[s] her spirit" (*Three Guineas*, 53). Women are, in Woolf's account, barred from positions for which they are best qualified, and even worse, their productive energies dissipate as they fight for equal social opportunities.[32] It is also at the point that Woolf explains her logic behind the gift economy of "three guineas."[33] If women had an independent income, she argues, they would spend money on their own pleasures, on liberties, but in reality they do not have this kind of economic freedom and so any "surplus fund that can be devoted to causes, pleasures or philanthropies gravitates mysteriously but indisputably toward those causes, pleasure and philanthropies which her husband enjoys, and of which the husband approves" (57).[34] Woolf's freely given gift of three guineas thus represents an alternative source of money that – because donated to the anti-war society, the women's college building fund, and the society for women's professional development – works to establish an alternative world of work and education that is divorced from masculine structures of wealth and status. In order for this gift economy to work, however, women must first recognize their collective interest in female economic independence. To this end, Woolf imagines women fighting for "a living wage in all professions," as well as state support for "mothers of educated men" (110). The economic remuneration of women's domestic labour is certainly a question of justice, but at the same time it also undercuts those socio-economic forces reinforcing the gendered spheres. Instead, an independent income ensures a woman's ability to choose freely among the many "attractive profession[s]" that best suit her interests or talents – even if that still means work within the home (111).

In the third and final letter of *Three Guineas* (1938), Woolf proposes a theory of "outsiderness" to describe this micro-political work of the female pressure group. Without this kind of collective refusal, women might continue to play a passive part ("like a gramophone whose needle is stuck") in reproducing socio-political structures of sexual exclusion and inequality (105). In order to be truly critical, then, women must pursue a path "outside" of any dominant gendered economy. "We believe," Woolf explains to the anti-war society, "we can help you most effectively by refusing to join your society; by working for our common ends – justice and equality and liberty for all men and women – outside your society, not within" (105–6). It is important to clarify, however, that the name "society of outsiders" does not refer to any real transcendence of dominant social structures, for as Pamela L. Caughie convincingly argues in *Virginia Woolf & Postmodernism*, when looking at Woolf's work on art and politics one must differentiate between content, or "what the text is about," and the text's formal innovations, or "what it brings about" (32).[35] Woolf's appeal to the "society of outsiders" (content) thus represents a certain aspiration to critical distance (form) similar to that described in her extended writings on aesthetics and cultural resistance. In this model, "outside" and "inside" are simply metaphors for rhetorical positions vis-à-vis dominant social narratives, and through the dialogic interrogation of gender roles, the feminist pressure group might help to write new narratives which are inclusive (not exclusive) of women's labour and economic independence. Economic autonomy would, the text continues, afford women the "freedom from unreal loyalties" and "freedom from interested motives which are at present assured them by the state" (113).[36] Once freed from financial dependency, women would instead take greater pleasure in, and work toward, an inclusive economy of cultural production: "It will be one of their aims to increase private beauty,"

Woolf explains, focusing equally on "the beauty which brims not only every field and wood but every barrow in Oxford Street" as well as "the scattered beauty which needs only to be combined by artists in order to become visible to all" (113–14).[37] By celebrating on equal terms creative talent that is both natural (in "every field and wood") as well as commercial (on "Oxford Street"), Woolf again returns to the idea of critical engagement that runs throughout so much of her work on art and economics; the pressure group fights for women's right to an independent income so that the female artists among them might bring to life beauty and talents hitherto unrecognized (or "scattered") by patriarchal capitalism.

This vision of democratic culture takes us full circle back to the concept of class privilege and its role in the political economy of art. Woolf's attention to the structural consequences of women's economic collaboration not only resists what Raymond Williams describes as self-serving bourgeois consumption, but it also illustrates a certain reciprocal relationship between gender and cultural production.[38] In fact, the model of feminist alliance outlined in *Three Guineas* fits better with what Williams himself describes as a kind of "avant-garde" movement at the turn of the century. In *Culture and Society, 1780–1950,* Williams traces the changing meaning of "culture," and the corresponding rise of "high art," as a consequence of modern industrial capitalism with its attendant class hierarchy. According to Williams, so-called high art was gradually elevated to a purely aesthetic dimension, beyond everyday politics and social production, thus reaffirming the ruling elite's special status as privilege consumers of the rarified artwork (think, for example, of Matthew Arnold's argument against the so-called "Barbarians" in *Culture and Anarchy* [1869], or Walter Benjamin's discussion of the cultic function of Art's "aura" in his "The Work of Art in the Age of Mechanical Reproduction" [1936]). Yet Williams also penned a later essay "The Politics of the Avant Garde" in which he describes how the transition to Modernism, beginning in the late nineteenth century, saw artists and writers assuming increased control over the means of cultural production and dissemination; this historic transition was accompanied by the formation of a radical or "avant-garde" counter-movement against the institutions and conventional meanings of both high and mainstream culture. In his now classic text *Theory of the Avant-Garde,* Peter Bürger explains how this vanguard movement distinguishes itself from those other Modernist efforts premised upon the assumption of art's apartness ("art for art's sake"); the latter is unable to recognize its own aesthetic aspiration to autonomy as complicit with capitalist ideology (mirroring commodity reification), while the vanguard artist instead recognizes the apolitical gesture implicit in "high art" and instead makes this contradiction the central theme of artwork (Bürger, 27). The "avant-garde" mode is therefore a product of, and takes as its very subject, the critical relationship between art and the socio-economic sphere of politics – a sphere that includes different classes and their relationship to cultural production, as opposed to a privileged few.

Woolf's representation of the female pressure group in *Three Guineas* fits with the self-reflexive impulses of the avant-garde movement in two ways: first, it refuses to settle upon any stable or autonomous entity that is divorced from its social context, and second, with respect to this embeddedness, her literary experiment is very much invested in the idea of critique as still participating in the political realm of cultural production. The pressure group is, as Woolf describes in her final letter, a strategic alliance among women who have come together for a variety of reasons, from the pursuit of "knowledge" (137), to the desire "to lead a rational existence without love" (137) or "to travel" (137–8). Woolf's narrative thus conceives of the female pressure group as a fluid collective of "women" whose composition and objectives are contingent upon attendant socio-political contexts. After all, Woolf asks, "what one word can sum up the variety of the things that [nineteenth-century gender feminists] wanted, and had wanted, consciously or subconsciously, for so long?" (138). "Josephine Butler's label – Justice, Equality, Liberty – is a fine one," Woolf continues, "but it is only a label, and in our age of innumerable labels, of multicoloured labels, we have become suspicious of labels; they kill and constrict" (138). Woolf's refusal to resolve the multiple "I"s that populate her feminist narratives into a single or coherent subject has, as Toril Moi argues, been the source of frustration for many humanist feminists; yet these critics misunderstand how the pluralistic viewpoint effectively counters any patriarchal impulse to contain the feminine through a singular or "phallic" construction of the "unified" self (*Sexual/Textual Politics*, 8).[39] Woolf's model of feminist critique instead celebrates the generative potential of strategic resistance, a mode of critical engagement through which the coalition forms in response to, and works to transform, its relevant gender economy. This is why, when asked to join the anti-war movement, Woolf concludes that the pressure group can best assist "not by joining your society but by remaining outside your society but in cooperation with its aim" (143). The feminist alliance functions as a self-reflexive reference to praxis that works to dissolve the boundary between art and cultural production, and through collaborative resistance, works to undermine structures of patriarchal authority – from educated men who jealously guard the way to paid professions, to men who wage war in the name of chivalrous protectionism regarding the gendered divisions of spheres.

Woolf's representation of the female pressure group draws attention to the persistent influence that Victorian gender roles and patriarchal structures of power, in particular, still exercise over Modernist women's lives. In the third letter of *Three Guineas*, she explains how the anti-war cause is, therefore, an extension of the same fight waged by gender radicals generations before: these nineteenth-century feminists "were fighting the same enemy that you are fighting and for the same reasons," she explains, adding that "they were fighting the tyranny of the patriarchal state as you are fighting the tyranny of the Fascist state" (102). Shari Benstock, in *Textualizing the Feminine*, argues that Woolf's feminist writings privilege women's relationship with their brothers, not their mothers, and that through mimetic dialogue *Three Guineas* undermines patriarchal narratives on the family and women's gender roles by making explicit the hidden fact of misogyny and sexual inequality.[40] Woolf's frequent references to Victorian feminists must also be understood as part of this larger effort to rethink the familial bond as a cultural narrative that is open to critique and thus malleable. This is not to say that Woolf's vision of gender reform does not focus on women's role in reproducing masculine authority, for she sees how girls are trained from a young age to defer to their fathers and that this kind of submission is both the product of, and reproduces, the same "sexual jealousy" that keeps women dependent and that preserves men's monopoly of sexual and economic power (132). In her critique of this Victorian sexual psychology, Woolf thus recognizes how modern feminists such as herself "are merely carrying on the same fight that our mothers and grandmothers fought" (102). She stages her intervention into this "fight" as an extension of the rhetorical practices modelled by many nineteenth-century feminist radicals (those unruly daughters who became Victorian Grandmothers) invested in women's right to an independent income and mobility beyond domestic plots (110).

As a work of creative labour itself, *Three Guineas* not only models, but also participates in the production of, this form of feminist inheritance. The text ends, not with an answer, but with a final invitation to continued dialogue among feminists. The narrator apologizes three times for leaving the letter unanswered for so long, but then adds that "the blame for that … rests upon you, for this letter would never have been written had you not asked for an answer to your own" (144). Like the official recipient of this letter, the reader implicitly desires some form of response or closure to Woolf's investigation, but rather than satisfy this need for answers, Woolf places the responsibility for this problem with "*you*," her reader. Woolf does not, in other words, deliver some fully developed or coherent vision of a feminist future neatly articulated from one foremother-author to her passive daughter-reader. Instead, Woolf reminds readers that feminist resistance is an ongoing and participatory project. By modelling this resistance to structure or closure, the narrative itself invites readers' participation in strategic collectivity and analysis, for we must decipher the points of debate and, hopefully, align ourselves with the stronger arguments asserted by the female pressure group. With this appeal to readers' participation, the text offers a glimpse of hope in the continuing dialogue and thus continuing possibilities of women's political resistance.

Conclusion: Feminist Futures and Cultural Inheritance

> The sun had risen, and the sky above the house wore an air of extraordinary beauty, simplicity and peace. (Virginia Woolf, *The Years*)

As Delia's party draws to a close and guests prepare to leave, Eleanor is suddenly captivated by the sight of a young couple across the street returning home by taxi. She watches as they draw out their latchkey and, when they pause "for a moment on the threshold," she emphatically repeats "There!" before the "door shut[s] with a little thud behind them" (434). Eleanor's proclamation is, in one way, meant as an answer to her own nagging question as to whether there is "a pattern" to the whole of life (369); the young couple on the "threshold" would seem to indicate to her a positive movement forward into a brighter future that is, as she insists in an earlier conversation, so much "happier" and "freer" (386).[41] The novel's closing reference to "beauty, simplicity and peace" is thus an impressionistic snapshot of Eleanor's own internal resolution that time is teleological and that things progress for the better. The optimism that pervades this closing scene is, in a second way, meant as a response to the novel's sustained interrogation of gender roles and the socio-economic limitations imposed upon women as a consequence of the persistent influence of Victorian domestic ideology. It is significant to note that, with respect to this second point, Eleanor's positive response occurred specifically in that moment when "they [the couple] stood on the threshold." Her audible proclamation "There!" is an almost involuntary response (as compared with her earlier "murmur[ings]") to the idea of a future that is entered into and shared between men and women. Dressed in a "tweed travelling suit," the young woman is equal to her male partner in mobility, and even though she trails behind as they approach the flat, she stands undifferentiated by gender as "they" both pass together across the "threshold."

Though Eleanor gets the last and optimistic word, Woolf's novel is not unifocal in its vision, and the plethora of characters' perspectives in fact undercut the possibility of any singular resolution. This can especially be seen in Peggy's ongoing and sceptical response to her aunt's hopeful interpretation of human relationships in the "Present Day." After insisting that things are indeed better or "freer," Eleanor also adds that she is now "happy in this world – happy with living people" and then "wave[s] her hand as if to embrace the miscellaneous company, the young, the old, the dancers, the talkers" (387). Yet Peggy's silent mimesis of this comment undermines its positive message: "Peggy sank back against the wall. Happy in this world, she thought, happy with living people!" (387). The bitterness implicit in Peggy's response speaks volumes about her own sense of social alienation and disconnect between genders and generations. Peggy belongs to the younger or supposedly (according to Eleanor) liberated cohort of women who can move more beyond the domestic sphere (and enter into new professions such as medicine), and yet she is clearly disappointed in her brother North's pursuit of masculine status, and she cannot understand or identify with the hopeful sentiments espoused by her aunt. This tension in world views between aunt and niece – of an older optimism checked by younger cynicism – represents a non-linear or, what I have described throughout this chapter as, "post-Victorian" model of kinship and the contested transmission of feminist culture between women. In his work on temporality in *The Years*, Steve Ellis describes how both generations share in common a critical rejection of their cultural contexts and that this collective critique effectively destabilizes the idea of a progressive move from the Victorian to the Modernist period. "The older generation's desire to escape from its past and the younger generation's being baffled and disaffected by its present … ensures that neither modernity nor the Victorian seems a particularly hospitable era," Ellis writes, "and the contrast between them (for good and bad) [is] not as productive a subject as hitherto for Woolf" (*Virginia Woolf and the Victorians*, 136). Peggy might look to her aunt in search of by-gone models of domestic femininity, and yet her inability to comprehend the latter's positive self-alignment with the present day confounds any such effort to keep the Victorian at a safe and separate distance. At the same time, Peggy's sceptical attitude toward her own historical context aligns her with, rather than differentiates her from, her aunt whose anti-Victorian optimism reads as a similar form of feminist resistance grounded in cultural critique.

As a kind of capstone chapter to *Critical Alliances*, my analysis of Woolf in this section is meant to demonstrate the ongoing conversations and, even, strategic collaborations among feminist writers across generations. Woolf might not, therefore, see periodization, or the distinction between Victorian and Modernism, as particularly fruitful to her larger project on women and economics, but this is not to say that she thereby embraces a model of kinship as a chronological or even (re)productive bond between women across generations. Rather, the tie that binds together her feminist characters is their shared investment in dialogical critique of their respective cultural contexts and corresponding social constructions of gendered economics as exclusionary. Woolf's later texts thereby propose a theory of Modernism which is engaged in an ongoing struggle against the persistent influence of Victorian gender roles but which also draws inspiration from, as well as replicates, the same deconstructivist techniques practised by nineteenth-century feminist predecessors. Like Schreiner and Levy, for example, Woolf imagines how a feminist mode of cultural kinship might undermine patriarchal structures of power, and like Egerton and Field, Woolf also recognizes the power of art and women's writing, in particular, to facilitate these cultural bonds between generations. Also, like women writers before her, Woolf leaves open this dialogue between generations in an effort to show that feminist inheritance is not linear (always forward-looking), nor is it easily resolved according to a single plotline or character formation. Rather, this dialogic conversation between generations of feminist writers must also necessarily look to the past, and wrestle with inherited gender roles, as women struggle to write new or present and future socio-economic plots. This persistent exchange between generations makes it hard to keep the Victorians at a safe or separate distance, and instead suggests how the present is, as Ellis argues, "backed" by the past (*Virginia Woolf and the Victorians*, 131). The plural perspectives and contestation between generations culminate in narratives that are, ultimately, open-ended invitations to the reader: we cannot help but anticipate Peggy's sceptical response to Eleanor's visions of "simplicity and peace" (*The Years*, 435), while Woolf's third and final letter in *Three Guineas* is deliberately left unsigned in defiance of a single-authored narrative.

With this representation of women's dialogical critique of gender roles, Woolf thus imagines an alternative mode of cultural inheritance that looks both backward and forward across generations. The closing interaction between Eleanor and her brother Morris invokes this dialectic by leaving open the question of how nineteenth-century men and women, and the gender roles they bring with them, might make the transition to a new era: "And Now?" Eleanor asks her brother, "holding out her hands to him," and though the latter's response is omitted, we know that the Victorian woman is happy to welcome the dawn of a new day (435). By leaving Eleanor's question unanswered, Woolf's novel would certainly seem to replicate, in both form and content, the dystopian strategies modelled by New Woman writers at the fin de siècle. Yet Woolf's attempt to rewrite gender – including the relationship between brother and sister – also involves a dialectical conversation that looks back at, and forms in response to, radical foremothers and their fight against sexual and economic inequality. After all, Eleanor's invitation to her brother – reaching out her hand as if in a gesture of good faith – would not only seem to echo the sexual equality represented by the young taxicab couple across the street, but it also reads as an attempt to undo the trauma of the past in favour of a new narrative built on patterns of connectedness. Morris's past is marked by trauma given that his son Charles (Peggy's brother) was killed in the First World War, but the novel's only reference to this death is quite tellingly preceded by a conversation between Peggy and Eleanor on women's filial obligations: On the way to Delia's party Peggy asks her aunt if she was "suppressed when you were young?" (335), to which Eleanor silently responds, "I do not want to go back into my past … I want the present" (336).[42] But Eleanor's past is always with her and makes her all the more attentive to the present, even in those moments of resistance. The bond between aunt and niece, in their attempt to make sense of this past, thus supersedes the masculine story of war as a traumatic break, and instead works as a kind of intergenerational conversation among women on feminist resistance and critical collaboration. Eleanor's final invitation to Morris, her brother, stands as an open-ended question to men and those invested in the divisive narratives on war and gender: will they look to the future with their feminist sisters, or will they cling to a past driven by sexual jealousy and competition?

Coda: The Post-Victorian Legacy of Women's Work

It is because so wide and gracious to us are the possibilities of the future; so impossible is a return to the past, so deadly is a passive acquiescence in the present, that to-day we are found everywhere raising our strange new cry – "Labor and the training that fits us for labor!"

– Olive Schreiner, *Woman and Labor*

Indeed it will be a long time still, I think, before a woman can sit down to write a book without finding a phantom to be slain, a rock to be dashed against. And if this is so in literature, the freest of all professions for women, how is it in the new professions which you are now for the first time entering?

– Virginia Woolf, "Professions for Women"

In the final paragraph to her touchstone work *Woman and Labor*, Olive Schreiner looks forward to a feminist future, imagining how the combined "cry" for gender reform has grown in volume and spread "everywhere." The Women's Movement is, in her account, driven by a kind of (re)productive energy or force in search of, and celebrating, the socio-sexual "possibilities of the future." This rallying cry to action is taken up by feminist writers after Schreiner, from New Woman novelist Amy Levy and sex radical George Egerton, to aesthetic poets Michael Field, and Modernist author Virginia Woolf. Yet these literary successors do not necessarily subscribe to the same brand of (re)productivist feminism, opting instead to focus on the gendered economics of kinship (Levy), the cosmopolitan professional woman (Egerton), lesbian aesthetics (Field), and the feminist community of outsiders (Woolf). Although each of these authors pursues a different representation of women's economic collaboration, they all share in common a similar commitment to narrative as a means to produce an alternative gendered economy for subsequent generations. Looking back at her nineteenth-century predecessors, Woolf also suggests how modern feminists are, in their attempt to deconstruct gender, still in a critical dialogue with the past – even while they look forward to, and write, new narratives for working women. In reflecting on the "new professions," Woolf acknowledges that modern women have made headway in literature, "the freest profession," and that it may indeed be their writings which will then pave the way for subsequent gains in gendered economics. Woolf's post-Victorian dialectic with foremothers such as Schreiner therein allows for an alternative or "feminist" model of cultural inheritance that acknowledges the afterlife of Victorian gender radicals and their writings into the twentieth century.

I have, here in *Critical Alliances*, attempted to showcase the economic advances made by women writers as working professionals at the turn of the century. At the same time, I have deliberately selected authors who represent the many different points of, and range among, feminist interventions into this gendered workforce. Taken together, these authors remind readers that inherited gender roles can take on varying forms – from gendered education and kinship structures, to the sexual gaze and artistic authority. Olive Schreiner's writings highlight the importance of women's education and show readers how access to cultural capital might facilitate women's transition from outmoded domestic labour to more modern or professional forms of care-giving, including teaching and work in medicine. Her proto feminist, Lyndall, ushers in a generation of radical New Woman thinkers who demand alternative social narratives befitting their economic ambitions and search for skilled vocations beyond the home. Amy Levy's fiction offers a similar, open-ended call for new representations of self-possessed women engaged in the urban marketplace, including women who own and operate independent businesses or specialize in modern art forms such as photography. In *The Romance of a Shop*, the four Lorimer sisters look to female-centred kinship systems in order to facilitate their fluid movement into public spaces of economics and their equal economic/sexual exchange with male counterparts. George Egerton's *The Wheel of God* is also interested in women and the city and focuses extensively on the sexual gaze limiting women's participation in the urban workforce. Our heroine, Mary Desmond (later, Mary Marriott), must form cosmopolitan bonds with other female professionals (from typists to modern journalists) in order to transcend the domestic plots barring her economic ambitions. Though not a work of fiction, Michael Field's *Sight and Song* raises similar questions about the literary inheritance of gender roles prohibiting women's access to socio-economic authority. The collection of poetic translations instead presents readers with a bold assertion of women's equal status as artistic connoisseurs who enjoy, as well as produce, art by and for women. Finally, writing in response to Victorian gender roles, Virginia Woolf celebrates the work of sexual radicals before her but also acknowledges differences in economic goals and strategies among women. She rejects Schreiner's emphasis on reproductivist self-sacrifice, but Woolf cannot help but express a certain respect for – and ongoing dialogue with – her Victorian sisters' attempts to write new economic narratives for women. In Woolf's hands, this feminist narrative focuses on women's role as professional authors of their own social and sexual plots.

The question remains as to what impact, if any, fin-de-siècle feminist writings had upon the modern Women's Movement and gendered economics after the First World War. Can we, in other words, trace some form of cultural legacy between these early articulations of feminine collaboration and the mass influx of women into the workforce in the second half of the twentieth century? For historian Ellen Jordan, the late nineteenth-century marked a high-water point in the feminist fight for women's employment equity and access to modern professions. The number of women working in new and high-ranking vocations rose significantly throughout the 1880s and 1890s, but at the turn of the century, women's economic advancement seemed to stall almost entirely. For example, a 1911 census, released the same year as Schreiner's *Woman and Labor*, counts only seven women among reported architects, nine women working as accountants, two hundred registered female pharmacists, and twelve female dentists.[1] The census also shows how women continued to advance in those modern professions to which they had already staked an early claim, including work as "author, editor, journalist" (from 452 women in 1881 to 1,756 in 1911 [or 13.2 per cent to 12.7 per cent of the category]), "Telegraph" (from 2,228 women to 14,308 [23.6 per cent to 52.2 per cent]), "civil service" (3,216 women to 22,034 [12.6 per cent to 26.5 per cent]), and "commercial clerks" (5,989 women to 117,057 [3.3 per cent to 24.5 per cent]).[2] At the same time, women continued to dominate those careers traditionally defined as "feminine," including teaching (183,298 or 72.7 per cent) and nursing (83,662 or 98.5 per cent). While women held strong to such professional gains, the advent of the twentieth century seemed to present new obstacles and women were unable to make any further headway in modern careers such as veterinary science, engineering, or law. According to Jordan's history, the problem with women's access to these latter professions has much to do with a change in priorities of modern feminism: "once the Women's Movement stopped targeting new occupations," she explains, "no new occupations opened" (*The Women's Movement*, 220).[3] Women's economic mobility always depended critically upon the collective deconstruction of gender roles underwriting labour and the modern workforce, Jordan argues, but by the early twentieth century, the feminist cause instead turned its attention to political debates on trades unionism and the suffrage movement.[4] For Jordan, the assumption that political reform would lead to more equitable working conditions (not the reverse causal chain from labour to politics) was shared by both labour unionists and suffragettes.

Yet women's political and legal rights were always at the very heart of Victorian feminism and its effort to redefine gender roles and women's work. Founding members of the Society for Promoting the Employment of Women (established in 1859),[5] Jessie Boucherett and Barbara Bodichon were keen supporters of women's suffrage and their organization also helped to push through the 1882 Married Women's Property Act guaranteeing wives legal property rights.[6] Because of their focus on exclusively middle-class women's rights, the move to liberal arguments regarding women's economic and political self-possession seemed almost intuitive to these early Victorian feminists. Still other turn-of-the-century feminists saw in political enfranchisement a means to infiltrate the structures of power informing women's labour rights. This seemingly circuitous path to economic reform through politics was often framed as a pragmatic response to women's failed attempts to penetrate many of the lucrative professions, such as medicine.[7] A leading advocate of female suffrage, Emmeline Pankhurst, explains how the right to vote would give women the power (or "status") to shape the institutions and social narratives that enforce gender roles.

> We women see so clearly the fact that the only way to deal with this thing is to raise the status of women; first the political status, then the industrial and the social status of women. You must make women count as much as men; you must have an equal standard of morals; and the only way to enforce that is through giving women political power so that you can get that equal moral standard registered in the laws of the country. ("Freedom or Death" [1913], 22)

For Pankhurst, the only way to "deal" with the problem (or "thing") of gender inequality is to give women the right to vote, through which they could then decide economic and moral laws. Indeed, women did see some gains in professions such as law, accounting, and civil service after the 1919 Sex Disqualification Removal Act, but the newly acquired right to vote did very little to open up new fields of employment to women or to break down the sexual segregation in those lucrative vocations dominated by men.[8] Still, by the 1920s, there were more women than ever studying at universities – even if most still took degrees in traditionally feminine fields such as the arts or humanities – and the professional woman was, by then, an established part of the everyday workforce.

Feminism in the early twentieth century continues this Victorian tendency to see in women's work, especially during the war effort, a means to wide-ranging social and political gains.[9] "Suddenly, campaigners for women's suffrage became avid patriots and organizers of women in support of the war effort," writes Joshua S. Goldstein, adding that "[m]any of these feminists hoped that patriotic support of the war would enhance the prospects for women's suffrage after the war, and this came true in a number of countries" (*War and Gender*, 318). Even Emmeline Pankhurst and her daughter Christabel temporarily suspended their campaign for women's suffrage in order to focus on the war: they "dedicated themselves instead to war work and fanatical patriotism," Sally Ledger explains, "changing the name of the Women's Social and Political Union journal from *The Suffragette* to *Britannica*" (*The New Woman*, 1).[10] Right from the start of the war effort in 1914, the British government employed as many as 262,000 women (another 505,000 worked in commerce), a move which gave these female employees both economic independence and social status as reward for their contributions to the nationalist mission.[11] Though many of the positions were not considered white-collar professions, they did allow women to enter into fields and public spaces typically dominated by men. Some of the more well-known roles for women in the First World War included work in munitions factories and shipyards or as intelligence collectors and spies.[12] The Women's Land Army encouraged members to take up farming labour that their dispatched brothers had left off, while organizations such as the Women's Royal Air Force gave women the opportunity to work on planes as mechanics and technicians. Of course, women continued to work in traditional professions such as nursing, but demand for medical care and the large number of wounded soldiers meant that many of these women (through the Women's Auxiliary Corps, the Voluntary Aid Detachment, or the First Aid Nursing Yeomanry) enjoyed new access to the frontlines of war. As Joshua S. Goldstein writes, these women workers "helped nurse the wounded, provide food and other supplies to the military, serve as telephone operators (the 'Hello Girls'), entertain troops, and work as journalists" (*War and Gender*, 318). A certain degree of innovation and assertive strength was also required of those women who also helped to create new labour organizations and auxiliary corps in support of women's service. For example, female nurses and doctors recognized that they were an invaluable part of the war effort and so, in 1916, together formed the Medical Women's Federation to fight against discriminatory practices within the profession, such as pay inequity and misogynistic training or working conditions.[13] Throughout the war effort, many suffragettes also devoted themselves to patriotic labour as a way to lobby for women's equal citizenship; such new forms of employment not only allowed women to break free of the gendered ideology binding middle-class ladies to the domestic sphere, but these jobs also allowed women to prove their citizenship through equal labour (318).[14] As this history suggests, then, women's labour was a critical precursor to – and not undermined by – the female suffrage movement.

A better explanation for the decline in modern women's infiltration of professional borderlands can be found in culture, particularly literary representations of feminine labour. *Critical Alliances* has argued throughout that literary representations of feminine collaboration helped rewrite the gendered workforce in the nineteenth century to include professional women working beyond the domestic sphere. By representing women working in a variety of modern fields – from nursing, teaching, business, photography, journalism, art criticism, and professional writing – the five authors in this study validate the working woman and her contribution to the modern workforce at the turn of the century. Yet it is not just in terms of content that these writers helped usher in a new generation of professional women. Through their innovations in narrative form, Amy Levy and Olive Schreiner pioneered the proto-New Woman novel with its open ending that looks forward to a time of socio-economic equality. While Lyndall's quest for social and sexual equality is left unfinished, Schreiner's non-fiction prose anticipates a future where feminists might bond together in the collective fight for educational and economic equality (as if carrying on where the dystopian novel's heroine left off). *The Romance of a Shop* (1888) is likewise left unresolved with its epilogue's final references to the shop (rented by unnamed proprietors) and unlet flat, two spaces rendered genderless as if to imply a possible future where women might move freely between domestic and professional plots. George Egerton's *The Wheel of God* (1898) also challenges readers to think beyond domestic plots as it quickly forgoes the comfortable romance story for a more expansive tale of emigration and cosmopolitan working women. And through sexually charged imagery and respect for the autonomous feminine muse, Michael Field's lyric poetry invites the reader to participate in a relationship of queer consumption that takes pleasure in beauty by and for women. In response to these "queer dead women" and gender radicals before her (*Three Guineas*, 102), Virginia Woolf continues the discussion of women's right to work as professional writers who might shape – and even challenge – the social narratives limiting access to the gendered marketplace. The literary texts discussed in this study thereby invite readers, through innovations in content or literary form, to see the correlation between, and to participate in, the generation of alternative plots that are inclusive of women's economic ambitions.

The correlation between literature and women's economic roles also played a critical role in the first half of the twentieth century, during which the resurgence in the Victorian ideal of feminine domesticity worked to undermine many of the economic gains made by independent-minded women in the growing middle class. On women's return to the private sphere, Martin Pugh explains how there was a widespread attempt "to elevate the status and prestige of housekeeping" during the interwar period, due in large part to a decline in domestic servants (*Women and the Women's Movement in Britain, 1914–1959*, 83). Though the supply in service stabilized by 1930, the virtues of domestic ideology had taken hold and many modern women learned to take pride in, as well as define themselves through, their work as wives and mothers.[15] At the same time, a proliferating number of new magazines and periodicals for modern women actively reinforced what Cynthia Leslie White describes as "the trend back to 'dear housewifeliness'" (*Women's Magazines 1693–1968*, 100). "Almost without exception," White argues, "the new periodicals dedicated themselves to upholding the traditional sphere of feminine interests and were united in recommending a purely domestic role for women" (100).[16]

Yet the picture is not entirely bleak, for there was some growth in literary representations of women's professional advances during the interwar period. Some texts, such as D.H. Lawrence's "Tickets, Please" (1922), implied that women's participation in typically masculine vocations (relief work at home as trolley drivers) would have a dire impact upon the forces of heterosexual attraction and, particularly, the presumption of masculine virility. Still other texts, such as Radclyffe Hall's *The Well of Loneliness* (1928), showed how the opportunity to contribute during the war effort (driving ambulance in the Women's Auxiliary Corps) gave sexual radicals, including protagonist Stephen Gordon, a self-identified gender "invert," a newfound sense of social belonging and economic possibility. There were also stories of women in traditional vocations such as nursing, including Mary Borden's "Blind. A Story" [1929]), which showed how the trauma of war forever altered their "perception" of feminine care-giving and the gendered dichotomy between public work and private affect. And J.G. Sime's "Munitions" (1919) suggests how many middle-class women jumped at the opportunity to support themselves and to serve their country through factory labour. Indeed, women's short-lived foray into factories was supported by feminists and suffragettes alike as part of an ongoing effort to challenge dominant gender roles, including the often exclusionary politics within the male-dominated labour movement. "Suffragettes supported the idea of getting women into factories, demanding that they be paid at the same rate as men," Muriel Whitaker explains, but "[t]he male-dominated labour movement opposed the employment of women, fearing (wrongly) that, because their wages were lower, they would continue to replace men when the war ended" (*Great Canadian War Stories*, 69). Despite the persistent influence of traditional gender roles, a cultural shift was clearly underway, and modern narratives on women's economic equality within the workforce continued to prove a powerful force for social reform, even well after the initial proliferation in women's careers at the fin de siècle.[17]

Critical Alliances argues that feminist cooperation was – and continues to be – integral to women's participation in the modern workforce. The modern workforce was expanding and adding new vocations at the turn of the century. In order to access these modern professions, fin-de-siècle gender radicals found it necessary to work together and find support in each other's collective deconstruction of domestic ideology limiting women's economic plots. While cooperation is the common theme, the form and function of these feminist alliances varied in direct relationship with the targeted site of market intervention. More specifically, different vocations or gendered employment required different forms of feminine bonds. Schreiner's writings, for example, stress the importance of women's intellectual cooperation, or of bonds forged through the transmission of cultural capital, in accessing skilled careers; as inheritors to this new form of cultural kinship (rivaling, if not displacing, reproductivist biology), later generations of women might enjoy working in modern vocations such as teaching and nursing, to the more elite medical professions earlier denied the domestic lady. Levy is also interested in structures of female kinship, and her fiction explores the idea of sisterly bonds (a matrilineal kinship system) as underwriting women's self-possessed sexual/economic exchange. *The Romance of a Shop* (1888) shows us how this kind of economic self-possession is requisite to women's equality within the world of business, including women's status as shop proprietors. Egerton shifts our attention to the modern cityscape and women's equal access to the urban workforce. *The Wheel of God* (1898) suggests that women's work in emergent vocations – from popular journalism to modern medicine – depends upon a cosmopolitan community of female professionals who recognize the sociopolitical value of women's work. Michael Field's lyric poetry explores the link between queer erotics and women's aesthetic authority; building upon a long tradition of women's art writing, *Sight and Song* (1892) shows us that women's status as modern art critics (connoisseurship) can only happen once women collectively take back the productive potential of beauty's body. Woolf is interested in women's status as professional writers and, like fin-de-siècle feminists, produces new socioeconomic plots for women in the early twentieth century. Yet Woolf's writings also encourage readers to return to the question of diversity or difference among feminine bonds; reflecting upon the generation of gender radicals before her, Woolf models a form of feminism that is both engaged with, but also critical of, women's economic strategies.

As Woolf thus encourages us to see, in the quotation at the outset of this Coda, women's role in the modern marketplace depends critically upon literature and the cultural construction of gender. In singling out literature as the new professional borderland for women, Woolf also underlines the importance of cultural inheritance and the ongoing conversation among generations of feminists. Woolf's post-Victorian stance – as engaged with, but also critical of, her nineteenth-century sisters – presents us with a new understanding of feminist kinship that isn't linear or rooted in reproductivist biology; instead, Woolf's response to the fin-de-siècle reformers before her invokes a new model of feminist inheritance that is grounded in dialogic resistance and cultural (re)construction of gender roles. This "critical" bond between generations of feminist reformers is firmly rooted in literature and the different – sometimes divergent – stories we tell ourselves about what constitutes a "woman" and her socio-economic role. Feminists' unrelenting pursuit of economic equality, throughout the twentieth century, in many ways confirms this idea of an open-ended conversation and the perpetual effort to write new and evolving social narratives for female professionals. The late-Victorian authors discussed here saw in literature a powerful medium through which to write into existence new socioeconomic opportunities for women. These independent-minded women continued to struggle against nineteenth-century gender roles and the very Victorian idea of women's work as tied to the home or domestic plots. This literary inheritance – writing against, and generating new, social narratives – was central to women's participation in the modern marketplace at the fin de siècle and well into the twentieth century, even during the post-war period when the pressure to return to domestic ideology was intensified. In this way, women's professional advancement was, and is still, a question of cultural inheritance and the importance of "critical" alliances (or dialogic resistance) among women working against social narratives of gendered labour. While she might be speaking back to her Victorian sisters, Woolf is nonetheless both prophetic and simply pragmatic in her proclamation that, "Indeed it will be a long time still, I think, before a woman can sit down to write a book without finding a phantom to be slain, a rock to be dashed against."

Notes

Introduction

1 See also Holcombe's *Victorian Ladies at Work*, 194.
2 For more on the influence of domestic ideology on the form and function of women's classed labour, see also Scott's *Gender and the Politics of History*, 73–4, and Jordan's *The Women's Movement*, 62–4.
3 See Stetz, "'George Egerton,'" 67–8.
4 See Schaffer's *The Forgotten Female Aesthetes*, 4–5.
5 See Jordan, *The Women's Movement*, 76.
6 See also Craik's *A Woman's Thoughts About Women*, 69, for more on working women and social (i.e., marriageable) status.
7 See also Jordan's *The Women's Movement*, 80–1, and Bird's 1911 study, *Women at Work*, 126–42, for a similar range of new professions for women.
8 See Jordan, *The Women's Movement*, 78–9, for the following census statistics.
9 "This entry of women into areas previously seen as appropriate only to men," Jordan explains, "seems to have been accompanied by a relaxation of the patriarchal constraints on working girls" (*The Women's Movement*, 81–2).
10 For more on late-Victorian women's increased access to the city and urban consumption, see also Vadillo's *Women Poets and Urban Aestheticism*, 12, Erika Rappaport's *Shopping for Pleasure*, 7, as well as Krueger's chapter, "Possessing London: *The Yellow Book*'s Women Writers," especially pages 101–3, in *British Women Writers and the Short Story, 1850–1930*.
11 See also Pedersen's "Victorian Liberal Feminism and the 'Idea' of Work," 37.
12 I discuss the Society for Promoting the Employment of Women (SPEW) in more detail in chapter 3.
13 See Gordon and Doughan, *Dictionary of British Women's Organizations, 1825–1960* for a more comprehensive list of feminist associations throughout the Victorian and Modernist periods.

14 Ledger also cites key figures in the history of feminism, including the country's first female medical doctors, Elizabeth Garrett Anderson and Sophia Jex-Blake, as proof that Victorian women "were becoming competitors in the more privileged sections of the economic marketplace to an extent that had never before been apparent" (*The New Woman*, 19).

15 See also Holcombe's *Victorian Ladies at Work*, 194.

16 For contemporary critical work sceptical of the transformative powers of female-female bonds, see also Helena Michie's *Sororophobiae*, 21–2, Dill's "Race, Class, and Gender," 132–8, and Spelman's *The Inessential Woman*, ix.

17 Helena Michie, in *Sororophobia*, acknowledges that sisterly bonds could provide "a place and a vocabulary" for women to explore feelings and relationships typically prohibited within dominant and heterosexist models of gender difference (21). This same mode of a "strategic" and "often, self-critical coalition is also helpful in thinking about the role of feminism in women's fin-de-siècle writings on modern labour and the fight for socio-sexual equality.

18 See Scott's *Gender and the Politics of History*, 37–8, and Jordan's *The Women's Movement*, 14–15. While Scott focuses largely on working-class histories, Jordan's more recent study looks at how the social construction of gender is important to understanding middle-class women's movement into the paid work force toward the end of the Victorian period.

19 For more on the cultural turn in the history of nineteenth-century women's work, see Scott's *Gender and the Politics of History*, 37–8, and Jordan's *The Women's Movement*, 14–15.

20 See also Davidoff's "Adam Spoke First and Named the Others of the World," 234–40, and Kessler-Harris's "Treating the Male as 'Other,'" 197, for more on this poststructuralist approach to gender and women's labour.

21 Jordan is writing in response to foremost feminist historians such as Lee Holcombe, whose touchstone *Victorian Ladies at Work*, 18, attempts an economic-determinist history of nineteenth-century women in the workplace.

22 There were also works, such as Linton's "The Wild Women as Social Insurgents" and Kenealy's *Feminism and Sex-Extinction*, which argued vehemently against women's participation in the public sphere of paid employment and politics as unnatural or even sexually degenerate.

23 See Amariglio and Ruccio's "From Unity to Dispersion," 145–7, for more on the 1870s Marginal Revolution and the changing definition of the economic body.

24 "Demand," in this new model, corresponds directly with the amount of happiness consumption of a given good produces in the consumer, and "happiness," Jevons quickly clarifies, "is a convenient name for the aggregate of the favorable balance of feeling produced – the sum

of the pleasure created and the pain prevented" (*The Theory of Political Economy*, 45).

25 For a similar theory of sex and economics, see also Michael Tratner's *Deficits and Desires*. Like Birken, Tratner argues that Victorian gender models are informed by a productivist logic that emphasizes restraint, saving, and labour. Alternatively, modern sexuality embraces the new economics and its emphasis upon circulation, spending, and pleasure.

26 For more on the link between the New Woman movement and political economy, see also Ledger's *The New Woman*, 39–43, and Richardson's *Love and Eugenics in the Late Nineteenth Century*, 37–8.

27 See also Gagnier's essay, "Women in British Aestheticism and the Decadence," 248.

28 See also the entry "The New Woman" in *The Cambridge Guide to Women's Writing*, 465, and King's *Discourses of Aging in Fiction and Feminism*, 33, for more on the relationship between mothers and daughters in New Woman writings.

29 Caird cites as an epigraph for her *Morality of Marriage* the following stanza from Charlotte Perkins Stetson's "To Mothers," another work that is very critical of compulsory motherhood: "We are Mothers. Through us in our bondage/ Through us with a brand in the face / Be we fettered with gold or with iron / Through us comes the race" (Stetson, ll. 5–8).

30 See also Norton's essay, "Anne Lister: The First Modern Lesbian," as well as Liddington's *Presenting the Past*.

31 See also Cameron's "The Pleasures of Looking and the Feminine Gaze in Michael Field's *Sight and Song*."

32 See also Vicinus's *Intimate Friends*, 113.

33 See Ledger's *The New Woman*, 37.

34 See also Ross's *Slum Travellers*, 8–10, for more on late-Victorian women's efforts to blend together feminism and social reform or socialism.

35 On the question of socio-economic and racial differences among women, Michie cites influential sources such as Dill's "Race, Class, and Gender" and Spelman's *The Inessential Woman*. On the subject of differences within sexual (or lesbian) bonds between women, Michie looks to Lindenbaum's essay "The Shattering of an Illusion."

36 See also Ehnenn's *Women's Literary Collaboration* and Oulton's *Romantic Friendship in Victorian Literature* for more on the range among feminine ties, including female friendships and lesbian marriage.

37 Vicinus's view of women's deliberate agency in self-fashioning sexual identities complements recent studies such as Doan's *Fashioning Sapphism*. This emphasis on feminist agency can also be read as a response to Jeffreys's *The Spinster and Her Enemies* and Faderman's *Surpassing the Love of Men* and *Odd Girls and Twilight Lovers*, which tend to read Victorian lesbianism

as a passive response to dominant nineteenth-century narratives (like sexology).

38 Even Helena Michie, in her move toward a deconstructive methodology, acknowledges that sisterly bonds could provide "a place and a vocabulary" for women to explore feelings and relationships typically prohibited within dominant and heterosexist models of gender difference (*Sororophobia*, 21).

39 Rich's "Compulsory Heterosexuality and the Lesbian Experience" helped to pioneer this first critical approach to female-female bonds as libratory.

40 Vicinus's work on female bonds ("Distance and Desire" and *Intimate Friends*) is a good example of the continuum model.

41 See Rubin's "Thinking Sex" for an example of this second approach, stressing the difference between gender and sex.

42 For examples of the tension model, see Cosslett's *Woman to Woman* and Smith-Rosenberg's "The Female World of Love and Ritual."

43 Judith Butler also looks to Fuss's *Essentially Speaking* as engaged in deconstructing the binary between discursive and essentialist models of gendered embodiment (*Gender Trouble*, 30).

44 See also Gallagher's *The Body Economic* regarding the novel's role in the formation of economic bodies and the regulation of pleasurable or productive subjects. Building upon Gallagher's important work, *Critical Alliances* argues that women and representations of feminine collaboration play a fundamental role in rewriting the gendered marketplace (including economic subjectivities) at the turn of the nineteenth century.

45 See also Spender's *The Education Papers* for more on this history of women's education and for examples of specific reforms enacted in the nineteenth century.

46 See also Hamilton, *Criminals, Idiots, Women, & Minors*, 208.

47 Maine's argument is in many ways a response to the 1857 Divorce and Matrimonial Causes Act, the first in a wave of reforms to marital coverture and property laws throughout the period. Subsequent passage of the Married Women's Property Acts in 1870 and 1882 would continue to extend wives' economic agency after marriage.

48 Critics such as Schaffer (*The Forgotten Female Aesthetes*) and Psomiades (*Beauty's Body*) focus specifically on women's contribution to aesthetic experiments intent on a detachment from, and artistic reflection upon, consumer practices and relationships. As Psomiades explains, the beautiful female is herself a site of contested meaning, embodying both "inaccessible psychological depth" and a "tangible material surface" (3). Beauty's body thus plays a critical role within the aesthetic tradition as an iconic representation of an irresolvable tension between pleasing surfaces (art) and underlying economic structures (including commodity culture).

49 Several critics have, over the past two decades, produced a wealth of research on Woolf's dual interests in women and economics. Recent examples of such scholarship include Froula's *Virginia Woolf and the Bloomsbury Avant-Garde* and Cuddy-Keane's *Virginia Woolf, the Intellectual, and the Public Sphere*. Still other scholars such as Tratner (*Deficits and Desires*) and Ellis (*Virginia Woolf and the Victorians*) compare Woolf's representations of gender economies with those of her Victorian predecessors.

50 Froula, in *Virginia Woolf and the Bloomsbury Avant-Garde*, argues that the author's decision to separate the two texts and write a single work of fiction – *The Years* – comes closer to the truth of femininity as a kind of performative act, a fiction in itself, especially given the suppression and repression involved in the public or published representation of femininity (228–9).

1. Educating New Women for Feminist Futures

1 See Brittain's *Testament of Youth*, 41.

2 See Ledger's *The New Woman*, 2.

3 See Ardis's *New Women, New Novels*, 68, and Ledger's *The New Woman*, 81.

4 See Walkowitz's *City of Dreadful Delight*, 140, for more on Schreiner's (romantic) relationship with Pearson.

5 See also Bland's *Banishing the Beast*, 10–11, particularly her opening chapter, "The Men and Women's Club," for more on this troubled friendship between Pearson and Schreiner.

6 For more on Schreiner's early relationships with Ellis and Carpenter via the New Life, see also Robin Hackett's *Sapphic Primitivism*, 40.

7 This essay was originally read to the Men and Women's Club in 1886, and then was later published in pamphlet form, and then again reprinted as *The Ethic of Freethought* (see Rive, *Olive Schreiner's Letters*, 125, n. 4).

8 See Livesey's "Morris, Carpenter, Wilde" for more on Schreiner and Carpenter, specifically. According to Livesey, Schreiner's writings serve as an example of socialist feminism that "deliberately blurred the distinction between masculine production and feminine reproduction" (609).

9 For more on Carpenter's influence on late nineteenth-century gender theorists, see Rowbotham and Weeks's *Socialism and the New Life*.

10 See also Levine's *Victorian Feminism, 1850–1900* for more on middle-class women in higher education and skilled positions.

11 Anderson earned her MD in the United States in 1859, and was finally admitted to the British Medical Association in 1873. After this, the British Medical Association voted to refuse future entry of female members, and so Anderson remained its only female member until 1889 (19 years), at

which point the policy was finally revoked. Jex-Blake had already passed the medical exams in 1877 at the University of Bern (in Switzerland).

12 Schreiner mentioned Jex-Blake`s practice in a letter to friend John Brown (30 April 1881): "Dr McDonald is out in the country so I've not been able to see Jex-Blake" (ll. 20–1. www.oliveschreiner.org/vre?view=collections&colid=58&letterid=1).

13 See Burstyn, *Victorian Education*, 130–1.

14 The emphasis on a domestic-skills-based curriculum for girls only began to change in the early twentieth century and in an effort to compete with other countries, particularly Germany. The thinking was, both Burstyn and Dyhouse explain, that England's middle-class women must be able to compete with other skilled women, particularly insofar as trained women raised smarter or more competitive sons (for military or national service).

15 See Purvis's *A History of Women's Education in England*, 74, for more on each of these four critical camps.

16 See Vicinus's *Independent Women*, 21–2, and Pedersen's *The Reform of Girls' Secondary and Higher Education in Victorian England*, 378, for more on the women's education movement as a product of changing social and economic gender roles.

17 As June Purvis argues, "This focus was established by Ray Strachey in her classic 1928 book, *The Cause: A Short History of the Women's Movement in Great Britain* and has been particularly continued by Olive Banks, Jane Rendall, Philippa Levin, and myself [Purvis]" (*A History of Women's Education in England*, 75).

18 Biographers First and Scott (*Olive Schreiner*) also discuss how Schreiner was a voracious reader and taught herself through an ambitious course of texts on philosophy and the sciences.

19 See First and Scott's *Olive Schreiner*, 112.

20 See Burstyn, *Victorian Education*, 119–27, for more on mid-Victorian women's shift from marriage plots to professional plots. Levine's *Victorian Feminism, 1850–1900*, 36–9, also discusses the 1871 National Union for the Improvement of the Education of Women of all Classes (1871) and the 1870s spike in teacher colleges which arose in response to the growing need to train women for careers independent of marriage.

21 See also Joan N. Burstyn, *Victorian Education*, 134, and Philippa Levine, *Victorian Feminism*, 37, for more on the Girls' Public Day School as a response to women's higher and skilled education.

22 See also Levine, *Victorian Feminism*, 38–9, for more on women's gendered education and domestic skills in girls' curriculum, specifically.

23 This list is taken from Lecaros's "The Victorian Heroine Goes a Governessing." Lecaros traces the earliest narrative representations of the governess figure back to eighteenth-century school stories, adding that it was not until the nineteenth century that writers shifted their

attention to the resident governess and her "relation to employers and pupils" (31).

24 See Lecaros, "The Victorian Heroine Goes a Governessing," 31.

25 See also Samuelian's introduction to the 2004 Broadview edition of *Emma* for more on this history of the governess (especially 23–36).

26 See also Tobin's "Aiding Impoverished Gentlewomen" and Looser's "The Duty of Women by Women."

27 Gilbert's analysis is also influenced by Adrienne Rich's "Jane Eyre: The Temptations of a Motherless Woman."

28 See Lecaros, "The Victorian Heroine Goes a Governessing," 31–2.

29 Alice Hall Petry, for example, characterizes James's novel as a "parody" in her article "Jamesian Parody, *Jane Eyre*, and 'The Turn of the Screw.'"

30 See Hughes, *The Victorian Governess*, 197.

31 Ibid., xiii.

32 See Peterson, "The Victorian Governess," 5.

33 For more on the oversupply of female teachers, especially music and arts teachers, see Jordan, *The Women's Movement*, 114.

34 Critics such as Ray Strachey (*The Cause*, 226) and Jane Rendall (*The Origins of Modern Feminisms*, 17–20) argue that the reforms to women's education are in part a response to the rise of economic liberalism after 1850.

35 See also Martin's *Women and the Politics of Schooling*, 22–3.

36 The growing number of public schools for both boys and, later, girls also made possible a new field of employment for women as secondary or high-school teachers (Bryant, *The Unexpected Revolution*, 76, 106).

37 See Jordan, *The Women's Movement*, 115–22, for more on this history of women's colleges and teacher-training schools.

38 See also Burstyn's *Victorian Education and the Ideal of Womanhood*, 91, and Green's *Educating Women*, 102.

39 See also Burstyn, *Victorian Education and the Ideal of Womanhood*, 94.

40 See also Marks's *Bicycles, Bangs, and Bloomers*, 103.

41 Ledger also reads Lyndall as a mouthpiece for Schreiner's critique of the domestic ideology limiting women's education: "Like her fictional and real-life successors, Lyndall attempts to get herself educated by taking herself off to boarding school," but, Ledger continues, "[t]he 'education' she received is, though, utterly useless in terms of enabling her to make her way independently in the world" (*The New Woman*, 81).

42 See Ardis's analysis of Schreiner's novel and, specifically, its critique of restrictive domestic plots in *New Women, New Novels*, 61–8.

43 See also Ledger and Luckhurst's essay, "The New Woman," 76, for more on Lyndall's investment in both women's education and maternal roles.

44 According to Ledger, Schreiner objected to modern women's exclusion from "meaningful work" without "any compensatory fields of activity" (*The New Woman*, 42).

45 See also Macura's "'Lifeless, inane, dawdling': Decadence, Femininity and Olive Schreiner's *Woman and Labor.*"
46 Karl Pearson was a good friend of the famous eugenicist, Francis Galton. In 1911, Pearson was named the University College of London's first Galton Professor of Eugenics and he also wrote a biography recording Galton's life and philosophies entitled *The Life, Letters and Labors of Francis Galton.*
47 We know from Schreiner's letter to Havelock Ellis, on 28 March 1884, that "the book that the Stranger gives to Waldo was intended to be Spencer's 'First Principles'" (Draznin, *My Other Self*, 39). In her introduction, page 11, to the Broadview edition, Patricia O'Neill also makes note of Spencer's influence on Schreiner, including that important scene when the Stranger gives Waldo the mysterious book. See also First and Scott's *Olive Schreiner*, 58–9, for more on the personal origins of this story.
48 In her own work on the New Woman, Angelique Richardson describes how the emphasis on maternity fits within an eugenic imperative: "the central goal of eugenic feminists was the construction of civic motherhood which sought political recognition for reproductive labor; in the wake of new biological knowledge they argued that their contribution to nation and empire might be expanded if they assumed responsibility for the rational selection of reproductive partners" (*Love and Eugenics in the Late Nineteenth Century*, 9).
49 See also Spencer's essay, "The Social Organism" in *Essays: Scientific, Political & Speculative.*
50 Schreiner typically aligned herself with, what Ruth First and Ann Scott describe as, smaller socialist organizations (including the FNL) that were equally committed to "sexual pleasure, the issue of love in a loveless world, [and] with a democratic creation of beauty" (*Olive Schreiner*, 110).
51 In her work *The Educated Woman*, Katharina Rowold describes such arguments as a form of race-based feminism, in which women's higher education and professional development are defensible because they advance the ongoing health of the "race" (61).
52 See also Nelson's introduction to *A New Woman Reader*, ix, for more on this history of the "New Woman's" public naming in printed discourse.
53 For more on this history, see also the entry "New Woman" in *The Cambridge Guide to Women's Writing in English*, 465–7: "Whilst the female New Women writers did not always agree on the value of motherhood, what they did agree on was the necessity of a broader education for women as well as access to a wider cultural world than that deemed suitable for the bulk of middle-class Victorian women" (465).
54 In a later 1897 interview, Grand reflected upon her own uncomfortable relationship with dominant discourses on women's education: "It must

be remembered that at that time I was but a mere girl, and took without question the reiterated prophecy which still leads a halting maimed existence to this day, that if a woman became a doctor, or did anything of an intellectual and capable kind, or made a career for herself, she must be hideously ugly, and hard, and utterly horrid, and like a man, so they said – just like a man" (quoted in Tooley, "Madame Sarah Grand at Home," 242).

55 See Heilmann, *New Woman Strategies*, 27.

56 Caird's later essay, "Emancipation of the Family" offers an even longer discussion on the gendered difference in education (*The Morality of Marriage and Other Essays*, 52).

57 Caird is counted by many critics – including Angelique Richardson (*Love and Eugenics*) and Anne Heilmann (*New Woman Strategies*) – as a primary example of anti-essentialist feminism at the fin de siècle.

58 See also Rowold's extended discussion of Caird and the "energy economy" in *The Educated Woman*, 61.

59 See also Angelique Richardson's "'People talk a lot of Nonsense about Heredity': Mona Caird and Anti-Eugenic Feminism."

60 Almost a decade later, in "Plain Words on the Woman Question," 12, Allen argues that most women must give birth to at least four children in order to perpetuate the human species.

61 For a similar analysis of Allen's educational program, see Cameron's "Grant Allen's *The Woman Who Did*: Spencerian Individualism and Teaching New Women to Be Mothers."

62 See also Sabine Ernst's "*The Woman Who Did* and 'The Girl Who Didn't,'" 87, Morton's "*The Busiest Man in England*," 153, and Ruddick's introduction, 34–5, to the Broadview edition of *The Woman Who Did*.

63 See also Berkman's *The Healing Imagination of Olive Schreiner* for more on Schreiner's rejection of "prevalent scientific views on sex and gender difference held by feminist and non-feminists alike" (128).

64 See also Walkowitz's *City of Dreadful Night*, 147–9, for more on this history and Pearson's cautionary approach to women's sexual emancipation.

65 See also Rowold's *The Educated Woman*, 54, for more on Pearson's conflicting views on education and his eugenic measures for the regulation of sexual reproduction.

66 For more on Schreiner and Race Theory, including the author's tendency to exclude people of colour from her models of social (re)production, see Krebs's "Olive Schreiner's Racialization of South Africa" and Monsman's "Writing the Self on the Imperial Frontier."

67 See chapter 4 in First and Scott's *Olive Schreiner*.

68 See O'Neill's introduction to the Broadview edition, 17.

69 Schreiner's representation of the book as a kind of intellectual catalyst echoes her own personal experience upon first encountering Mill's

political writings: in a letter to Rev. J.T. Lloyd (29 October 1892), for example, she insists that "the only man to whose moral teaching I am conscious of owing a profound and unending debt is John Stuart Mill" (Rive, *Olive Schreiner Letters*, 213), and in another letter to Betty Molteno (on 22 May 1896), Schreiner writes that "the book which has had most effect on my spiritual life was Mill's *Logic*, and more or less all his works, especially his *Political Economy*" (Rive, *Olive Schreiner Letters*, 277).

70 This theory of "capital" and the following quotations are taken from Bourdieu's touchstone essay, "The Forms of Capital."

71 See also Laura Morgan Green's *Educating Women*, 105, for more on education as a form of "cultural capital" and Victorian women's socio-economic mobility.

72 In her note to the Broadview edition, O'Neill explains how Schreiner's book is in part a response to Pearson's "Woman and Labor," in which he proposed state funding for mothers (*The Story of an African Farm*, 342 n.1).

73 See Hilton and Hirsch's *Practical Visionaries*, 12, for more on Froebel's innovative contributions to early childhood education.

74 For more on Schreiner and modernized labour, see also Burdett's *Olive Schreiner and the Progress of Feminism*.

75 See also Rowold, *The Educated Woman*, 63, for more on this inversion of classed domesticity.

76 See also First and Scott, *Olive Schreiner*, 265.

77 As her biographers Ruth First and Ann Scott note, many of the reviews were "inconsequential" or "shallow in their approval," while still others offer substantial yet diametrically opposed reading to the novel (*Olive Schreiner*, 123).

78 Aveling also describes the book as "cosmopolitan and human," and claims the characters are so well drawn that "we were so interested in what they [the characters] think and say" (quoted in First and Scott, *Olive Schreiner*, 124).

79 McClintock (*Imperial Leather*) is particularly interested in Schreiner's status as a white woman born to poor missionary parents, a liminal social status that gave Schreiner unique insight into both labour politics and dominant middle-class constructions of femininity (267).

80 Schreiner, "Letter to Andre" (1911) in *The Oliver Schreiner Letters Online* www.oliveschreiner.org/vre?view=collections&colid=45&letterid=41.

2. Sisterly Kinship and the Modern Sexual Contract

1 The same year she left, at only twenty years of age, Levy published her first volume of poetry entitled *Xantippe and Other Verse* (1881).

2 By calling Levy "pallid-faced," Allen also rather callously alludes to the author's poor health and eventual suicide in 1889.

3 See also Tanner's *Adultery in the Novel* for more on how, in the typical domestic plot, "patterns of passion and patterns of property" are always "br[ought] into harmonious alignment" (15). Miller's "Emphasis Added" also looks at how feminine purity is confirmed by marriage and domestic closure.

4 See my introduction (pp. 12–13) and, specifically, references to Shanley (*Feminism, Marriage, and the Law in Victorian England, 1850–1895*) and Frank (*Law, Literature, and the Transmission of Culture in England, 1837–1925*) for more on this history and women's limited autonomy under the 1882 Act.

5 See Shanley, *Feminism, Marriage, and the Law in Victorian England*, 177.

6 Linton singles out contemporary feminists ("the grimmer designs of women's rights") and the 1882 Act for specific mention as threatening the Victorian family (692).

7 Hunt describes this as a clash between an old value system "stressing obligation toward kin" and the new system "concerned with individual profit and loss" (*Middling Sort*, 29).

8 See also Phegley's *Courtship and Marriage* for more on the economic pressures shaping the Victorian family, particularly after the industrial revolution. "[M]arriage was still largely an economic decision," Phegley explains, and "[a]s the economy moved from communal aggregating modes of production toward waged manufacturing and commercial systems, the increasing separation of the home and the workplace precipitated the wider division between male and female domains" (13–14).

9 Pollak also cites Rubin's careful reworking of foundational psychoanalytic theories like the "Incest Taboo" as a social, not an innate drive (*Incest and the English Novel*, 6).

10 See also Juliet Mitchell's *Psychoanalysis and Feminism* for more on how kinship continues to play a central role in women's right to economic contract. "[M]en enter into the class-dominated structures of history," she explains, "while women (as women, whatever their actual work in production) remain defined by the kinship patterns of organization … harnessed into the family" (13).

11 Both Michie ("Rich Woman, Poor Woman") and Psomiades ("The Marriage Plot in Theory") pay homage to Armstrong's *Desire and Domestic Fiction* for its powerful articulation of the political and economic forces inherent within, and constantly reproduced through, Victorian fiction on marriage and the domestic sphere.

12 See also Psomiades's "Heterosexual Exchange and Other Victorian Fictions" for another example of her extensive work on Victorian structures of kinship and gendered/ sexual exchange.

13 See also Michie's earlier essay "Rich Woman, Poor Woman," which explains how the "nineteenth-century marriage plot is anthropological in

the sense that it works the historical pressures of the period by providing a symbolic form in which those pressures can be both encoded and denied" (425).

14 For more on the history of middle-class women's participation in the urban workforce, see Wojtczak's *Women of Victorian Sussex* and Holcombe's *Victorian Ladies at Work.* Wojtczak cites examples of numerous middle-class women who owned their own businesses (granted the aforementioned book limits its study to Sussex), and Holcombe's study looks at women's increasing demand for white-collar work, such as teaching, nursing, and clerical work.

15 See also Liggins, "Women of True Respectability?"; Robertson's "'It was Just a Real Camaraderie Thing'"; and Cowman and Jackson's *Women and Work Culture.* Both Liggins and Robertson look at middle-class Victorian women's effort to redefine shop-keeping as a respectable profession, while Cowman and Jackson both cite the wide range in strategies among women's fight for labour opportunity and equality.

16 Older women and widows are the only exception to this Victorian social rule (Claudia Nelson, *Family Ties in Victorian England,* 101).

17 The sisterly home provides a sanctuary for women who could not find husbands, or "[i]n other cases," Nelson continues, "sisterly love might serve as a socially approved rehearsal for romantic love" (*Family Ties in Victorian England,* 101).

18 See Perry's *Novel Relations,* 129, and Staves's *Married Women's Separate Property in England, 1660–1833* for more on this history surrounding women's inherited property rights and marital coverture.

19 J.H. Morgan was himself a British general and lawyer, and his introduction to the 1917 edition described the lasting influence of *Ancient Law,* adding that "its epoch-making influence may not unfitly be compared to that exercised by Darwin's *Origins of Species*" (vii).

20 See Frank's *Law, Literature, and the Transmission of Culture in England, 1837–1925,* which explains Maine's theory on the familial transmission of property "by showing how the modern primacy of the individual ... is actually an inversion of the ancient primacy of the family – understood as a corporation – of which the patriarch is no more than a 'public officer' or temporary representative" (40).

21 In *Novel Relations,* 117, Perry describes how the legacy of this familial structure can be found in the abundance of names or ways to think of sibling bonds through subsequent generations (niece, nephew, etc); yet there are few ways to discuss relations acquired through marriage, or what we now call "in-laws."

22 Psomiades characterizes *Ancient Law* as "an origin story that could substitute for the social contract, a historical story of how law actually emerged" ("The Marriage Plot in Theory," 54).

23 See Wordsworth's "Tintern Abbey."

24 See also Brown's discussion of Samuel Taylor Coleridge per, what she describes as, the effect of his "passionate attachment to the memory of his own dead sister on his relationships with the Fricker sisters" (*Devoted Sisters*, 111).

25 For more on the idealized relationship between siblings and sisters, specifically, see also Brown's *Devoted Sisters*, vii–viii, May's *Disorderly Sisters*, 81–5, and Davidoff's *Thicker Than Water*, 124–6.

26 See Gruner's "Born and Made," 427.

27 See also Wion's "The Absent Mother in *Wuthering Heights*" for a longer discussion of this sibling bond as a pre-social or primal "oneness" (364).

28 See also Brown, *Devoted Sisters*, 110–11, for more on "strong bonds of friendship" between Maggie and Tom.

29 See also May's *Disorderly Sisters*, 81, for more on the critical debate surrounding Eliot's representation of childhood psycho-sexual development.

30 Leacock describes this as the historic "shift" in women's position "from valued people who cement networks of reciprocal relations and who have access to various publicly recognized mechanisms for adjudicating their interests as women, into that of service workers in the households of husbands and their kin group" ("Interpreting the Origins of Gender Inequality," 270).

31 In *Family Ties in Victorian England*, Nelson explains how "[m]iddle-class fathers typically considered that they had a duty to provide financially for their daughters," while sons were expected to pave their own way, forming and assuming responsibility for their own private families (88).

32 See also Merrell's *The Accidental Bond* for more on this cross-sex sibling bond as preparation for the conjugal private family; siblings are, Merrell explains, our "first real partners in life" training us for those private and linear relations to come (12).

33 See also Sacks's *Sisters and Wives* for a Marxist reading of this history and the "perennial subordination" of wives and daughters within the patricorporation (123).

34 The 1835 Act was, as Gruner explains, "designed to bring English common law into line with canon law of the Anglican church" ("Born and Made," 424). See also Brown's *Devoted Sisters* for more on this legal history and the Act as prohibiting, what Brown refers to as, "Incest by surrogacy" (111).

35 See also Gruner's "Born and Made," 436, for more on A.J. Beresford-Hope and his role in the debates surrounding the Deceased Wife's Sister Act.

36 See also Chambers's "Triangular Desire and the Sororal Bond" for more on Beresford-Hope and the controversy surrounding the "Deceased Wife's Sister's Bill."

37 For more on *Tess* and sisterly sameness, see also Chambers's "Triangular Desire and the Sororal Bond," 8, and Brown's *Devoted Sisters*, 107–8.

38 Elsewhere in his study, Maine refers to the "[f]iction of Adoption which permits the family tie to be artificially created" (*Ancient Law*, 16).
39 See also Harders's essay "Agnatio, Cognation, Consanguinitus."
40 See also Evans's "We Are Photographers, Not Mountebanks!" for more on Levy's progressive representation of women in urban business. As Evans explains, Levy's novel is "unique" insofar as the female protagonists "are shop proprietors, not paid assistants" and because the sisters "are the producers of spectacles, not the subjects of them" (26).
41 This is also the reason that Gertrude expressly limits sororal support to sisters, insisting that the sisters "couldn't go on taking Fred's guineas for ever [*sic*]" (*The Romance of a Shop*, 90).
42 For more on Black's political writings, see also Cameron's "Women's Slum Journalism, 1885–1910."
43 See Bernstein's introduction to the 2006 Broadview edition of *The Romance of a Shop*, 27–8.
44 As Linda Hunt Beckman writes, in *Amy Levy: Her Life and Letters*, "It was most likely at the British Museum ... that Levy became acquainted with Eleanor Marx (Karl Marx's daughter), Olive Schreiner, Margaret Harkness, Beatrice Potter (later Webb), and Dollie Maitland [later Radford] ... The women were all socialists or social reformers" (79).
45 See also Ledger, *The New Woman*, 160–1.
46 See also Lise Shapiro Sanders, *Consuming Fantasies*, 7–8.
47 In *Women of Victorian Sussex*, Wojtczak also cites several examples of real-life Victorian women who worked as employees or proprietors of successful businesses.
48 See Holcombe's *Victorian Ladies at Work*, 104–6, for more on how deskilling contributed to the feminization of this workforce (shop-keeping) (18); Davidoff and Hall's *Family Fortunes*, 302, looks at how, over the centuries, shop-keeping transformed into a specialized form of labour with a "fixed retail distribution" (302); and Jordan's *The Women's Movement*, 11–12, argues that many employers simply exploited the already existent knowledge among the labourers (this is particularly the case in dress shops, where the number of female assistants grew the most).
49 For more on middle-class women's work in trade and business, see also Liggins's "Women of True Respectability? Investigating the London Work-girl, 1880–1900" and Robertson's "'It was Just a Real Camaraderie Thing.'"
50 See Jordan, *The Women's Movement*, 114.
51 See Boucherett, *Hints on Self-Help*, 27–8.
52 See Jordan, *The Women's Movement*, 114.
53 Marien, *Photography*, 97. See also Weaver's chapters 12 and 13 on Lady Hawarden and Julia Margaret Cameron, respectively, in *British Photography in the Nineteenth Century*, 141–61.

54 See also Di Bello, *Women's Albums and Photography*, 19–21.

55 In his review of the novel, George Orwell focuses on the "pressure of social conventions" that limit women's economic freedoms, and each character's unhappy ending is thus the direct result of "obeying the accepted social code, or in not having enough money to circumvent it" ("George Gissing," n.p.).

56 See also Cameron's article, "'She is Not a Lady, but a Legal Document': The Tattoo as Contract in *Mr. Meeson's Will*."

57 For more on Levy and the urban gaze, see Flint's "hour of pink twilight"; Goody's "Passing in The City"; Walkowitz's *City of Dreadful Delight*; and Vadillo's *Women Poets and Urban Aestheticism*. Goody discusses Levy's investment in liminal urban spaces (163), while Flint focuses on fleeting and erotically charged encounters (693–4). Vadillo describes Levy's novel (and poems in *A London Plane-Tree*) as an example of the late-Victorian *flâneuse* (71–3), and Walkowitz describes how the *flâneuse*'s "disorderly sexual conduct in the city" flaunts "non-familial attachments" (6).

58 See also Levy's "Ballade of an Omnibus" in *A London Plane-Tree, and Other Verses* for another example of Levy's interest in women urban wandering, omnibuses, and visual aesthetics.

59 See also Georg Simmel's *Philosophische Kulture* (1911), quoted in David Frisby's *Simmel and Science*.

60 As Parsons explains, in *Streetwalking the Metropolis*, Baudelaire's original writings "[did] not use the term flâneur" but instead borrowed and "expanded" upon the English concept of the dandy (20). See also Moers's *The Dandy in Literature* for more on this history and the changing meaning of the dandy after Beau Brummell and Max Beerbohm.

61 See Evans's "We Are Photographers, Not Mountebanks!" 34, and Nord's *Walking the Victorian Streets*, 202.

62 See also Kerber's "Separate Spheres," for more on this anthropological history of the shift from mother-right to father-right and a patrilineal descent of blood and property.

63 As Rubin defines it, "[c]apitalism is a set of social relations – in which production takes the form of turning money, things, and people into capital. And capital is a quantity of goods or money which, when exchanged for labour, reproduces and augments itself by extracting unpaid labour, or surplus value, from labour and into itself" ("The Traffic in Women," 108).

64 As Phegley explains, in *Courtship and Marriage in Victorian England*, "[d]uring the Victorian period the aspiration to achieve companionate marriage based on mutual affection, respect, and love was pervasive" (2).

65 Several critics have made similar points in their analyses of Levy's own female desire; Beckman, for example, describes Levy as "a woman whose

desire was homoerotic" (*Amy Levy*, 7), while Goody, by contrast, discusses the "complexities of Levy's sexuality" and how it troubles simple classification of her as an "independent New Woman" ("Passing in the City," 168).

66 For more on Amy Levy's poetry as a critique of heteronormativity, see also Francis's "Amy Levy: Contradictions?" 193, and Scheinberg's *Women's Poetry and Religion in Victorian England*, 194–5.

67 In her work "Heterosexual Exchange and Other Victorian Fictions," Psomiades describes this as a kind of "Gender indifferen[ce]" in which sex is merely something exchanged between partners, adding that "[s]kill at producing orgasms" is the real measure of value within this contractual economy (114).

68 See also Radner's "Introduction: Queering the Girl" for more on this new sexual economy of mutual pleasure. "If pleasure replaces reproduction as the goal of sexuality," Radner writes, "then the 'sex' of either partner is significant only to the extent that it increases or lessens pleasure given or received" (19).

69 Ardis also invokes Adrienne Rich's work on "woman-centerednesss" in her analysis of these narratives and their emphasis on the sisterly bond over and above the heterosexual romance plot (*New Women, New Novels*, 135).

70 Evans, "We Are Photographers, Not Mountebanks!" also notes that the "gender of this young photographer is left ambiguous" (40).

71 Bernstein makes a similar claim in her introduction to the 2006 Broadview edition of *The Romance of a Shop* (28). She explains how James Thomson's *The City of Dreadful Night* applied Baudelaire's concept to Victorian London, thus ushering in the *flâneur* as an international term for the city wanderer.

72 According to Chris Jenks's definition, in "Watching Your Step," "the *flâneur* possesses a power, it walks at will, freely and seemingly without purpose, but simultaneously with an inquisitive wonder and an infinite capacity to absorb the activities collected – often formulated as the 'crowd'" (146).

73 In Charles Baudelaire's account there is no separation between the personal and the public; instead, the *flâneur* is "away from home" and yet "feel[s] oneself everywhere at home" ("The Painter of Modern Life," 9).

74 Janet Wolff claims that the female *flâneur* (or "*flâneuse*") "was rendered impossible by the sexual divisions of the nineteenth century" (*Feminine Sentences*, 47), for example, while Griselda Pollock is even more pessimistic in her claim that "there is no female equivalent of the quintessential masculine figure, the flâneur: there is not and could not be a female flâneuse" ("Modernity and the Spaces of Femininity," in *Vision and Difference*, 71).

75 See Cameron and Bird's essay, "Sisterly Bonds."

3. Cosmopolitan Communities of Female Professionals

1 Egerton also published two short stories, "The Lost Masterpiece" (April 1894) and "The Captain's Book" (July 1895), both in *The Yellow Book*, as well as a translation of Ola Hansson's *Young Ofeg's Ditties* in 1895.

2 Egerton had planned to call her "life study" novel *The Hazard of the Hill*, but as the 1898 publication date drew near, she wrote to her new publisher Grant Richards telling him to change the title to *The Wheel of God* (see also Stetz, "'George Egerton,'" 116).

3 Much like its precursor the bildungsroman, the life novel is an extended narrative focused on a single character's social maturation or "apprenticeship to life," to use the terms set forth by Johann Wolfgang von Goethe's *Wilhelm Meister's Apprenticeship*, 96.

4 "In Benjaminian terms, a parallel can be drawn between the eyes of the prostitutes in Baudelaire's poems and the windows of the shopping industry" (Parsons, *Streetwalking the Metropolis*, 25).

5 See also Wolff's *Feminine Sentences*, 45.

6 Chavelita was, as Stetz records, "appalled to hear 'George Egerton' hailed as a new Olive Schreiner or 'Sarah Grand' (Frances MacFall [*sic*]), leading women out of bondage to men and proposing an Amazonian ideal" ("'George Egerton,'" 67). Instead, "What [Egerton] wanted," Stetz argues, "what she argued for in every book – were not civil rights but *sexual* rights for women" (68, emphasis in original).

7 See also Schaffer ("Nothing But Foolscap and Ink") and Willis ("Packaging the New Woman for Mass Consumption") for more on second-generation New Woman novelists and their popular take on sex-positive feminism.

8 Here I echo Stetz's "'George Egerton,'" which claims that "Mary's hunger for a feeling of union will be the motive for all her behavior and the source of all her frustration" (124).

9 See also Kate Krueger's earlier article, "Mobility and Modern Consciousness in George Egerton's and Charlotte Mew's *Yellow Book Stories*" (as Kate Krueger Henderson).

10 See also Linda Nochlin's "Foreword" to *The New Woman International* for more on this urban feminist figure in late-Victorian London (1880–1900).

11 Regarding the urban New Woman as socially situated, see also Hager's "A Community of Women" for more on class difference in Egerton's female-female bonds, and Jusová's "George Egerton and the Project of British Colonialism" and *The New Woman and Empire* for more on Egerton's representation of race and nationalism.

12 Parsons's theory of women's situated cosmopolitanism is also draws from Rose's *States of Fantasy*, 13 and 129.

13 Stetz ("'George Egerton'") and O'Toole (*Irish New Woman*) also read *The Wheel of God* as anticipating the kind of experiments in narrative point of view and stream of consciousness made famous by later writers such as James Joyce and Virginia Woolf.

14 This scene bears a strong resemblance to events in Egerton's own early childhood. See also the *Dictionary of Literary Biography* entry, by Anita Moss, for more on Egerton's own "bitterness toward those who did nothing to help her family, even during the ordeal of her mother's death" (n.p).

15 O'Toole reads the novel as essentially the story of "a young Irish woman who immigrates to America late in the nineteenth century, fleeing destitution and a dysfunctional family" – a woman whose life follows a pattern not that dissimilar from Edgerton's own (*The Irish New Woman*, 141).

16 The specific dates for her arrival to and departure from these countries are not known (see O'Toole, *The Irish New Woman*, 140–1).

17 See also Stetz and Lasner's *England in the 1890s*.

18 As Stetz writes, "*The Wheel of God* picks up where the short stories had left off in portraying the three most important figures in the author's life – Captain Dunne, Higginson, and Clairmonte – and treats in greater depth her complicated feelings towards them" ("'George Egerton,'" 131).

19 See Pencak's introduction to *Immigration to New York* and Bogen's *Immigration in New York*.

20 Bayor and Meagher, *The New York Irish*, 20. Stansell claims that, "by 1855, the Irish accounted for 28 per cent of New York's populace" (*City of Women*, 44).

21 In *The New York Irish* Bayor and Meagher argue that the numbers "reflected an immigration that was coming from the distressed rural districts where the land war was in full swing. Emigration from the more prosperous northeast and Leinster was not at the same level" (289).

22 See also Russell's essay, "Escaping the Examined Life in George Moore's 'Home Sickness.'"

23 "By 1860," Stansell explains, "there were again 125 women of marrying age for every 100 men" (*City of Women*, 83).

24 See Aron's introduction to *The Long Day*, xi, as well as Weiner's *From Working Girl to Working Mother*, 4, and Hill's *Women in Gainful Occupations*, 16 and 13.

25 This date also suggests a certain parallel between Mary's and Egerton's own lives.

26 *The Census of the State of New York for 1875* also lists 526,534 working women to 500,098 working males. Of these numbers, 306,908 were single women and 313,161 were single men (218, 228).

27 To make this point, Walkowitz cites Sennett's study *The Fall of Public Man*, which describes cosmopolitanism as the "experience of diversity in the city as opposed to a relatively confined localism" (Sennett, 137).
28 In his revised essay, "On Some Motifs in Baudelaire," Benjamin draws the even stronger conclusion that "[t]he man of the crowd is no *flâneur*" (326). See also Buck-Morss's *The Dialectics of Seeing* for more on Benjamin's revisions and how his later essay pursues a Marxist reading of the *flâneur* as a bourgeois figure of leisure.
29 See Sante's *Low Life* for more on Broadway and urban congestion. As Sante explains, the avenue was the centre of "commerce and fashion" and was therefore "plied by every sort of truck, wagon, cart, and coach" (47).
30 See also Homberger's *The Historical Atlas of New York City*: "By the end of the century, Fifth Avenue was dominated by the ostentatious mansions of the super-rich of the Gilded Age" (101).
31 In *Washington Square* James writes of the area as characterized by an "established repose" (13).
32 Richardson's *The Long Day* describes one aspect of the village, "though for the most part eminently respectable, [as] dotted here and there, near the riverfront, with some of the worst plague-spots of moral and physical foulness to be found in New York" (121). Even the class-conscious Marches in Howells's *A Hazard of New Fortunes* are careful to assess apartments within the village on a case-by-case basis, even though the area itself falls within the "east and west line" designating "self-respect" (58).
33 See Sante's *Low Life*, which describes the area around Washington Square as a "bohemian nexus" comprised of "elements of gentility and genteel poverty" (333).
34 See Sante's *Low Life*, 18, for more on class tensions and race riots in nineteenth-century New York.
35 "In 1871, the Ninth Avenue 'el,' operated by the New York Elevated Co., opened as far as 30th street, and was extended northwards in 1878. The Rapid Transit commission, empowered by the State Legislature to lay out routes and assign franchises to private operatives, was formed on July 1, 1875. Routes were awarded on Second, Third, and Sixth Avenues, and by 1880 the 'el' had reached the Harlem River" (Homberger, *The Historical Atlas of New York City*, 106–7).
36 See Sante's *Low Life*, 51, for more on late nineteenth-century New York City's elevated trains as a kind of kaleidoscopic theatre of city spaces.
37 See Vadillo, *Women Poets and Urban Aestheticism*, 21, and T.C. Barker and Michael Robbins, *A History of London Transport*, 166.
38 See Christopher Hibbert, *London*, 184 and 190.

39 See also Vadillo, *Women Poets and Urban Aestheticism*, 21, as well as Seaman, *Life in Victorian London*, 73, and Barker and Robbins, *A History of London Transport*, vol. 1: 261 and 263.
40 For more on the rise of the modern department store and female shoppers, see also Parsons's *Streetwalking the Metropolis*, 48–9, and Bowlby's *Just Looking*, 11.
41 While SPEW remained active into the twentieth century, it later evolved into a largely "philanthropic" organization designed to help women interested in business.
42 See A. James Hammerton, "Feminism and Female Emigration, 1861–1886," 54.
43 In Tom Gallon's *The Girl Behind the Keys* (1903), Bella Thorn plays the part of both professional typist and detective heroine. And in Gissing's *The Odd Women*, gender pioneers Rhoda Nunn and Mary Barfoot co-establish a training school for middle-class women who must work for a living but who lack any real saleable skills. For more about the female typewriter as novel heroine, see also Young's "The Rise of the Victorian Working Lady."
44 For more on this history, see Davies's *Woman's Place is at the Typewriter*, 55–9, Keep's "Cultural Work of the Type-writer Girl," 412, and Olwell's "Typewriters and the Vote," 58–60.
45 Delgado's *The Enormous File* explains that the number of female office workers in England rose by 500 per cent (or fivefold) between 1861 and 1911.
46 Of course much of this has to do with the gendered difference in pay, which was a product of the so-called individual and living wage; the latter was the exclusive domain of men who presumably needed to support (or would eventually establish) a family of wife and children (see Keep, "Cultural Work of the Typewriter Girl," 410).
47 For more on the typewriter as a rather vexed means to women's economic and social mobility, see Wicke's "Vampiric Typewriting," 476–7, Doane's "Technophilia," 167, as well as Price's "Grant Allen's Impersonal Secretaries," 129–30, and her collection (co-edited with Pamela Thurschwell) *Literary Secretaries/Secretarial Culture*, 66.
48 See also Cameron's "Sister of the Type" for more on typewriting and the erasure of feminine "aura."
49 See also Livesey's *Socialism, Sex, and the Culture of Aestheticism in Britain*, 54–5, and Gordon and Doughan's *British Women's Organizations, 1825–1960*, 184–5.
50 See also Krueger's *British Women Writers and the Short Story*, 105.
51 See also O'Toole's discussion of the library scene, in which Mary is mentally transported "away" to a "magical world" where she finds comfort in the form of fictional companions (*The Irish New Woman*, 145).

52 Again, my interpretation of Egerton's feminist figure is influenced by Deborah Parsons's claim that the modern cosmopolitan woman is limited by the material conditions of the city, including gender and class (*Streetwalking the Metropolis*, 14).
53 See also O'Neill and Lloyd's edited collection, *The Black and Green Atlantic*, for more on transatlantic exchanges among Irish and American reformers throughout the Victorian and Modernist periods.
54 See McWilliams's "'Avenging Bridget,'" 100, for more on the female migrant's conflicted feelings of alienation and ambition, as well as her subversive access to middle-class domestic secrets.
55 For more on Irish women's anti-emigration writings, see Nichols's *The Women Who Leave*. Nichols is writing against critics such as Patrick Ward who, in *Exile, Emigration, and Irish Writing*, argues that women were "almost totally silent in the discourses surrounding emigration" (152) and therefore focuses almost exclusively on male authors such as Kickham, Mangan, Joyce, and Moore (see Nichols, 6).
56 See also Nichols's *The Women Who Leave*, 42, for more on Butler's anti-emigration feminist fiction.
57 See also Nichol's *The Women Who Leave*, 51, as well as Rosa Mulholland's *A Fair Emigrant* and her essay, "Emigrants."
58 See Nichols's *The Women Who Leave*, 63.
59 See ibid., 66.
60 See also O'Toole's *The Irish New Woman*, 141 and 146–8, for a similar comparison of Egerton's writings with representations of the Irish migrant in works by Joyce and Moore.
61 Joyce's "Eveline" was first published in 1904 and then republished in his 1914 collection of short stories *The Dubliners*.
62 Daisy Miller is even described by her author, Henry James, as an "unsuspecting creature" who is then "sacrificed, as it were, to a social rumpus that went on quite over her head & to which she stood in no measurable relation" ("Reply to Eliza Lynn Linton," 104 in the Broadview edition).
63 Egerton's representation anticipates Anaïs Nin's later impressionistic accounts of the city as a psychological-scape through which the migrant filters and compares her present urban experiences (see Parsons, *Streetwalking the Metropolis*, 152 and 162).
64 See also Poovey's *Uneven Developments* and Cohen's *Professional Domesticity in the Victorian Novel*. Both critics consider how bourgeois domesticity itself took on an almost professional dimension as a form of service work straddling the private and public spheres.
65 See also Helmstadter and Godden's *Nursing before Nightingale*.
66 More recently, Jill Rappoport's *Giving Women* frames Nightingale as part of a larger mid-century effort among Anglican women to find service work for so-called surplus women (93).

67 For more on the "lady" journalist in popular fiction, see Liggins's *George Gissing, the Working Woman, and Urban Culture.*

68 See also Stetz's "Publishing Industries and Practices" and Sally Mitchell's "Careers for Girls" for more on the role of the Writer's Club in supporting women's contributions to professional journalism and publishing.

69 I am also thinking about Benedict Anderson's work on newspapers and the cultural role of print media as outlined in his touchstone text, *Imagined Communities.*

70 See Rubery's *The Novelty of Newspapers* and Gray's edited collection *Women in Journalism at the Fin de Siècle* for the popularization of women's journalism in the nineteenth century.

71 For more on popular literature and women's sports, see also Nancy Fix Anderson's *The Sporting Life: Victorian Sports and Games* and Collins's *Physical Fitness, Sports, and the Rise of the New Woman.*

72 See also Buck-Morss's "The *Flâneur*, the Sandwichman and the Whore."

73 See also Parsons, 25, in *Streetwalking the Metropolis*, for more on Baudelaire's objectification of urban female figures.

74 Parsons singles out Janet Wolff's *Feminine Sentences* and Pollock's *Vision and Difference* as representative feminist texts that, in relying on Benjamin, still overlook women's contribution to other forms or figures of urban wandering (*Streetwalking the Metropolis*, 40).

75 See my earlier discussion of mass transportation, page 113 n. 39.

76 See Vadillo's *Women Poets and Urban Aestheticism*, 24–5, and Kate Krueger's *British Women Writers and the Short Story, 1850–1930*, 115.

77 See also the *Dictionary of Nineteenth-Century Journalism*'s entry "Yellow Journalism," 694.

78 For more on the different types of journalism by women, see also Dillane, "A Fair Field and no Favour," 148–64.

79 Literary examples of the emancipated female journalist include Henry James's Henrietta Stackpole (*The Portrait of a Lady*), Ella Hepworth Dixon's Mary Erle (*Story of a Modern Woman*), Grant Allen's Juliet Appleton (*The Type-Writer Girl*), and Dorothy Richardson's unnamed narrator in *The Long Day.*

80 See also Shelley's "Female Journalists and Journalism."

81 See also Koven's chapter "The American Girl in London: Gender, Journalism, and Social Investigation in the Late Victorian Metropolis," in *Slumming*, 140–80.

82 See also Ross's *Slum Travelers* and Cameron's "Women's Slum Journalism, 1885–1910."

83 See also Stetz and Lasner's *England in the 1890s.*

84 Aubrey Beardsley illustrated works for Oscar Wilde, the earliest editions of the *Yellow Book*, and Egerton's *Keynotes.*

85 As Stetz notes in "'George Egerton'" the trials contributed to the "slow death" of the *Yellow Book*: "By May of 1897, that once colorful and now pallid journal, stripped of the controversial elements which had made it notorious, had ceased publication" (98).

86 For an example of a positive review, see the 25 June 1898 "Review of *The Wheel of God*, by George Egerton" in the *Spectator*, which begrudgingly admits that the novel displays a "certain lurid power and picturesqueness" (913).

87 As Stetz records, Egerton only found some measure of success and, thus, financial security once she "stopped fighting and changed sides, becoming an 'adapter' herself of other people's plays" ("'George Egerton,'" 156).

4. Women's Artistic Connoisseurship and the Pleasures of a Lesbian Aesthetic

1 Clarke's study also references Bradley and Cooper's use of pseudonyms – or what Yeats describes as "hid[ing]" behind a masculine pen-name – in order to obtain a fair review of their work, as well as the tendency among periodicals to favour anonymous authorship and the general so-called ephemerality of women's writings (*Critical Voices*, 155).

2 See Clarke and Ventrella, "Women's Expertise and the Culture of Connoisseurship," 2, and Clarke, *Critical Voices*, 159, for more on women's struggle to be accepted as equal authorities on artistic subjects.

3 Yeats thus misses the point when he assumes that "song" is the stuff of subjective feeling (wishing the poets would "sing out of their own hearts"), for in Field's account the "pictures sing in themselves."

4 For more on Field's erotic gaze and gendered translation, see also Cameron's "'Where Twilight Touches Ripeness Amorously': The Gaze in Michael Field's *Sight and Song*," and "The Pleasure of Looking and the Feminine Gaze in Michael Field's *Sight and Song*."

5 See Gagnier's touchstone work in *Idylls of the Marketplace*.

6 See Psomiades's *Beauty's Body* for another account of the fin-de-siècle female aesthete's critical resistance against the gendered gaze.

7 Or as Krista Lysack explains in her study of late-Victorian aesthetes, at the very heart of their artistic projects was a rejection of the mass marketplace, and yet, she continues, "[t]he art for art's sake credo of the aesthetes attests to aestheticism's dependence on the very commercial forms it would seek to renounce" (*Come Buy, Come Buy*, 112).

8 Writing in response to Theodor W. Adorno's work, *Aesthetic Theory*, Jonathan L. Freedman takes particular issue with what he suggests is a "facile" attempt to "bracket" off the world of commodities, as if it were possible for *l'art pour l'art* to somehow transcend such material market forces (Adorno, 336–7).

9 See also Ehnenn's *Women's Literary Collaboration*.

10 The full account reads as follows: "This is when I said to him there was one sentence of Mr. Pater`s [which] I would not say I could never forgive, because I recognised its justice; but from [which] I suffered – [and which] was hard to bear – that in [which] he speaks of the scholarly conscience as male – adding I did not remember where the passage occurred" – Katharine Bradley (quoted in Thain and Vadillo, *Michael Field the Poet*, 241).

11 This latter phrase is a reference to Matthew Arnold's essay "The Function of Criticism," though originally published in his lesser-known work "On Translating Homer."

12 See Fraser's *Women Writing Art History*, 64.

13 See Saville's "The Poetic Imaging of Michael Field," 179, and Siegel's *Desire and Excess*, 133–5, for more on the public museum and art gallery.

14 For more on women and travel writing, see also Scholl's *Translation, Authorship and the Victorian Processional Woman* and Johnston's *Victorian Women and the Economies of Travel*.

15 See Fraser's chapter "Girl Guides: Travel, Translation, Ekphrasis" in *Women Writing Art History*, especially 62–98.

16 As an accomplished illustrator, Maria Graham not only provided the etchings for her own volumes, but she was also drawn to the local arts and artists of her host countries and was later inspired to write *Memoirs of the Life of Nicholas Poussin* on the eponymous French baroque painter.

17 Mariana Starke's "Sonnet to Grief" is singled out by Hilary Fraser as an example of how "vision and affect" are both central to the female traveller's "empathetic encounter" with the cultural landscape (*Women Writing Art History*, 68).

18 Eastlake, "Lady Travellers," 98–137. See also Fraser, *Women Writing Art History*, 68.

19 Elizabeth Eastlake was invited to contribute to the *Quarterly Review* by editor J.G. Lockhart following the popular success of her *A Residence on the Shores of the Baltic* (as "Elizabeth Rigby").

20 Jameson also wrote a guidebook *Companion to the Most Celebrated Private Galleries of Art in London* on artwork collections in London, while her *Memoirs of the Early Italian Painters* features detailed descriptions of both public and private galleries in Italy.

21 See Kingsley's review, "The Poetry of Sacred and Legendary Art" (March 1849), in *Fraser's Magazine*.

22 See the entry "Anna Jameson" for the *Dictionary of Art Historians* online (https://dictionaryofarthistorians.org/jamesona.htm), and "Ruskin to His Father, September 28, 1845," in Shapiro, *Ruskin in Italy: Letters to His Parents*, 215.

23 Robinson's "Etruscan Tombs" sequence represents a unique take on the traditional Elizabethan sonnet sequence, which usually explores themes such as love and romantic relationship. While the beloved is an important figure in her poems, Robinson is better compared with Romantic-era writers such as Charlotte Smith who focused on more melancholic meditations of their current situation, and "Etruscan Tombs" also seems to draw inspiration from eighteenth-century graveyard poetry as well as the nineteenth-century obsession with the dead (as evidenced by the popularization of memento mori images).
24 See also Vadillo's *Women Poets and Urban Aestheticism*, 88 and 160, as well as Vadillo's "Immaterial Poetics," 233, for more on Field's relationship with Robinson.
25 See also Fraser, *Women Writing Art History*, 65, for more on Lee's *Euphorion* and its formative role in women's art criticism.
26 See John Plunkett et al.'s entry "Vernon Lee: *Euphorion*" in *Victorian Literature*, 171–3.
27 As Fraser argues, Lee "authorises a view of the past that is avowedly subjective and partial, particular to herself" (*Women Writing Art History*, 116).
28 See also Evangelista's "Vernon Lee and the Gender of Aestheticism," 94.
29 See also Zorn's *Vernon Lee*, 13, for more on these critical references.
30 See also Colby's *Vernon Lee*, 72.
31 See Zorn, *Vernon Lee*, 13.
32 See also Evangelista, "Vernon Lee and the Gender of Aestheticism," 91–7, for more on the sexual politics implicit in Lee's aesthetic gaze.
33 See also Meaghan Clarke's "1894: The Year of the New Woman Art Critic" for another account of Alice Meynell's essay and its larger contribution to women's art criticism, especially per French Impressionism and literary realism.
34 As Leighton and Reynolds write in their introduction to the poet, "It would seem highly likely that May Probyn knew Dante Gabriel Rossetti's painting and one wonders how much she knew of Lizzie Siddal's story" ("May Probyn," 526).
35 See also Flint's "Identity and the Victorian Woman Poet" for more on the differences between these two generations of feminist poets. As Flint explains, later writers do away with the motif of the male poet-observer to instead focus on the female poet looking at herself and attempting to resolve the divide between subject and object (162).
36 "This figure," write Leighton and Reynolds, "where the woman poet makes herself into her own Muse, does appear in Victorian poetry – see the opening passages of Barrett Browning's *Aurora Leigh* – but it is much

more common in the work of twentieth-century writers" ("Caroline Lindsay," 476).

37 See also Braun's "'Set the Crystal Surface Free!': Mary E. Coleridge and the Self-Conscious Femme Fatale" for more on the erotic undertones and often lesbian subtext in Coleridge's poetry.

38 Ruskin rejected the Fields following Bradley's 1877 letter proclaiming she had "lost God and found a Skye Terrier" (see Thain and Vadillo, *Michael Field, The Poet*, 306).

39 On 24 November 1890, Edith Cooper recorded her and Bradley's visit to the London Institute to hear Pater's lecture on Prosper Mérimée (Thain and Vadillo, *Michael Field, The Poet*, 241).

40 In an entry dated 10 June 1890, Cooper recounts how, during a trip to the Louvre, she and Bradley "met Mr. Berenson, a young Russian, qualifying to become Art-historian, introduced to us by Mrs. Moulton" (*Michael Field, the Poet*, 243). See also Saville's "The Poetic Imaging of Michael Field," 183; Michael Field's *Works and Days* (1933); and Samuels, *Bernard Berenson*, 137–8.

41 In their journals, Bradley and Cooper describe *Sight and Sound* as "too wholly due to our friendship with Bernard" (qtd in Fraser, *Women Writing Art History*, 83).

42 Yopie Prins argues that the signature M.F., which appears underneath the volume's preface, suggests a kind of play between genders: the author is both "masculine" (M) and "feminine" (F) (*Victorian Sappho*, 82).

43 See also Vadillo's more recent book, *Women Poets and Urban Aestheticism*.

44 The success of Field's project, Vadillo adds, can be measured in the object's final autonomy: "*Sight and Song* emerges thus as a series of transparent translations where Field projects a theory of visuality that values the autonomy of the object, foreseeing the avant-garde revolution of the object" ("Sight and Song: Transparent Translations," 32).

45 Pater's "Prosper Mérimée" was first published by the *Fortnightly Review* 48 (December 1890), 852–64. He later republished the essay in his *Miscellaneous Studies* (1895).

46 As Julia Saville convincingly argues, Field learned from Pater to "turn to Flaubert as the master of impersonality, and like Pater, they accept an inevitable alteration between self-suppression and self-expression" ("The Poetic Imagining of Michael Field," 181).

47 Regarding the first point on aesthetic distance, Donnelly, in *Reading Dante Gabriel Rossetti*, explains how Rossetti, as poetic translator, "does little to describe the painting directly" and that, instead, "the constant reimagining of the virgin is reliant on the sonnet form for its efficacy" (38).

48 See Thain and Vadillo, *Michael Field, The Poet*, 316 n. 4.

49 See also Wise's "Michael Field's Translations into Verse," 206, for more on translation as a collaborative enterprise.

50 For example, the poem doesn't recount La Gioconda as "smiling," but rather the poem describes an image of La Gioconda with "the smile that leads upward" (l. 3). These verbal phrases remind us of the lack of temporality (and narrative action) in poetic translation. The poem thus sings of events that have already happened prior to, and independent of, the observer.

51 Krista Lysack sees in Michael Field's translation of *Mona Lisa* a representation of the feminized artwork as "an unreadable text" ("Aesthetic Consumption and the Cultural Production of Michael Field's *Sight and Song*," 948–9).

52 Hilary Fraser, by contrast, argues that this moment of "implication" does not fold back on the poets' themselves; instead, the poetic translation explores a mode of non-possessive looking, or what she describes as a "dynamic stereoscopic gaze intersected by homoerotic desire, a gaze of gays, a way of looking at art" ("A Visual Field: Michael Field and the Gaze," 555).

53 Using Marion Thain's theory of "synaesthesia," I therefore diverge from critics like Nicholas Frankel ("The Concrete Poetics of Michael Field's *Sight and Song*," 212) who believe that Field's poetic translations successfully suppress the subjective function of sight.

54 Explaining this in terms of "synaesthesia," Marion Thain characterizes Field's aesthetic mode as "a process which is not dependent on abstracting content from form in order to represent it within another mode, but a more complete apprehension of something designed for one sense through another sensory channel" ("*Michael Field*," 71).

55 See also Lysack's earlier work in "Aesthetic Consumption," 936.

56 Hilary Fraser describes this as a "dynamic stereoscopic gaze," in which the pseudonym (the monocular gaze of the heterosexual subject) combines with the lesbian co-authorship (or binocular gaze) to produce a way of looking that "enables decentring of the observing subject and the radical destabilisation of the gendered binary" (*Women Writing Art History*, 84). Julia Saville also insists that the pseudonym "provide[s] the heterosexual female viewer with an aesthetic alibi for scrutinizing images of the male nude, even as [Bradley and Cooper] speak as the manly poet authorized to gaze on the male nude by virtue of his Berensonian objectivity and austere Paterian self-restraint" ("The Poetic Imaging of Michael Field," 183–4).

57 As Nicholas Frankel notes, the dancing boy is the embodiment of indifference which Field's translations find so alluring ("The Concrete Poetics of Michael Field's *Sight and Song*," 218).

58 Looking at these italicized addresses, Julie Wise argues that the translation recreates Watteau's work and, with it, the "feeling of artistic detachment it depicts by rendering it in poetry as an incomplete conversation" ("Michael Field's Translations into Verse," 208). By contrast, Julia Saville reads the address as the poets' desire to see and impose "verbal imagery on the visual image" ("The Poetic Imaging of Michael Field," 186).

59 See also Laird's *Women Coauthors*, 83–4, for more on Michael Field's collaborative poetics and sexual erotics.

60 The collection contains several poems on Sandro Botticelli's paintings of Venus, including "Botticelli's *Birth of Venus*" (13), "Botticelli's *Venus and Mars*" (42), and "*The Venus* in Botticelli's *Spring*" (85). As Vadillo rightly argues, it is as if Venus is at the very centre of Field's ekphrastic project (see "*Sight and Song*: Transparent Translations," 31).

61 Ana Parejo Vadillo makes this same point regarding the returned gaze in "*Sight and Song*: Transparent Translations," 32.

62 In her analysis of the poem, Krista Lysack argues that this final stanza "disrupts a sense of conventional temporality in the poem to signal a shift to an expansive future, which will guarantee Venus's future self and her gaze beyond the text" ("Aesthetic Consumption and the Cultural Production of Michael Field's *Sight and Song*," 955).

63 Krista Lysack, too, offers a feminist reading of this scene as an "excess" of "sensual" pleasure contained and sustained within a "community of women" ("Aesthetic Consumption and the Cultural Production of Michael Field's *Sight and Song*," 954).

64 See Bloom's *The Ringers in the Tower*.

65 Jameson's profiles of Italian painters for the *Penny Magazine* were later reprinted in *Memoirs of the Early Italian Painters*.

66 See also Clarke's "1894: The Year of the New Woman Art Critics" for more on this later history of women's art journalism in the nineteenth century.

67 Ricketts's memoir was prepared as source material for Mary Sturgeon's *Michael Field*.

5. Virginia Woolf's Post-Victorian Feminism

1 The scholarship on Virginia Woolf's interest in androgyny as a transformative force can be traced back as early as Bazin's *Virginia Woolf and the Androgynous Vision* and Minow-Pinkney's *Virginia Woolf and the Problem of the Subject*.

2 See *Critical Alliances*, page 32.

3 See also Boyd's *Bloomsbury Heritage* for more on Woolf as part of a Bloomsbury "rebel[ion] against the Victorian world" (77).

4 Jane Marcus also argues that *The Years,*in particular, represents "the most brilliant indictment in modern literature of the world of empire, class, and privilege," while adding to the list of power structures both "capitalism and patriarchy" ("Storming the Tool Shed," 636).
5 For other examples of this line of criticism complicating the Victorian/ Modernist divide in Woolf's writings see also McNees's "Colonizing Virginia Woolf" and Cuddy-Keane's "Virginia Woolf and the Varieties of Historicist Experience."
6 By focusing on the author's critique of gender as a narrative construct, I am building upon work by feminist scholars whose analyses of Woolf's writings draw attention to the author's deconstructivist textual practices. See, for example, Shari Benstock's *Textualizing the Feminine*, 152, for Woolf's use of mimesis to undermine misogynist narratives.
7 Froula, in *Virginia Woolf and the Bloomsbury Avant-Garde*, 223, explains how narrative resistance – as opposed to an absolute break in period or convention – transforms the text into something of a "talking cure" whereby the author works through and mimetically critiques dominant narratives of power and exclusion.
8 In "The Novels of the 1930s and the Impact of History," Briggs argues that this same scepticism toward narrative authority also informs Woolf's rejection of history as linear or episodic with a masculine hero whose sacrifice in death is regenerative (n.p.).
9 Spencer also notes how such stories are based on, and therein perpetuate, a distinctly patriarchal structure of inheritance (*Literary Relations*, 9–10).
10 See Sale, *Literary Inheritance*, 144–5, or Law and Pinnington's introduction, 12, to the Broadview edition of *Great Expectations* for more on this autobiographical thread in Dickens's fiction.
11 In her 2012 dissertation, "What Violently Elects Us: Filiation, Ethics, and War in the Contemporary British Novel," 14–17, Cynthia Quarrie provides an overview of contemporary critical approaches to Modernist writings on filial kinship.
12 Heffernan cites as support Frank Kermode's work "Lawrence and Apocalyptic Types" as also interested in the war as fracturing any sense of communal temporality or shared history (Heffernan, *Post-Apocalyptic Culture*, 34).
13 In her article "Enchantment, Disenchantment, War, Literature," 1633, Cole argues that the Great War is often represented as synonymous with violent death and the violated body, neither of which could figure as sites for cultural renewal or regeneration.
14 See also Quarrie, "What Violently Elects Us," 17, for more on this history. Quarrie also mentions E.M. Forster's *The Longest Journey* as another example of the Modernist's adamant rejection of literary kinship. "'Let

them die out' is the rallying cry," Forster writes, so "that suggests certain lineages need not continue merely for the sake of continuance" (quoted in Allan Hepburn, introduction, 19).

15 See also Silver's "The Authority of Anger" for more on Woolf's use of trauma and anger, specifically, as a part of a larger rhetorical strategy interested in critical resistance.

16 Steve Ellis is also interested in the role that the Great War played in the Modernist's negotiation of the post-Victorian past; in Woolf's novels, he argues, "the War is either effaced in the historical record or treated as one event among many, examples practically of a fictional 'indifference' that anticipates the argument of *Three Guineas*" (*Virginia Woolf and the Victorians*, 112).

17 See also Patrick Anderson's 1970 review for *The Spectator*: "*Howard's End*, posing its question of 'who shall inherit England?' against a background of Anglo-German rivalry," is ultimately the product of the author's larger and persistent interest in questions of "human sympathy based upon reason and tolerance" – a focus in fairness that therein shifts questions of power from filial descent to a new bond based on affiliation and equity ("E.M. Forester," 29).

18 See also Tim Armstrong's *Modernism*, 76–7, for more on this question of rightful inheritance in *Howard's End*.

19 This movement from the past to the present and future thereby affects what Joshua Kavaloski describes as a "chiasmatic model of time" which draws attention to the "incongruity" between characters' stories and their "incommensurable temporalit[ies]" (*High Modernism*, 30).

20 See also Ellis's *Virginia Woolf and The Victorians*, particularly his use of the "Post-Victorian" in order to describe how all of Woolf's novels present the readers with "narratives that evaluate and balance past and present and that resist the War's threat to continuity and to its creating precisely such a gulf between pre- and post-War partisanship" (116).

21 See also Showalter's touchstone essay "Killing the Angel in the House," 345–6, for more on Woolf's work on women and artistic autonomy.

22 See also Jane Marcus's "'No More Horses'" for more on Woolf's theory of art and/as political propaganda.

23 See Cuddy-Keane, *Virginia Woolf, the Intellectual, and the Public Sphere*, 63.

24 For more on the relationship between Keynes and the Bloomsbury Group, particularly on the relationship between art and economics in Keynes's writings, see also Goodwin's "The Value of Things in the Imaginative Life" and "The Art of an Ethical Life."

25 See also Goodwin's "The Art of an Ethical Life," 222.

26 Theoretically, social intervention is meant to ensure individuals' rights to free choice; the Group's project of civilization is, Raymond Williams

summarizes, "against cant, superstition, hypocrisy, pretension and public show,"and it also prohibited "ignorance, poverty, sexual and racial discrimination, militarism, and imperialism" ("The Bloomsbury Fraction," 244).

27 See also Froula's *Virginia Woolf and the Bloomsbury Avant-Garde*, 4.

28 See also Laura Marcus's "Woolf's Feminism and Feminism's Woolf" for more on Woolf's interest in literary texts as disseminating feminist ideas and for more on second-generation feminists' subsequent relationship to (and recovery of) the Modernist author.

29 For an alternative interpretation of *The Years* that focuses specifically on heteronormative sexuality, see also Hanson's "Virginia Woolf in the House of Love."

30 It is worth noting that this line comes from a conversation between Peggy and Eleanor, during which the latter muses on the change in romantic relationships between the sexes. Eleanor mentions how she is struck by Renny and Maggie's marriage ("I said to myself, That's a happy Marriage" [386]), and wonders if she would have married Renny had she known him when she was younger.

31 Patricia Cramer, in "'Pearls and the Porpoise': *The Years* – A Lesbian Memoir," 226, argues that Kitty's freedom, particularly her attachment to the rural landscape, is a kind of code for Woolf's lesbian desire. For more on lesbian desire in Woolf's fiction, see also Barrett and Cramer, *Virginia Woolf and Lesbian Readings*.

32 In "More than *A Room* and *Three Guineas*," 2, Bechtold makes this same argument regarding *Three Guineas* and women's wasted productive potential.

33 This is what economists today call a corner solution or a restricted gift. It is used by neoclassicals to describe the efficiency losses that occur when you give people gifts but force them to spend on certain things. For more on this theory, see Waldfogel's "The Efficiency of Gift Giving."

34 For more on women and self-censorship in Woolf, see also Froula's *Virginia Woolf and the Bloomsbury Avant-Garde*, 24, and Barbara Green's *Spectacular Confessions*, 162.

35 Pamela L. Caughie takes particular aim at Jane Marcus on this point (see Caughie, *Virginia Woolf & Postmodernism*, 115–16).

36 'Disinterested' is also a key concept in fellow Bloomsburyites Fry's ("Essay in Aesthetics" and Bell's (*Civilization and Old Friends*) post-impressionist writings.

37 On this point, *Three Guineas* is in dialogue with fellow Bloomsbury member Clive Bell who, in *Civilization and Old Friends*, 146, argues for a leisure-class of artists that will produce culture on the backs of a pseudo-slave class of labourers.

38 See also Froula, *Virginia Woolf and the Bloomsbury Avant-Garde*, 4.
39 Moi cites Showalter's *A Literature of Their Own* and Holly's "Consciousness and Authenticity" per this anxiety towards Woolf's multiple Is (*Sexual/ Textual Politics*, 8).
40 See Benstock's chapter, "Ellipses: Figuring Feminism in *Three Guineas*," which looks at Woolf's mimetic reproduction of arguments by C.E.M. Joad and H.G. Wells.
41 See also Sim's *Virginia Woolf: The Patterns of Ordinary Experience*, 167, for more on Eleanor's search for meaningful patterns in *The Years*.
42 See also Panken's *Virginia Woolf and the Lust of Creation*, 125–6, for more on Peggy and her relationships with her brothers (alive and dead) after the First World War.

Coda: The Post-Victorian Legacy of Women's Work

1 Jordan, *The Women's Movement*, 219. See also Bird, *Women at Work*, 195–6, for more on women's work in new medical professions, including pharmaceuticals and dentistry.
2 See Jordan, *The Women's Movement*, 79, for the table of these census statistics.
3 It would, Jordan continues, fall upon second-wave feminists almost three quarters of a century later to return to the original question of gendered economics and the fight for women's right to equal work and pay (*The Women's Movement*, 221).
4 See Rowbotham's early essay "Women's Liberation and the New Politics," 19, for more on how the Women's Movement was eventually supplanted by a much broader feminism interested in women's liberal freedoms and political rights. Rowbotham's essay was first published in 1969 as a Spokesman pamphlet by the May Day Manifesto, a socialist organization. A slightly modified version was later published in Michelene Wandor's *The Body Politic*.
5 Adelaide Anne Procter was also a founding member of the Society for Promoting the Employment of Women, but passed away in 1864 before the 1882 Married Woman's Property Act.
6 Barbara Bodichon also organized the first Women's Suffrage Committee in 1866, whose petition John Stuart Mill would later present to the House of Commons, while Jessie Boucherett helped found *The Women's Suffrage Journal* in 1870 (with Lydia Becker, who was equally inspired by Bodichon's work).
7 Jordan, *The Women's Movement*, 220, explains how the right to vote would give women the authority to influence political institutions to which individual professions or certification boards must answer.

8 Jordan, *The Women's Movement*, 220.
9 On one side of the critical debate, Jordan (*The Women's Movement*, 19), maintains that the women's suffrage movement in the early twentieth century supplanted the feminist fight for careers and economic mobility, while still other historians such as Joshua S. Goldstein (*War and Gender*, 318), claim that women's political gains, including the right to vote, were the result of women's advances in the workforce, especially service in a wide range of new occupations during the First World War.
10 See also Anderson and Zinsser's *A History of Their Own*, vol. 2:366.
11 See "Work, Not Surrogates, Won Women the Vote" in *Express*.
12 See Smith's "All Quiet on the Woolwich Front?" and Noakes "Eve in Khaki."
13 See Michaelsen, "'Union is Strength,'" 161–2.
14 Still other scholars doubt that women's work during the First World War was a source of liberation and personal happiness. See for example Woollacott's *On Her Their Lives Depend*, especially 209–11, and Goldstein's *War and Gender*, 385, for more on this debate.
15 See also Keating, *A Child for Keeps*, 13.
16 See also Gittins's *Fair Sex*, 56, for more on the reciprocal relationship between modern women's magazines and the popularization of feminine domesticity.
17 The impact of this cultural shift away from domestic ideology would not be felt again in England until the 1960s and 1970s as middle-class women flooded into the workforce, signaling a return to the collective measures of the Women's Movement. See Noakes's "Eve in Khaki," 213, McCloskey's "Paid Work," 165, and Dyhouse's *Feminism and the Family*, 5.

Bibliography

Primary

Alger, Horatio. *Ragged Dick: or, Street Life in New York*. Boston: Joseph H. Allen, 1867.

Allen, Grant. "The Girl of the Future." *Universal Review* 7 (May 1890): 49–64.

– "Plain Words on the Woman Question." *Fortnightly Review* 52 (October 1889): 448–58.

– *The Type-Writer Girl*. 1897. Edited by Clarissa Suranyi. Peterborough: Broadview Press, 2003.

– *The Woman Who Did*. 1895. Edited by Nicholas Ruddick. Peterborough: Broadview Press, 2004.

Arnold, Matthew. *Culture and Anarchy: An Essay in Political and Social Criticism*. London: Smith, Elder, 1869.

– "The Function of Criticism at the Present Time." 1864. In *Arnold: "Culture and Anarchy" and Other Writings*, edited by Stefan Collini, 26–52. Cambridge: Cambridge University Press, 1993.

– *On Translating Homer: Last Words. A Lecture Given at Oxford*. London: Longman Green, 1862.

"Artistic Professions for Women." *All the Year Round* 43 (29 September 1888): 296–300.

Austen, Jane. *Emma*. 1815. Edited by Alistair Duckworth. New York: Bedford/St Martins, 2002.

Banks, Elizabeth. *Campaigns of Curiosity: Journalistic Adventures of an American Girl in London*. New York: F. Tennyson Neely, 1894. https://archive.org/details/campaignsofcurio00bank.

Barrett Browning, Elizabeth. *Aurora Leigh*. 1856. Oxford: Oxford University Press, 1993.

– *Sonnets from the Portuguese*. London: Chapman and Hall, 1850.

Baudelaire, Charles. "The Painter of Modern Life." 1863. In *The Painter of Modern Life and Other Essays*, 1–41. 1965, 1995. London: Phaidon, 1995.

– "The Rag-Picker's Wine." 1857. http://fleursdumal.org/poem/193.

– "The Way Her Silky Garments …" 1857. In *The Flowers of Evil*. Translated by James McGowen, 55–6. Oxford: Oxford University Press, 1993.

Bell, Clive. *Civilization and Old Friends*. 1928 & 1956, respectively. Chicago: University of Chicago Press, 1973.

Beresford-Hope, A.J. "The Lords and the Deceased Wife's Sister Bill." *National Review* 1 (1883): 758–66.

– *The Report of Her Majesty's Commission on the Laws of Marriage, Relative to Marriage with a Deceased Wife's Sister, Examined in a Letter to Sir Robert Harry Inglis, Bart. M.P.* 6 books; 1849–56. London: James Rigby, 1850.

Besant, Annie. "White Slavery in London." 1888. In *Slum Travelers: Ladies and London Poverty, 1860–1900*, edited by Ellen Ross, 48–51. Los Angeles: University of California Press, 2007.

Bird, M. Mostyn. *Women at Work: A Study of the Different Ways of Earning A Living Open to Women*. London: Chapman and Hall, 1911.

Black, Clementina, and Adèle Meyer. *Makers of Our Clothes: A Case for Trade Boards*. London: Duckworth, 1909. https://archive.org/details/makersofourcloth00meyerich.

– "The Organization of Working Women." 1889. In *The Romance of a Shop*, edited by Susan David Bernstein, 258–62. Peterborough: Broadview Press, 2006.

– *Sweated Industry and the Minimum Wage*. London: Duckworth, 1907.

Blessington, Marguerite. *The Governess*. London: Longman, Orme, Brown, Green, and Longmans, 1839.

"Books of the Week: Review of 'Vernon Lee's Renaissance Essays.'" *Times* (December 1895): 13.

Borden, Mary. "Blind. A Story." In *The Forbidden Zone*. London: W. Heinemann, 1929. www.ourstory.info/library/2-ww1/Borden2/fz.html.

Boucherett, Jessie. *Hints on Self-Help: A Book for Young Women*. London: S.W. Patridge, 1863.

Brennan, Maeve. "The Anachronism." In *The New Yorker* (30 January 1954): 20.

– "The Bride." *The New Yorker* (8 August 1953): 19.

– "The Servants' Dance." *The New Yorker* (22 May 1954): 32.

– "The View from the Kitchen." *The New Yorker* (14 November 1953): 40.

Brittain, Vera. *Testament of Youth: An Autobiographical Study of the Years 1900–1925*. (1933). London: Virago, 1978.

Brontë, Charlotte. *Jane Eyre*. 1847. Edited by Richard Nemesvari. Peterborough: Broadview Press, 1999.

Brontë, Emily. *Wuthering Heights*. 1847. Edited by Linda H. Peterson. New York: Bedford/St Martin's, 2003.

Brooke, Rupert. "The Soldier." (1914). www.poetryfoundation.org/poetrymagazine/poems/detail/13076.
Browning, Elizabeth Barrett. "Sonnets from the Portuguese." 1850. In *The Poetical Works of Elizabeth Barrett Browning*, vol. 4, 33–82. London: Smith, Elder, 1890.
Buckley, Julia. *Emily, the Governess*. London: J. Farrow, 1836.
Bulley, A. Amy, and Margaret Whitley. *Women's Work*. London: Methuen, 1894.
Butler, Josephine E. *The Education and Employment of Women*. Liverpool: T. Brakell, 1868.
Butler, Mary E.L. *The Ring of Day*. London: Hutchinson, 1906.
Caird, Mona. *The Daughters of Danaus*. 1894. New York: Feminist Press, 1989.
– "A Defence of the So-Called 'Wild Women.'" 1892. In *"Criminals, Idiots, Women, and Minors": Victorian Writing by Women on Women*, edited by Susan Hamilton, 287–307. Peterborough: Broadview Press, 1995.
– "Marriage." 1888. In *The Fin de Siècle: A Reader in Cultural History c. 1880–1900*, edited by Sally Ledger and Roger Luckhurst, 77–80. Oxford: Oxford University Press, 2000.
– *The Morality of Marriage, and Other Essays on the Status and Destiny of Women*. London: G. Redway, 1897. https://archive.org/details/moralityofmarria00cairrich.
Cameron, Charles. *Marriage with a Deceased Wife's Sister*. London: Marriage Law Reform Association, 1883.
Carpenter, Edward. *Love's Coming-of-Age*. New York: Mitchell Kennerley, 1911. http://archive.org/details/lovescomingagea02carpgoog.
– "Marriage in Free Society." *Labour Press Society*. 1894. http://archive.org/details/marriageinfrees00carpgoog.
Census of the State of New York for 1875: Compiled from the Original Returns Under the Direction of the Secretary of State by C. W. Seaton, Superintendent of the Census. Albany: Weed, Parsons, 1975. https://archive.org/details/censusofstateofn1875newy.
Clifton, Irene. *The Little Governess*. London: S.W. Partridge, 1900.
Cobbe, Francis Power. *Life as Told by Herself*. London: Swan Sonnenshein, 1904.
Coleridge, Mary E. "The Other Side of a Mirror." 1896. In *Victorian Women Poets: An Anthology*, edited by Angela Leighton and Margaret Reynolds, 613. Oxford: Blackwell, 1995.
Collins, Wilkie. *No Name* 1862. New York: Harper, 1893. https://archive.org/details/nonameanovel00collgoog.
Craik, Dinah Mulock. *Bread upon the Waters: A Governess's Life*. London: Governesses' Benevolent Institution, 1852.
– *Hannah*. New York: Harper & Brothers, 1872.
– *A Woman's Thoughts about Women*. London: Hurst and Blackett, 1858.

Dickens, Charles. *David Copperfield*. 1850. Peterborough: Broadview Press, 2001.
– *Great Expectations*. 1861. Edited by Graham Law and Adrian J. Pinnington. Peterborough: Broadview Press, 1998.
– *Oliver Twist*. 1838. New York: Penguin Classics, 2003.
Dixie, Florence. *Gloriana, Or the Revolution of 1900*. London: Henry, 1890.
Dixon, Ella Hepworth. *The Story of a Modern Woman*. 1894. Edited by Steve Farmer. Peterborough: Broadview Press, 2004.
– "Why Women Are Ceasing to Marry." 1899. In *The Fin de Siècle: A Reader in Cultural History c. 1880–1900*, edited by Sally Ledger and Roger Luckhurst, 83–8. Oxford: Oxford University Press, 2000.
Eastlake, Elizabeth. *Five Great Painters: Essays Reprinted from the Edinburgh and Quarterly Review*. London: Longmans, 1883.
– "Lady Travellers." *Quarterly Review* 76 (1845): 98–137.
– "Photography." *Quarterly Review* 101 (April 1857): 442–68.
– (as "Elizabeth Rigby"). *A Residence on the Shores of the Baltic*. London: John Murray, 1841.
Egerton, George (Mary Chavelita Dunne Bright). "The Captain's Book." *The Yellow Book*. Vol. 6 (July 1895): 103–16.
– *Keynotes*. London: Elkin Matthews and John Lane, 1893.
– "A Lost Masterpiece." *The Yellow Book*. Vol. 1 (April 1894): 189–96.
– *The Wheel of God*. New York/London: G.P. Putnam's Sons, 1898.
Eliot, George. *Middlemarch*. 1872. Edited by Gregory Maertz. Peterborough: Broadview Press, 2004.
– *The Mill on the Floss*. 1860. Edited by Oliver Lovesey. Peterborough: Broadview Press, 2003.
Ellis, Sarah Stickney. *Women of England: Social Duties and Domestic Habits*. New York: D. Appleton, 1843.
Engels, Friedrich. *The Origin of the Family, Private Property and the State*. 1884. New York: Penguin Books, 1986.
"Euphorion." Book Review in *The Australasian 966* (Saturday, 4 October 1884): 632.
Faulkner, William. *As I Lay Dying*. New York: Jonathan Cape & Harrison Smith, 1930.
Field, Michael (as Arran and Isla Leigh). *Bellerophôn*. London: C. Kegan Paul, 1881.
– *Sight and Song 1892 with Underneath the Bough 1893*. New York: Woodstock Books, 1993.
– *Works and Days: From the Journal of Michael Field*. Edited by T. and D.C. Sturge Moore. London: John Murray, 1933.
Ford, Isabella O. *Women and Socialism*. London: The Independent Labour Party, 1907.
Forster, E.M. *Howard's End*. London: Edward Arnold, 1910.

– "Not New Books." *Books and Authors*. Listener (28 December 1932), 651.
Fry, Roger. "Essay in Aesthetics." 1909. In *Vision and Design*, 11–25. London: Chatto and Windus, 1920.
Gallon, Tom. *The Girl Behind the Keys*. 1903. Peterborough: Broadview Press, 2005.
Gissing, George. *The Odd Women*. New York: Palgrave Macmillan, 1893.
Goethe, Johann Wolfgang von. *Wilhelm Meister's Apprenticeship and Travels*. 1795–6. London: Chapman and Hall, 1842.
Graham, Maria. *Journal of a Residence in Chile*. London: Longman, 1824.
– *Journal of a Residence in India*. Edinburgh/London: Archibald Constable, 1812.
– *Journal of a Voyage to Brazil*. London: Longman, 1824.
– *Memoirs of the Life of Nicolas Poussin*. London: Longman, 1820.
Grand, Sarah. *The Beth Book: Being a Study of the Life of Elizabeth Caldwell Maclure, a Woman of Genius*. 1897. London: Heinemann, 1898.
– *Heavenly Twins*. London: Cassell, 1893.
– "The New Aspect of the Woman Question." *The North American Review* 158.448 (1894): 270–6.
Grey, Maria G., and Emily Shirreff. *Thoughts on Self-Culture Addressed to Women*. London: Edward Moxon, 1850.
Haggard, H. Rider. "About Fiction." 1887. In *The Story of an African Farm*, edited by Patricia O'Neill, 362–3. Peterborough: Broadview Press, 2003.
– *Mr. Meeson's Will*. London: Spencer Blackett, 1888.
Hall, Anna Maria. *Stories of the Governess*. London: J. Nisbet, 1852.
Hall, Radclyffe. *The Well of Loneliness*. 1828. London: Virago Modern Classics, 1982.
Hamsun, Knut. *Hunger*. 1899. New York: Penguin Books, 1998.
Hansson, Ola. *Young Ofeg's Ditties*. Translated by George Egerton. London: John Lane, 1895.
Hardy, Thomas. *The Hand of Ethelberta: A Comedy in Chapters*. London: Smith, Elder, 1876.
– *Tess of the D'Urbervilles*. 1891. Edited by John Paul Riquelme. New York: Bedford/St Martin's, 1998.
Harkness, Margaret (as "John Law"). *A City Girl*. 1887. Brighton: Victorian Secrets, 2015.
– *In Darkest London*. 1889. Cambridge: Black Apollo Press, 2003.
– *Out of Work*. 1888. Lanham, MD: Ivan R. Dee, 1990.
– ("Anon.") *Tempted London: Young Men*. London: Hodder and Stoughton, 1888.
– ("John Law.") *Toilers in London: or, Inquiries Concerning Female Labour in the Metropolis*. London: Hodder and Stoughton, 1889. https://archive.org/details/toilersinlondono00brituoft.

Harper, Charles G. *Revolted Woman: Past, Present and to Come*. London: Elkin Matthews, 1894.
Hill, Joseph A. *Women in Gainful Occupations, 1870–1920*. Washington, DC: United States Government Printing Office, 1929.
"Hints on the Modern Governess System." 1844. In *Jane Eyre.*, edited by Richard Nemesvari, 567–77. Peterborough: Broadview Press, 1999.
Howells, William Dean. *A Hazard of New Fortunes*. 1890. New York: Modern Library, 2002.
James, Henry. *Daisy Miller*. 1879. Edited by Kristin Boudreau and Megan Stoner Morgan. Peterborough: Broadview Press, 2012.
– *The Portrait of a Lady*. 1881. Oxford: Oxford University Press, 2009.
– *The Princess Casamassima*. 1886. Rev. 2nd edition. New York: Penguin Classics, 1987.
– "Reply to Eliza Lynn Linton." 1901. In *Daisy Miller*, edited by Kristin Boudreau and Megan Stoner Morgan, 103–4. Peterborough: Broadview Press, 2012.
– *The Turn of the Screw*. 1898. London: Martin Secker, 1915.
– *Washington Square*. 1881. Oxford: Oxford University Press, 1982, 1998, 2010.
Jameson, Anna Brownell. *Companion to the Most Celebrated Private Galleries of Art in London*. London: Saunders and Otley, 1844.
– *Diary of an Ennuyée*. London: Henry Colburn, 1826.
– *The History of Our Lord in Art*. London: Longman, 1864.
– *Memoirs of the Early Italian Painters, and the Progress of Painting in Italy*. London: Charles Knight, 1845.
– *Poetry of Sacred and Legendary Art*. London: Longman, 1848.
– *Visits and Sketches Abroad*. New York: Harper, 1834.
Jevons, William Stanley. *Principles of Economics: A Fragment of a Treatise on the Industrial Mechanism of Society and Other Papers*. London: Palgrave Macmillan, 1905.
– *The Theory of Political Economy*. 5th edition. 1871. New York: Kelley & Millman, 1957.
Joyce, James. "Eveline." 1904. In *Dubliners*, 42–8. London: Grant Richards, 1914.
Kenealy, Arabella. *Feminism and Sex-Extinction*. London: T. Fisher Unwin, 1920. https://archive.org/details/feminismsexextin00kenerich.
Keynes, John Maynard. *Collected Writings*. New York: Palgrave Macmillan, 1972.
– *The General Theory of Employment, Interest, and Money*. 1936. New York: Prometheus Books, 1997.
Kingsley, Charles. "The Poetry of Sacred and Legendary Art." *Fraser's Magazine* 39 (1849): 283–98.
Lang, Andrew. "Theological Romances." 1888. In *The Story of An African Farm*, edited by Patricia O'Neill, 363. Peterborough: Broadview Press, 2003.
Lawrence, D.H. "Tickets, Please." In *England, My England, and Other Stories*, 51–68. New York: Thomas Seltzer, 1922. https://archive.org/details/englandmyengland00lawrrich.

Lee, Vernon. *Euphorion: Being Studies of the Antique and the Medieval in the Renaissance.* 2 vols. London: T. Fisher Unwin, 1884.

Levy, Amy. *A London Plane-Tree: And Other Verse.* London: T. Fisher Unwin, 1889.

– *The Romance of a Shop.* 1888. Edited by Susan Bernstein. Peterborough: Broadview Press, 2006.

– *Xantippe and Other Verse.* Cambridge: E. Johnson, 1881.

Lindsay, Caroline. "To My Own Face." 1889. In *Victorian Women Poets: An Anthology*, edited by Angela Leighton and Margaret Reynolds, 476–7. Oxford: Blackwell, 1995.

Linton, Eliza Lynn. "The Higher Education of Women." December 1886. *Popular Science Monthly* 30 (November 1886–April 1887). 168–80. https://archive.org/details/popularsciencemo30newy.

– "The Judicial Shock to Marriage." May 1891. *The Nineteenth Century: A Monthly Review*, edited by James Knowles. 29 (January–June 1891): 691–700.

– "The Wild Women: as Politicians." 1891. In *Criminal, Idiots, Women, & Minors: Victorian Writing by Women on Women*, edited by Susan Hamilton, 188–97. Peterborough: Broadview Press, 1995.

– "The Wild Women: as Social Insurgents." 1891. In *Criminals, Idiots, Women, & Minors: Victorian Writing by Women on Women*, edited by Susan Hamilton, 198–208. Peterborough: Broadview Press, 1995.

Lister, Anne. *I Know My Own Heart: The Diaries of Anne Lister, 1791–1840.* Edited by Helena Whitbread. London: Virago, 1988, 1992.

MacColl, Canon Malcolm. "An Agnostic Novel." 1887. In *The Story of an African Farm.* 1883, edited by Patricia O'Neill, 356–62. Peterborough: Broadview Press, 2003.

Maine, Henry Sumner. *Ancient Law.* 1861. New York: J.M. Dent, 1917. www.gutenberg.org/files/22910/22910-h/22910-h.htm.

Mansfield, Katherine. "The Tiredness of Rosabel." 1908. *The Katherine Mansfield Society* Web: 24 October 2018. www.katherinemansfieldsociety.org.

Marinetti, Filippo Tommaso. "The Futurist Manifesto." 1909. In *Critical Writings: New Edition*, edited by Gunter Berghaus and translated by Doug Thompson, 11–17. New York: Farrar, Strauss, and Giroux, 2006.

Maudsley, Henry. "Sex in Mind and in Education." *Fortnightly Review* 21 (1874): 466–83.

Meynell, Alice. "Pictures of the Hill Collection." *The Magazine of Art*, 80–4. London: Cassell, Petter, Galpin, 1882.

Mill, J.S. *Principles of Political Economy.* 1848. Edited by Jonathan Riley. New York: Oxford University Press, 1994.

Moore, George. "Home Sickness." In *The Untilled Field*, 155–72. London: Unwin, 1903.

More, Hannah. *Strictures on the Modern System of Female Education*. London: T. Cadell Jun and W. Davies, 1799.
Morgan, J.H. Introduction. In *Ancient Law*, vii–xv. New York: J.M. Dent, 1917.
Morgan, Lewis Henry. *Ancient Society*. London: Palgrave Macmillan, 1877.
Mulholland, Rosa. "Emigrants." *The Irish Monthly* (1893): 236.
– *A Fair Emigrant*. New York: D. Appleton, 1896.
– *Father Tim*. London: Sands, 1910.
– *Norah of Waterford*. New York: P.J. Kenedy, 1915.
Olive Schreiner Letters Online. www.oliveschreiner.org/vre?page=home.
Owen, Wilfred. "Dulce et Decorum Est." 1920. www.poetryfoundation.org/poems-and-poets/poems/detail/46560.
Pankhurst, Emmeline. "Freedom or Death." 1913. *Gleeditions: Guided Literary E-Text Editions* (Web): 26pages. www.gleeditions.com/freedomordeathspeech/students/pages.asp?lid=418&pg=3.
Pater, Walter. "Preface." In *The Renaissance: Studies in Art and Poetry*, xxix–xxxiii. 1873. Oxford: Oxford University Press, 1986.
– "Prosper Mérimée." (1890). In *Miscellaneous Studies*, 1–25. London: Palgrave Macmillan, 1895. https://archive.org/details/miscellaneousstu01pate.
– *The Renaissance: Studies in Art and Poetry*. (1873). Oxford: Oxford University Press, 1986.
– "The School of Giorgione." In *The Renaissance: Studies in Art and Poetry*, 83–98. 1873. Oxford: Oxford University Press, 1986.
Pearson, Karl. *Socialism and Sex*. William Reeves, 1887. Google Books. Web. 14 August 2013. http://books.google.ca/books/about/Socialism_and_Sex.html?id=DZ7COwAACAAJ&redir_esc=y.
– "The Woman's Question." In *The Ethic of Freethought: A Selection of Essays and Lectures*, 370–94. London: T. Fisher Unwin, 1888.
Probyn, May. "The Model." 1883. In *Victorian Women Poets: An Anthology*, edited by Angela Leighton and Margaret Reynolds, 526–9. Oxford: Blackwell, 1995.
Purcell, E. "Review of The Beautiful." *Academy* 19 (July 1884): 37–8.
"Review of *The Wheel of God*, by George Egerton." *Spectator* 25 (June 1898): 913.
Richardson, Dorothy (American Author). *The Long Day: The Story of a New York Working Girl*. 1905. Charlottesville: University of Virginia Press, 1990.
Richardson, Dorothy (British Author). *The Tunnel*. London: Duckworth, 1919. https://archive.org/details/tunnelri00richuoft.
Ricketts, Charles. *Michael Field*. Edited by Paul Delaney. Edinburgh: Tragara Press, 1976.
"The Romance of a Shop." *The Jewish Chronicle*, 2 November 1888: 13. In *The Romance of a Shop*, 195–6. 1888. Peterborough: Broadview Press, 2006.

Robinson, A. Mary F. "Etruscan Tombs." 1887. In *Lyrics: Selected from the Works of A. Mary F. Robinson* 93–6. London: T.F. Unwin, 1891. https://archive.org/details/cu31924013343631.

– "Venetian Nocturne." 1886. In *Victorian Women Poets: An Anthology*, edited by Angela Leighton and Margaret Reynolds, 539–40. Oxford: Blackwell, 1995.

Romanes, George J. "Mental Differences between Men and Women." 1887. In *The Education Papers: Women's Quest for Equality in Britain 1850–1912*, edited by Dale Spender, 10–31. New York: Routledge, 1987.

Ross, Miss. *The Governess: or, Politics in Private Life*. London: Smith, Elder, 1843.

Rossetti, Christina. "In an Artist's Studio." 1856. In *New Poems by Christina Rossetti*, edited by William Michael Rossetti, 114. New York: Macmillan and Co, 1896.

Ruskin, John. *The Elements of Drawing: In Three Letters to Beginners*. London: Smith, Elder, 1857. http://ruskinhistory.org/John_Ruskin_Books/The_Elements_of_Drawing.pdf.

Saintsbury, George. "New Novels." Review for *The Academy*, 10 November 1888. In *The Romance of a Shop*, 197–8. Peterborough: Broadview Press, 2006.

Schreiner, Olive. *The Story of an African Farm*. 1883. Edited by Patricia O'Neill. Peterborough: Broadview Press, 2003.

– *Woman and Labor*. 7th edition. New York: Frederick A. Stokes, 1911. http://archive.org/details/cu31924021878099.

Selous, Henry Courtney. *The Young Governess: A Tale for Girls*. 1871. London: Griffith & Farran, 1891.

Sherwood, Mary Martha. *Caroline Mordaunt, or: The Governess*. London: William Darton and Son, 1835.

Shirreff, Emily. *Intellectual Education and Its Influence on the Character and Happiness of Women*. London: John W. Parker and Son, 1858.

Siddal, Elizabeth. "The Lust of the Eyes." 1850s. In *Poems and Drawings of Elizabeth Siddal*, edited by Roger C. Lewis and Mark Samuels Lasner, 14. Wolfville, NS: Wombat Press, 1978.

Sime, J.G. "Munitions." 1919. In *Great Canadian War Stories*, edited by Muriel Whitaker, 70–6. Edmonton: University of Alberta Press, 2001.

Simmel, Georg. "The Metropolis and Mental Life." 1903. In *The Sociology of Georg Simmel*, translated by Kurt H. Wolff, 409–24. Glencoe, IL: Free Press, 1950.

Spencer, Herbert. *The Principles of Biology* 2. London, 1867. http://archive.org/details/principlesbiolo22spengoog.

– "The Social Organism." In *Essays: Scientific, Political, & Speculative*. Vol. 1:265–307. London: Williams and Norgate, 1891. Print. Project Gutenberg, 5 June 2011.

– *Social Statistics: Or, the Conditions Essential to Human Happiness Specified, and the First of Them Developed*. New York: D. Appleton, 1915. http://archive.org/details/socialstatistics00spenuoft.

Starke, Mariana. *Information and Directions for Travellers on the Continent*. 9th edition. Orig. 1824. Paris: A. and W. Galignani, 1839.

Stetson, Charlotte Perkins. "To Mothers." 1893. In *This Our World: Poems*, 37–9. Oakland: McCombs & Vaughan, 1893.

Stourton, Margaret. *Margaret Stourton, or a Year of Governess Life*. London, 1863.

Strachey, Ray. *"The Cause": A Short History of the Women's Movement in Great Britain*. London: G. Bell & Sons, 1928.

"Studies of the Renaissance." *The Atlantic Monthly* 55 (1885): 132–6.

Sturgeon, Mary. *Michael Field*. London: Harrap, 1921.

Thomson, James. "The City of Dreadful Delight." 1874. In *The City of Dreadful Delight and Other Poems*, 1–55. London: Reeves and Turner, 1880.

Tynan, Katharine. *The French Wife*. Philadelphia: J.B. Lippincott Company, 1904.

Webb, Sydney, and Beatrice Webb. *The History of Trade Unionism*. London: Longmans, Green, 1894.

– *Industrial Democracy*. London: Longmans, Green, 1897.

Wharton, Edith. *The Age of Innocence*. Boston: D. Appleton & Company, 1920.

Wollstonecraft, Mary. *A Vindication of the Rights of Woman*. 1792. New York: Oxford University Press, 1999.

"Woman and Labor." *Good Health* 46.10 (1911): 915–16.

Woolf, Virginia. *The Common Reader*. 1923. https://ebooks.adelaide.edu.au/w/woolf/virginia/w91c/.

– "Middlebrow." In *The Death of the Moth, and Other Essays*. 1942. https://ebooks.adelaide.edu.au/w/woolf/virginia/w91d/chapter22.html.

– "Modern Fiction." In *The Common Reader*. 1923. https://ebooks.adelaide.edu.au/w/woolf/virginia/w91c/.

– *Night and Day*. London: Duckworth Overlook, 1919.

– "Olive Schreiner." *The New Republic* (18 March 1925): 103.

– *The Pargiters: The Novel-Essay Portion of "The Years."* Edited by Mitchel A. Leska. London: Hogarth, 1978.

– "Professions for Women." 1931. https://ebooks.adelaide.edu.au/w/woolf/virginia/w91d/chapter27.html.

– *To the Lighthouse*. London: Hogarth Press, 1927.

– *Three Guineas*. (1938). New York: Harcourt, 1966.

– *A Room of One's Own*. London: Harcourt, 1929.

– *The Voyage Out*. London: Duckworth Overlook, 1915.

– *The Years*. New York: Harcourt, Brace, 1937.

Wordsworth, William. "Lines Written a Few Miles Above Tintern Abbey." 1798.

"Work, Not Surrogates, Won Women the Vote." *Express* (10 March 2014): n.p. www.express.co.uk/life-style/life/461332/Work-not-suffragettes-won-women-the-vote.

Yeats, W.B. "Review of Sight and Song." July 1982; *The Bookman*. In Michael Field, *The Poet: Published and Manuscript Materials*, edited by Marion Thain and Ana Parėjo Vadillo, 361–3. Peterborough: Broadview Press, 2009.

Yonge, Charlotte M. *Womankind*. London: Mozley & Smith, 1877.

Secondary Sources

Adorno, Theodor. *Aesthetic Theory*. 1970. Translated by C. Lenhardt. London: Routledge & Kegan Paul, 1984.

Amariglio, Jack, and David F. Ruccio. "From Unity to Dispersion: The Body in Modern Economic Discourse." In *Postmodernism, Economics, and Knowledge*, edited by Stephen Cullenberg, Jack Amariglio, and David F. Ruccio, 143–65. New York: Routledge, 2001.

Anderson, Benedict. *Imagined Communities: Reflections on the Origin and Spread of Nationalism*. New York: Verso, 1983, 1991.

Anderson, Bonnie S., and Judith P. Zinsser. *A History of Their Own: Women in Europe from Prehistory to the Present*. Vol 2. New York: Harper & Row, 1988.

Anderson, Nancy Fix. *The Sporting Life: Victorian Sports and Games*. Santa Barbara, CA: Praeger, 2010.

Anderson, Patrick. "E.M. Forester." *The Spectator* (12 June 1970), 29. http://archive.spectator.co.uk/article/13th-june-1970/29/e-m-forster.

"Anna Jameson." *Dictionary of Art Historians*. Websource. https://dictionaryofarthistorians.org/jamesona.htm.

Ardis, Ann L. *New Women, New Novels: Feminism and Early Modernism*. New Brunswick, NJ: Rutgers University Press, 1990.

Armstrong, Nancy. *Desire and Domestic Fiction: A Political History of the Novel*. Oxford: Oxford University Press, 1987.

Armstrong, Tim. *Modernism: A Cultural History*. Cambridge: Polity Press, 2005.

Aron, Cindy Sondik. Introduction to *The Long Day: The Story of a New York Working Girl*, ix–xxxvii. 1905. Charlottesville: University of Virginia Press, 1990.

Banks, J.A. *Prosperity and Parenthood: A Study of Family Planning among the Victorian Middle Classes*. London: Routledge & Kegan Paul, 1954.

Barker, T.C., and Michael Robbins. *A History of London Transport: Passenger Travel and the Development of the Metropolis*. 2 vols. London: George Allen & Unwin, 1963.

Barrett, Eileen, and Patricia Cramer, eds. *Virginia Woolf: Lesbian Readings*. New York: New York University Press, 1997.

Bayor, Ronald, and Timothy J. Meagher. *The New York Irish*. Baltimore, MD: Johns Hopkins University Press, 1996.

Bazin, Nancy Topping. *Virginia Woolf and the Androgynous Vision*. New Brunswick, NJ: Rutgers University Press, 1973.

Bechtold, Brigitte. "More than a Room and Three Guineas: Understanding Virginia Woolf's Social Thought." *Journal of International Women's Studies* 1.2 (2000): 1–11.

Beckman, Linda Hunt. *Amy Levy: Her Life and Letters*. Athens: Ohio University Press, 2000.

Bell, Quentin. *Virginia Woolf: A Biography*. 2 vols. London: Hogarth, 1972.

Benjamin, Walter. "The Paris of the Second Empire in Baudelaire." 1938. In *Walter Benjamin: Selected Writings*, Vol. 4, *1938–1940*, translated by Edmund Jephcott et al., edited by Howard Eiland and Michael W. Jennings, 3–92. Cambridge: The Belknap Press of Harvard University Press, 2003.

– "On Some Motifs in Baudelaire." 1939. In *Walter Benjamin: Selected Writings*, Vol. 4, *1938–1940*, translated by Edmund Jephcott et al., edited by Howard Eiland and Michael W. Jennings, 313–55. Cambridge: The Belknap Press of Harvard University Press, 2003.

– "The Work of Art in the Age of Mechanical Reproduction." 1936. In *Illuminations: Essays and Reflections*, edited by Hannah Arendt, 217–42. New York: Schocken Books, 1968.

Benstock, Shari. *Textualizing the Feminine: On the Limits of Genre*. Norman: University of Oklahoma Press, 1991.

Berkman, Joyce Avrech. *The Healing Imagination of Olive Schreiner: Beyond South African Colonialism*. Amherst: University of Massachusetts Press, 1989.

Bernstein, Susan David. Introduction to *The Romance of a Shop*, 11–41. Peterborough: Broadview Press, 2006.

Birken, Lawrence. *Consuming Desire: Sexual Science and the Emergence of a Culture of Abundance, 1871–1914*. Ithaca: Cornell University Press, 1988.

Bland, Lucy. *Banishing the Beast: Feminism, Sex and Morality*. New York: Tauris Parke Paperbacks, 2001.

Bloom, Harold. *The Ringers in the Tower: Studies in Romantic Tradition*. Chicago: University of Chicago, 1971.

Bogen, Elizabeth. *Immigration in New York*. New York: Praeger, 1987.

Bonca, Teddi Chichester. *Shelley's Mirrors of Love: Narcissism, Sacrifice, and Sorority*. Albany: State University of New York Press, 1999.

Bourdieu, Pierre. "The Forms of Capital."In *Handbook of Theory and Research for the Sociology of Education*, edited by John G. Richardson, 241–58. New York: Greenwood Press, 1986.

Bowlby, Rachel. *Just Looking: Consumer Culture in Dreiser, Gissing, and Zola*. New York: Methuen, 1985.

Boyd, Elizabeth French. *Bloomsbury Heritage: Their Mothers and Their Aunts.* New York: Taplinger, 1976.

Braidotti, Rosi. *Nomadic Subjects: Embodiment and Sexual Difference in Contemporary Feminist Thought.* New York: Columbia University Press, 1994.

– *Nomadic Theory: The Portable Rosi Braidotti.* New York: Columbia University Press, 2011.

Braun, Heather L. "'Set the Crystal Surface Free!': Mary E. Coleridge and the Self-Conscious Femme Fatale." *Women's Writing* 14.3 (2007): 496–509.

Briggs, Julia. "The Novels of the 1930s and the Impact of History." In *The Cambridge Companion to Virginia Woolf*, edited by Susan Roe and Susan Sellers, 72–90. Cambridge: Cambridge University Press, 2000.

Brown, Sarah Annes. *Devoted Sisters: Representations of the Sister Relationship in Nineteenth-Century British and American Literature.* Burlington, VT: Ashgate, 2003.

Bryant, Margaret. *The Unexpected Revolution: A Study in the History of the Education of Women and Girls in the Nineteenth Century.* London: University of London, Institute of Education, 1979.

Buck-Morss, Susan. *Dialectics of Seeing: Walter Benjamin and the Arcades Project.* Cambridge, MA: MIT Press, 1989.

– "The *Flâneur*, the Sandwichman and the Whore: The Politics of Loitering." *New German Critique* 39 (1986b): 99–140.

Burdett, Carolyn. *Olive Schreiner and the Progress of Feminism: Evolution, Gender, Empire.* New York: Palgrave Macmillan, 2001.

Bürger, Peter. *Theory of the Avant-Garde.* 1974. Minneapolis: University of Minnesota Press, 1984.

Burrow, John. *Whigs and Liberals: Community and Change in English Political Thought.* Oxford: Clarendon, 1988.

Burstyn, Joan N. *Victorian Education and the Ideal of Womanhood.* Totowa, NJ: Barnes and Noble Books, 1980.

Butler, Judith. *Gender Trouble: Feminism and the Subversion of Identity.* New York: Routledge, 1990.

Cameron, S. Brooke. "Grant Allen's The Woman Who Did: Spencerian Individualism and Teaching New Women to Be Mothers." *ELT: English Literature in Transition* 51.3 (2008): 281–301.

– "The Pleasures of Looking and the Feminine Gaze in Michael Field's Sight and Song." *Victorian Poetry* 51.2 (2013): 147–75.

– "'She is Not a Lady, but a Legal Document': The Tattoo as Contract in Mr. Meeson's Will." *Studies in the Novel* 45.2 (2013): 178–97.

– "Sister of the Type: The Feminist Collective in Grant Allen's *The Type-Writer Girl.*" *Victorian Literature and Culture* 40.1 (2012): 229–44.

– "'Where Twilight Touches Ripeness Amorously': The Gaze in Michael Field's Sight and Song." In *Michael Field and Their World*, edited by Margaret

D. Stetz and Cheryl A. Wilson, 147–54. High Wycomb: Rivendale Press, 2007.

– "Women's Slum Journalism, 1885–1910." In *The History of British Women's Writing, 1880–1920*, edited by Holly A. Laird, 245–57. London: Palgrave Macmillan, 2016.

Cameron, S. Brooke, and Danielle Bird. "Sisterly Bonds and Rewriting Urban Gendered Spheres in Amy Levy's *The Romance of a Shop*." *Victorian Review* 40.1 (2014): 77–96.

Caughie, Pamela L. *Virginia Woolf & Postmodernism: Literature in Quest & Question of Itself*. Chicago: University of Illinois Press, 1991.

Chambers, Diane M. "Triangular Desire and the Sororal Bond: The Deceased Wife's Sister Bill." *Mosaic* 29.1 (1996): 19–36.

Clarke, Meaghan. *Critical Voices: Women and Art Criticism in Britain 1880–1905*. Burlington, VT: Ashgate, 2005.

– "1894: The Year of the New Woman Art Critic."In *BRANCH: Britain, Representation and Nineteenth-Century History*. Online. n.p.

Clarke, Meaghan, and Francesco Ventrella. "Women's Expertise and the Culture of Connoisseurship." *Visual Resources: An International Journal on Images and Their Uses* 33.1–2 (2017): 1–10.

Clayton, Cherry. *Beyond the Frame: Feminism and Visual Culture, Britain 1850–1900*. New York: Routledge, 2000.

– *Olive Schreiner*. New York: Twayne, 1997.

Cohen, Monica F. *Professional Domesticity in the Victorian Novel: Women, Work, and Home*. Cambridge: Cambridge University Press, 1998.

Colby, Vineta. *Vernon Lee: A Literary Biography*. Charlottesville: University of Virginia Press, 2003.

Cole, Sarah. "Enchantment, Disenchantment, War, Literature." *PMLA* 124.5 (2009): 1632–47.

Collins, Tracy J.R. "Physical Fitness, Sports, and the Rise of the New Woman." Diss. Purdue University, 2007.

Cosslett, Tess. *Woman to Woman: Female Friendship in Victorian Fiction*. Atlantic Highlands, NJ: Humanities Press International, 1988.

Cowman, Krista, and Louise A. Jackson, eds. *Women and Work Culture: Britain c. 1850–1950*. London: Ashgate, 2005.

Cramer, Patricia. "'Pearls and the Porpoise': *The Years* – A Lesbian Memoir." In *Virginia Woolf: Lesbian Readings*, edited by Eileen Barrett and Patricia Cramer, 222–40. New York: New York University Press, 1997.

Cuddy-Keane, Melba. *Virginia Woolf, the Intellectual, and the Public Sphere*. Cambridge: Cambridge University Press, 2003.

– "Virginia Woolf and the Varieties of Historicist Experience." In *Virginia Woolf and the Essay*, edited by Beth Carole Rosenberg and Jeanne Dubino, 59–77. New York: St Martin's, 1997.

Davidoff, Leonore. "'Adam Spoke First and Named the Others of the World': Masculine and Feminine Domains in History and Sociology." In *Politics of Everyday Life: Continuity and Change in Work and the Family*, edited by H. Corr and L. Jamieson, 226–55. London: Palgrave Macmillan, 1990.

– *Thicker Than Water: Siblings and Their Relations, 1780–1920*. Oxford: Oxford University Press, 2012.

Davidoff, Leonore, and Catherine Hall. *Family Fortunes: Men and Women of the English Middle Class, 1780–1850*. London: Hutchinson, 1987.

Davies, Margery W. *Woman's Place Is at the Typewriter: Office Work and Office Workers 1870–1930*. Philadelphia: Temple University Press, 1982.

Delgado, Alan. *The Enormous File: A Social History of the Office*. London: John Murray, 1979.

Di Bello, Patrizia. *Women's Albums and Photography in Victorian England: Ladies, Mothers, and Flirts*. Aldershot, UK: Ashgate, 2007.

Dill, Bonnie Thornton. "Race, Class, and Gender: Prospects for and All-Inclusive Sisterhood." *Feminist Studies* 9 (1983): 131–50.

Dillane, Fionnuala. "A Fair Field and no Favour: Hulda Friederichs, the Interview, and the New Woman." In *Women in Journalism at the Fin de Siècle*, edited by F. Elizabeth Gray, 148–64. New York: Palgrave Macmillan, 2012.

Doan, Laura. *Fashioning Sapphism: The Origins of a Modern English Lesbian Culture*. New York: Columbia University Press, 2001.

Doane, Mary Ann. "Technophilia: Technology, Representation, and the Feminine." In *Body/Politics: Women and the Discourses of Science*, edited by Mary Jacobus et al., 163–76. New York: Routledge, 1990.

Donnelly, Brian. *Reading Dante Gabriel Rossetti: The Painter as Poet*. Burlington, VT: Ashgate, 2015.

Donoghue, Emma. *We Are Michael Field*. Somerset: Absolute Press, 1998.

Draznin, Yaffa Claire, ed. *My Other Self: The Letters of Olive Schreiner and Havelock Ellis, 1884–1920*. New York: Peter Lang, 1992.

Dyhouse, Carol. *Feminism and the Family in England 1880–1939*. Oxford: Blackwell, 1989.

– "Social Darwinistic Ideas and the Development of Women's Education in England 1880–1920." *History of Education* 5.1 (1976): 41–58.

Ehnenn, Jill. *Women's Literary Collaboration, Queerness, and Late-Victorian Culture*. Burlington, VT: Ashgate, 2008.

Ellis, Steven. *Virginia Woolf and the Victorians*. New York: Cambridge University Press, 2007.

Ernst, Sabine. "The Woman Who Did and 'The Girl Who Didn't': The Romance of Sexual Selection in Grant Allen and Ménie Muriel Dowie." In *Grant Allen: Literature and Cultural Politics at the Fin de Siècle*, edited by William Greenslade and Terence Rodgers, 81–94. Burlington, VT: Ashgate, 2005.

Evangelista, Stefano. "Vernon Lee and the Gender of Aestheticism." In *Vernon Lee: Decadence, Ethics, Aesthetics*, edited by Catherine Maxwell and Patricia Pulham, 91–111. New York: Palgrave Macmillan, 2006.

Evans, Elizabeth F. "'We are photographers, not mountebanks!': Spectacle, Commercial Space, and the New Public Woman." In *Amy Levy: Critical Essays*, edited by Naomi Hetherington and Nadia Valman, 25–46. Athens: Ohio University Press, 2010.

Faderman, Lillian. *Odd Girls and Twilight Lovers: A History of Lesbian Life in Twentieth-Century America*. New York: Columbia University Press, 1991.

– *Surpassing the Love of Men: Romantic Friendship between Women from the Renaissance to the Present*. New York: William Morrow, 1981.

Felski, Rita. *The Gender of Modernity*. Cambridge, MA: Harvard University Press, 1995.

– *Literature after Feminism*. Chicago: University of Chicago Press, 2003.

First, Ruth, and Ann Scott. *Olive Schreiner*. New York: Schocken Books, 1980.

Flint, Kate. "The 'hour of pink twilight': Lesbian Poetics and Queer Encounters on the Fin-de-Siècle Street." *Victorian Studies* 51.4 (2009): 687–712.

– "Identity and the Victorian Woman Poet." In *Rewriting the Self: Histories from the Middle Ages to the Present*, edited by Roy Parker, 156–66. New York: Routledge, 1997.

– *The Victorians and the Visual Imagination*. Cambridge: Cambridge University Press, 2000.

Francis, Emma. "Amy Levy: Contradictions? – Feminism and Semitic Discourse." In *Women's Poetry, Late Romantic to Late Victorian: Gender and Genre, 1830–1900*, edited by Isobel Armstrong and Virginia Blain, 183–204. London: Palgrave Macmillan, 1999.

– "Why wasn't Amy Levy more of a socialist? Levy, Clementina Black, and Liza of Lambeth." In *Amy Levy: Critical Essays*, edited by Naomi Hetherington and Nadia Valman, 47–69. Athens: Ohio University Press, 2010.

Frank, Cathrine O. *Law, Literature, and the Transmission of Culture in England, 1837–1925*. Burlington, VT: Ashgate, 2010.

Frankel, Nicholas. "The Concrete Poetics of Michael Field's *Sight and Song*." In *Michael Field and Their World*, edited by Margaret D. Stetz and Cheryl A. Wilson, 211–22. High Wycomb: Rivendale Press, 2007.

Fraser, Hilary. "A Visual Field: Michael Field and the Gaze." *Victorian Literature and Culture* 34 (2006): 553–71.

– *Women Writing Art History in the Nineteenth Century: Looking Like a Woman*. Cambridge: Cambridge University Press, 2014.

Freedman, Johnathan L. *Professions of Taste: Henry James, British Aestheticism, and Commodity Culture*. Stanford: Stanford University Press, 1990.

Frisby, David. *Simmel and Science*. London: Routledge, 1992.

Froula, Christine. *Virginia Woolf and the Bloomsbury Avant-Garde: War, Civilization, Modernity*. New York: Columbia University Press, 2005.

Fuss, Diana. *Essentially Speaking: Feminism, Nature, & Difference*. New York: Routledge, 1989.

Gagnier, Regenia. *Idylls of the Marketplace: Oscar Wilde and the Victorian Public*. Stanford: Stanford University Press, 1986.

– *The Insatiability of Human Wants: Economics and Aesthetics in Market Society*. Chicago: University of Chicago Press, 2000.

– "Women in British Aestheticism and the Decadence." In *New Woman in Fiction and Fact: Fin-de-Siècle Feminisms*, edited by Angelique Richardson and Chris Willis, 239–49. New York: Palgrave Macmillan, 2001.

Gallagher, Catherine. *The Body Economic: Life, Death, and Sensation in Political Economy and the Victorian Novel*. Princeton: Princeton University Press, 2006.

– *The Industrial Reformation of English Fiction*. Chicago: University of Chicago Press, 1985.

Gilbert, Sandra M. "Plain Jane's Progress." In *Jane Eyre*, edited by Beth Newman, 475–501. New York: Bedford/St Martin's, 1996.

Gilbert, Sandra M., and Susan Gubar. *The Madwoman in the Attic: The Woman Writer and the Nineteenth-Century Literary Imagination*. New Haven: Yale University Press, 1979.

Gittins, Diana. *Fair Sex: Family Size and Structure 1900–39*. London: Hutchinson, 1982.

Goldstein, Joshua S. *War and Gender: How Gender Shapes the War System and Vice Versa*. Cambridge: Cambridge University Press, 2001.

Goodwin, Craufurd D. "The Art of an Ethical Life: Keynes and Bloomsbury." In *The Cambridge Companion to Keynes*, edited by Roger E. Backhouse and Bradley W. Bateman, 217–36. Cambridge: Cambridge University Press, 2006.

– "The Value of Things in the Imaginative Life: Microeconomics in the Bloomsbury Group." *History of Economic Review* 34 (2001): 56–73.

Goody, Alex. "Passing in the City: The Liminal Spaces of Amy Levy's Late Work." In *Amy Levy: Critical Essays*, edited by Naomi Hetherington and Nadia Valman, 157–79. Athens: Ohio University Press, 2010.

Gordon, Peter, and David Doughan. *Dictionary of British Women's Organisations, 1825–1960*. London: Woburn Press, 2001.

Gray, F. Elizabeth, ed. *Women in Journalism at the Fin de Siècle*. New York: Palgrave Macmillan, 2012.

Green, Barbara. *Spectacular Confessions: Autobiography, Performative Activism, and the Sites of Suffrage, 1905–1938*. New York: St Martin's, 1997.

Green, Laura Morgan. *Educating Women: Cultural Conflict and Victorian Literature.* Athens: Ohio University Press, 2001.

Gruner, Elisabeth Rose. "Born and Made: Sisters, Brothers, and the Deceased Wife's Sister Bill." *Signs* 24.2 (winter 1999): 423–47.

Hackett, Robin. *Sapphic Primitivism: Productions of Race, Class, and Sexuality in Key Works of Modern Fiction.* New Brunswick, NJ: Rutgers University Press, 2004.

Hager, Lisa. "A Community of Women: Women's Agency and Sexuality in George Egerton's *Keynotes* and *Discords.*" *Nineteenth-Century Gender Studies* 2.2 (2006): n.p.

Hamilton, Susan, ed. *Criminals, Idiots, Women, & Minors: Victorian Writing by Women on Women.* Peterborough: Broadview Press, 1995.

Hammerton, A. James. "Feminism and Female Emigration, 1861–1886." In *A Widening Sphere: Changing Roles of Victorian Women,* edited by Martha Vicinus, 52–71. Bloomington: Indiana University Press, 1977.

Hanson, Clare. "Virginia Woolf in the House of Love: Compulsory Heterosexuality in *The Years.*" *Journal of Gender Studies* 6.1 (1997): 55–62.

Harders, Ann-Cathrin. "Agnatio, Cognation, Consanguinitus: Kinship and Blood in Ancient Rome." In *Blood & Kinship: Matter for Metaphor from Ancient Rome to the Present,* edited by Christopher H. Johnson et al., 18–39. New York: Berghahn Books, 2013.

Heffernan, Teresa. *Post-Apocalyptic Culture: Modernism, Post-Modernism, and the Twentieth-Century Novel.* Toronto: University of Toronto Press, 2008.

Heilmann, Anne. *New Woman Strategies: Sarah Grand, Olive Schreiner, Mona Caird.* Manchester: Manchester University Press, 2004.

Heinzelman, Kurt. *Make It New: The Rise of Modernism.* Austin: University of Texas Press, 2003.

Helmstadter, Carol, and Judith Godden. *Nursing before Nightingale, 1815–1899.* Burlington, VT: Ashgate, 2011.

Hepburn, Allan. "Introduction: Inheritance and Disinheritance in the Novel." In *Troubled Legacies: Narrative and Inheritance,* 3–25. Toronto: University of Toronto Press, 2007.

Hibbert, Christopher. *London: The Biography of a City.* 1969. Harmondsworth: Penguin Books, 1980.

Hilton, Mary, and Pam Hirsch. *Practical Visionaries: Women, Education and Social Progress 1790–1930.* New York: Pearson Education, 2000.

Holcombe, Lee. *Victorian Ladies at Work: Middle-Class Working Women in England and Wales, 1850–1914.* North Haven: Shoe String, 1973.

Holly, Marcia. "Consciousness and Authenticity: Towards a Feminist Aesthetic." In *Feminist Literary Criticism: Explorations in Theory,* edited by Josephine Donavan, 38–47. Lexington: University of Kentucky Press, 1975.

Holton, Sandra Stanley. "Religion and the Meaning of Work: Four Cases from among the Bright Circle of Women Quakers." In *Women and Work Culture: Britain c. 1850–1950*, edited by Krista Cowman and Louise A. Jackson, 48–69. London: Ashgate, 2005.

Homberger, Eric. *The Historical Atlas of New York City: A Visual Celebration of 400 Years of New York City's History*. New York: Holt Paperbacks, 1994.

Hughes, Kathryn. *The Victorian Governess*. London: Hambleton Press, 1993.

Hunt, Margaret. *The Middling Sort: Commerce, Gender, and the Family in England, 1680–1780*. Berkeley: University of California Press, 1996.

Jeffreys, Sheila. *The Spinster and Her Enemies: Feminism and Sexuality, 1880–1930*. North Melbourne, VIC: Spinifex, 1977.

Jenks, Chris. "Watching Your Step: The History and Practice of the Flâneur." In *Visual Culture*, edited by Chris Jenks, 142–60. London: Routledge, 1995.

Johnston, Judith. *Victorian Women and the Economies of Travel, Translation and Culture, 1830–1870*. Aldershot, UK: Ashgate, 2012.

Jordan, Ellen. *The Women's Movement and Women's Employment in Nineteenth Century Britain*. New York: Routledge, 1999.

Jusová, Iveta. "George Egerton and the Project of British Colonialism." *Tulsa Studies in Women's Literature* 19.1 (2000): 27–56.

– *The New Woman and the Empire*. Columbus: Ohio State University Press, 2005.

Kanwit, John Paul M. *Victorian Art Criticism and the Woman Writer*. Columbus: Ohio State University Press, 2013.

Kavaloski, Joshua. *High Modernism: Aestheticism and Performativity in Literature of the 1920s*. New York: Camden House, 2014.

Keating, Jenny. *A Child for Keeps: The History of Adoption in England, 1918–45*. New York: Palgrave Macmillan, 2009.

Keep, Christopher. "The Cultural Work of the Type-Writer Girl." *Victorian Studies* 40.3 (1997): 401–26.

Kerber, Linda K. "Separate Spheres, Female Worlds, Woman's Place: The Rhetoric of Women's History." *Journal of American History* 75.1 (1988): 9–39.

Kermode, Frank. "Lawrence and Apocalyptic Types." *Critical Inquiry* 10 (1968): 14–38.

Kessler-Harris, Alice. "Treating the Male as 'Other': Redefining the Parameters of Labor History." *Labor History* 34.2–3 (1993): 190–204.

King, Jeannette. *Discourses of Aging in Fiction and Feminism*. New York: Springer Press, 2012.

Knechtel, Ruth. "George Egerton." In *The Yellow Nineties Online*. Edited by Dennis Denisoff and Lorraine Janzen Kooistra. http://www.1890s.ca. 2010.

Koven, Seth. *Slumming: Sexual and Social Politics in Victorian London*. Princeton, NJ: Princeton University Press, 2003.

Krebs, Paula. "Olive Schreiner's Racialization of South Africa." *Victorian Studies* 40.3 (spring 1997): 427–45.

Kreisel, Deanna K. *Economic Woman: Demand, Gender, and Narrative Closure in Eliot and Hardy*. Toronto: University of Toronto Press, 2012.

Krueger, Kate. *British Women Writers and the Short Story, 1850–1930: Reclaiming Social Space*. New York: Palgrave Macmillan, 2014.

– (as Kate Krueger Henderson). "Mobility and Modern Consciousness in George Egerton's and Charlotte Mew's *Yellow Book* Stories." *ELT* 54.2 (2011): 185–211.

Kwolek-Folland, Angel. *Engendering Business: Men and Women in the Corporate Office, 1870–1930*. Baltimore, MD: Johns Hopkins University Press, 1994.

Laird, Holly. *Women Coauthors*. Chicago: University of Illinois Press, 2000.

Law, Graham, and Adrian J. Pinnington. Introductionto *Great Expectations*, edited by Graham Law and Adrian J. Pinnington, 7–27. Peterborough: Broadview Press, 1998.

Leacock, Eleanor. "Interpreting the Origins of Gender Inequality: Conceptual and Historical Problems." *Dialectical Anthropology* 7.4 (1983): 263–84.

Lecaros, Cecilia Wadsö. "The Victorian Heroine Goes a Governessing." In *Silent Voices: Forgotten Novels by Victorian Women Writers*, edited by Brenda Ayers, 27–56. London: Praeger, 2003.

Ledger, Sally. *The New Woman: Fiction and Feminism at the Fin de Siècle*. Manchester: Manchester University Press, 1997.

Ledger, Sally, and Roger Luckhurst. "The New Woman." In *The Fin de Siècle: A Reader in Cultural History c. 1880–1900*, edited by Sally Ledger and Roger Luckhurst, 75–6. Oxford: Oxford University Press, 2000.

Lee, Hermione. *Virginia Woolf*. London: Chatto & Windus, 1996.

Leighton, Angela, and Margaret Reynolds. "Caroline Lindsay." In *Victorian Women Poets: An Anthology*, edited by Angela Leighton and Margaret Reynolds, 475–6. Oxford: Blackwell, 1995.

– "Mary E. Coleridge." In *Victorian Women Poets: An Anthology*, edited by Angela Leighton and Margaret Reynolds, 610–13. Oxford: Blackwell, 1995.

– "May Probyn." In *Victorian Women Poets: An Anthology*, edited by Angela Leighton and Margaret Reynolds, 525–6. Oxford: Blackwell, 1995.

Levinas, Emmanuel. *Totality and Infinity: Conversations with Philippe Nemo*. 1961. Translated by Richard A. Cohen. Pittsburg: Duquesne University Press, 1982.

Levine, Philippa. *Victorian Feminism, 1850–1900*. London: Hutchinson, 1987.

Lewis, Wyndham. *Blast 1*. 1914. Edited by Paul Edwards. Santa Rosa: Black Sparrow Press, 1997.

Liddington, Jill. *Presenting the Past: Anne Lister of Halifax 1791–1840*. Hebden Bridge, West Yorkshire: Pennine Pens, 1994.

Liggins, Emma. *George Gissing, the Working Woman, and Urban Culture.* Burlington, VT: Ashgate, 2006.

– *Odd Women? Spinsters, Lesbians and Widows in British Women's Fiction, 1850s–1930s.* Manchester: Manchester University Press, 2014.

– "'Women of True Respectability?' Investigating the London Work-Girl, 1880–1900." In *Women and Work Culture: Britain c. 1850–1950,* edited by Krista Cowman and Louise A. Jackson, 89–106. London: Ashgate, 2005.

Lindenbaum, Joyce P. "The Shattering of an Illusion: The Problem of Competition in Lesbian Relationships." In *Competition: A Feminist Taboo?,* edited by Valerie Miner and Helen E. Longino, 195–208. New York: Feminist Press, 1987.

Livesey, Ruth. "Morris, Carpenter, Wilde, and the Political Aesthetics of Labor." *Victorian Literature and Culture* 32.2 (2004): 601–16.

– *Socialism, Sex, and the Culture of Aestheticism in Britain, 1880–1914.* Oxford: The British Academy by Oxford University Press, 2007.

Looser, Devoney. "'The Duty of Women by Women': Reforming Feminism in *Emma.*" In *Emma,* edited by Alistair Duckworth, 577–93. New York: Bedford/St Martin's, 2002.

Lysack, Krista. "Aesthetic Consumption and the Cultural Production of Michael Field's Sight and Song." *SEL* 45.4 (2005): 935–60.

– *Come Buy, Come Buy: Shopping and the Culture of Consumption in Victorian Women's Writing.* Athens: Ohio University Press, 2008.

Macfarlane, Alan. *Marriage and Love in England 1300–1840.* Oxford: Blackwell, 1986.

MacKay, Carol Hanbery, ed. *Autobiographical Sketches: Annie Besant.* Peterborough: Broadview Press, 2009.

Macura, Ewa. "'Lifeless, inane, dawdling': Decadence, Femininity and Olive Schreiner's *Woman and Labour.*" In *Decadences: Morality and Aesthetics in British Literature,* edited by Paul Fox, 121–50. Stittgart: ibidem-Verlag, 2006.

Marcus, Jane. "'No More Horses': Virginia Woolf on Art and Propaganda." *Women's Studies* 4 (1977): 265–90.

– "Storming the Tool Shed." *Signs* 7.3 (1982): 622–40.

– *Virginia Woolf and the Languages of Patriarchy.* Bloomington: Indiana University Press, 1987.

Marcus, Laura. "Woolf's Feminism and Feminism's Woolf." In *The Cambridge Companion to Virginia Woolf,* edited by Susan Roe and Susan Sellers, 209–44. Cambridge: Cambridge University Press, 2000.

Marcus, Sharon. *Between Women: Friendship, Desires, and Marriage in Victorian England.* Princeton, NJ: Princeton University Press, 2007.

Marien, Mary Warner. *Photography: A Cultural History.* London: Lawrence King, 2002.

Marks, Patricia. *Bicycles, Bangs, and Bloomers: The New Woman in the Popular Press*. Lexington: University Press of Kentucky, 1990.

Martin, Jane. *Women and the Politics of Schooling in Victorian and Edwardian England.* New York: Leicester University Press, 1999.

May, Leila Silvana. *Disorderly Sisters: Sibling Relations and Sororal Resistance in Nineteenth-Century British Literature*. Lewisburg: Becknell University Press, 2001.

McClintock, Anne. *Imperial Leather: Race, Gender and Sexuality in the Colonial Contest*. New York: Routledge, 1995.

McCloskey, Deirdre. "Paid Work." In *Women in Twentieth Century Britain*, edited by Ina Zweiniger-Bargielowska, 165–79. Edinburgh: Pearson Education Limited, 2001.

McNees, Eleanor. "Colonizing Virginia Woolf: Scrutiny and Contemporary Cultural Views." In *Virginia Woolf and the Essay*, edited by Beth Carole Rosenberg and Jeanne Dubino, 41–58. Basingstoke: Palgrave Macmillan, 1997.

McWilliams, Ellen. "'Avenging Bridget': Irish Domestic Servants and Middle-Class America in the Short Stories of Maeve Brennan." *Irish Studies Review* 21.1 (2013): 99–113.

Merrell, Susan. *The Accidental Bond: The Power of Sibling Relationships*. New York: Random House, 1995.

Michaelsen, Kaarin. "'Union is Strength': The Medical Women's Federation and the Politics of Professionalism, 1917–30." In *Women and Work Culture: Britain c. 1850–1950*, edited by Krista Cowman and Louise A. Jackson, 161–76. London: Ashgate, 2005.

Michie, Elsie B. "Rich Woman, Poor Woman: Toward an Anthropology of the Nineteenth-Century Marriage Plot." *PMLA* 124.2 (2009): 421–36.

– *The Vulgar Question of Money: Heiresses, Materialism, and the Novel of Manners from Jane Austen to Henry James*. Baltimore, MD: Johns Hopkins University Press, 2011.

Michie, Helena. *Sororophobia: Differences among Women in Literature and Culture*. Oxford: Oxford University Press, 1992.

Miller, Nancy K. "Emphasis Added: Plots and Possibilities in Women's Fiction." *PMLA* 96 (January 1981): 36–48.

Minow-Pinkney, Makiko. *Virginia Woolf and the Problem of the Subject*. Brighton: Harvest, 1987.

Mitchell, Juliet. *Psychoanalysis and Feminism*. New York: Vintage Books, 1975.

Mitchell, Sally. "Careers for Girls: Writing Trash." *Victorian Periodicals Review* 25.3 (1992): 109–13.

Moers, Ellen. *The Dandy in Literature: Brummell to Beerbohm*. London: Secker and Warburg, 1960.

Moi, Toril. *Sexual/Textual Politics: Feminist Literary Theory*. New York: Methuen, 1985.

Moine, Fabienne. "Italian Rewritings by Nineteenth-Century Women Poets: From Constructing a Community of Women to Creating a Place of Poetical Freedom." In *Travel and Translations: Anglo-Italian Cultural Transactions*, edited by Alison Yarrington, Stefano Villani, and Julia Kelly, 205–18. New York: Rodopi, 2013.

Monsman, Gerald. "Writing the Self on the Imperial Frontier: Olive Schreiner and the Stories of Africa." *The Bucknell Review* 37.1 (1993): 134–55.

Morton, Peter. *The Busiest Man in England: Grant Allen and the Writing Trade, 1875–1900*. New York: Palgrave Macmillan, 2005.

Moss, Anita. "George Egerton." In *British Short-Fiction Writers, 1880–1914: The Realist Tradition*, edited by William B. Thesing. Detroit: Gale Research, 1994. *Dictionary of Literary Biography*. Vol. 135. Literature Resource Center.

Nelson, Carolyn Christensen, ed. Introduction to *A New Woman Reader: Fiction, Articles, Drama of the 1890s*, ix–xiv. Peterborough: Broadview Press, 2001.

Nelson, Claudia. *Family Ties in Victorian England*. Westport, CT: Praeger, 2007.

"The New Woman." In *The Cambridge Guide to Women's Writing in English*, edited by Lorna Sage, Elaine Showalter, and Germaine Greer, 465–7. Cambridge: Cambridge University Press, 1999.

Nichols, K. Madolyn. "The Women Who Leave: Irish Women Writing on Emigration." Diss. University of Warwick, 2014.

Noakes, Lucy. "Eve in Khaki: Women Working with the British Military, 1915–18." In *Women and Work Culture: Britain c. 1850–1950*, edited by Krista Cowman and Louise A. Jackson, 213–28. London: Ashgate, 2005.

Nochlin, Linda. Foreword in *The New Woman International: Representations in Photography and Film from the 1870s through the 1960s*, edited by Elizabeth Otto and Vanessa Rocco, vii–xi. Ann Arbor: University of Michigan Press, 2011.

Nord, Deborah. *Walking the Victorian Streets: Women, Representation, and the City*. Ithaca: Cornell University Press, 1995.

Norton, Rictor. "Anne Lister: The First Modern Lesbian." http://rictornorton.co.uk/lister.htm.

Nunn, Pamela Gerrish. "Critically Speaking." In *Women in the Victorian Art World*, edited by Clarissa Campbell Orr, 107–24. Manchester: Manchester University Press, 1995.

Olwell, Victoria. "Typewriters and the Vote." *Signs* 29.1 (2003): 55–83.

O Muirithe, Diarmaid. *A Seat behind the Coachman: Travellers in Ireland 1800–1900*. Dublin: Gill and Palgrave Macmillan, 1972.

O'Neill, Patricia. Introduction to *The Story of An African Farm*, 9–29. Peterborough: Broadview Press, 2003.

O'Neill, Peter D., and David Lloyd. *The Black and Green Atlantic: Cross-Currents of the African and Irish Diasporas*. New York: Palgrave Macmillan, 2009.

Orwell, George. "George Gissing." 1960. http://orwell.ru/library/reviews/gissing/english/e_gis.

Oulton, Carolyn. *Romantic Friendship in Victorian Literature*. Burlington, VT: Ashgate, 2007.

O'Toole, Tina. *The Irish New Woman*. New York: Palgrave Macmillan, 2013.

Panken, Shirley. *Virginia Woolf and the "Lust of Creation": A Psychoanalytic Exploration*. Albany: State University of New York Press, 1987.

Parsons, Deborah L. *Streetwalking the Metropolis: Women, the City and Modernity*. Oxford: Oxford University Press, 2000.

Pedersen, Joyce Senders. *The Reform of Girls' Secondary and Higher Education in Victorian England, a Study of Elites and Educational Change*. New York/London: Garland, Series of Outstanding Dissertations, 1987.

– "Victorian Liberal Feminism and the 'Idea' of Work." In *Women and Work Culture: Britain c. 1850–1950*, edited by Krista Cowman and Louise A. Jackson, 27–47. London: Ashgate, 2005.

Pencak, William. Introduction to *Immigration to New York*, edited by William Pencak, Selma Berrol, and Randall M. Miller, 3–5. Philadelphia, PA: Balch Institute Press, 1991.

Perry, Ruth. *Novel Relations: The Transformation of Kinship in English Literature and Culture 1748–1818*. Cambridge: Cambridge University Press, 2004.

Peterson, M. Jeanne. "The Victorian Governess: Status Incongruence in Family and Society."In *Suffer and be Still: Women in the Victorian Age*, edited by Martha Vicinus, 3–19. Bloomington: Indiana University Press, 1972.

Petry, Alice Hall. "Jamesian Parody, Jane Eyre, and 'The Turn of the Screw.'" *Modern Language Studies* 13.4 (autumn 1983): 61–78.

Phegley, Jennifer. *Courtship and Marriage in Victorian England*. Denver, CO: Praeger, 2012.

Plunkett, John, et al., eds. *Victorian Literature: A Sourcebook*. New York: Palgrave Macmillan, 2012.

Pollak, Ellen. *Incest and the English Novel, 1684–1814*. Baltimore, MD: Johns Hopkins University Press, 2003.

Pollock, Griselda. "Modernity and the Spaces of Femininity." In *Vision and Difference: Femininity, Feminism, and the Histories of Art*, 50–90. London: Routledge, 1988.

Poovey, Mary. *Uneven Developments: The Ideological Work of Gender in Mid-Victorian England*. Chicago: University of Chicago Press, 1988.

Price, Leah. "Grant Allen's Impersonal Secretaries: Rereading *The Type-Writer Girl*." In *Grant Allen: Literature and Cultural Politics at the Fin de Siècle*, edited by William Greenslade and Terence Rodgers, 129–42. Burlington, VT: Ashgate, 2005.

Price, Leah, and Pamela Thurschwell. *Literary Secretaries/ Secretarial Culture*. Burlington, VT: Ashgate, 2005.

Prins, Yopie. *Victorian Sappho*. Princeton, NJ: Princeton University Press, 1999.

Pugh, Martin. *Women and the Women's Movement in Britain, 1914–1959*. London: Palgrave Macmillan, 1992.

Purvis, June. *A History of Women's Education in England*. Philadelphia, PA: Open University Press, 1991.

Psomiades, Kathy Alexis. *Beauty's Body: Femininity and Representation in British Aestheticism*. Stanford: Stanford University Press, 1997.

– "Heterosexual Exchange and Other Victorian Fictions: The Eustace Diamonds and Victorian Anthropology." *NOVEL: A Forum on Fiction* 33.1 (1999): 93–118.

– "The Marriage Plot in Theory." *NOVEL: A Forum on Fiction* 43.1 (2010): 53–9.

Quarrie, Cynthia. "What Violently Elects Us: Filiation, Ethics, and War in the Contemporary British Novel." Diss. University of Toronto, 2012.

Radner, Hilary. "Introduction: Queering the Girl."In *Swinging Single: Representing Sexuality in the 1960s*, edited by Hilary Radner and Moya Luckett, 1–35. Minneapolis: University of Minnesota Press, 1999.

Rappaport, Erika. *Shopping for Pleasure: Women in the Making of London's West End*. Princeton, NJ: Princeton University Press, 2001.

Rappoport, Jill. *Giving Women: Alliance and Exchange in Victorian Culture*. Oxford: Oxford University Press, 2012.

Rendall, Jane. *The Origins of Modern Feminisms: Women in Britain, France and the United States, 1780 1960*. London: Palgrave Macmillan, 1985.

Rich, Adrienne. "Compulsory Heterosexuality and Lesbian Existence." In *The Signs Reader: Women, Gender, and Scholarship*, edited by Elizabeth Abel and Emily K. Abel, 139–68. Chicago: University of Chicago Press, 1980, 1983.

– "Jane Eyre: The Temptations of a Motherless Woman." In *On Lies, Secrets, and Silence: Selected Prose 1966–1978*, 89–106. New York: W.W. Norton, 1979.

Richardson, Angelique. *Love and Eugenics in the Late Nineteenth Century: Rational Reproduction and the New Woman*. New York: Oxford University Press, 2003.

– "'People talk a lot of Nonsense about Heredity': Mona Caird and Anti-Eugenic Feminism." In *The New Woman in Fiction and in Fact: Fin de Siècle Feminisms*, edited by Angelique Richardson and Chris Willis, 183–211. Basingstroke: Palgrave Macmillan, 2000.

Rive, Richard, ed. *Olive Schreiner Letters*, Vol. 1, *1871–1899*. New York: Oxford University Press, 1988.

Robertson, Emma. "'It Was Just a Real Camaraderie Thing': Socialising, Socialisation and Shopfloor Culture at the Rowntree Factory, York." In

Women and Work Culture: Britain c. 1850–1950, edited by Krista Cowman and Louise A. Jackson, 107–20. London: Ashgate, 2005.

Rose, Jacqueline. *States of Fantasy*. Oxford: Clarendon Press, 1996.

Ross, Ellen. "Annie (Wood) Besant." *Slum Travelers: Ladies and London Poverty, 1860–1920*, 45–8. Los Angeles: University of California Press, 2007.

– *Slum Travelers: Ladies and London Poverty, 1860–1920*. Los Angeles: University of California Press, 2007.

Rowbotham, Sheila. *Dreamers of a New Day: Women Who Invented the Twentieth Century*. New York: Verso, 2010.

– "Women's Liberation and the New Politics." 1969. In *Dreams and Dilemmas: Collected Writings*, 5–32. London: Virago Press, 1983.

Rowbotham, Sheila, and Jeffrey Weeks. *Socialism and the New Life: The Personal and Sexual Politics of Edward Carpenter and Havelock Ellis*. London: Pluto Press, 1977.

Rowold, Katharina. *The Educated Woman: Minds, Bodies, and Women's Higher Education in Britain, Germany, and Spain, 1865–1914*. New York: Routledge, 2010.

Rubery, Matthew. *The Novelty of Newspapers: Victorian Fiction after the Invention of the News*. Oxford: Oxford University Press, 2009.

Rubin, Gayle. "Thinking Sex: Notes for a Radical Theory of the Politics of Sexuality." In *Pleasure and Danger: Exploring Female Sexuality*, edited by Carole S. Vance, 267–319. Boston: Routledge & Kegan Paul, 1984.

– "The Traffic in Women: Notes on the 'Political Economy of Sex.'" 1975. In *Feminism & Histor*, edited by Joan Wallach Scott, 105–51. Oxford: Oxford University Press, 1996.

Ruddick, Nicholas. Introduction to *The Woman Who Did*, 11–43. Peterborough: Broadview Press, 2004.

Russell, Richard Rankin. "Escaping the Examined Life in George Moore's 'Home Sickness.'" *Journal of the Short Story in English* 45 (2005): 2–12.

Sacks, Karen. *Sisters and Wives: The Past and Future of Sexual Equality*. Chicago: University of Illinois Press, 1982.

Sale, Roger. *Literary Inheritance*. Amherst: University of Massachusetts Press, 1985.

Samuelian, Kristin Flieger. Introduction to Jane Austen's *Emma*, 9–46. Peterborough: Broadview Press, 2004.

Samuels, Ernest. *Bernard Berenson: The Making of a Connoisseur*. Cambridge, MA: The Belknap Press of Harvard University Press, 1979.

Sanders, Lise Shapiro. *Consuming Fantasies: Labor, Leisure, and the London Shopgirl, 1880–1920*. Columbus: Ohio University State Press, 2006.

Sanders, Valerie. *The Brother-Sister Culture in Nineteenth-Century Literature: From Austen to Woolf*. New York: Palgrave Macmillan, 2002.

Sante, Luc. *Low Life: Lures and Snares of Old New York*. New York: Farrar, Straus and Giroux, 2003.

Saville, Julia. "The Poetic Imaging of Michael Field." In *The Fin-de-Siècle Poem: English Literature and Culture and the 1890s*, edited by Joe Bristow, 178–206. Athens: Ohio University Press, 2005.

Scarry, Elaine. *The Body in Pain: The Making and Unmaking of the World*. Oxford: Oxford University Press, 1985.

Schaffer, Talia. *The Forgotten Female Aesthetes: Literary Culture in Late-Victorian England*. Charlottesville: University Press of Virginia, 2000.

– "'Nothing but Foolscap and Ink': Inventing the New Woman." In *The New Woman in Fiction and Fact: Fin-de-Siècle Feminisms*, edited by Angelique Richardson and Chris Willis, 39–52. New York: Palgrave Macmillan, 2001.

Scheinberg, Cynthia. *Women's Poetry and Religion in Victorian England: Jewish Identity and Christian Culture*. Cambridge: Cambridge University Press, 2002.

Scholl, Lesa. *Translation, Authorship and the Victorian Processional Woman: Charlotte Brontë, Harriet Martineau and George Eliot*. Aldershot, UK: Ashgate, 2011.

Scott, Joan Wallach. *Gender and the Politics of History*, revised edition. 1988. New York: Columbia University Press, 1999.

Seaman, L.C.B. *Life in Victorian London*. London: B.T. Batsford, 1973.

Sennett, Richard. *The Fall of Public Man*. Cambridge: Cambridge University Press, 1973.

Shanley, Mary Lyndon. *Feminism, Marriage, and the Law in Victorian England, 1850–1895*. Princeton, NJ: Princeton University Press, 1993.

Shapiro, Harold I., ed. *Ruskin in Italy: Letters to His Parents 1845*. Oxford: Clarendon, 1972.

Shelley, Lorna. "Female Journalists and Journalism in Fin-de-Siècle Magazine Stories." *Nineteenth-Century Gender Studies* 5.2 (summer 2009): n.p.

Showalter, Elaine. "Killing the Angel in the House: The Autonomy of Women Writers." *Antioch Review* 32.3 (1972): 339–53.

– *A Literature of Their Own: British Women Novelists from Brontë to Lessing*. Princeton, NJ: Princeton University Press, 1977.

Siegel, Jonah. *Desire and Excess: The Nineteenth-Century Culture of Art*. Princeton, NJ: Princeton University Press, 2000.

Silver, Brenda. "The Authority of Anger; '*Three Guineas*' as Case Study." *Signs* 16.2 (winter 1991): 340–70.

Sim, Lorraine. *Virginia Woolf: The Patterns of Ordinary Experience*. New York: Routledge, 2010.

Smith, Angela K. "All Quiet on the Woolwich Front? Literary and Cultural Constructions of Women Munitions Workers in the First World War." In *Women and Work Culture: Britain c. 1850–1950*, edited by Krista Cowman and Louise A. Jackson, 197–212. London: Ashgate, 2005.

Smith-Rosenberg, Carroll. "The Female World of Love and Ritual." In *Feminism and History*, edited by Joan Scott, 366–97. Oxford: Oxford University Press, 1996.

Spelman, Elizabeth V. *The Inessential Woman: Problems of Exclusion in Feminist Thought*. Boston: Beacon Press, 1988.

Spencer, Jane. *Literary Relations: Kinship and the Canon, 1660–1830*. Oxford: Oxford University Press, 2005.

Spender, Dale, ed. *The Education Papers: Women's Quest for Equality in Britain, 1850–1912*. New York: Routledge & Kegan Paul, 1987.

Stanley, Liz. *Imperialism, Labour and the New Woman: Olive Schreiner's Social Theory*. Durham: Sociology Press, 2002.

Stansell, Christine. *City of Women: Sex and Class in New York, 1789–1860*. New York: Alfred A. Knopf, 1986.

Staves, Susan. *Married Women's Separate Property in England, 1660–1833*. Cambridge, MA: Harvard University Press, 1990.

Stetz, Margaret D. "'George Egerton': Woman and Writer of the Eighteen-Nineties." Diss. Harvard University, 1982.

– "Publishing Industries and Practices." In *The Cambridge Companion to the Fin de Siècle*, edited by Gail Marshall, 113–30. Cambridge: Cambridge University Press, 1997.

Stetz, Margaret D., and Mark Samuels Lasner. *England in the 1890s: Literary Publishing at the Bodley Head*. Georgetown: Georgetown University Press, 1990.

Sutherland, Gillian. *In Search of the New Woman: Middle-Class Women and Work in Britain 1870–1914*. Cambridge: Cambridge University Press, 2015.

Tanner, Tony. *Adultery in the Novel: Contract and Transgression*. Baltimore, MD and London: Johns Hopkins University Press, 1979.

Thain, Marion. *"Michael Field": Poetry, Aestheticism and the Fin de Siècle*. New York: Cambridge University Press, 2007.

Thain, Marion, and Ana I. Parejo Vadillo. *Michael Field, The Poet: Published and Manuscript Materials*. Peterborough: Broadview Press, 2009.

Tobin, Beth Fowkes. "Aiding Impoverished Gentlewomen: Power and Class in *Emma*." In Jane Austen's *Emma*, edited by Alistair Duckworth, 437–87. New York: Bedford/St Martin's, 2002.

Tooley, Sarah A. "Madame Sarah Grand at Home." In *Sex, Social Purity and Sarah Grand: Journalistic Writings and Contemporary Reception*, edited by Ann Heilmann and Stephanie Forward, 239–47. London: Routledge, 2000.

Tratner, Michael. *Deficits and Desires: Economics and Sexuality in Twentieth-Century Literature*. Stanford: Stanford University Press, 2001.

Vadillo, Ana I. Parejo. "Immaterial Poetics: A. Mary F. Robinson and the Fin-de-Siècle Poem." In *The Fin-de-Siècle Poem: English Literary Culture and the 1890s*, edited by Joe Bristow, 231–60. Athens: Ohio University Press, 2005.

– "Sight and Song: Transparent Translations and a Manifesto for the Observer." *Victorian Poetry* 38.1 (2000): 15–34.
– *Women Poets and Urban Aestheticism: Passengers of Modernity*. New York: Palgrave Macmillian, 2005.
Vicinus, Martha. "The Adolescent Boy: Fin-de-Siècle Femme Fatale?" In *Victorian Sexual Dissidence*, edited by Richard Dellamora, 83–106. Chicago: University of Chicago Press, 1999.
– "Distance and Desire: English Boarding-School Friendships." *Signs* 9.4 (summer 1984): 600–22.
– *Independent Women, Work and Community for Single Women, 1850–1920*. London: Virago, 1985.
– *Intimate Friends: Women Who Loved Women, 1778–1928*. Chicago: University of Chicago Press, 2004.
Waldfogel, Joel. "The Efficiency of Gift Giving." *American Economic Review* 83.5 (December 1993): 1328–36.
Walkowitz, Judith. *City of Dreadful Delight: Narratives of Sexual Danger in Late Victorian London*. Chicago: University of Chicago Press, 1992.
Wandor, Michelene, ed. *The Body Politic: Writings from the Women's Liberation Movement in Britain, 1969–72*. London: Stage 1, 1972.
Ward, Patrick. *Exile, Emigration, and Irish Writing*. Dublin/Portland, OR: Irish Academic Press, 2002.
Weaver, Mike. *British Photography in the Nineteenth Century: The Fine Art Tradition*. Cambridge: Cambridge University Press, 1989.
Weiner, Lynn Y. *From Working Girl to Working Mother: The Female Labor Force in the United States, 1820–1980*. Chapel Hill: University of North Carolina Press, 1985.
Whitaker, Muriel. *Great Canadian War Stories*. Edmonton: University of Alberta Press, 2001.
White, Cynthia Leslie. *Women's Magazines 1693–1968*. London: Michael Joseph, 1970.
Wicke, Jennifer. "Vampiric Typewriting: Dracula and Its Media." *ELH* 59.2 (1992): 467–93.
Williams, Raymond. "The Bloomsbury Fraction." In *Problems in Materialism and Culture*, 148–69. New York: Verso, 1980.
– *Culture and Society, 1780–1950*. London: Chatto and Windus, 1958.
– "The Politics of the Avant Garde." In *The Politics of Modernism*, 49–63. London: Verso, 1989.
Willis, Chris. "'Heaven defend me from political or highly educated women!': Packaging the New Woman for Mass Consumption." In *The New Woman in Fiction and Fact: Fin-de-Siècle Feminisms*, edited by Angelique Richardson and Chris Willis, 53–65. New York: Palgrave Macmillan, 2001.

Wion, Philip K. "The Absent Mother in *Wuthering Heights*." In *Wuthering Heights*, edited by Linda H. Peterson, 364–78. New York: Bedford/St Martin's, 2003.

Wise, Julie. "Michael Field's Translations into Verse." In *Michael Field and Their World*, edited by Margaret D. Stetz and Cheryl A. Wilson, 203–10. High Wycomb: Rivendale Press, 2007.

Wojtczak, Helena. *Women of Victorian Sussex: Their Status, Occupations, and Dealings with the Law, 1830–1870*. Hastings: Hastings Press, 2004.

Wolff, Janet. *Feminine Sentences: Essays on Women and Culture*. Los Angeles: University of California Press, 1990.

– "The Invisible Flâneuse: Women and the Literature of Modernity." *Theory, Culture and Society* 2.3 (1985): 37–45.

Woollacott, Angela. *On Her Their Lives Depend: Munitions Workers in the Great War*. Berkeley: University of California Press, 1994.

"Yellow Journalism." In *Dictionary of Nineteenth-Century Journalism*, edited by Laurel Brake and Marysa Demoor, 694. London: Academia Press and the British Library, 2009.

Young, Arlene. "The Rise of the Victorian Working Lady: The New-Style Nurse and the Typewriter, 1840–1900." *BRANCH: Britain, Representation and Nineteenth-Century History*. Online. n.p.

Zorn, Christa. *Vernon Lee: Aesthetics, History, and the Victorian Female Intellectual*. Athens: Ohio University Press, 2003.

Zwerdling, Alex. *Virginia Woolf and the Real World*. Los Angeles: University of California Press, 1986.

Index